Lessons from Regional Responses to Security, Health, and Environmental Challenges in Latin America

Edited by

Ivo Ganchev

Founder of the Centre for Regional Integration, UK

Series in Politics

VERNON PRESS

Copyright © 2024 by the Authors.

All rights reserved. No part of this publication may be reproduced, stored in a retrieval system, or transmitted in any form or by any means, electronic, mechanical, photocopying, recording, or otherwise, without the prior permission of Vernon Art and Science Inc.
www.vernonpress.com

In the Americas:
Vernon Press
1000 N West Street, Suite 1200,
Wilmington, Delaware 19801
United States

In the rest of the world:
Vernon Press
C/Sancti Espiritu 17,
Malaga, 29006
Spain

Series in Politics

Library of Congress Control Number: 2023946578

ISBN: 978-1-64889-935-5

Also available: 978-1-64889-773-3 [Hardback]; 978-1-64889-827-3 [PDF, E-Book]

Product and company names mentioned in this work are the trademarks of their respective owners. While every care has been taken in preparing this work, neither the authors nor Vernon Art and Science Inc. may be held responsible for any loss or damage caused or alleged to be caused directly or indirectly by the information contained in it.

Every effort has been made to trace all copyright holders, but if any have been inadvertently overlooked the publisher will be pleased to include any necessary credits in any subsequent reprint or edition.

Cover designed by Vernon Press with resources from Freepik.

Table of contents

List of tables vii

List of figures ix

Acknowledgements xi
Ivo Ganchev
Founder of the Centre for Regional Integration, UK

Notes on contributors xv

Introduction xix
Ivo Ganchev
Founder of the Centre for Regional Integration, UK

PART I:
REGIONAL RESPONSES TO COLLECTIVE SECURITY
CHALLENGES 1

Chapter 1
Responses of Latin American organizations to coup attempts: Power play between political ideologies in post-hegemonic regionalism 3
Ivo Ganchev
Founder of the Centre for Regional Integration, UK

Chapter 2
The impact of deglobalization on the security agenda of contemporary Latin American regionalism 37
Kseniya Konovalova
Saint-Petersburg State University, Russia
Victor Jeifets
Saint-Petersburg State University, Russia

Chapter 3
Security governance in the Andean borderlands: Hybrid formations and the rising armed violence   61
Rafael A. Duarte Villa
University of São Paulo, Brazil
Camila de Macedo Braga
University of São Paulo, Brazil
Rafael Enrique Piñeros Ayala
Universidad Externado de Colombia, Colombia

Chapter 4
Lessons from forced partnerships: The Alliance for the Prosperity of the Northern Triangle (2015–2020)   91
Miguel Gomis
Pontificia Universidad Javeriana, Colombia

PART II:
REGIONAL RESPONSES TO COLLECTIVE HEALTH CHALLENGES   121

Chapter 5
Institutional factors influencing the success of Latin American organizations confronting epidemics   123
Octavio González Segovia
National Autonomous University of Mexico, Mexico
Alfonso Sánchez Mugica
National Autonomous University of Mexico, Mexico

Chapter 6
The impact of COVID-19 on the national power of Latin American countries   163
Daniel Morales Ruvalcaba
Sun Yat-sen University, China

Chapter 7
Regional integration and presidential elections in Latin America in the context of COVID-19   191
Ignacio Medina Núñez
El Colegio de Jalisco, México

Chapter 8
Interactions of Brazil, Peru, PAHO and ACTO in overcoming the effects of COVID-19   217
Alla Yurievna Borzova
Peoples' Friendship University of Russia, Russia

**PART III:
REGIONAL RESPONSES TO COLLECTIVE ENVIRONMENTAL CHALLENGES**   233

Chapter 9
MERCOSUR's environmental policy: Institutional evolution and limitations   235
Tatiana de Souza Leite Garcia
University of São Paulo and Inter-American Institute for Cooperation on Agriculture, Brazil

Chapter 10
Regional environmental efforts in Mesoamerica: Achievements and modes of cooperation   263
Alina Gamboa Combs
Universidad Anáhuac México, México
Dircea Arroyo Buganza
Universidad Anáhuac México, México

Chapter 11
Lessons from the Escazú Agreement for environmental and human rights protection in Africa   293
Fernand Guevara Mekongo Mballa
Centre for Regional Integration, Cameroon

Index   317

List of tables

Table 3.1	Border security incidents in Colombia and Venezuela (2002–2010)	69
Table 3.2	NSAGs in the borderlands of Colombia and Venezuela	72
Table 3.3	Reconfiguration of armed conflict groups	80
Table 3.4	Production efficiency of coca paste and cocaine in Colombia	82
Table 5.1	Main features of TGNs and IGOs	129
Table 5.2	External and internal factors for joining a TGN	131
Table 5.3	Flexibility of various organizations	140
Table 5.4	Respondents' replies to "Why are selected organizations flexible?"	141
Table 5.5	Which organization learns faster (rank from 1 to 9)?	143
Table 5.6	When are TGNs more effective than IGOs?	153
Table 6.1.	Real gross domestic product (percentage change from the previous year)	166
Table 6.2.	Annual growth rate of the total GDP in 2020	167
Table 6.3.	Geostructure of Latin America, with categories and positions of states as of 2021	176
Table 7.1	COVID-19 deaths in Latin American countries	194
Table 7.2	Electoral processes in 2021 in Latin America	196
Table 7.3	Schedule of CELAC summits	208
Table 8.1	Data on COVID-19 in selected Latin American countries, as of 21 December 2022	218
Table 8.2	Comparative data on sustainable development in Peru and Brazil	220
Table 8.3	The main indicators of the health system in Brazil and Peru	222
Table 9.1.	GMC resolutions with environmental themes (direct or indirect) (2009–2019)	250
Table 9.2.	CMC decisions on environmental themes (direct or indirect) (2009–2019)	252

Table 9.3.	CMC declarations on environmental themes (direct or indirect) (2009–2019)	253
Table 10.1	Overlapping environmental regionalisms in Mesoamerica	275
Table 10.2	The EMSA 2013–2016 plan of action	281

List of figures

Figure 4.1	Total net official development assistance and official assistance received by Guatemala, Honduras, and El Salvador (USD millions at 2020 prices)	99
Figure 4.2	US cooperation disbursements to Guatemala from 2001 to 2020 (in millions of 2020 USD)	101
Figure 4.3	US disbursements in El Salvador from 2001 to 2020 (in millions of 2020 USD)	103
Figure 4.4	US disbursements in Honduras from 2001 to 2020 (in millions of 2020 USD)	105
Figure 5.1	Effectiveness of organizations	137
Figure 5.2	Flexibility of organizations in dealing with PHEICs	139
Figure 5.3	Which organization learns faster?	142
Figure 5.4	Capability of organizations (most assessed organizations)	144
Figure 5.5	Capability of Organizations	145
Figure 5.6	Under what circumstances are TGNs more effective than IGOs?	149
Figure 6.1	Variation of the currencies of Latin America and the Caribbean against the US dollar, December 2019–December 2020	169
Figure 6.2	Latin American countries least affected in terms of national power by the COVID-19 pandemic, according to the WPI	177
Figure 6.3	Latin American countries moderately affected in terms of national power by the COVID-19 pandemic, according to the WPI	179
Figure 6.4	Latin American countries strongly affected in terms of national power by the COVID-19 pandemic, according to the WPI	182

Acknowledgements

Ivo Ganchev

Founder of the Centre for Regional Integration, UK

In our increasingly interconnected world, both opportunities and challenges spread quickly across states more quickly than ever. Before and after these processes take place at the global level, they begin and end at the regional level. To help manage relevant opportunities and challenges, the number of regional organizations, treaties, associations, and other similar forms of collective governance has increased substantially in number since WWII. This is a major trend in international politics and it has emerged in order to satisfy the ever-increasing demand for new mechanisms of regional cooperation, integration, and coordination.

Latin America and the Caribbean (LAC) is a region where a substantial number of regional organizations and treaties co-exist, evolve, and adapt simultaneously. Since the start of the twenty-first century, the landscape of frameworks governing the region has undergone a process of continuous transformation while constantly accommodating dynamic adjustments for both political and pragmatic reasons. When the COVID-19 pandemic started, some regional bodies provided much needed support to governments and people alike, while others did not have the mandate or resources to do so, and a third group that had previously functioned well suspended their operations due to a lack of member state capacity, but maintained a façade of activity nevertheless.

Observing these trends, some of my colleagues decided to focus their research agenda specifically on the LAC regional responses to the COVID-19 pandemic, producing excellent specialized books and papers on the topic. As important as the lessons from the pandemic are, I always thought that examining them in a broader context would help to make research works more relevant in the long run and link them to the broader theme of collective challenges that LAC states are facing. In early 2021, I conducted a brief survey among 78 fellow political scientists about their views on the most pressing collective challenges for Latin America in terms of areas of regional governance where research is still lacking.

After grouping the responses thematically, three areas stood out: security, healthcare, and environmental protection. Upon further reflection, I realized that the areas indicated in the survey responses are essential for protecting the borders, lives and land that constitute the social and environmental ecosystems of

LAC. Security, healthcare, and environmental protection are interrelated, but they are also reshaped through collective governance, which provides various fruitful research threads to explore. Understanding that the need to conduct such work was too large to ignore, I realized that exploring these topics requires a collaborative effort.

This inspired me to conceptualize this edited volume, which explores how regional, sub-regional and national frameworks for LAC governance address collective security, healthcare and environmental protection challenges and are reshaped by them. Engagement with these topics has produced valuable findings and lessons for students, scholars and practitioners of regionalism, Latin American studies and political science more broadly, as well as for those who engage with regional or international organizations related to LAC.

This volume took more than two years to compile and it is the result of a group effort by numerous scholars and organizations. Without them, it would not be possible. I would like to express my profound gratitude to everyone who helped to make this book a reality, in the order of their involvement. I hope to show my appreciation to everyone involved in its publication and to help readers understand key aspects of the process that produced the end result.

First, I would like to thank Vernon Press for trusting in this research project from the start, as well as for allowing me the creative freedom to design the conceptual framework that underpins this volume and to make final decisions about its content. This has greatly facilitated my work as an editor and enabled me to create a coherent compilation of contributions.

Second, I highly appreciate the help of my team at the Centre for Regional Integration, as they were extremely supportive in the early days of this project. My colleagues provided me with invaluable assistance in terms of technical aspects, such as preparing and mailing feedback forms and formatting the chapter manuscripts. In addition, thanks to the vast network of scholars who are friends or fellows at the Centre, I was able to build a small community of potential contributors during the first few weeks of promoting the call for chapters. Our organization provided a solid basis for the foundation of this project.

Third, I am very grateful to the organizers of the annual academic conferences, where many of the contributors originally met each other and where I got to know them as well. Some of these conferences are organized by the International Studies Association, the Latin American Studies Association, and the World International Studies Committee, among other structures and communities. The circulation of the call for chapters was also actively supported by the International Political Science Association and by the Colombian academic community, RedIntercol. Any academic knows how much effort it takes to operate these kinds of organizations and all contributors appreciate the work that academic communities do to provide us with platforms for sharing and exchanging ideas.

Fourth, and most crucially, I deeply appreciate the work of all the contributors who took this project to heart and worked tirelessly to produce high-quality chapters. It was heartwarming to see the determination that motivated everyone to improve their work through multiple rounds of edits and to help each other in the process as well. Seeing colleagues pro-actively provide valuable suggestions to each other and finding time for engaging in discussions about their work truly created a sense of team spirit.

Finally, on behalf of all contributors, I would also like to thank the external peer reviewers who shall remain anonymous. These colleagues generously gave us their time and provided us with elaborate feedback and tips that improved our work and the quality of the book over several months prior to finalizing the manuscript. This is a testament to their genuine desire and selfless commitment to help.

Similar to the way that various governmental and non-governmental organizations work together to provide a framework for supporting and deepening Latin American regionalism, everyone involved in the creation of this edited volume also had a crucial role to play. The collaboration, cooperation and, ultimately, integration of our efforts made this project, and it has been an honour for me to work with everyone involved.

We hope that you will enjoy reading the book!

Notes on contributors

Introduction to the Editor

Ivo Ganchev is the Founding Director of the Centre for Regional Integration. He has taught at several universities, including Queen Mary University of London and Beijing Foreign Studies University. Ivo holds a PhD from Peking University. His research has appeared in academic journals such as *World Affairs, Strategic Analysis* and *International Studies*.

Introduction to the contributors (in alphabetical order)

Dircea Arroyo Buganza is an Academic Coordinator of Regional and Legal Studies at Universidad Anáhuac México. She holds a PhD from the National Autonomous University of Mexico. Her research has appeared in several books and in academic journals such as *Red de Estudios Superiores Asia-Pacífico*.

Alla Yurievna Borzova is a Professor of Theory and History at the International Relations Department of Peoples' Friendship University of Russia (RUDN). She holds a PhD from the same institution. Alla has authored or co-authored over 100 research publications, which have appeared in academic journals such as *Latinskaya Amerika, Vestnik RUDN* and *Asia and Africa Today*.

Camila de Macedo Braga is a Post-doctoral Fellow at the Institute of International Relations, University of São Paulo. She holds a PhD in Political Science from the same institution, where she is also currently the Coordinator of the Center for Peace and Conflict Studies (CCP-NUPRI). Camila has also served as a Global Fellow at the Center for Human Rights and Humanitarian Studies, Brown University, since 2016.

Rafael A. Duarte Villa is a Professor at the University of Sao Paulo and holds a PhD from the same institution. He is also the Director of the Political Science Department at the same university. Rafael has served as the Director of the International Research Center there and as a Fellow at Columbia University and at the International University of Andalucia. He has authored numerous books and recently co-edited the volume *Power Dynamics and Regional Security in Latin America* (Palgrave Macmillan, 2017).

Alina Gamboa Combs is a Lecturer and Researcher at Universidad Anáhuac México. She holds a PhD from the University of Warwick. She has authored the book *Regional Integration, Development and Governance in Mesoamerica*

(Springer, 2019), and her research articles has have appeared in journals such as *Foreign Affairs Latinoamérica*.

Tatiana de Souza Leite Garcia is an Associate Researcher at the Department of Geography of the University of São Paulo and a Consultant for the Inter-American Institute for Cooperation on Agriculture (IICA). She holds a PhD from the University of São Paulo. Tatiana has authored articles for academic journals such as *Confins Revue Franco-Brésilienne de Géographie* and she has recently co-edited the book *América do Sul: geopolítica, arranjos regionais e relações internacionais* (Edições FFLCH/USP, 2022).

Miguel Gomis is an Assistant Professor at Pontificia Universidad Javeriana. He holds a PhD from Universidad Complutense. Miguel has authored numerous book chapters and research articles on governance, policy, and institutional change, which have appeared in academic journals such as *Ciencia y Poder Aéreo* and *Papel Político*.

Octavio González Segovia is a regular lecturer at the National Autonomous University of Mexico (UNAM), where he recently concluded a postdoctoral stay. He has taught at the University of Potsdam, the Hertie School of Governance and Universidad de las Américas Puebla, among others institutions. Octavio holds a PhD from Universidad Autónoma de Baja California. He has authored book chapters and research articles on global health governance, which have appeared in academic journals such as *Face à Face: Regards sur la Santé*.

Victor Jeifets is a Professor at Saint-Petersburg State University. He holds a PhD from the same institution and has published over 250 research articles in academic journals in Russia, Mexico, Colombia, Argentina, Spain and Portugal. He has authored numerous books and recently co-edited the volume *Rethinking Post-Cold War Russian–Latin American Relations* (Routledge, 2022) and edited the volume *The Comintern in Latin America: Historical Traditions and Political Processes* (Ves' Mir, 2021). He is also the Editor-in-Chief of *Latinskaya Amerika*, a journal of the Russian Academy of Sciences, and a leading researcher at the Institute for Latin American Studies in Moscow.

Kseniya Konovalova is an Assistant (Teaching Fellow) at Saint-Petersburg State University. She holds a PhD from the same institution and has published over 30 research articles in academic journals. Her research has appeared in academic journals such as *World Economy and International Relations*, *Latinskaya Amerika*, and *Iberoamerica*.

Ignacio Medina Núñez is a Research Professor at El Colegio de Jalisco in Zapopan, Mexico. He previously served as the Head of the Department of Iberian and Latin American Studies at the University of Guadalajara and holds a PhD from the same institution. He is a Level III member of the Mexican

National Research System and has authored numerous research articles, as well as books such as *Presidential Elections in Latin America: The Ascent of the Left* (2013) and *Política, Democracia y Educación Ciudadana: De la Antiguedad a la Época Moderna* (2015).

Fernand Guevara Mekongo Mballa is an Africa Fellow at the Centre for Regional Integration and a Doctoral Candidate at the Catholic University of Central Africa. Fernand has authored and presented papers at several global conferences, which have subsequently appeared in academic journals such as the *Journal of Law and Emerging Technology*.

Daniel Morales Ruvalcaba is an Associate Professor at Sun Yat-sen University (China) and a Member of the National System of Researchers of Mexico. He holds a PhD from the University of Guadalajara. Daniel is the creator of the World Power Index and the author of numerous research articles, which have appeared in academic journals such as *Cambridge Review of International Affairs, Third World Quarterly, International Studies, Geopolitica(s), Colombia Internacional,* and *Estudios Internacionales,* among others, as well as in the *Oxford Research Encyclopedia of Politics*.

Rafael Enrique Piñeros Ayala is a PhD Candidate and an Associate Professor (Docente) at Universidad Externado de Colombia. He holds a MA in International Relations from the same institution and his research has appeared in various books and in academic journals such as *Relaciones Internacionales and Revista Desafíos.*

Alfonso Sánchez Mugica is a Professor at the National Autonomous University of Mexico. He holds a PhD from the same institution. Alfonso has authored dozens of articles in journals such as *Revista Mexicana de Ciencias Políticas y Sociales*. He has also edited or co-edited numerous books, such as *La política exterior de México y la Constitución de 1917 en su Centenario* (UNAM, 2020).

Introduction

Ivo Ganchev

Founder of the Centre for Regional Integration, UK

The development of regionalism in Latin America and the Caribbean (LAC) is a very long and resilient historical process. Conceptually, it can be traced back to early ideas about Pan-Americanism, a concept which first emerged at the Congress of Panama, organized by Simon Bolivar in 1826. Institutionally, the world's first regional organization was established in 1889-90 in the Americas under the name International Union of American Republics (later transformed into the Pan-American Union). Since then, many political leaders have traditionally used phrases such as "we, the Latinos" (Spanish: *nosotros los latinos*) to address their people.

Since 1945, dozens of regional agreements and initiatives have shaped LAC regionalism. At least 19 of them can be classified as regional organizations and they are driven by engagement between governments, which are the only actors possessing both the legitimacy and the resources to make large strides in promoting greater engagement on a large scale across the region. While scholars have rightly pointed out that the involvement of non-state actors in regional projects requires more attention and in some parts, this book engages with this emerging field of research, Latin American regionalism remains de facto state-centric when it comes to collective governance. This consideration has influenced the topics and methods selected by the contributors in many of the chapters.

LAC regionalism is characterized by a complex web of institutionalized organizations which overlap in various ways to form a so-called "alphabet soup" or "spaghetti bowl" of regional bodies. This forms a landscape of dynamic and flexible mechanisms that serve to help states cooperate, coordinate, and pursue greater integration. These mechanisms form complex processes which are sometimes heavily politicized and difficult to evaluate. Hence, academic studies have produced widely varied and often ostensibly contradictory evaluations of LAC regionalism. They generally fall within three broad categories. Drawing on the work of Thomas Legler (2013), Cintia Quiliconi and Raúl Salgado Espinoza (2017, p. 20) accurately divide relevant authors into three types: optimists, sceptics and innovators.

Optimists examine Latin American regional integration empirically and argue that it is sufficiently resilient to resist shifts in the ideological inclinations of both intra-regional and extra-regional political tides. These scholars believe that this is possible because organizations in the region have changed their form and focus over time while maintaining a relatively stable overall aim of deepening integration. They argue that the post-1945 history of LAC regionalism has developed in four waves; the first one was an effort to industrialize the region during the 1950s and 1960s, which only had limited success. The second wave has been labelled revisionist (Rosenthal, 1991). It was characterized by disappointment with the outcomes of the first one and inspired efforts to create more mechanisms for coordination on economic and political matters during the 1970s and 1980s. The third wave was an effort to promote economic liberalization starting with the end of the Cold War during the 1990s and it has been often referred to as open regionalism.

The fourth and most recent wave is viewed as a response to the failures of the third one and it is often referred to as "post-liberal/neoliberal" or "post-hegemonic" as these terms indicate an effort to move beyond economic reforms shaped by US influence (which some see as negative and hegemonic) according to a liberal/neoliberal economic model. The past two decades of LAC regionalism have been characterized by a shift in priorities from trade and finance to social and political concerns (da Motta Veiga and Ríos, 2007; Riggirozzi and Tussie, 2012; Serbin et al., 2012). This has led to the emergence of new regional organizations and to a change in the priorities of earlier ones as non-economic topics have become increasingly central. Academic scholarship since the start of the 21st century has reflected that and, in a way, the themes covered in this book and the research interests of its contributors are also reflective of this trend.

Sceptics, as their label suggests, are critical of LAC regionalism. Some of them have argued that it has produced organizations which are largely dysfunctional (Baquero-Herrera, 2005) and characterized by institutional weaknesses (Coral, 2011; Malamud and Gardini, 2012; Gómez-Mera, 2014). Others hold that regional integration in Latin America is a "failure" due to the lack of sovereignty transfer from national governments to supra-national organizations (Buelvas, 2013). A third group argues about the terminology that should be employed to characterize Latin American regionalism – some scholars who do this suggest that existing processes should be labelled as "cooperation", and believe that the term "integration" should be reserved for other regions (Malamud, 2013). While some of the criticisms that sceptics make are well-reasoned, they are rarely followed by any constructive suggestions; the proposals of most scholars in this category are often either direct or indirect encouragement for LAC states to move closer to the EU model. However, given the political polarization among LAC governments and the limited resources they have, it seems to me that this is simply wishful thinking. This book does not aim to, nor could it possibly refute these criticisms but instead seeks to learn from their limitations and offer more constructive proposals.

Innovators are dissatisfied with the state of mainstream scholarship on LAC regionalism and they seek ways to present new concepts that can help to explain its development. For instance, Briceño-Ruiz (2006) applies concepts such as "strategic regionalism" (Deblock and Brunelle, 1993, p. 596) to the Free Trade Area of the Americas (FTAA), discussing the use of economic policy to develop comparative advantages in international markets. His other works emphasize the relevance of various concepts to Latin America; they include "social regionalism", which is centred around poverty reduction and improvements in public services and "productive regionalism", which emphasizes mechanisms for integrating the production of multiple countries (Briceño-Ruiz, 2018). Another example is the work of Mariana Vázquez (2011, p. 175), which proposes the concept of "inclusive regionalism" to emphasize shared concerns regarding the protection of civil, political, economic, and cultural rights. While such studies make admirable efforts to pursue intellectual innovation, they ultimately have limited potential to produce insights of practical relevance because of the high degree of abstraction that characterises their intended aim. The contributors to this book have been mindful of the limitations that conceptual discussions create and while some of them engage in relevant discussions, most of them remain largely concerned with empirical discussions and seek to offer rather practical insights.

This edited volume represents a departure from the approaches of most recent books on LAC regionalism. It does not focus on one or several specific regional organizations (as in Cusack, 2019; Tigre, 2017; Gómez-Mera, 2013), or on a single event (as in Meireles, de Conti and Guevara, 2023); it also does not seek to employ an overly-abstract umbrella theme such as "resilience" to unite the chapters (as in Briceño-Ruiz, 2021; Briceño-Ruiz and Puntigliano, 2013). Instead, this volume groups the contributions according to the types of policy challenges that they address in three specific areas: security, healthcare, and environmental protection. This is a conscious move and it seeks to help readers orient themselves more easily and to bring awareness to these three areas which deserve more attention in the study of LAC regionalism. After all, security, healthcare, and environmental governance and environmental protection share a fundamental common characteristic as they are issues related to the safety of the general public (Nunes, 2012). Besides, addressing them is a necessary precondition for achieving sustainable economic development; hence, challenges in these areas must be tackled for economic development and regional integration to proceed further and generate greater prosperity for the region.

The challenges that LAC faces in terms of security, health and environmental concerns are considerable and emerge in conditions that are specific to the region. There is broad consensus that LAC is characterized by "violent peace", a phrase which was first coined by David Mares (2001) to explain inter-state bargaining processes, but later scholars began to quote in a variety of contexts. Traditional wars between LAC states have been rare: since gaining their independence over two centuries ago, they have waged 12 inter-state wars in total, with 10 of them within the region and only 3 taking place since WWII (Sarkees and Wayman, 2010). While occasional diplomatic skirmishes do happen and there are several unresolved border disputes, they rarely escalate to the point of armed conflict. However, the security of governments and citizens is under various forms of threat; the former often face rather frequent attempts for both violent and non-violent coups, which ultimately undermine the legitimacy of political mechanisms and create negative spillover effects across the region. Meanwhile, citizens must ensure that they avoid engaging with organized crime groups who could pose a serious threat to them. The annual number of homicides in Latin America fluctuates around 150,000, which is 30 times higher than that of all estimated casualties in the three intra-state wars that took place in LAC since 1945 (Igarapé Institute, 2015). This means that many of the regional security threats in Latin America are non-traditional and, thus, often challenging to isolate and tackle appropriately.

Environmental protection is another area where LAC states face collective challenges. The region is home to highly biodiverse areas, including the Amazon region which takes up 40% of South America's land area and is home to one-fifth of all species of animals and plants in the world, while the Amazon River Basin contains the same proportion of all freshwater entering the oceans globally. This aquatic system plays an important role in the global carbon cycle, influencing the maintenance of the hydrological cycle and climate in several subregions of Latin America (Goulding et al., 2003). In addition to their natural beauty and role in the regional ecosystem, LAC forests and rivers provide sources of energy and food while also serving as tourist attractions. Whether for reasons of principle, as a means of pursuing sustainable development, or as a means to pursue the concept of "living well" (Spanish: *buen vivir*), it is necessary for LAC states and their people to tackle collective environmental challenges.

Protecting and improving public health is another area where LAC faces collective challenges. Most recently, the prolonged COVID-19 crisis highlighted the weaknesses of the region's health and social protection systems (CEPAL, 2022), drawing more attention to the topic, which inspired relevant academic research as well. LAC states face various issues, such as a lack of quality healthcare availability in remote regions and inequality of access to healthcare due to wealth disparity. When the COVID-19 pandemic began, there was a clear necessity for deeper regional coordination, but instead, what happened was that many regional organizations slowed down their work as governments focused on national priorities. This revealed that the severity of a health crisis can impact the way that national and regional bodies respond but also that its impact can be curbed when appropriate action is taken.

This book explores the way that security, health-related and environmental challenges are collectively addressed in various parts of LAC. The chapters are methodologically diverse as the approaches have been chosen to fit appropriately with the research questions explored by the contributors. Each of them presents key findings and attempts to draw lessons from or for regionalism in LAC and beyond.

The book contains eleven chapters, which are grouped into three parts. The first part examines how LAC regional organizations and actors have addressed various security challenges, such as coup attempts, deglobalization and hybrid threats. In chapter one, I compare the ways that LAC regional organizations have responded to coup attempts since the rise of post-hegemonic regionalism and evaluate their performance vis-à-vis the US-promoted OAS. I argue that during this time period, LAC organizations were moderately successful in their efforts to produce responses diverging from US interests and to articulate distinctly Latin American positions. The introduction of the first chapter aims to contextualize recent developments in LAC regionalism and its body contains detailed empirical descriptions, while the main findings are only presented in the conclusion. This is deliberate because the chapter is intended to serve as an entry point to the book, so it was designed to contain analysis that appeals to both experts on Latin American studies and readers who might require a broader overview of the political shifts underpinning the development of LAC regionalism since the start of the twenty-first century.

In chapter two, Kseniya Konovalova and Victor Jeifets explore how "deglobalization" relates to changes in the security agenda of LAC. They use historical and case study methods to examine PROSUR, the Venezuelan issue in the OAS, and contemporary Latin America-NATO dialogue as examples. The authors of this chapter reveal why the integration process has not produced a joint vision for LAC governments to face pressing security challenges. In chapter three, Rafael A. Duarte Villa, Camila de Macedo Braga, and Rafael Enrique Piñeros Ayala analyse the concept of hybrid security as it applies to the Colombia-Venezuela and Colombia-Ecuador border areas. The three co-authors use a critical and empirical perspective to understand grey areas in which control of territory, solutions to social problems, and the provision of services are determined both by the presence of the state and by various actors outside the law. In chapter four, Miguel Gomis explores the impact of the Alliance for

Prosperity of the Northern Triangle (APNT) on Guatemala, El Salvador, and Honduras. He relies on institutional documents, field interviews, and an extensive press review to show that APNT benefited donors and NT elites while having little impact on national socio-economic conditions or institutions in the three relevant countries.

The second part of the book investigates how LAC regional organizations and actors have dealt with health challenges, such as epidemics (including COVID-19), and how these challenges have affected national power and domestic elections. In chapter five, Octavio González Segovia and Alfonso Sánchez Mugica argue that during epidemic outbreaks, LAC transgovernmental networks (TGNs) are more effective than intergovernmental organizations (IGOs), largely due to the faster speed at which they can operate. To build this argument, the authors employ semi-structured interviews with health and foreign affairs senior officials and international bureaucrats who have worked for regional organizations. In chapter six, Daniel Morales Ruvalcaba evaluates the impact of the COVID-19 pandemic on the national power of the 14 best-positioned LAC countries in the international geostructure. He measures a wide range of variables that make up national power and the World Power Index (WPI) to categorize them according to the impact of the pandemic. He finds that some countries, such as Guatemala and Ecuador, experienced minor impacts, while others, such as Argentina, Brazil, and Venezuela, suffered significant decreases in terms of their national power.

In chapter seven, Ignacio Medina Núñez discusses the influence of the COVID-19 pandemic on the presidential electoral processes in LAC. He reveals that the pandemic affected elections because it involved crowds in assemblies and rallies and also impacted the physical process of casting votes in person. In chapter eight, Alla Yurievna Borzova examines the interactions of Brazil, Peru, PAHO and ACTO in helping to overcome the consequences of COVID-19. She shows that these actors cooperated to improve healthcare systems and support the efforts of national governments to respond to the pandemic. She also shows that Brazil and Peru cooperate within the framework of the Organization for Cooperation in the Amazon River Basin (ACTO) on various issues related to health and development more broadly.

The third part of the book analyses how LAC regional organizations and actors have tackled environmental challenges, including various aspects of policy-making in terms of protecting ecosystems and human rights, while also drawing some lessons based on the findings. In chapter nine, Tatiana de Souza Leite Garcia presents MERCOSUR's institutional evolution in terms of its environmental policy. Based on both primary and secondary sources, she identifies and analyses the domestic, regional, and international variables that resulted in advances and limitations of MERCOSUR's environmental policy. In chapter ten, Alina Gamboa Combs and Dircea Arroyo Buganza study the activities and efficacy of the environmental efforts of Proyecto Mesoamerica, a regional cooperation and integration project that includes the south-eastern states of Mexico, Central America, Colombia, and the Dominican Republic. They focus on the Mesoamerican Biological Corridor (MBC) project to reveal that when it involved international bodies that required accountability and reporting results, promising results were delivered. However, when the MBC and other environmental projects of the PM needed funding from and were accountable only to each of the member governments, little or no progress ensued. Finally, in chapter eleven, Fernand Guevara Mekongo Mballa explores the lessons that can be learnt from the Escazú Agreement for environmental and human rights protection in Africa. He uses a comparative analysis to highlight the similarities and differences between LAC and Africa on environmental issues. He shows that the Escazú Agreement is an innovative legal instrument that contains specific provisions for Environmental Human Rights Defenders (EHRDs) in LAC and argues that a similar instrument could be useful for Africa to address its own environmental challenges.

The book contributes to the academic literature on LAC regionalism by analyzing pertinent issues through a variety of theoretical and methodological perspectives, so it is likely that different readers will find value in different chapters. Hence, I have refrained from adding a conclusion as this would inevitably draw more attention to some findings and observations than to others. I hope that the contributions which have been compiled in this volume will stimulate further research and debate on the role and impact of regional responses to collective challenges in LAC, inviting the readers to discover the richness and complexity of regional governance.

References

Baquero-Herrera, M. (2005) 'Open regionalism in Latin America: an appraisal', *Law and Business Review of the Americas*, 11 (2), pp. 139–184.

Briceño-Ruiz, J. (2006) 'The FTAA and the EU: models for Latin American integration', Jean Monnet-Robert Schuman Paper Series, 6 (2), pp. 1–20.

Briceño-Ruiz, J. (2018) 'El estudio de la integración regional y del regionalismo en América Latina: entre la influencia europea y el pensamiento propio', *Análisis Político*, 31 (94), pp. 49–74.

Briceño-Ruiz, J. (2021) *Regionalism in Latin America: Agents: Systems and Resilience*. New York: Routledge.

Briceño-Ruiz, J. and Puntigliano, A. R. (2013) *Resilience of Regionalism in Latin America and the Caribbean: Development and Autonomy*. Basingstoke: Palgrave Macmillan.

Buelvas, E. P. (2013) 'Why regionalism has failed in Latin America: lack of stateness as an important factor for failure of sovereignty transfer in integration projects', *Contexto Internacional*, 35 (2), pp. 443–469.

CEPAL (2022) 'Two years of the COVID-19 pandemic in Latin America and the Caribbean: reflections for advancing towards universal, comprehensive, sustainable and resilient health and social protection systems', United Nations. Available at: https://www.cepal.org/en/notes/two-years-covid-19-pandemic-latin-america-and-caribbean-reflections-advancing-towards (Accessed: 5 February 2023).

Coral, M. L. (2011) 'La Unión Europea y la nueva integración latinoamericana: parámetros de comparación aplicados en diferentes estudios sobre los procesos de integración', *Comentario Internacional: Revista del Centro Andino de Estudios Internacionales*, 11 (1), pp. 217–251.

Cusack, A. (2019) *Venezuela, ALBA, and the Limits of Postneoliberal Regionalism in Latin America and the Caribbean*. Basingstoke: Palgrave Macmillan.

da Motta Veiga, P. and Ríos, S. P. (2007) 'O regionalismo pós-liberal, na América do Sul: origens, iniciativas e dilemas', *SERIE Comercio Internacional*, 82, Santiago, Chile: United Nations. Available at: https://repositorio.cepal.org/bitstream/handle/11362/4428/S2007612_pt.pdf?sequence=1&isAllowed=y (Accessed: 3 March 2023).

Deblock, C. and Brunelle, D. (1993) 'Une intégration régionale stratégique: le cas nord-américain', *Revue Études Internationales*, 24 (3), pp. 595–629.

Gómez-Mera, L. (2013) *Power and Regionalism in Latin America: The Politics of MERCOSUR*. Notre Dame: University of Notre Dame Press.

Goulding, M., Barthem, R. and Ferreira, E. G. (2003) *Smithsonian Atlas of the Amazon*. Washington: Smithsonian Books.

Gómez-Mera, L. (2014) 'International regime complexity and regional governance: evidence from the Americas', Presented at the FLACSO-ISA Joint International Conference, Buenos Aires, July 23–25.

Igarapé Institute (2015) 'Homicides and homicide rates 2000 to 2014 – Brazil'. Available at: https://igarape.org.br/en/issues/citizen-security/homicide-monitor/ (Accessed: 13 January 2023).

Legler, T. (2013), 'Post-hegemonic regionalism and sovereignty in Latin America: optimists, skeptics, and an emerging research agenda', *Contexto Internacional*, 32 (2), pp. 325–352.

Malamud, A. (2013) 'Overlapping regionalism, no integration: conceptual issues and the Latin American experiences', European University Institute Working Paper from the Robert Schuman Centre for Advanced Studies, pp. 2–4.

Malamud, A. and Gardini, G. L. (2012), 'Has regionalism peaked? The Latin American quagmire and its lessons', *The International Spectator*, Vol. 47, No. 1, pp. 116–133.

Mares, D. (2001) *Violent Peace: Militarized Interstate Bargaining in Latin America*. New York: Columbia University Press.

Meireles, M., de Conti, B., and Guevara, D. (2023). *COVID-19 and Economic Development in Latin America: Theoretical Debates, Financing Dilemmas and Post-Pandemic Scenarios*. London: Routledge.

Nunes, J. (2012) 'Health, politics and security', *Debates Contemporâneos*, 15, pp. 142–164.

Quiliconi, C. and Espinoza, R. S. (2017) 'Latin American integration: regionalism à la carte in a multipolar world?', *Colombia Internacional*, 92, pp. 15–41.

Riggirozzi, P. and Tussie, D. (2012) *The rise of post-hegemonic regionalism: The case of Latin America*. London: Springer.

Rosenthal, G. (1991) 'Un informe crítico a 30 años de integración en América Latina', *Nueva Sociedad*, Vol. 113, pp. 60–65.

Sarkees, M. and Wayman, F. (2010) *Resort to War: 1816–2007*. Washington, DC: CQ Press.

Serbin, A., Martínez, L. and Júnior, H. R. (2012) 'El regionalismo "post-liberal" en América Latina y el Caribe: nuevos actors, nuevos temas, nuevos desafíos', Buenos Aires, Argentina: Coordinatora Regional de Investigaciones Económicas y Sociales, pp. 19–72.

Tigre, M. A. (2017) *Regional Cooperation in Amazonia: A Comparative Environmental Law Analysis*. Leiden/Boston: Brill/Nijhoff.

Vázquez, M. (2011) 'El MERCOSUR social: Cambio político y nueva identidad para el proceso de integración regional en América del Sur,' in: Caetano, G. (ed.), *MERCOSUR: 20 años*, Montevideo: Centro de Formación para la Integración Regional – CEFIR, pp. 165-187.

PART I:
REGIONAL RESPONSES TO COLLECTIVE SECURITY CHALLENGES

Chapter 1

Responses of Latin American organizations to coup attempts: Power play between political ideologies in post-hegemonic regionalism

Ivo Ganchev

Founder of the Centre for Regional Integration, UK

Abstract

This chapter analyses the responses of regional organizations to coup attempts in Latin America during the rise, peak, and decline of post-hegemonic regionalism. Non-democratic challenges to power are frequent in the region and have widespread implications for government legitimacy, which makes responses to them a key element of security policy. The cases examined in this chapter include both successful and unsuccessful coup attempts, such as those of Bolivia (2008), Honduras (2009), Ecuador (2010), Paraguay (2012), Brazil (2016) and Venezuela (2019). The chapter argues that Latin American organisations were moderately successful in their pro-active efforts to counter-balance both direct and indirect US interests and influence in Latin American regional security. The discussion compares responses to coups by various organisations such as the OAS, UNASUR, MERCOSUR, ALBA, CELAC, CARICOM, SICA and PROSUR, as well as the positions of the Lima Group and the Montevideo Mechanism on the Venezuelan crisis.

Keywords: Latin American organizations, coup d'état, post-hegemonic regionalism, Pink Tide, US influence, Venezuela, Blue Tide

***

1.1. Introduction

Writing in 1978, Howard Wiarda once remarked that "the incidence of Latin American coups has been so constant over such a long period of time [that they] could be considered... a 'normal', or 'regular' part of the political process" (p. 43). The cases he examined include military dictatorships established in Brazil (1964), Chile (1973), Uruguay (1973), and Argentina (1976), among others. These events brought about a wave of authoritarian regimes which remained in power until the 1980s. At that point, most Latin American countries experienced profound and promising political transitions towards democracy. However, during the past four decades, coups have continued to occasionally take place, albeit often in a "softer" form. Rather than seeking to undermine the model of democratic governance, more recent challengers to government power have often (though not always) aimed to assume control over the presidency through legal mechanisms such as impeachments or declarations of presidential incapacity.

Since 1978, there have been dozens of unsuccessful challenges to Latin American and Caribbean (LAC) governments in power, as well as at least 19 successful changes of government which the academic community broadly categorizes as coups (Pérez-Liñán and Polga-Hecimovich, 2016 p. 1). There are diverse definitions of the term "coup", and its use also sometimes differs between politicians and academics. The former often employ this word to characterize attacks against the legitimacy of their government and present themselves as victims or gain political support through rallying support from their base. The latter tend to study coups from an analytical perspective and categorize them according to various criteria, such as the extent to which force is used (e.g., hard and soft coups) or the mode through which a challenge to power is issued (e.g., military, constitutional and judicial coups; see Marsteintredet and Malamud, 2019). Some scholars have also proposed the use of other terms to categorize specific events, such as "white" coup (de Oliveira and de Souza, 2016) to indicate a shift in government orchestrated by the elites as opposed to the masses.

Coups are not only a security threat to LAC governments but also to maintaining peace and order in the region more broadly. There are also other regional security threats, such as inter-state disputes (notably about border or territorial control) and transnational organized crime (Dominguez, 2017, pp. 61–62). However, tackling coups is a particularly high priority for governments as this is essential to protect their political survival as well as norms of establishing and maintaining political legitimacy through democratic processes across the region at large. In addition to governments, regional organizations also possess important voices that shape responses to coups, and the oldest of them is the pan-regional Organization of American States (OAS).

The OAS has a broad mandate, which involves engagement in security matters enshrined in its founding document, where it is defined as a regional agency for UN purposes (Chapter VIII in the UN Charter; United Nations, 1945). The OAS designates the strengthening of peace and security and the promotion of democracy (Article 2 in OAS, 1948) as some of its basic tenets, which is rare for a regional organization. Although the OAS does not pursue direct interference and claims to be a collective instrument, it is, in fact, sometimes employed as a mechanism of US influence on LAC affairs. Historically, the US has viewed LAC as "America's backyard" (Livingstone, 2009) and in addition to its role in the OAS, it has also been engaged in regional security through partnerships with governments and involvement of various extents in orchestrating or supporting coups. Even though Washington often denies allegations of direct interference in Latin American affairs, declassified documents show several such instances in the latter half of the 20th century (Dietz, 1984) and this gives a reason for governments to have occasional doubts about the intentions of US actions or stances.

In contrast to earlier periods of Latin American regionalism, since the dawn of the new century, many LAC organizations have sought to frame their voices as independent from US influence. Scholars often describe this period of Latin American regionalism as post-hegemonic or post-liberal, referring to the desire to achieve greater independence from the influence of US hegemony or the US-backed ideology of neo-liberal economic development. This trend was driven by disillusionment with the mixed results that economic opening produced during the 1990s, which spurred the Pink Tide (Spanish: *marea rosa*), a term referring to the rise to power of leftist leaders in many LAC states during the early years of the 21st century (Ganchev, 2020). This led to changes in the landscape of regional governance – existing organizations, such as the Andean Community of Nations (CAN) and the Southern Common Market (MERCOSUR), would soon be joined by new ones, formed with strong support from leftist governments which were motivated to decrease US influence in the region. First, the Bolivarian Alliance for the Peoples of Our America (ALBA) was launched in 2004 under Venezuela's leadership and began to propagate radical opposition to the US. Then, the Union of South American Nations (UNASUR) was established in 2008 with major involvement from Brazil, partially with the aim of re-conceptualizing South America as a region separate from US influence. After that, the Community of Latin American and Caribbean States (CELAC) was launched with 33 member states, including Mexico, but excluding the US and Canada, seeking to conceptually separate LAC as a distinct region (rather than as a part of the Americas). These regional organizations soon developed their own voices and began to express positions and take action on a variety of issues, including both successful and failed coup attempts which shaped the context of regional security.

This chapter aims to analyze the responses of Latin American organizations when challenges to the power of incumbent governments have occurred. To what extent have LAC organizations addressed de facto coup attempts independently from US influence and from the OAS since the rise of post-hegemonic regionalism? How efficient were they and why so? Through addressing these questions, the chapter evaluates the performance of Latin American regional organizations vis-à-vis the US-promoted OAS, focusing on their successes and failures to promote and support peaceful and orderly resolutions to coup attempts. It offers comparative analysis and a retrospective evaluation which aims to present both conceptual and practical findings, including lessons for practitioners working on the design and operations of Latin American regional organizations.

The time period of post-hegemonic regionalism is defined through the rise and fall of the Pink Tide and its impact on Latin American politics, which effectively began with the evolution of ALBA from an agreement to a regional organization in 2004, reached a peak around the early 2010s and has been gradually subsiding from around 2015 to date. The case studies include all major events which have been broadly viewed as attempts or instances of a coup, broadly defined as a targeted attempt to overthrow a government with a clear opposition openly challenging an incumbent government and seeking to either replace it or position itself in a way that would make its election highly likely. It is important to note that cases of social unrest due to non-coordinated mass discontent or aiming to organize snap elections with largely unpredictable elections (Ecuador in 2004 and 2005, Bolivia in 2003 and 2005, as well as Chile in 2019) do not satisfy the criteria in the the above-discussed definition of a coup and are thus not discussed in this chapter.

The main body of the chapter is divided into four parts. The first one begins by briefly discussing coup attempts (Venezuela 2002 and Haiti 2004) in the early days of the Pink Tide and analyzes in more detail the responses of regional organizations to unsuccessful coup attempts at its peak (Bolivia 2008 and Ecuador 2010). The second part compares said responses to those addressing successful coup attempts around the same time period (Honduras 2009 and Paraguay 2012). The third part discusses regional responses to two cases of successful coup attempts (Brazil 2016 and Bolivia 2019) after the Pink Tide began to be gradually replaced with a Blue Tide (Spanish: *marea azul*), involving the election of many conservative governments starting in the mid-2010s. The fourth part discusses the case of regional responses to events leading up to and following a coup attempt in Venezuela (2019) from 2014 until now. Finally, the chapter presents a conclusion which summarizes the main findings, arguing that LAC regional organizations were moderately successful in their efforts to address coup attempts in ways that do not align with US interests.

1.2 Rise of the Pink Tide and regional responses to failed coup attempts in Bolivia (2008) and Ecuador (2010)

Prior to the formation of new regional organizations in the post-hegemonic era, the OAS played a key role as a regional mechanism for coordinating collective responses to attempts at coups. This is well-exemplified in the stance that the organization took during a coup attempt against Venezuelan leader Hugo Chavez in 2002. Curiously, Chavez himself had been a key leader in a failed coup in 1992 but eventually came to power through elections in 1998 and promoted the adoption of a new constitution in 1999, which received public support through a popular referendum at the time. However, three years later, the opposition gathered considerable popular support for their claims that the incumbent government was becoming undemocratic; hence, it sought to dissolve the Supreme Court and denounce the 1999 Constitution. This led to a military coup against Chavez on 11 April 2002, in which he was briefly removed from power and businessman Pedro Carmona was installed as interim president. Backed by the military and by a large portion of the general population which encircled the presidential palace and took control over television stations, Chavez returned to power after 47 hours.

Despite allegations of US support for the coup (see McCaughan, 2005), Chavez acknowledged post-factum that there was little evidence for this (Rory, 2014, pp. 82–3). Although the OAS (including the US) only met one day after the coup was effectively over and its position did not affect the outcome, it officially condemned perpetrators and dispatched the OAS Secretary General on a fact-finding and diplomatic mission to Venezuela (Parish et al., 2007, pp. 218–219). This vocal response was ultimately based on a defence of democratic principles and diplomatic dialogue. While there was some antagonism between the governments in Caracas and Washington in the early 2000s, it was still rather minor and did not substantially affect regional organization dynamics in the Americas at the time. This reveals that before the Pink Tide started to have a considerable impact on regional politics, there was much less polarization and hostility between the US and rising leftist leaders in Latin America (excluding the case of Cuba).

Another coup in the early days of the Pink Tide era took place in Haiti and unlike that against Chavez, this case illustrates the capacity of the US to interfere in LAC security much more directly. On 29 February 2004, after several weeks of conflict, Haitian President Jean-Bertrand Aristide was overthrown by a rebel group, including soldiers who were allegedly trained by the US. Upon the request of his successor, Boniface Alexandre, the United Nations Stabilization Mission in Haiti (MINUSTAH) was established and dispatched within hours to help stabilize the country, while Aristide was deported by American guards and eventually sought asylum in South Africa. Meanwhile, US

Marines swiftly arrived in Haiti and became the first external forces to intervene, although they would later be joined by Canadian, French and Chilean troops (Fishel and Saenz, 2007). In 2022, the French ambassador to Haiti at the time, Thierry Burkard, told The New York Times that France and the United States had "effectively orchestrated 'a coup' against Aristide by pressuring him to step down and taking him into exile" (Méheut et al., 2022), but his US counterpart James Brendan Foley (2022), refuted these claims, stating that there was "no evidence" in support of this claim. Regardless, the US response to the 2004 coup was clear, namely intervention in line with the desire of Haitian elites; two more similar events have taken place in Haiti over the past 30 years (Katz, 2022), so the 2004 occurrence is not an isolated case.

Other actors which responded to the coup include the Caribbean Community (CARICOM), which denounced the removal of Aristide and questioned the legality of the new government. It suspended Haiti from the organization and Jamaican Prime Minister Patterson expressed concerns that this sets "a dangerous precedent" (The Economist, 2004). However, these criticisms were not paired with substantial measures that would yield any lasting pressure on Haiti and after the election of its next president René Préval in 2006, the island country returned to CARICOM. This rather inconsequential response contrasts starkly with the US-led intervention described above. While one could reasonably argue that US direct involvement in Latin American politics has become less common over time, the case of Haiti showcases the capability and extent of the US to effectively determine the fate of some governments in the region as recently as 2004. These types of occurrences feed into a broader narrative of "anti-Americanism" which is grounded in the doubts and suspicions of Latin American politicians about the intention and outcome of US engagement in regional affairs, echoing the views of Simon Bolivar (1967), who once wrote that "the United States appear to be destined by Providence to plague America with misery in the name of liberty".

The pursuit of greater independence from the US influenced the discourse and actions of many Latin American leaders who were elected in the early years of the twenty-first century and began to reshape the landscape of LAC organizations around the same time. In 2003, as soon as Lula da Silva was sworn in, he began to work towards the establishment of the South American Community of Nations (CSN), which would eventually serve as a predecessor to UNASUR (Turner, 2006). In 2004, Venezuela and Cuba formally established ALBA (although they had already signed prior relevant agreements as well), an organization which would later gradually expand. The elections of other leftist leaders across Latin America in the following years would tilt the balance of political interests across Latin America in favour of seeking regional solutions to regional issues. Two of these leaders were Bolivian President Evo

Morales and Ecuadorian President Rafael Correa, who were elected in 2005 and 2006, respectively; both soon faced challenges to power, which ultimately proved unsuccessful.

In 2008, protests emerged against Bolivian President Evo Morales and they were followed by calls for greater autonomy for the country's eastern areas. These calls reached their peak on 11 September, when prefectural authorities of the Bolivian Department of Pando organized an assault on farmers supporting President Morales, which resulted in at least 12 deaths; this became known as the Porvenir massacre (Bjork-James, 2012).

When the authority of Evo Morales was briefly questioned, a considerable number of leftist Latin American governments explicitly expressed their support for him. The most radical statement came from Chávez, who warned that if Morales was overthrown or killed, then Venezuela would give a "green light" to conduct military operations in Bolivia. While the Bolivian army responded by rejecting "external intervention of any nature" (Notimérica, 2008), Chavez's statement was a clear sign that the Pink Tide was at the core of re-shaping regional security politics. This contributed to an ongoing deterioration in the relations of Bolivia and Venezuela with the US – Evo Morales accused the latter of supporting the opposition and declared the US ambassador persona non grata, while Washington issued a reciprocal response. To express solidarity, Venezuela echoed Bolivia's accusations of the US and expelled its ambassador.

At the same time, several LAC governments expressed their support for Evo Morales in various forms. The presidents of Ecuador and Nicaragua directly stated their support for the expulsion of the US ambassador from Bolivia, while Honduras delayed by a week a ceremony at which the US ambassador was supposed to present his credentials. Brazil issued a more measured but crucially important response by announcing that it will guarantee gas supplies to Bolivia and offering to potentially mediate discussions between Morales and his opposition. At this point, it became clear that leftist governments in Latin America were using diplomatic tools to effectively support Morales.

Many international organizations refrained from taking a side in the Bolivian political conflict and some regional ones followed suit; for instance, CAN echoed statements by the UN and the EU and condemned any form of violence, making calls for a peaceful resolution. However, the OAS and the newly established UNASUR had a greater focus on security and the opportunity to support a resolution of the crisis. The President Pro Tempore of UNASUR, Chilean head of state Michelle Bachelet, called a special summit in Santiago and invited the Secretary-General of the OAS, José Miguel Insulza. At the time, an ongoing diplomatic skirmish between Bolivia and the US, as well as the fact that the Bolivian opposition believed the Secretary General of the OAS was supportive of Evo Morales (Tussie 2016, pp. 76–79) made the organization seem less credible than UNASUR as a potential mediator. Hence, UNASUR sent its own separate mission to Bolivia, which was supposed to only coordinate its activities with the OAS. While the OAS did support the territorial integrity of Bolivia in principle, it was in a worse position than UNASUR to take the lead in facilitating crisis resolution.

Meanwhile, UNASUR had a strong incentive to engage in order to gain visibility (Nolte, 2018, pp. 135) as it was recently established and sought to deepen the extent of trust it garnered from LAC governments. Brazil, which was de facto the leading state in UNASUR, had already proposed to serve as an honest broker, mediating between the Morales government and his opposition. This pro-active stance as well as the quick and constructive response by UNASUR to the Bolivian crisis, differs starkly from the delayed response by the OAS to the 2002 coup attempt in Venezuela, which only came after the issue was already resolved.

Soon, UNASUR would have one more opportunity to play a key role in responding to a coup against another leftist leader, namely Ecuadorian President Rafael Correa. In September 2010, he began to face backlash from security forces regarding discussions about the potential adoption of a new Public Service Organic Law, which would have restructured the regulations determining the bonuses and awards that officers receive (de la Torre, 2017). Many officers did not appear to be aware that Correa had expressed a partial objection to the law and felt it was unfair to them. On 30 September 2010, large parts of the Armed Forces and the National Police protested across nine provinces in Ecuador. They demanded special bonuses and blocked roads and airports in Quito and Guayaquil, causing chaos and looting.

Correa went to a police barracks in Quito intending to help calm down the situation but in fact, there he was attacked and injured by the protesters. This prompted him to famously respond, "If you want to kill the president, here he is". He was taken to a hospital, where he was trapped by the police and declared a state of emergency from there. A loyal group of security officers rescued him from the hospital in a televised raid. Correa then returned to the palace and delivered a speech, denouncing the coup attempt and thanking his supporters and Latin American allies. He announced a three-day national mourning for the 8 people who died and the 274 who were hurt in the unrest, which became known as 30-S.

Many Latin American states declared their support for President Rafael Correa. Key UNASUR members such as Brazil, Argentina and Venezuela recognized the unrest as a coup but some, such as Chile, did not share this assessment. The ruling government of Honduras, where a coup had recently taken place in 2009 (analyzed in the next section) as well as various other LAC governments, expressed hope that the events of 30-S will not end in the same way.

While many in Ecuador suspect that the US had helped to orchestrate the unrest, later, it officially expressed support for Correa through its ambassador to the OAS and Ecuadorian foreign minister Ricardo Patiño stated he believes that he sees no evidence of interference by the US government. The OAS approved a resolution supporting Correa's government and asked relevant stakeholders to avoid "exacerbating" political instability. While this was a show of international solidarity, it was not paired with any concrete action. It did not indicate willingness or capacity to effectively address the security crisis and de facto resembled responses of third-party organizations, such as an expression of concern by the UN and a call for respecting law and order by the EU.

In contrast to the OAS, UNASUR called an emergency meeting on the evening of September 30. Responding to events almost in real time, heads of state from Argentina, Bolivia, Chile, Uruguay, Venezuela, Colombia, and Peru attended the meeting; the four remaining member states sent representatives and their leaders were absent only because of urgent political or health-related reasons. The Secretary General of UNASUR, Néstor Kirchner, notably stated that "South America cannot tolerate that corporate interests threaten and put pressure on democratically elected governments for fear of losing undue privileges". At this point, Colombia and Peru had already closed their borders with Ecuador in solidarity with the Correa government and the other member states of UNASUR agreed that if unrest continues to escalate, they will do the same and further suspend commerce, air traffic and other forms of engagement with Ecuador temporarily. Furthermore, it was also decided that the foreign ministers of UNASUR countries travel to Quito on the morning of 1 October. During the following Heads of State summit of the organization on 26 November, a democratic clause was adopted as an additional protocol to the Constitutive Treaty of the organization.

The cases analyzed so far reveal that the dynamics of regional responses to coup attempts in South America changed considerably from the early to the late 2000s. This shift resulted in the establishment of UNASUR, which began to offer faster and more constructive responses than the OAS to address crises of political legitimacy in South America, becoming a preferred option for leftist governments to engage with. This development is effectively an outcome of the rise of the Pink Tide and it was largely driven by the leadership of Brazil in UNASUR as well as by the vocal stance of Venezuela on various issues which was instrumental in the effort of South American governments to diminish the extent of US influence on politics in LAC. The next section moves on to discuss regional responses addressing successful coups in Honduras and Paraguay.

1.3 Regional responses to successful coup attempts in Honduras (2009) and Paraguay (2012) at the peak of the Pink Tide

Unlike the failed coup attempts in Bolivia and Ecuador, those in Honduras and Paraguay succeeded in overthrowing incumbent governments. On 28 June 2009, the Honduran Army, following orders from the Supreme Court, ousted liberal (leftist) president Manuel Zelaya and sent him into exile. Roberto Micheletti was installed to serve as an interim de facto president for the rest of 2009. Meanwhile, new elections were held and won by conservative Porfirio Lobo Sosa who assumed the presidency in early 2010; Lobo had previously lost to Manuel Zelaya in 2005 but was now able to win against much weaker opposition. The 2009 coup was widely condemned by the international community, including both global and regional organizations.

Initially, it was condemnation by the OAS that had the potential to carry more weight than other organizations because it could express a collective voice of all states in the Americas. The organization reacted by applying its Inter-American Democratic Charter (IADC), which was adopted in 2001 as a mechanism to protect and promote democracy. The OAS issued a resolution on June 28 that condemned the events as a "military coup d'état", demanding the immediate and unconditional restoration of Zelaya's government. The resolution also invoked Article 20 of the IADC, which allows any member state or the Secretary General to request an immediate convocation of the Permanent Council to undertake a collective assessment of the situation and take appropriate decisions. On July 1, following a failed diplomatic mission led by Secretary General José Miguel Insulza to Honduras, the OAS issued an ultimatum to the Micheletti regime to reinstate Zelaya within 72 hours or face suspension from the organization. On July 4, after the deadline expired without compliance from the de facto authorities, the OAS voted unanimously (with Honduras abstaining) to suspend Honduras from its membership, invoking Article 21 of the IADC for the first time in its history. The suspension was intended to isolate and pressure the Micheletti regime to accept a negotiated solution that would restore Zelaya to power until the end of his term in January 2010 (OAS, 2009a; 2009b).

At the time, one could make a reasonably strong case that the response of the OAS had the potential to fulfil its purpose of defending democratic principles and showcasing that countries which violate them might find themselves in isolation from the Americas. However, retrospectively it is now clear that the response was too rushed and too blunt to be successful. As Thomas Legler (2012, pp. 78–79) rightly points out, the OAS "ignored the longstanding diplomatic principle of a graduated, flexible response to crises that it shares with the United Nations" as stipulated in Articles 17 to 22 of the Democratic Charter. The stance of the organization was such that creating leeway to discuss an eventual normalization of relations with Honduras meant that either the organization would have to roll back its position, undermining the strength of its own voice, or the Honduran elites would have to allow the return of a president who was forced out of power, neither of which was realistic.

In early November 2009, the US unilaterally made a move that effectively dismantled the unity that had been previously achieved among states in the Americas. At the time, Assistant Secretary of State Thomas Shannon gave an interview to the Spanish-language news channel of CNN, indicating that the US would likely recognize the upcoming election which was to take place on 29 November in Honduras. This inspired a division between OAS states after the election; one group, which included traditionally closer US allies and other states with non-leftist governments from South and Central America (e.g., Colombia, Costa Rica, Guatemala, Panama, and Peru), aligned with the statement of Thomas Shannon. Another group, which included many influential UNASUR member countries with leftist governments in power (e.g., Argentina, Bolivia, Brazil, Ecuador, and Venezuela), maintained the original stance of the OAS, demanding that Zelaya return to power. However, once international unity was broken by the US, it became clear that eventually, the relations of Honduras with LAC states and organizations would normalize over time.

It is difficult to believe that the statement of Thomas Shannon and the subsequent division it caused in the stance of the OAS was an accident, as the response to the Honduran coup was such a contentious issue that it was even discussed in domestic US political debates. Prior to the emergence of divisions among OAS members, Noam Chomsky (2009) already wrote in October that he sees signs that US criticism of the coup is weak and suspected that Washington would eventually passively support the coup in hopes "to maintain and probably expand its military base at Soto Cano" and possibly to seek further establishment of other bases in Honduras as well; furthermore, he also correctly pointed out that many officers of the Honduran military have been trained by the US, so some degree of coordination between security forces from both sides was likely. Critical observers have continued to make similar arguments (e.g., Johnston, 2017) for an extended time period following the coup. While it is difficult to pinpoint with certainty the exact considerations of the US, military strategy clearly played some role in its decisions and ultimately produced broader implications that impacted the stance of the OAS.

A smaller regional organization which took a more principled stance but had limited influence was ALBA, which Honduras had recently joined in 2008 under Manuel Zelaya's presidency. Its member states expressed solidarity and assisted the ousted president in various ways, such as providing him with a plane to travel to Nicaragua after his exile in Costa Rica (Fernández, 2021), offering him asylum in their countries (The Guardian, 2009), expelling or recalling their ambassadors from Honduras (but leaving other diplomatic staff; Reuters, 2009), suspending trade and cooperation agreements with Tegucigalpa (ALBA-TCP, 2009), closing their borders with Honduras temporarily, and threatening military intervention if Zelaya was harmed (de la Torre, 2017). ALBA also issued a warning that it would expel Honduras from its membership unless Zelaya was restored to power (ALBA-TCP, 2009), although before this could happen President Roberto Micheletti deposited a request to withdraw from the organization after ratifying it through Congress.

The role of ALBA in the Honduran crisis was driven by ideological affinity with Zelaya and antagonism toward Micheletti and his allies (de la Torre, 2017), as well as by strategic interests in maintaining or expanding its influence and presence in Central America (Malamud and Gardini, 2012). This had some rhetorical impact on the shaping of regional responses to the coup and contributed to the effort to counter-balance voices arguing for the recognition of the new government after the 2009 elections. However, ultimately the statements and actions of ALBA had much less real impact on Honduran politics compared to those of the US and the OAS. This is both due to the smaller weight that Venezuela and ALBA carry and because of the organization's general lack of institutional capacity, resources, and legitimacy to mediate or resolve conflicts.

As mentioned above, many South American states took a highly critical stance against the Honduran coup within the OAS; they also expressed this position through UNASUR, showing solidarity and support for Zelaya by sending a delegation of foreign ministers to accompany him in his attempted return to Honduras on July 5, 2009, which was blocked by the Micheletti regime. UNASUR also refused to recognize any government that emerged from the November 29 elections and stated that it would not restore diplomatic relations with Honduras until Zelaya was restored to power (UNASUR, 2009).

UNASUR's role in the Honduran crisis was driven by a commitment to defend democratic principles and constitutional order in the region, as well as by a desire to enhance its visibility and credibility as a regional actor. The organization sought to differentiate itself from the OAS by adopting a more proactive and coherent stance on the Honduran crisis. Notably, in November 2009, UNASUR adopted a democratic clause as an additional protocol to its constitutive treaty, which establishes sanctions for any member state that suffers or perpetrates a rupture of the democratic order (UNASUR, 2010). However, this move seemed intended for strengthening the general legitimacy of the organization as a security mechanism in the future, rather than a tool for addressing the Honduran crisis. In fact, the potential of UNASUR to exert any real influence on Honduras was limited to begin with, as it was designed to function as an organization of South American rather than Central American states.

A sub-regional mechanism which had considerable economic leverage was the Central American Integration System (SICA). It condemned the Honduran coup and temporarily suspended the country while instating an immediate economic blockage. The members of SICA, which account for around one-fifth of the imports and exports of Honduras, suspended any economic engagement with the country, which resulted in an estimated loss in exports of 2.85 million dollars in two days. Furthermore, the new government was temporarily not allowed access to loans and disbursements from the Central American Integration Bank (Castro, Fonseca and Garro, 2012). These sanctions would have had a profound impact if they were maintained; however, this was not sustainable as the member states of SICA eventually became divided in their stances: Costa Rica, Guatemala, and Panama became more aligned with the position that the US suggestively expressed in early November, while others, such as Nicaragua and El Salvador, remained sympathetic to Zelaya. Hence, it became impossible for SICA to maintain a strong stance and attempt to force change in Honduran politics after its initial position became more watered down.

The coup in Paraguay on 22 June 2012 was another case that tested the responses of different regional organizations in Latin America to a democratic crisis. The coup, which ousted President Fernando Lugo and installed Vice President Federico Franco as the de facto leader, was carried out by the Paraguayan Congress, which impeached Lugo by a vote of 39 to 4 in a summary trial lasting less than 24 hours and giving him only two hours to defend himself. The accusation against Lugo was that he had failed to fulfil his duties as president, especially in relation to a violent clash between police and landless peasants that resulted in 17 deaths on 15 June 2012. His impeachment was widely condemned by the international community, including the United Nations, the European Union, and the OAS, as a "parliamentary coup" or a "constitutional coup" that violated due process and democratic principles (Dangl, 2012; Nickson, 2012).

The OAS reacted to the Paraguayan coup by sending a delegation of foreign ministers to Paraguay on 26 June 2012 to assess the situation and conduct dialogue with the different actors involved. The delegation issued a report on 10 July 2012, expressing concern for the lack of due process and guarantees for Lugo's defence in the impeachment trial but also recognizing that the trial was based on constitutional provisions and that there was no evidence of violence or coercion by the security forces. The report also recommended that the OAS should not suspend Paraguay from its membership but rather accompany and support the country in its electoral process and institutional strengthening.

This recommendation was approved by the OAS Permanent Council on 13 July 2012, with only Venezuela dissenting.

A subsequent visit by OAS representatives was arranged as well and it resulted in a second report which reiterated the findings and recommendations of the first one, urging the OAS to continue to assist Paraguay in strengthening its democratic institutions and processes, as well as to promote social inclusion and development. The OAS thus adopted a more cautious and conciliatory approach to the Paraguayan crisis than it did in the Honduran case, partly due to the legal ambiguity and complexity of the impeachment process and due to the reluctance of some member states to impose sanctions on Paraguay (OAS, 2012a; 2012b).

This careful OAS response was shaped by both technical and political factors. First, it was not clear from the norms of the OAS charter and of the IADC whether the organization should view the case as a coup and the final decision was left to interpretation by political actors. And second, the US stance influenced that of other member states as it did not recognize the case as a violation of democracy but rather saw it as a constitutional matter that should be resolved internally by Paraguayans. There were various pragmatic motivations that made this decision optimal for the US. It had a strategic interest in maintaining stability and security in Paraguay and the region in order to continue bilateral cooperation in relation to drug trafficking and maintain its military base in Mariscal Estigarribia. Meanwhile, Washington also had doubts about the extent to which a government led by Lugo would continue to be a reliable partner, given his moderately leftist orientation – although he did not propagate an anti-American ideology as vocally as Hugo Chavez or other more prominent leftist leaders, his ideas were often not aligned with US policy either.

Latin American regional organizations took different stances in response to the coup in Paraguay. MERCOSUR and UNASUR were the first to respond and they both had previously adopted democracy clauses; the former introduced one in 1998, while the latter did so as a response to the Honduran coup in 2009, as discussed above. The suspension of Paraguay from MERCOSUR brought much more tangible consequences for Paraguay and caused a reshuffle in regional politics. For the duration of the suspension, the country lost its eligibility for loans from the MERCOSUR Structural Convergence Fund (which had financed several infrastructure and social development initiatives) as well as its voice within the region.

The other member states of MERCOSUR took advantage of the opportunity to advance pending proposals that had been previously blocked by Paraguay's opposition. The most notable one was the full incorporation of Venezuela into MERCOSUR, which had been approved by Argentina, Brazil, and Uruguay in 2006, but had not been ratified by Paraguay's Congress due to ideological differences with Venezuela's leftist government. Taking advantage of Paraguay's absence, the presidents of Argentina, Brazil, and Uruguay decided to admit Venezuela as a full member of MERCOSUR on 31 July 2012, arguing that there was no legal obstacle since Paraguay had been suspended. This was seen as a strategic move to strengthen the bloc's economic and political weight in the region and beyond, as well as to counterbalance the influence of the United States. However, it was also controversial: Paraguay denounced it as illegal and appealed to the MERCOSUR Permanent Review Tribunal (TPR), a judicial body created by the Olivos Protocol in 2002 to settle disputes within the bloc, challenging the legality of its suspension and Venezuela's incorporation. However, the TPR did not rule on the merits of the case but only on procedural issues and effectively dismissed Paraguay's appeal.

The actions of MERCOSUR and UNASUR were certainly shaped by the strategic interests of their member states, and perhaps most notably by those of Brazil. In addition to the blockage on admitting Venezuela to MEROCSUR, the Brazilian government was also annoyed about several other disagreements with the Lugo administration. These included proposals for land reform in Paraguay (where many landowners are Brazilian immigrants) and Lugo's campaign to renegotiate the terms of the Itaipu treaty with Brazil. Besides, counter-narcotics efforts and the military presence of Brazil in Paraguay could have been threatened if the country was destabilized. Eventually, Brazil supported Paraguay's reintegration into MERCOSUR and UNASUR after new elections were held in 2013.

Other regional organizations which were critical of the coup include ALBA and CELAC. The response of the former had little practical relevance in this case, as Paraguay was not a full member of ALBA to begin with. CELAC was established in 2011 as a regional political coordination mechanism primarily hosts forums and discussions. Hence, its decision to suspend which Paraguay had a mostly symbolical meaning in this case.

Comparing regional responses to the coups in Honduras and Paraguay reveals that the dynamics that determine their formation are highly complex. Broadly speaking, they involve a contradiction of interests between the US and governments of states which seek to align with its policy vis-à-vis South American blocs that were dominated by leftist governments at the time. There were some inconsistencies in regional responses to the two cases but generally, the OAS and MERCOSUR appeared to operate more ad-hoc and their decisions were highly impacted by national interests, while UNASUR provided more principled responses, which gave it greater credibility in terms of addressing Latin American security issues at the time. Other organizations had less de facto impact for various reasons, such as internal divergence of stances (SICA), lack of real leverage (ALBA) or little ability to project political/economic impact by design (CELAC). Soon, the Pink Tide began to subside, which also led to changes in the landscape of Latin American regional politics. The next section discusses this development and analyzes responses to subsequent coups in Brazil and Bolivia.

1.4 Rise of the Blue Tide and regional responses to successful coup attempts in Brazil (2016) and Bolivia (2019)

By the early 2010s, the political conditions in Latin America had already begun to change. First, Lula was replaced by Dilma Rousseff in 2011; then, Venezuela saw the passing away of Chavez and the beginning of a polarizing political period marked by financial instability in 2013. It soon became apparent that this would change the landscape of post-hegemonic regional organizations. When the VI UNASUR Summit took place in Lima in 2012, the presidents of Argentina, Brazil and Venezuela, who had suspended Paraguay from UNASUR, were all absent. At the VII UNASUR Summit, four out of twelve heads of state were absent, which prevented the organization from appointing a new Secretary General. Although the organization continued to develop on paper, it had de facto stalled and ultimately became completely dysfunctional by 2018. Meanwhile, ALBA also began to lose its political appeal as the Pink Tide had clearly subsided and was gradually replaced by a wave of right-wing governments that emerged in LAC during the mid-2010s, causing the Blue Tide. This context shaped regional responses to two successful coup attempts in Brazil (2016) and Bolivia (2019).

The OAS did not condemn the impeachment as a coup or a violation of democracy and human rights. Instead, the organisation recognized Temer as the legitimate president and respected Brazil's internal affairs and constitutional process. The OAS Secretary General Luis Almagro met with Dilma Rousseff and expressed his concern for the situation, but he did not invoke the Inter-American Democratic Charter or propose any collective actions or measures to address the crisis (OAS, 2016). The OAS also did not issue any statement or resolution on Brazil through its General Assembly or Permanent Council.

This response was in line with the position of the US and other OAS members which also recognized the legitimacy of Temer. The US had previously had a somewhat adversarial relationship with Rousseff and her predecessor, Lula, who had pursued an independent and assertive foreign policy that often clashed with US interests on issues such as trade, development, and human rights among others (Burges, 2017). The OAS response to the coup in Brazil also reflected the position of other member states such as Argentina, Chile, Colombia, Mexico, and Peru. These countries had a pragmatic and strategic relationship with Brazil and it was in their interest to maintain economic ties with the country after the fall of Rousseff. Hence, their response was not motivated by a desire to uphold democratic principles but rather by their own interests.

Three organizations which had emerged directly from the rise of the Pink Tide, UNASUR, CELAC and ALBA, issued more critical responses, but none of them translated into concrete actions or measures that could affect Brazil. The then Secretary General of UNASUR, Ernesto Samper, denounced the impeachment process as a "serious threat to regional democracy and hemispheric legal certainty" (Jacomino, 2016). He also expressed his solidarity with Rousseff and warned that her removal would have negative consequences for regional integration and cooperation. He called for an extraordinary meeting of the foreign ministers of UNASUR to discuss the situation in Brazil and seek a common position on the impeachment of Rousseff. The meeting took place on April 22, 2016, in Quito, Ecuador, and resulted in a statement that reaffirmed UNASUR's commitment to democracy and constitutional order, rejected any form of coup d'état or rupture of institutional legitimacy, and urged dialogue and respect for due process in Brazil.

CELAC produced a response which was similar to that of UNASUR. On 18 April 2016, the then Pro Tempore Presidency of CELAC, held by the Dominican Republic, issued a statement that expressed its concern for the political situation in Brazil and its solidarity with Rousseff. A meeting of CELAC foreign ministers and the release of a statement in support of democracy followed; however, this was not paired with any concrete action. There were various reasons for this; first, there was a division of opinions within both organizations; and second, Brazil had played a leading role in both of them, so taking concrete measures to delegitimize Temer's government would have risked triggering their potentially rapid collapse.

ALBA issued the most vocal and critical response of all regional organizations. Its then Secretary General, David Choquehuanca, denounced the impeachment process as a "parliamentary coup" and a "conspiracy" against Rousseff, making a stronger statement than those of UNASUR and CELAC. He also expressed his solidarity with Rousseff and warned that her removal would have negative consequences for regional integration and cooperation. Following a meeting of the foreign ministers of ALBA, the organization condemned the impeachment as a coup d'état and a violation of democracy and human rights. Nevertheless, this did not inspire any further concrete measures as they would have likely been ineffective – ALBA lacked institutional mechanisms and had little leverage over Brazil, to begin with. The instalment of Michel Temer as Brazilian President in 2016 was a notable event in the rise of the Blue Tide and it weakened the voice of post-hegemonic regional organizations.

Another coup that took place against the backdrop of these new dynamics in Latin American regional politics unfolded in Bolivia in late 2019. After fourteen years in power, Evo Morales, the first indigenous president of Bolivia and one of the most prominent leaders of the Pink Tide, was forced to resign amid allegations of electoral fraud and pressure from the military and the police. His departure triggered a wave of protests by his supporters, mainly from indigenous and rural sectors, who faced violent repression by the security forces and paramilitary groups. Jeanine Áñez, a conservative senator from the opposition, assumed the interim presidency with the support of the right-wing parties and civic committees that had led the anti-Morales mobilizations. The interim government quickly reversed many of Morales's policies, both domestically and internationally, and initiated a campaign of persecution against his party, the Movement for Socialism (MAS), and its allies.

The OAS had sent an electoral observation mission to monitor the general elections held on October 20, 2019, in which Morales sought a fourth term in office. The preliminary results showed a close race between Morales and his main challenger, Carlos Mesa, a former president and leader of the Civic Community coalition. However, after a pause in the transmission of the official vote count, Morales's lead increased and surpassed the 10 percentage points needed to avoid a runoff. This sparked accusations of fraud coming from Mesa and his supporters, who took to the streets to demand a second round or new elections.

The OAS mission issued a statement on October 21 expressing its "deep concern and surprise at the drastic and hard-to-explain change in the trend of the preliminary results" and calling for maximum transparency in the process (OAS 2019b). The OAS then agreed with the Bolivian government to conduct an audit of the electoral results, which began on October 31 with the participation of experts from several countries. However, before completing the audit, the OAS issued another statement on November 10, in which it claimed to have found "clear manipulations" and "serious irregularities" in the election, such as hidden servers, forged signatures, and altered tally sheets. The OAS recommended appointing a new electoral authority and holding new elections; it also urged all political actors to contribute to restoring peace and social harmony (OAS 2019a). This statement was released hours after Morales had announced that he would call for new elections and renew the electoral body following a report by the Bolivian police that revealed a plot to alter the results by some officials of the Supreme Electoral Tribunal (TSE). The OAS statement was widely interpreted as a confirmation of fraud and a rejection of Morales's legitimacy, which emboldened his opponents to demand his resignation.

The role of the OAS in the Bolivian crisis has been criticized by several analysts and observers who have questioned its impartiality, methodology, and timing. Some have argued that the OAS acted as an instrument of US foreign policy, which sought to undermine Morales's government and support the opposition forces (Johnston et al., 2021). The US had long been hostile to Morales's government, which had expelled the US ambassador and the Drug Enforcement Administration (DEA) agents from Bolivia during the 2008 coup attempt discussed above, accusing them of conspiring against him. Morales had also denounced the US for supporting the opposition forces and for seeking to undermine his socialist and anti-imperialist project (Reuters, 2019). The US was one of the first countries to recognize Áñez as the interim president and to congratulate her for "leading her nation through this democratic transition" (US Department of State, 2019).

Others have pointed out that the OAS did not provide conclusive evidence of fraud and that its allegations were based on flawed statistical analysis and selective use of data (Curiel and Williams 2019). Moreover, some have suggested that the OAS violated its own protocols and procedures by issuing statements before completing its audit and by exceeding its mandate as an observer (Zegada, 2020). Naturally, the OAS has rejected these accusations and criticisms (OAS 2020) but its response was clearly aligned with the interests of non-leftist governments. It is also worth noting that by this point, Venezuela had already announced its departure from the OAS and was close to finalizing the leaving procedure. Hence, the country which would have been the strongest supporter of Evo Morales in the organization had no voice within its structure at the time.

Among the countries that recognized Áñez as the interim president and endorsed the OAS's findings were most of the members of the Lima Group, a coalition of fourteen American countries that was created in 2017 to address the Venezuelan crisis and that has adopted a critical stance towards the Maduro government (explained further in the next section). The position of the Lima Group reflected the alignment of these countries with US interests and policies in the region, as well as a collective opposition to leftist governments and movements.

By this point in time, UNASUR had de facto stalled; other American organizations faced internal disagreement regarding the stance that they should take in terms of the Bolivian coup. One of them was CAN, which includes Bolivia as well as other members with diverging stances, namely the right-wing governments of Colombia and Peru that recognized Áñez as interim president and the left-wing government of Ecuador which denounced the coup. In MERCOSUR, there was a very clear divergence between the positions of its member states. On the one hand, the right-wing governments of Brazil and Paraguay recognized Áñez and supported the OAS, while on the other hand the left-wing governments of Uruguay and Argentina denounced the coup against Morales and condemned the statement of the OAS.

Certain Latin American states as well as ALBA, expressed strong support for Morales. Notably, the Mexican government stood out as it openly voiced its criticism of the coup and defended Morales, while offering him political asylum as well. This stance appears to have been largely principled and rooted in the leftist leanings of Mexican President Andrés Manuel López Obrador, rather than based on pragmatic considerations. Meanwhile, ALBA issued a statement on November 14 that categorically condemned the coup, expressing support with "brother" Evo Morales and repudiating the stance and statements of then-US President Donald Trump, who had been supportive of Áñez. However, at this stage, leftist governments in Latin America were already facing various issues in areas such as economic growth and international legitimacy, among others; hence, this statement had little real impact.

The regional responses to the two coups analyzed here reveal that after the Blue Tide replaced the Pink Tide, the voice of Latin American regional organizations substantially weakened while that of the OAS became stronger and this allowed the US a greater platform to exert more influence in accordance with its interests. Both newly formed organizations that emerged as symbols of post-hegemonic regionalism (notably, UNASUR, ALBA and CELAC) and older ones which had temporarily supported greater independence of Latin American affairs declined in terms of their prominence. This happened partially because the driving force of UNASUR and CELAC, Brazil, experienced a coup that brought a conservative government in power and questioning its legitimacy would have caused regional tension that would be of little benefit to any country. Meanwhile, the general orientation of the US and the mechanisms of the OAS had remained relatively stable, which made them more appealing in the absence of alternative modes of forming consensus. All of this enabled the creation of channels for exerting regional pressure on Venezuela, where Nicolas Maduro has been facing a deepening crisis since 2014 and had to fend off a coup attempt in 2019; the next section discusses regional responses to these events.

1.5 Division in regional responses to the Venezuelan crisis (2014-on) and coup attempt (2019)

Venezuela has been suffering an ongoing socioeconomic and political crisis that began during the final years of Chávez and continued to worsen throughout Nicolás Maduro's presidency. A fall in oil prices was a main trigger for the crisis, as this would eventually cause hyperinflation and hunger as well as increased poverty and crime rates, leading to massive emigration from the country. The crisis culminated on 23 January 2019 when the assembly's president, Juan Guaidó, declared himself interim president of Venezuela, effectively seeking to oust Maduro. At the time, there were various allegations against the Maduro government of having manipulated the 2018 elections, where voter turnout was only 46%, nearly twice lower than the 79.7% and 81.5% turnout rates at previous elections in 2013 and 2012. Both the crisis escalating from 2014 on and the challenge that Guaidó issued to the power of the Maduro government prompted numerous international and regional responses.

One organization which became actively involved in addressing the crisis in Venezuela early on in 2014 was the OAS. At the time, it adopted a resolution expressing solidarity with the Venezuelan people and calling for dialogue and respect for human rights (OAS, 2014). However, over time, the OAS also faced divisions and disagreements among its member states over how to deal with the Maduro government and its legitimacy.

At the most fundamental level, the source of the divisions in the OAS was similar to that in the cases of other regional organizations, namely divergences between the political positioning of its member states. The then OAS secretary-general, Luis Almagro, who has been a vocal critic of Maduro and a supporter of Guaidó, has repeatedly argued that Maduro's government has violated the IADC by undermining democratic institutions, repressing dissent, holding fraudulent elections and violating human rights. He has also advocated for stronger sanctions and diplomatic pressure on Maduro, as well as "not excluding any action" to restore democracy in Venezuela (Al Jazeera, 2018).

On the one hand, Almagro's stance has been backed by some OAS member states, especially those aligned with the Lima Group (its role is explained further below), such as Argentina, Brazil, Canada, Colombia, Peru and the United States. These countries recognized Guaidó as Venezuela's legitimate president and imposed sanctions on Maduro's regime. They also supported Almagro's re-election as secretary-general in 2020 despite opposition from other countries that favoured a more conciliatory approach towards Maduro.

On the other hand, some OAS member states have rejected Almagro's interventionist posture and have defended Maduro's sovereignty and right to self-determination. These countries include Bolivia, Cuba, Dominica, Nicaragua and Suriname, which are members of ALBA (discussed further below), an alliance of leftist governments that was founded by Chavez in 2004. They were also joined by Mexico and Uruguay, which adopted a neutral position on Venezuela's internal affairs and proposed a dialogue-based solution through the Montevideo mechanism. These countries criticized Almagro for exceeding his mandate and for undermining the OAS's credibility and unity.

Divisions within the OAS have prevented it from reaching a consensus on how to address the crisis in Venezuela. The OAS Permanent Council, which is composed of representatives of all member states, has held several meetings and debates on Venezuela since 2014 but has failed to adopt any binding resolutions or actions due to a lack of agreement or veto by some countries. The OAS General Assembly, which is composed of foreign ministers or heads of state of all member states, has also discussed the Venezuelan crisis in its annual sessions since 2014 but has only issued non-binding declarations or resolutions that reflect different positions or perspectives on the situation.

One of the most controversial moments in the OAS's involvement in Venezuela occurred in April 2017, when Almagro convened a special session of the Permanent Council to discuss Venezuela's constitutional crisis following a Supreme Court ruling that annulled the powers of the National Assembly. The session was held without consulting or notifying Venezuela's representative at the OAS, so naturally, the Maduro government reacted angrily to Almagro's initiative and accused him of interfering in its internal affairs and violating the OAS charter. In April 2017, Venezuela announced its decision to withdraw from the OAS, becoming the first member state to do so in the history of the organization. The withdrawal process took two years and was completed in April 2019 (Garcia, 2019). Venezuela's foreign minister at the time, Delcy Rodríguez, said that the move was a "free and sovereign decision" in the face of "interventionist abuses" by the OAS.

The OAS's involvement in taking a stance on the crisis and coup attempt in Venezuela has been controversial and divisive, not only within the organization but also among external actors and observers. Some have praised Almagro for his leadership and courage in denouncing Maduro's authoritarianism and defending democracy and human rights (Reuters, 2017). Others have criticized him for being biased and partisan, acting as an agent of US interests and undermining the OAS's credibility and legitimacy as a regional forum for dialogue and cooperation. A third group of observers have also questioned the effectiveness and impact of the OAS's actions on resolving the crisis in Venezuela, arguing that they have failed to produce any concrete results or changes on the ground (Cobb, 2019). Regardless, the result was that the OAS did not manage to induce Maduro to step down.

One development that emerged out of the lack of capacity of the OAS in terms of the limited strength of its actions in response to the crisis in Venezuela took place in August 2017 when Canada and 13 Latin American countries formed the Lima Group, an ad hoc coalition officially claiming to work to address the crisis in Venezuela. Although it was not an organization in itself, the Lima Group became a part of the landscape of regional bodies that shaped responses to the Venezuelan crisis. The Lima Group issued numerous declarations condemning Maduro's actions, calling for free and fair elections, demanding respect for human rights and democracy and offering humanitarian aid to Venezuela. Ultimately, in 2019 it supported Guaidó's claim to the presidency and imposed sanctions on Maduro's regime and its officials, such as travel bans, asset freezes and arms embargoes. Although it stated that its aim was to advocate for a peaceful solution to the prolonged crisis, its methods for achieving this were quite strong.

The formation of the Lima Group has been influenced by several factors that have shaped its development and evolution. One factor is the ideological alignment of most of its members with a centre-right or conservative orientation in opposition to Maduro's socialism. Another factor is the geopolitical interest of some of its members in containing Venezuela's influence. A third factor is the economic interest of some of its members in maintaining or expanding trade and investment ties with Venezuela or its oil sector. A fourth factor is the humanitarian concern of some of its members over the plight of millions of Venezuelan refugees and migrants that have fled to their territories or neighbouring countries.

Venezuela has rejected the Lima Group's stance and accused it of being a tool of US interventionism and imperialism. Caracas has also denounced the Lima Group's interference in its internal affairs and its violation of international law and the UN charter. Venezuela has also challenged the legitimacy and representativeness of the Lima Group, arguing that it does not speak for the majority of LAC countries or for the regional organizations that Venezuela belongs to, such as ALBA, CELAC and UNASUR (Gallardo, 2020).

The Lima Group's involvement in Venezuela has been influential and controversial, not only within the region but also among external actors and observers. Some have praised this ad-hoc coalition for its leadership and solidarity in supporting democracy and human rights in Venezuela and for its efforts to find a peaceful and negotiated solution to the crisis (O'Neil, 2019). Others have criticized the Lima Group for its bias and partisanship, acting as an agent of US interests and undermining the sovereignty and self-determination of Venezuela (Chaves Garcia, 2020). Another group of observers has questioned the effectiveness and impact of its actions on resolving the crisis in Venezuela, arguing that they have failed to produce any concrete results or changes on the ground or to foster dialogue among Venezuelans. Regardless of one's view, the Lima Group represented an initiative that started to undermine the balance of power in the landscape of Latin American regional organizations by weakening the strength of leftist coalitions and serving as a rightist alternative.

As mentioned in the previous section, by 2019 UNASUR was already defunct as most member states were in the process of leaving the organization. Its dissolution has been lamented by some as a setback for regional integration and cooperation in South America, as well as for the promotion of a more autonomous and multipolar regional order (Mijares and Nolte, 2022). Others have welcomed UNASUR's demise as an opportunity to create new and more effective regional mechanisms that are more closely aligned with the current political and economic realities and interests of South America.

One of these new mechanisms is the Forum for the Progress and Integration of South America (PROSUR), which was created in March 2019 as an alternative to UNASUR by eight states, seven of which had left UNASUR in 2018 or 2019. At the time, the governments of these states had a centre-right or conservative orientation; hence, one would have expected from PROSUR to take a strong stance on the crisis and coup in Venezuela, but in fact, its involvement has been limited and marginal. While the organization issued a declaration in support of Guaidó as interim president and called for free and fair elections as well as respect for human rights in Venezuela (MercoPress, 2019), it did not adopt any concrete actions to address the crisis in Venezuela or to foster dialogue among Venezuelans.

Like other South American regional organizations, PROSUR soon began to face internal divisions and disagreements among its members over how to deal with Maduro's government and its legitimacy. For example, Argentina's President Alberto Fernández criticized the alignment of PROSUR with US interests and its hostility towards Maduro. Chile's President Sebastián Piñera announced his country's withdrawal from PROSUR in April 2021 after his successor, Gabriel Boric, won the presidential election on a left-wing campaign (DW, 2022). Suriname joined PROSUR in 2022, despite being one of the few countries that still recognize Maduro as Venezuela's President (Office of the President of Suriname, 2022). Hence, PROSUR turned out to be a rather unimpactful organization both in regard to addressing the situation in Venezuela and in general as well.

Another regional initiative that has emerged in response to the crisis in Venezuela is the Montevideo Mechanism, which was proposed by Mexico and Uruguay in February 2019 with the support of CARICOM and CELAC. The main aim of the Montevideo Mechanism at the time was to facilitate a peaceful and democratic solution to the conflict in Venezuela through dialogue and negotiation among all relevant actors without imposing any preconditions or external interference (Mexican Secretariat of Foreign Relations, 2019).

The Montevideo Mechanism was endorsed by some countries and organizations that have adopted a neutral or conciliatory position on Venezuela's internal affairs, such as Bolivia, Cuba, Nicaragua, Suriname, the Vatican, as well as the UN Secretary-General. However, it has also faced rejection or indifference from other countries and actors that have taken a more assertive or confrontational stance towards Maduro's government and its legitimacy, such as the Lima Group, the US, the EU and Guaidó (BBC, 2019). In the end, the Montevideo Mechanism was plagued by political divisions and it failed to initiate or facilitate any meaningful dialogue or negotiation among the conflicting parties in Venezuela, nor has it been able to influence or modify their positions or actions.

Although it was largely paralyzed around 2019, and Brazil suspended its participation in the organization starting in 2020, CELAC surprisingly began to be revived under the leadership of Mexico at the time. The organization attempted to serve as a mechanism for engagement with Venezuela; after it renewed its activity, it recognized Maduro as Venezuela's legitimate president and has recently invited him to participate in its meetings and summits. CELAC has also rejected any sanctions or interventions against Venezuela that violate international law or threaten its sovereignty. Despite receiving some criticisms for this move, this was a reasonable attempt to help address the crisis in Venezuela as it had become clear in 2019 that taking a tough stance can result in even deeper disengagement and would also undermine the possibility of any dialogue.

Since Venezuela is the leading state in ALBA, the organization adopted a supportive and loyal stance towards Maduro's government and its legitimacy. ALBA expressed its solidarity with Venezuela and offered their assistance to overcome the crisis. It has also sought to denounce the US's role and influence in the region and its policies towards Venezuela (ALBA-TCP, 2020). Furthermore, Maduro has received support from the states of Petrocaribe, a regional oil procurement agreement between Venezuela and Caribbean member states of ALBA. However, by 2019 both ALBA and Petrocaribe had largely stalled; the former saw Ecuador leave in 2018 and then Bolivia also withdrew after the coup discussed above, while the latter has been characterized by highly diminished activity because of Venezuela's eroded domestic production and refining.

The factors that have shaped regional responses to the ongoing crisis and the coup in Venezuela are complex. They involve both considerations of alignment with and opposition to US interests, but also the ideological positioning of Latin American governments, geopolitical interests, economic ties and humanitarian concerns. The situation in Venezuela has posed significant challenges for regional governance and cooperation in Latin America as responding either way can be seen as controversial and divisive, not only within the region but also among external actors and observers. In continuation of the analysis in the previous section, it is important to point out that as the Pink Tide was replaced by the Blue Tide, the landscape of regional initiatives that were proposed (often specifically to address the Venezuelan crisis) also developed as new ones were introduced and older ones sometimes became defunct. Intriguingly, despite the diverse responses to the Venezuelan crisis that this produced, none of them have had a substantial impact in terms of either strengthening or weakening considerably the Maduro administration which, for better or worse it has been able to consolidate its position.

There is a good reason to believe that while tracking the responses of regional organizations helps to untangle the complexity of the regional security landscape in Latin America, they might have been unable to influence Venezuelan politics to begin with. After fleeing to the US, former director of the Bolivarian National Intelligence Service and Venezuelan General Manuel Ricardo Cristopher Figuera (Schifrin, 2020) publicly stated that he believes the main obstacle to strengthening the possibility that Juan Guaidó succeeds in his coup attempt was the excessive ambition of Maikel Moreno, who was serving as President of the Venezuelan Supreme Court but in fact hoped to become leader of the country as well. This suggests that when internal dynamics or the strength of the military is a deciding factor, it is likely that regional (or, for that matter, almost any external) responses might only have a very diminished impact on the politics surrounding a coup attempt.

1.6 Conclusion

This chapter has analyzed the responses of Latin American regional organizations to coup attempts in the context of the rise and fall of post-hegemonic regionalism. It has examined six cases of both failed and successful coups that occurred in Bolivia, Brazil, Ecuador, Honduras, Paraguay and Venezuela between 2008 and 2019 and compared the reactions and actions of different regional organizations (OAS, UNASUR, MERCOSUR, CARICOM, ALBA, CELAC, SICA and PROSUR) as well as of relevant ad-hoc response mechanisms (e.g., Lima Group and Montevideo Mechanism).

The reactions of Latin American regional organizations to coup attempts have been influenced by both internal and external factors. Internal factors include institutional design and capacity, membership composition, the decision-making process, and the leadership role of some countries within each organization. External factors include the role and interests of the US, the positions and actions of other global or regional actors, and the norms and principles of international law and democracy. Even at the height of the Pink Tide, the US stance on Latin American coup attempts still matters for the way the dynamics of regional responses are shaped.

The motivations that shape the ideas that have guided governments reveal that US positions on Latin American regional coups have an indirect impact which serves as an anchor in relation to which (either supporting or opposing the US position) LAC governments and, hence, bodies of which they are members, shape their stances. Thus, this chapter argues that on one hand, LAC regional bodies have been taking decisions in ways which are moderately independent from US influence and the US; however, on the other hand, the fundamental factors that shape their stances are still highly influenced (albeit not necessarily shaped) by the US.

LAC organizations have been moderately efficient in addressing coup attempts since the rise of post-hegemonic regionalism. They have been able to influence or modify the behaviour or position of some actors involved in some coup attempts, such as those in Bolivia (2008) and Ecuador (2010). However, they have also failed to produce any concrete results or changes on the ground in the cases of other coups, such as those in Paraguay (2012) and Brazil (2016). They have also polarized or antagonized some actors involved in some coups, such as those in Honduras (2009) and Venezuela (2019).

Assuming the aim of maintaining peace, order and democratic principles of government legitimacy, this chapter reveals that South American responses to South American coups were more efficient than either sub-regional or pan-regional responses to coups in Central America or the Caribbean. First, South American states are more likely to agree on the benefits of steering away from US influence since their economies and armed forces are less dependent on cooperation with the US as opposed to Central America and the Caribbean. Second, South American countries have a greater stake and interest in addressing coup attempts in their sub-region, which makes up a large part of LAC. Third, organizations that are based in South America, such as UNASUR and ALBA, respond faster to coup attempts when compared to organizations that are Pan American or Latin American, such as the OAS and CELAC. This is because South American heads of state or foreign ministers can physically meet more easily and quickly, as well as because they face less sensitivity or resistance from their domestic audiences or external actors. Overall, this demonstrates that physical distance still matters when coordinating regional responses to security issues in our age.

There are various lessons that should be drawn from the analysis in this chapter. First, to respond more efficiently to coup attempts, Latin American regional organizations should seek to enhance their institutional design and capacity, especially in terms of decision-making processes, dispute settlement mechanisms, monitoring and evaluation systems. Second, Latin American regional organizations should seek to balance their respect for sovereignty and non-interference with their commitment to democracy and human rights, especially when dealing with cases of coups or attempted coups. And third, in cases where member states of regional organizations have a genuine desire to address coup attempts appropriately, they should seek to adopt a graduated, flexible, and dialogue-based approach to address coup attempts, rather than a rushed, rigid, or confrontational one. Otherwise, they risk preventing the possibility of dialogue before it has started.

Since the Pink Tide subsided, the rise of the Blue Tide has led to some de facto changes in the landscape of Latin American regional bodies by creating the Lima Group and PROSUR, among other initiatives, while the influence of

UNASUR and ALBA subsided. However, it is not clear whether post-hegemonic regionalism is currently reforming, already passé or is due for a reboot very soon. The inauguration of Lula da Silva on 1 January 2023 gave a great impetus for potentially reviving UNASUR, although it is not clear whether he will remain in power long enough to do this and have allies in the process. Meanwhile, Nicolas Maduro was recently invited to attend a meeting with CELAC leaders, and this could also potentially open a pathway to the partial reintegration of Venezuela into the landscape of LAC regional organizations, driving relations with the Bolivarian republic closer to normalization.

Whether Latin American states manage to revive the pillars of regional organizations that characterized post-hegemonic regionalism, the practice of counter-balancing US influence will remain in some form. Unlike previous waves of LAC integration, such as the pro-development efforts in the 1950s and 1960s or the open regionalism of the 1990s, post-hegemonic regionalism did not follow advice or a model suggested from outside (e.g., the UN, the US or through economic advisors), but rather emerged as a regional method of opposing external influence in LAC affairs. The tendency to do this will continue to exist in some form, whether the era of post-hegemonic regionalism continues or comes to an end. This will likely continue to be reflected in the way that regional responses to both successful and unsuccessful coups are formed.

References

Al Jazeera (2018) 'Lima Group rules out military intervention in Venezuela', 17 September. Available at: https://www.aljazeera.com/news/2018/9/17/lima-group-rules-out-military-intervention-in-venezuela (Accessed: 8 December 2022).

ALBA-TCP (2009) *Declaración conjunta.* 17 October. Available at: https://www.albatcp.org/acta/declaracion-conjunta-5/ (Accessed: 11 January 2023).

ALBA-TCP (2020) *Declaración conjunta del xx consejo político y x consejo de complementación económico.* 29 June. Available at: https://www.albatcp.org/acta/declaracion-conjunta-del-xx-consejo-politico-y-x-consejo-de-complementacion-economico-caracas-29-de-junio-de-2020/ (Accessed: 3 January 2023).

BBC (2019) 'Venezuela crisis: Juan Guaidó backed by Lima Group', 5 February. Available at: https://www.bbc.com/news/world-latin-america-47126434 (Accessed: 8 December 2022).

Bjork-James, C. (2019) 'Race and the right to speak for the city: Political violence in Bolivia's 2006–2009 stalemate', *Urban Anthropology and Studies of Cultural Systems and World Economic Development*, 48 (3–4), pp. 263–305.

Bolívar, S. (1967) *Carta De Jamaica,* Los Teques, Venezuela: Casa de la Cultura.

Burges, S. W. (2017) *Brazil in the World: The International Relations of a South American Giant.* Manchester: Manchester University Press.

Castro, B., Fonseca, C. and Garro, F. (2012) *El golpe de estado en Honduras contra el presidente Manuel Zelaya en junio del 2009, repercusiones en la integración centroamericana.* Costa Rica: Universidad Nacional.

Chaves Garcia, C. A. (2020) 'The political crisis in Venezuela and the role of the Lima Group: stocktaking and challenges of its diplomatic action', *Revista de Relaciones Internacionales, Estrategia y Seguridad*, 15 (1), pp. 177–193.

Chomsky, N. (2009) 'Coups, UNASUR, and the U.S.', *Z Magazine*, October. Available at: https://chomsky.info/200910__/ (Accessed: 19 January 2023).

Cobb, J. S. (2019) 'OAS must avoid "extremes," push for dialogue, leadership candidate says', 4 December. Available at: https://www.reuters.com/article/us-venezuela-politics-oas-idCAKBN1Y72LS (Accessed: 5 December 2022).

Curiel, J. and Williams, J. R. (2019) 'Bolivia dismissed its October elections as fraudulent. Our research found no reason to suspect fraud', *Washington Post*, 27 February. Available at: https://www.washingtonpost.com/politics/2020/02/26/bolivia-dismissed-its-october-elections-fraudulent-our-research-found-no-reason-suspect-fraud/ (Accessed: 23 December 2022).

Dangl, B. (2012) 'Behind Paraguay's coup', *Al Jazeera*, 26 July. Available at: https://www.aljazeera.com/opinions/2012/7/26/behind-paraguays-coup (Accessed: 11 February 2023).

de la Torre, C. (2017) 'A populist international? ALBA's democratic and autocratic promotion', *SAIS Review of International Affairs*, 37 (1), pp. 83–94.

de Oliveira, M. G., and de Souza, D. R. (2016) 'Brazil's "white coup": Back to the old elite political culture', *World Affairs*, 20 (2), pp. 142-151.

Dietz, J. L. (1984) 'Destabilization and intervention in Latin America and the Caribbean', *Latin American Perspectives*, 11 (3), pp. 3–14.

Dominguez, R. (2017) 'Security governance in Latin America', in: Suarez, M. A. G., Villa, R. D., and Weiffen, B. (eds.), *Power Dynamics and Regional Security in Latin America*. London: Palgrave Macmillan, pp. 53–76.

DW (2022) 'Boric suspende participación de Chile en foro Prosur', 4 April. Available at: https://www.dw.com/es/boric-suspende-participaci%C3%B3n-de-chile-en-foro-prosur/a-61348627 (Accessed: 17 December 2022).

The Economist (2004) 'After Aristide, what?', 4 March. Available at: https://www.economist.com/unknown/2004/03/04/after-aristide-what (Accessed: 10 October 2022).

Fernández, B. (2021) 'Memories of a Honduran coup', *Al Jazeera*, 28 June. Available at: https://www.aljazeera.com/opinions/2021/6/28/memories-of-a-honduran-coup (Accessed: 11 February 2023).

Fishel, J. T. and Saenz, A. (2007) *Capacity Building for Peacekeeping: The Case of Haiti*. Washington, DC: Potomac Books.

Foley, J. B. (2022) 'No, the U.S. did not try to overthrow President Jean-Bertrand Aristide in Haiti', *Miami Herald*, 24 May. Available from: https://www.miamiherald.com/opinion/op-ed/article261734482.html (Accessed: 4 February 2023).

Gallardo, O. (2020) 'Estado venezolano presenta informe "La verdad sobre Venezuela contra infamia del Grupo de Lima"', *Ministry of People's Power for Foreign Affairs of Venezuela*, 23 September. Available at: https://mppre.gob.ve/2020/09/23/estado-venezolano-presenta-informe-verdad-sobre-venezuela-contra-infamia-grupo-lima/ (Accessed: 18 December 2022).

Ganchev, I. (2020) 'China pushed the pink tide and the pink tide pulled China: intertwining economic interests and ideology in Ecuador and Bolivia (2005–2014)', *World Affairs*, 183 (4), pp. 359–388.

Garcia, S. (2019) 'Venezuela ceases membership in the OAS this Saturday: what motivates this sovereign decision?', *Ministry of People's Power for Foreign Affairs of Venezuela*, 26 April. Available at: http://mppre.gob.ve/en/2019/04/26/venezuela-ceases-membership-oas-sovereign-decision/ (Accessed: 7 January 2022).

The Guardian (2009) 'Zelaya refuses to leave Honduras as political exile', 10 December. Available at: https://www.theguardian.com/world/2009/dec/10/manuel-zelaya-refuses-political-asylum (Accessed: 15 December 2022).

Jacomino, P. (2016) 'UNASUR labels Brazil coup a threat to democracy in the region', *Radio Habana Cuba*, 12 May. Available at: https://www.radiohc.cu/en/noticias/internacionales/93283-unasur-labels-brazil-coup-a-threat-to-democracy-in-the-region (Accessed: 1 February 2023).

Johnston, J. (2017) 'How Pentagon officials may have encouraged a 2009 coup in Honduras', *The Intercept*, 29 August. Available at: https://theintercept.com/2017/08/29/honduras-coup-us-defense-departmetnt-center-hemispheric-defense-studies-chds/ (Accessed: 18 January 2023).

Johnston, J., Sammut, J., Weisbrot, M. and Carvalho, M. (2021) 'Bolivia after the 2019 coup: economic policy', *Center for Economic and Policy Research*, 1 June. Available at: https://cepr.net/report/bolivia-after-the-2019-coup-economic-policy/ (Accessed: 17 January 2023).

Katz, J. M. (2022) 'Haiti's elites keep calling for the U.S. marines', *Foreign Policy*, 22 October. Available at: https://foreignpolicy.com/2022/10/31/haiti-us-intervention-gangs-united-nations/ (Accessed: 3 January 2023).

Legler, T. (2012) 'The democratic charter in action: reflections on the Honduran crisis', *Latin American Policy*, 3 (1), pp. 74–87.

Livingstone, G. (2009) *America's Backyard: The United States and Latin America from the Monroe Doctrine to the War on Terror*. London: Zed Books.

Malamud, A. and Gardini G. L. (2012) 'Has regionalism peaked? The Latin American quagmire and its lessons', *The International Spectator*, 47 (1), pp. 116–133.

Marsteintredet, L. and Malamud, A. (2019) 'Coup with adjectives: conceptual stretching or innovation in comparative research?', *Political Studies*, 68 (4), pp. 1–22.

McCaughan, M. (2005) *The Battle of Venezuela*. New York: Seven Stories Press.

Méheut, C., Porter, C., Gebrekidan, S. and Apuzzo, M. (2022) Demanding reparations and ending up in exile', *New York Times*, 26 May. Available at: https://www.nytimes.com/2022/05/20/world/americas/haiti-aristide-reparations-france.html (Accessed: 28 January 2023).

MercoPress (2019) 'Prosur aguarda de brazos abiertos a Venezuela y al presidente interino Guaidó', 23 March. Available at: https://es.mercopress.com/2019/03/23/prosur-aguarda-de-brazos-abiertos-a-venezuela-y-al-presidente-interino-guaido (Accessed: 8 December 2022).

Mexican Secretariat of Foreign Relations (2019) 'Mexico, Uruguay and CARICOM present Montevideo Mechanism', *Government of Mexico*, 6 February. Available at: https://www.gob.mx/sre/articulos/mexico-uruguay-and-caricom-present-montevideo-mechanism-189816 (Accessed: 15 January 2023).

Mijares, V. and Nolte, D. (2022) 'UNASUR: an eclectic analytical perspective of its disintegration', *Colombia Internacional*, 111, pp. 83–109.

Nickson, A. (2012) 'Paraguay's presidential coup: the inside story', *openDemocracy*, 10 July. Available at: https://www.opendemocracy.net/en/paraguays-presidential-coup-inside-story (Accessed 11 July 2023).

Nolte, D. (2018) 'Costs and benefits of overlapping regional organizations in Latin America: the case of the OAS and UNASUR', *Latin American Politics and Society*, 60 (1), pp. 128–153.

Notimérica (2008) 'Bolivia/Venezuela – El ejército boliviano rechaza la "intromisión" de Chávez, que ofreció su ayuda a Morales', 12 September. Available at: https://www.notimerica.com/politica/noticia-bolivia-venezuela-ejercito-boliviano-rechaza-intromision-chavez-ofrecio-ayuda-morales-20080912202914.html (Accessed: 11 December 2022).

OAS (1948) *Charter of the Organization of American States*, 30 April. Available at: https://www.refworld.org/docid/3ae6b3624.html (Accessed: 11 January 2023).

OAS (2009a) 'OAS Permanent Council adopts resolution on the situation in Honduras', *Organization of American States*, June 26. Available at: https://www.oas.org/en/media_center/press_release.asp?sCodigo=E-211/09 (Accessed: 19 November 2022).

OAS (2009b) 'OAS suspends membership of Honduras', *Organization of American States*, June 26. Available at: https://www.oas.org/en/media_center/press_release.asp?sCodigo=e-219/09 (Accessed: 19 November 2022).

OAS (2012a) 'OAS Permanent Council receives report of the Secretary General and delegation to Paraguay', 10 July. Available from: https://www.oas.org/en/media_center/press_release.asp?sCodigo=E-247/12 (Accessed: 5 March 2023).

OAS (2012b) 'Report by the mission of the OAS Secretary General and delegation to the Republic of Paraguay', 10 July. Available from: https://www.oas.org/en/about/speech_secretary_general.asp?sCodigo=12-0058 (Accessed: 7 March 2023).

OAS (2014) 'OAS Permanent Council approved declaration on the situation in Venezuela', *Organization of American States*, March 7. Available at: https://www.oas.org/en/media_center/press_release.asp?sCodigo=E-084/14 (Accessed: 19 November 2022).

OAS (2016) 'Statement by OAS Secretary General Luis Almagro after meeting with the Constitutional President of Brazil, Dilma Rousseff', *Organization of American States*, March 7. Available at: https://www.oas.org/en/media_center/press_release.asp?sCodigo=E-044/16 (Accessed: 21 November 2022).

OAS (2019a) 'Final report of the audit of the elections in Bolivia: Intentional manipulation and serious irregularities made it impossible to validate the results', 4 December. Available from: https://www.oas.org/en/media_center/press_release.asp?sCodigo=E-109/19 (Accessed: 15 March 2023).

OAS (2019b) 'Statement of the OAS electoral observation mission in Bolivia', 21 October. Available from: https://www.oas.org/en/media_center/press_release.asp?sCodigo=E-085/19 (Accessed: 12 March 2023).

OAS (2020) 'Press release on disinformation campaign regarding the role of the OAS in the Bolivian elections', 16 June. Available from: https://www.oas.org/en/media_center/press_release.asp?sCodigo=E-064/20 (Accessed: 12 March 2023).

O'Neil, S. K. (2019) 'Mexico is making the wrong bet on Venezuela', *Council on Foreign Relations*, 20 February. Available at: https://www.cfr.org/blog/mexico-making-wrong-bet-venezuela (Accessed: 21 November 2022).

Office of the President of Suriname (2022) 'Suriname officieel lid PROSUR', 8 April. Available at: https://cds.gov.sr/de-boodschap/suriname-officieel-lid-prosur/ (Accessed: 5 January 2023).

Parish, R., Peceny, M. and Delacour, J. (2007) 'Venezuela and the collective defence of democracy regime in the Americas', *Democratization*, 14 (2), pp. 207–231.

Pérez-Liñán and Polga-Hecimovich (2016) 'Explaining military coups and impeachments in Latin America', *Democratization*, 24 (5), pp. 839–858.

Reuters (2009) 'Venezuela won't withdraw diplomats from Honduras', 23 July. Available at: https://www.reuters.com/article/us-honduras-venezuela-sb-idUSTRE56L6BS20090723 (Accessed: 13 January 2023).

Reuters (2017) 'OAS head accuses Venezuela's Maduro of "self-coup"', 31 March. Available at: https://www.reuters.com/article/venezuela-politics-oas-idUSKBN1712WC (Accessed: 15 January 2023).

Reuters (2019) 'Morales decries U.S. recognition of new Bolivian government', 14 November. Available at: https://www.reuters.com/article/us-bolivia-election-trump-idUSKBN1XO01V (Accessed: 15 December 2022).

Rory, C. (2014) *Comandante: Hugo Chavez's Venezuela*. New York: Penguin Books.

Schlifrin, N. (2020) 'Former Maduro intelligence chief on why Guaido's revolt failed', *PBS NewsHour*, 24 July. Available at: https://www.pbs.org/newshour/show/former-maduro-intelligence-chief-on-why-guaidos-revolt-failed (Accessed: 17 February 2023).

Turner, B. (2005) 'South American Community of Nations (CSN/SACN)', *The Statesman's Yearbook*. London: Palgrave Macmillan.

Tussie, D. (2016) 'Presidential diplomacy in UNASUR: coming together for crisis management or marking turfs?', in: Mace, G., Thérien, J., Tussie, D. and Dabène, O. (eds.), *Summits and Regional Governance: The Americas in Comparative Perspective*. London: Routledge, pp. 71–87.

UNASUR (2009) *Declaración Presidencial de Quito*, III Ordinary Meeting of the Council of Heads of State and Government of the UNASUR, 10 August. Available at: https://encod.org/app/uploads/2011/01/UNASUR2009.pdf (Accessed: 22 January 2023).

UNASUR (2010) *Protocolo Adicional ao Tratado Constitutivo da Unasul sobre o Compromisso com a Democracia, Georgetown*, Guiana. Available at: https://legis.senado.leg.br/sdleg-getter/documento?dm=5079280&disposition=inline (Accessed: 25 January 2023).

United Nations (1945) *Charter of the United Nations*, 24 October. Available at: https://www.refworld.org/docid/3ae6b3930.html (Accessed: 17 February 2023).

US Department of State (2019) 'Congratulations to Bolivian Senator Anez for assuming the role of Interim President', 13 November. Available at: https://2017-2021.state.gov/congratulations-to-bolivian-senator-anez-for-assuming-the-role-of-interim-president/ (Accessed: 5 February 2023).

Wiarda, H. (1978) *Critical Elections and Critical Coups: State, Society and the Military in the Processes of Latin American Development*. Athens, Ohio: Ohio University Center for International Studies.

Zegada, M. T. (2020) 'La crisis del sistema de representación política: los partidos opositores al MAS en el interregno post y preelectoral (2019-2020)', in: Souverein, J. and José Luis, E. (eds.), *Nuevo Mapa de Actores en Bolivia: Crisis, Polarización e Incertidumbre (2019-2020)*. La Paz: Friedrich Ebert Stiftung.

Chapter 2

The impact of deglobalization on the security agenda of contemporary Latin American regionalism

Kseniya Konovalova

Saint-Petersburg State University, Russia

Victor Jeifets

Saint-Petersburg State University, Russia

Abstract

This chapter explores how the current trend of deglobalization in international politics impacts the security agenda of Latin American regional integration organisations, both from a symbolic and from a practical perspective. It employs historical analysis and case study methods, focusing in depth on the role of PROSUR, the way that the OAS has addressed a string of issues in Venezuela and the contemporary Latin America – NATO dialogue. The chapter argues that Latin American integration organisations have been unable to develop a coherent regional security vision that member state governments can agree on. Hence, it is challenging to coordinate regional responses to relevant challenges such as the legacy of the COVID-19 pandemic, growing nationalism and geopolitical conflict between the West and its challengers, mainly China and Russia. This makes Latin America vulnerable to the imposition of external security agendas and ultimately hinders its ability to exercise agency in international politics.

Keywords: Latin American regionalism, deglobalization, security, PROSUR, OAS, Venezuela

***

2.1 Introduction

A number of recent phenomena—such as the Trumpism that has generated an authoritarian-nationalist wave all over the world, the US–China trade rivalry, the novel coronavirus pandemic, and the military conflict in Ukraine—have dealt a deep blow to global interconnectedness. All these occurrences indicate that the liberal world order is in crisis; platforms for multilateral dialogue are paralyzed; the bloc logic has been revived; and the importance of national borders has become extremely exaggerated. On the one hand, against this background, nations in general have become more vulnerable, since human socio-economic security, as well as issues of war and peace, have grown more pressing than they were in the twenty-first century. On the other hand, the peculiarity of Latin America is that the US hegemony and, indeed, the stability of the liberal international order have historically been important drivers for both the internal dynamics of the region and its participation in global affairs, with Latin American diplomacy traditionally laying special emphasis on international law and universal multilateral institutions. The breakdown of such pillars itself brings great tumult, while Latin America's ties with China and Russia, having expanded in the beginning of the twenty-first century (Rouvinsky and Jeifets, 2022, pp. 178–190), may plunge the region into major geopolitical confrontation. Meanwhile, the late 2010s and early 2020s in Latin America were complex in terms of intra-regional security, which prompted nations to revise their understanding of the role of a nation-state as its key actor and referent. We could say that this happened due to the accumulation of many factors at once: the negative consequences of the recession in 2014–2015, when commodity prices collapsed, reversing the progressive reforms of the so-called "golden decade"; the subsequent political protest, violence, and aggravation of intermestic challenges of organized crime; and the spread of COVID-19, which, according to the United Nations (2020), "represents a massive… shock with an immense human toll for the countries of Latin America and the Caribbean". All these circumstances, which affected the modus of international cooperation and security in all dimensions, inevitably had an impact on the agenda of Latin American regionalism.

This chapter is an attempt to look at how current trends in deglobalization are related to changes in the security agenda of Latin America's integration projects. We first track the general relationship between the evolution of regionalism, globalization and its rollbacks, and security, and then proceed to examine some emblematic formats of intergovernmental cooperation. We seek to discover to what extent the integration groups can adapt to these changes and how this adaptation affects them and the region's global positioning. We assume that the security agenda in Latin America is now influenced by both new transnational challenges and the re-emergence of hard security issues, and although a plethora of formal frameworks and mechanisms of security governance have been created in the region, multilateral groups fail to make a unified and fruitful effort to counter them. The side effects of this seem to be the intrusion of external security agendas into the region's fields of concern, the growing influence of current international conflict on the lives of its people, and the eventual decrease of its own global agency.

2.2 Looking at Latin American regionalism in terms of (de)globalization

Regionalism has historically played a pivotal role in shaping the structure of international relations within Latin America as well as its interaction with the outer world. At the same time, globalization, being immanent to the international environment, has always been one of the universal frameworks to define meanings and forms of Latin American integration.

In the twentieth century, both closed and open regionalisms were largely configured by the same set of factors that influenced globalization: the Yalta-Potsdam system that was global instead of Eurocentric for the first time in history; the inequality across global economies; the spread and universalization of Western political values; and liberal democracy. The hegemony of the United States, which has long been the most influential country in the affairs of the Western hemisphere, where the tribunes of the Organization of American States (OAS) played a significant role, later spilt over the region and became the pillar of unipolarity. As part of the philosophy of the "closed" regionalism of the 1960s and 70s, integration served as a tool to help Latin America adapt to globalization. For instance, the creation of groups such as the Latin American Free Trade Area or the Central American Free Trade Area sought to mitigate negative structural factors—for instance, the region's position on the periphery of global capitalism and its division of labour, which constantly affected the regional economic complexes. The popularity of open regionalism embodied the acceptance of globalization. For the original MERCOSUR, North American Free Trade Area, or Pan American Free Trade Area (the Spanish is ALCA), integration meant—in a narrow sense—to step into the transnational neoliberal economy and, in a broad sense, to combine national and universal goals and values and join the "civilized" global community after the triumph of the Western democracies over the socialist camp (Jeifets and Konovalova, 2019, po. 218–221).

However, the twenty-first century provides a much more mosaic and heterogeneous picture. After examining integration concepts and formats through the prism of attitudes towards globalization, we find two distinct periods.

The first one lasted from the 2000s to the early 2010s —a period of dominance of forces representative of the transnational contemporary left movement (the so-called *marea rosa*). Latin American politicians from the marea rosa decade denounced the socio-economic, environmental, cultural, and spiritual costs of neo-liberal globalization, called for solidarity with the developing world and, in general, promoted the idea of multipolarity. At this time, regionalism received a powerful impetus, correlating with the reality of globalization in different ways. Firstly, the spirit of the integration groups brought with it a critical reflection on the content and results of neoliberal globalization and the desire of Latin American nations to move from the status of its objects to its protagonists. In the conceptual domain, this was the reason that this stage of regionalism was labelled "postliberal" and "posthegemonic" (Briceño Ruiz, 2017; Riggirozzi and Tussie, 2012). Characteristic, practical examples of the postliberal period were the launch of non-trade integration in the Southern Common Market (MERCOSUR), which developed non-trade integration; the Buenos Aires Consensus in 2003; the restart of the Central American Integration System with the signing of San Salvador Protocol in 2010; and the emergence of the Bolivarian Alliance for the Peoples of Our America (ALBA), where, in the words of Hugo Chavez—who stood out not only as its most emblematic leader but also as a bright alter-globalist—capitalism "must be transcended" (Woods, 2006). Secondly, there was a simultaneous discussion about Latin American civilizational and cultural identity, its irreducibility to Western universals, and pan-regional sovereignty. It translated into a distrust of Pan-Americanism, which the region expressed by torpedoing ALCA, disregarding the OAS, and creating the Community of Latin American and Caribbean States (CELAC) as its alleged "counterweight" (Jeifets and Khadorich, 2015). Finally, at this time, Latin American self-determination was developing in terms of global regionalization: the Union of South American Nations (UNASUR) and CELAC's agendas appealed to the Global South, while the creation of the Pacific Alliance emphasized the Asia Pacific. These moments were significant for the world's economic, technological, and logistical ties.

Despite the fact that the ideas and rhetoric of postliberal integration often contained criticism of globalization, in practice, the governments promoting them continued to rely on transnationalism, openness, and interdependency. In this regard, it seems significant that even after the left and centre–left ceded power to moderate liberal–conservatives in the mid-2010s—for instance, left-wing Peronists stepped out in Argentina to cede the presidency to Mauricio Macri in 2015; Dilma Rousseff was ousted in 2016 in Brazil and Michel Temer came to power— aspirations to pursue global interconnectedness remained in force, and their alignments in Latin American regionalism did not change.

Meanwhile, since the second half of the 2010s, there have been profound transformations in regionalism due not only to the changes in political leadership but also to the hemispheric and global dynamics to which the integration responded. To begin with, in the late 2010s, Latin America was influenced in many ways by the phenomenon of Trumpism. On the one hand, it led to a trend of rising national-populist leaders in general, referred to as *derechas neopatriotas* by Sanahuja and López Burian (2020), among which Jair Bolsonaro stood out as the most consistent opponent of globalism and cosmopolitanism. On the other hand, it generally strengthened the right ideological flank. Under these conditions, pan-regional structures that tried to establish ideas of the "special way" of Latin America in the community of civilizations were outdated, and multilateralism moved towards economization and minimalist institutional design. As a result, CELAC, as a Pan-Latin American project, was weakened, and UNASUR also fell apart. This made room for the Forum for the Progress and Integration of South America (PROSUR), which aspires to de-ideologize integration and make it more agile. Not only did MERCOSUR—which embraced non-trade integration—turn to discussions about the need to go back to its origins, but also the North American Free Trade Agreement (NAFTA) was modified: under Trump in the USA, it went from an open agreement into a preferential one. Meanwhile, from an aspiration for "socialism of the twenty-first century", ALBA now became isolated, and Venezuela's severe internal crisis due to the distortions of its development model with Nicolas Maduro turned into an occasion for ultra right-wing unity. At the same time, Trumpism meant that the US was fatigued from the burden of leading and sponsoring neo-liberal globalization, and planetary trade and technological competition with China became its most obvious symptom. Because of Trump's indifference toward Latin American socio-economic and humanitarian problems, which were especially acute in the face of the COVID-19 pandemic, the region began to associate China with constructive tendencies in global cooperation (Jeifets and Konovalova, 2021, pp. 24–25). Thus, China's actions have a growing influence over CELAC. On the suggestion of Uruguay, negotiations on a free trade agreement with China entered MERCOSUR's agenda in 2021–2022. The role of the Pacific Alliance as Latin America's gateway to Asia, has grown, including in the context of solidarity with Beijing on the issue of the US interrupting the Trans-Pacific Partnership. Moreover, the economic agenda of Latin American integration structures are now developing against the backdrop of a dwindling of free trade and WTO rules not only because of ongoing US–China tensions, but also due to the war of sanctions between Western countries and Russia that has followed the current military conflict in Ukraine.

To sum up, we see two simultaneous trends characterizing the contemporary stage of Latin American integration. It seems to have lost its momentum in the face of splits within the region, hemisphere, and world system that, to our mind, contribute to the big picture of deglobalization. At the same time, regionalism has produced new formats and changed earlier ones in order to adapt to geopolitical division lines as well as to back up new prevailing ideological–political coalitions.

2.3 Shifting focus to security

Since the period of postliberal and posthegemonic regionalism began, a number of trends and mechanisms related to security issues have come into existence.

First, the concept of multidimensional security appeared. On the one hand, it addressed the challenges of both traditional (military) conflicts and non-traditional (societal, criminal, terroristic) conflicts to build "peaceful and prosperous societies" (Stein, 2009, p. 31). On the other hand, it represented security as consisting of "different levels: from personal, local and national to regional and global… considered to be closely intertangled and interconnected with each other" (Eremin, 2017, p. 48). The OAS formulated the concept of multidimensional security while adapting to the realities of the twenty-first century, with unconventional threats gaining strength and the circle of security referents expanding. The starting point was the Special Conference on Security in Mexico City in 2003 and its adoption of the Declaration on Security in the Americas and the creation of the Secretariat for Multidimensional Security of the OAS in 2005. Subsequently, Latin American integration bodies also embraced such integrated approaches to security. At the same time, the multidimensional approach allowed them to 'customize' security agendas according to sub-regional differences. For example, CAIS formulated its Central American Security Strategy with four pillars: the fight against crime; prevention of violence; rehabilitation, reinsertion, and safety as core principles of the penitentiary system; and the strengthening of institutions. MERCOSUR lays special focus on the complex issue of the Argentine–Brazilian–Paraguayan Triple-Border Area, including both social and criminal components. The Pacific Alliance was initially oriented toward economic goals, but over time its integration agenda embraced security issues as well. Considering that Mexico and Colombia are part of the Pacific Alliance, it places a special emphasis on the migration control and prevention of narco-crimes (Ripoll de Castro and Quintero, 2016).

Second, international regimes with qualities of "zones of peace" and "democratic clauses" have come into existence. As Riquelme Rivera (2018) shows, their creation in particular within the Andean Community of Nations (ACN) or MERCOSUR reflected not only deepening integration, but also a regional effort to address the global issues of war, peace, and the weakening of democracy.

Third, in the experience of Latin American regionalism, there were attempts to build security communities. From a theoretical point of view, a security community is a spatial continuum formed by cooperating countries with close perceptions of challenges and threats, high levels of mutual trust, and potentially zero or negligible conflict within their borders (Tusicisny, 2007). According to Riquelme Rivera (2018), Alda Mejías (2010, pp. 235–236), and Fuentes (2005), at the sub-regional level, the concept of a security community has inspired integration in MERCOSUR, ACN, and ALBA, especially given Chavez's intentions to form a "South American NATO", but UNASUR is the most mature example of this. Within its framework, several specialized councils worked on various aspects of security—from the fight against tropical diseases to defence—and the emphasis was not only on coordinating intergovernmental efforts but also on the formation of a common, regionalist way of thinking in order to provide multidimensional security and avoid externally imposed agendas. Thus, as per Flemes, Nolte and Wehner (2011), the South American Defence Council (SADC), focused not only on practical and operative issues, such as confidence-building measures or the coordination of international peacekeeping efforts of South American countries but also on the creation of a common strategic identity free from external influence—specifically, the doctrines of the US. The concept of a security community at the heart of UNASUR, therefore, represented an emblematic link between postliberal regionalism and Latin American (South American) pan-nationalism.

We must note that the postliberal stage brought significant proliferation of initiatives for regional and subregional security, which sometimes overlapped, and a trend of securitization, in the words of Buzan (1998), of socio-economic issues and obstacles for development by the leftist governments. The issues of hard power were relevant to not only resolving some attendant problems—such as the creation of intra-regional strategic culture or fostering the buildup of national military-industrial complexes—but also to backing the (sub)region's self-representation in the external environment.

Simultaneously, such impulses for integration in security stemmed from several big-picture factors that existed at the beginning of the twenty-first century:

- A convenient political context (the dominance of social reformists and left-wing populists) and economic opportunities (the period of growth of the commodities-driven economies of Latin America in 2003–2013) that shaped an integral view of security and promoted it by financing social protection programmes, increasing international donorship, or defence spending;
- Internal stability, international proactivity, and strategic alignment between the leading integrating actors, primarily Brazil and Venezuela. During the period of postliberal regionalism, Mexico remained oriented towards the North American security complex;
- A global environment in which attention to non-traditional threats was growing, and the factor of hard power was becoming, in general, less significant.

In the Latin American context, it was of particular importance that the United States under George W. Bush prioritized the problem of international terrorism and other regions more susceptible to it. In contrast, under Barack Obama, the US leaned towards benevolent hegemony, diminishing pressure on the region. Revisionist powers such as Iran, China, and Russia acted in the interest of a multipolar world based on a balance of interests and, therefore, behaved more cooperatively towards the West than they do now. The latter is worth noting because Latin American integration in the domain of defence, as in ALBA or UNASUR, contributed to a serious expansion of the region's contact with revisionist actors, but the US has not articulated this as a considerable challenge.

By the mid-2010s, there was a change in the three mentioned modalities that had an impact on the state of affairs in Latin American security integration.

First, the economic downturn and the emergence of COVID-19 worsened the human and public security situation in most countries. The pandemic has proved to be both a transnational security challenge on its own—unprecedented in the twenty-first century—and a catalyst for poverty, the increased precarity of labour, and crime. Since no Latin American country besides Cuba has been able to produce and distribute its own anti-COVID-19 vaccine even nationally, the pandemic has also revealed that from the perspectives of science and technology, solving global humanitarian problems, and international cooperation for development, Latin America holds a dependent status. Moreover, Latin America turned out to be a field for the "vaccine race" of external powers—the US, EU, China, and Russia—which, by promoting their medicines here, combined humanitarian aid and trade with the consolidation of their political influence. Against this background, on the one hand, the Latin American authorities stimulated the search for regional mechanisms to strengthen its sanitary sovereignty and improve healthcare and social protection systems. Various leaders began to talk about this—for example, Andres Manuel López Obrador, who hosted the CELAC summit in September 2021, or Salvador's president Nayib Bukele, who stressed the need to further deepen Central American integration in the light of "critical circumstances" (Pérez, 2022). But in practice, this has not brought about any significant results. Indeed, the COVID-19 outbreak seemed to destroy the philosophy of free international contact, mobility, and transparent borders and, as Frenkel and Dasso-Martorell (2021) argue, contributed to the re-securitization of neighbouring countries by South American governments, drawing internal division lines in (sub)regional groups and therefore subverting the idea of the security community.

Both Brazil and Venezuela, which were early proponents of integration, have fallen out of this circle. Brazil was influenced by the far-right turn—the administration of Jair Bolsonaro radically revised its attitude towards the region, which it declared to be a source of tension and insecurity in the

Brazilian White Paper of National Defence of 2020 (Brazilian Ministry of Defence, 2020).

Venezuela's resources were undermined by the crisis, which had a political dimension (the struggle between the Bolivarians united around Maduro's personality and the opposition) and a humanitarian one (the impoverishment and mass emigration of Venezuelans). Under such circumstances, Venezuela itself became the cause and object of a kind of regional consolidation on security issues. The Venezuelan crisis has become central to the Lima Group, created in 2017, as well as to the OAS. It also reformatted the entire architecture of regionalism, collapsing UNASUR and thus freezing ALBA and MERCOSUR's deep integration.

Even though Brazil and Venezuela's absence pushed Colombia and Chile forward as potential new integrators (Jeifets and Konovalova, 2022), they faced several challenges. Both countries face internal security problems, such as the continued conflict with the Revolutionary Armed Forces of Colombia (FARC) under Iván Duque and violent civil protests in Chile during Sebastián Piñera's second presidential term. In addition, they were unable to foster international cooperation in multidimensional security due to their national affairs, for example, Duque's negationism in the sphere of international obligations for human rights protection or Piñera's reluctance to support collective ecological security efforts, as Chile abstained from signing the Escazú Agreement. Both ideological differences that existed between Duque and Piñera in 2018–2022, as well as the recent drastic changes that brought the leftist administrations of Gabriel Boric and Gustavo Petro to power in Chile and Colombia, prevent these nations from creating a "*núcleo de poder*" (power core) for a potential new security community, as Brazil and Venezuela previously did.

Numerous right-wing governments were elected across Latin America during the second half of the 2010s as part of the so-called conservative wave; this led to new conversations about a number of specific approaches to security, which, as we will discuss later, influenced their collective mode of thinking and the dynamics of the multilateral formats. Among issues of human security, they focused on crime, choosing hard-handed methods. They did not pay attention to the prevention of delinquency through socio-economic development, for which they needed multilateral efforts to pool resources (Jeifets and Konovalova, 2022). Since right-wing governments polarized the society, their strategy was based on the securitization of political democracy. In many cases, this involved not so much the strengthening of institutions but criticism and pressure on those associating with the left, as well as the discrediting and dismantling of their political legacy. In addition to Bolsonaro of Brazil, characteristic examples were the government of Juan Guaido in Venezuela, Colombia under Duque, and Bolivia when Jeanine Añez was in office (2019–2020). The interpretation of security as multidimensional—which in principle turned it into a political construct—

might have played into their hand. Moreover, the right preferred to prioritize ties with extra-regional actors who naturally brought to Latin America both new issues and new tools in the field of security. Such shifts—compared to the times of postliberal regionalism, when Latin Americans sought to nurture relatively self-sufficient communities that could define (sub)regional concerns and approaches in the sphere of security—had far-reaching consequences. Even after the right stopped ruling Brazil, Argentina, Colombia, and Chile during 2019–2023, major issues, such as environmental security in the Amazon, problematic tri-border area management and, in general, the fight against organized crime, continued to sound loudly in the context of these countries' relations with the USA or Europe. In addition to this, ties with Western governments in the field of defence and arms supplies (see data from the Stockholm International Peace Research Institute; SIPRI, 2023) continue to be highly relevant. Thus, the trend of growing attention and participation of outside actors in Latin American security affairs is fed by its internal socio-political circumstances.

At the system level, global confrontation is unfolding between the United States and its partners, with Russia on one side and China on the other. This is already associated with the biggest challenge to the liberal order (Fukuyama, 2022) and is referred to as the new Cold War (Malamud, Milosevich-Juaristi and Núñez Castellano, 2022). It has several major implications in the regional dimension. To begin with, it dramatically increases the cost of military–technical and political ties with Russia, China, and Iran, given that today they are seen as threats in the "backyard" of the United States and, at the same time as its global opponents who can boost each other (Ellis, 2022). According to, in our opinion, to a fair remark by the experts of the Elcano Institute (Malamud, Milosevich-Juaristi and Núñez Castellano, 2022), Latin America may be turning into a "victim" of the current geopolitical confrontation. While governments are faced with a political–moral choice—to declare solidarity with the West or bet on challenging powers—their economies suffer from the adverse effects of the US–China tariff war and anti-Russia sanctions. Finally, universal platforms within the UN or informal clubs such as G-20 are experiencing a crisis of legitimacy, becoming less effective in enabling Latin American players to leverage the global security agenda and calling international attention to their own problems. Meanwhile, channels for Latin American global positioning that are closely connected with the interests of confronting powers are nearing actualization. These relate to Pan-Americanism (especially the OAS) as well as the region's potentially wider participation in transatlantic relations.

The changing context has influenced the interaction of states and, therefore, the dynamics of integration. On the one hand, under the new conditions, the demand for collective action to address the topics of security in its broad interpretation still remains. On the other hand, the emphasis on multidimensional security has shifted due to new governments that construct new agendas, focusing on a new set of concerns, and new systemic effects emerging on the hemispheric and global scene. In the next section, we proceed to discuss these trends, providing some examples.

2.4 PROSUR's security agenda

With the collapse of UNASUR in 2018–2019, its sectoral councils, which had been working in the domains of defence, health protection, and civil security, ceased to function. Created quite literally on the ruins of UNASUR, the Forum for the Progress and Integration of South America positions itself as a "rebuilder" of South American universal integration without ideological limitations and excessive bureaucracy. Since the demand for integration in South American societies has remained consistently high (Corporación Latinobarómetro, 2020), PROSUR became an opportunity for the right-wing rise in the 2018–2019 electoral cycle, not only to establish their political authority but also to legitimize it. The domain of security has provided a suitable opportunity for their growth, given the novelty and acuteness of the challenges affecting South America, from COVID-19 and the crisis in Venezuela to the rising levels of crime and socio-political protests even in usually safe countries such as Chile.

PROSUR, like its predecessor, seeks to present its security agenda as pluralistic, which is evident both from the documentation of the forum and from its structure, which is represented by a set profile of groups and subgroups. Nevertheless, there are several specificities that can be attributed to the turbulent reality of the region: the devotion of PROSUR's founders to functional, institutionally and politically minimalist integration design and right-wing ideological consensus.

As part of its security thematic portfolio, PROSUR focuses on civil security issues, especially transnational organized crime. Its defence agenda includes the tasks of modernizing national ministries of defence and cyber defence and cooperation in the field of the military–industrial complex. Health and disaster risk management groups focus on human security issues. In theory, such a discrete vision could help build a realistic hierarchy of challenges, threats, and cooperative priorities, which surged in UNASUR, that was prone to tie security and defence as a whole to the idea of South American pan-nationalism ("*sudamericanización*"; see Comini, 2015, p. 110).

Nevertheless, the politicization of the security agenda in PROSUR is still present, at least as it refers to democracy as the "foundation of civil security" (Colombian Ministry of Foreign Affairs, 2022). The priority commitment to the protection of democracy and human rights was fixed in the Santiago Declaration of March 2019 (PROSUR, 2019), and then strengthened during the *presidencias pro témpore* of Colombia and Paraguay (2021–2022), which were ruled by the conservative governments of Duque and Mario Abdo Benitez respectively. We argue that PROSUR's approach presents democracy as reducible to its electoral–legalist aspect that captures the anti-Bolivarian vector of the integration group and presents a case of securitized democracy as an integration strategy.

The absolute hallmark of PROSUR is its focus on COVID-19. In fact, no integration association in South America has previously prioritized sanitary threats (Jeifets, 2019, pp. 107–108). Meanwhile, PROSUR promoted action on this issue, analyzing the recent coronavirus crisis in terms of the weakness of preventive and anti-epidemic measures and ensuring equal access of developing South American countries to vaccines and medicines. We must note that PROSUR formulates the challenge of the pandemic precisely in the context of the contradictions of globalization: on the one hand, it has appeared due to the transparency of borders and free mobility; on the other hand, it cannot be adequately addressed by nations on their own, without common efforts in control and prevention (PROSUR, 2021).

One should acknowledge that, given the state of South American affairs from the late 2010s to the early 2020s and its original idea, PROSUR has managed to find its niche. However, its integration efforts in security show the limitations of this format of regionalism.

First, despite the promised functionality of its integration model and its ability to solve the pressing problems of member-states, there is little evidence that PROSUR has brought practical change. Summits and virtual meetings of politicians and officials remain its predominant form of work, and the implementation of decisions is very limited precisely by the minimalist design of integration, which functions without binding multilateral agreements. For example, PROSUR's health group developed detailed recommendations for monitoring the status of international tourists and migrants during the pandemic, but these are impossible to expand into the rest of South America. Unlike UNASUR, which assisted in the international peacekeeping of Argentina, Chile, and Brazil; reacted to the political crises in Bolivia (2008), Ecuador (2010), and Paraguay (2013); and even sought, albeit unsuccessfully, to mediate between Maduro and the opposition in Venezuela, PROSUR has not yet conducted any practical collective work in the area of "democracy protection" besides the political and diplomatic isolation of the Bolivarian Venezuela. For instance, it did not take any action to calm the violent Chilean Spring in 2019–2020, the wave of crime engulfing Chile in 2022–2023, large anti-governmental protests in Colombia in 2021, or the insurrection of indigenous people in Ecuador in 2022.

Second, partly due to the problem of mutual distrust and the difference in national strategies, their unwillingness to bring their internal problems into the supranational field, and the ideological orientations of its members, the forum has already encountered many smaller empty-chair crises. In 2020, Colombia indicated that it was not ready to coordinate the subgroup on countering terrorism, and Brazil refused to participate in the subgroup on modernizing ministries of defence. Until Ernesto Aráujo was replaced by the more pragmatic Carlos França as the Foreign Minister of Brazil, PROSUR also ignored collective efforts in healthcare. Brazil's passivity in PROSUR—although the forum, in general, was also an amalgamation of right-wing forces—may be explained by the differences between Bolsonaro, who was "neo-patriotic far right" and sceptical about multilateralism, and his more moderate colleagues Piñera, Temer, and Macri (Sanahuja and López Burian, 2020, pp. 43–46). In 2022, Chile, which was first the leader of PROSUR in the domains of cyber security and the digitalization of anti-pandemic efforts, decided to leave the group after the election of Boric. Argentina under Alberto Fernandez formally participates in PROSUR, but does not contribute to any of its divisions. All these absences hinder the functionality of PROSUR, of which Paraguay under Abdo Benitez appears to be its only consistent enthusiast.

The third limitation stems from these problems—PROSUR is not able to play the role of even an imperfect security community, as UNASUR did. Indeed, it does not position itself that way. By actively resorting to the assistance of Pan-American structures—the Inter-American Defence Board, Inter-American Development Bank (IADB), and Pan-American Health Organization (PAHO)—PROSUR abandons the concept of *sudamericanización* and turns into a kind of truncated "non-left CELAC". At the same time, PROSUR does not express the collective voice of its members in the international arena. A striking example is its latest declaration on regional security (PROSUR, 2022), where PROSUR touched upon the aggravation between Russia and the West and only briefly mentioned the perspective of economic and social externalities for South America at the end of the document.

2.5 OAS and the crisis in Venezuela—security, the defence of democracy, and geopolitics

As we have already mentioned, under current systemic conditions, the weight of the Pan-American dimension of Latin American security efforts may increase. While the OAS pioneered the very idea of multidimensional security, the complex ongoing Venezuelan crisis seems to be a perfect test of relevance for this institution, especially if we consider that CELAC and UNASUR were unable to cope with it, and that PROSUR has limited itself to marginalizing Maduro.

The "Venezuelan cause" has consistently been a part of the OAS agenda since 2016, when the Secretary General Luis Almagro began issuing reports on it and convening special sessions of the OAS Permanent Council. We can state that by now, OAS' efforts to address the crisis have been rather awkward.

First, by placing the Venezuelan issue in the framework of democracy protection, the OAS has actually only contributed to the isolation of the Bolivarianists. This is because they insist on the resignation of Maduro as a precondition to further prompt the country's national reconciliation and the legitimization of Juán Guaidó, the opposition parliamentarian and self-proclaimed President, in January 2019. As of the beginning of 2023, it was clear that Guaidó was unable to ensure normalcy in Venezuela and gradually lost support all over the region; however, the OAS has not provided other channels of brokering. The option of using the Inter-American Democratic Charter against Venezuela was perceived by Caracas as interference in internal affairs and prompted it to leave the OAS in 2019.

Second, the OAS could not play the role of the main regional framework in the international response to the collapse of human security in the massive exodus of Venezuelan migrants. The reasons for this were its break-up with the official Caracas, its inability to coordinate the national migration policies of governments and countries hosting refugees throughout the hemisphere, and the interception of the initiative by more politically neutral international institutions. So in 2018, when the OAS launched the ad hoc Working Group on the migration crisis in Venezuela, the UN created the Inter-Agency Coordination Platform for Refugees and Migrants from Venezuela (R4W) at the suggestion of the International Organization for Migration and the UN High Commissioner for Refugees. This became the core effort in addressing the humanitarian collapse. In what seems emblematic, the United Nations cooperates with the OAS, but not as a "political whole" acting in the area of both Americas under the auspices of the UN, but at the level of a branch of the OAS profile. For example, in October 2021, R4W enlisted the assistance of the OAS Secretariat for Access to Rights and Equity to study the impact of COVID-19 on refugees and migrants from Venezuela (R4W, 2021).

Third, by articulating the Venezuelan crisis as a "threat to peace and security on the continent" (Organization of American States, 2019), the OAS could not legitimize its vision at the Latin American level. The Venezuelan crisis became the second time in the twenty-first century, after the events of 11 September 2001, when the Rio Pact was legally activated in 2019, but the region did not agree on collective action against the Bolivarian Republic except for personal sanctions against the Maduro government. While the Trump administration dropped hints in favour of removing Maduro by force, Latin American governments, including the majority of those united in PROSUR and evidently anti-Bolivarianist by nature, were firmly against such an option.

Evidently, the crisis in Venezuela has already made it an object to both the international regime for the protection of democracy and collective security in the Pan-American context, although without significant results. On the one hand, considering the OAS's deep power asymmetry— which for the US has the explicit function of guaranteeing its presence and bargaining power in the Latin American geopolitical space—and, on the other hand, the close ties of Bolivarian Venezuela with several of the US's geopolitical rivals, it is important to pay attention to how today's conflict between Russia and the West influences the presentation of the Venezuelan issue in the context of hemispheric security.

The idea of viewing Russia as one of the key allies of the official Caracas, which facilitated the Maduro government's resistance, took shape in the Pan-American multilateral structures long before the current aggravation caused by the events in Ukraine. In 2019, the Lima Group adopted a declaration in which it spoke of Russian support for the "illegitimate Maduro regime" as "having a negative effect on the region" (Examen ONU Venezuela, 2019). At the same time, US representatives raised in the OAS raised concerns about, as they put it, the "malicious influence" of Russia, which they argued undermined regional security and values of human rights and democracy both in Venezuela and the entire American continent, thus "dividing" its countries (Misión de los Estados Unidos ante la Organización de los Estados Americanos, 2019). In general, some view the role of Russia in Venezuelan affairs and its military, economic, and diplomatic support for Maduro from the perspective of the containment of the United States in response to the expansion of its military infrastructure into the post-Soviet area (Rouvinsky, 2019, pp. 173–174); Russia's struggle against Western narratives; and its backing of illiberal regimes in Latin America to undermine the moral authority of the West (Boersner Herrera and Chaguaceda, 2022; Mijares, 2017).

The conflict in Ukraine theoretically gives the OAS a new chance to rehabilitate its regional monopoly over stability at the expense of the Venezuelan issue. This view is justified because at present, the Venezuelan regional and Russian global "threats" are linked in the information agenda of the Organization. Although the OAS is territorially far from the European war, it has turned out to be an extremely active multilateral body in discussing the conflict and condemning Russia's actions. Moreover, in this respect, the OAS appeals not only to its regional responsibility but also to its status as the UN's hemispheric "herald" (Organization of American States, 2022a and 2022b). The US plays a major role in addressing the Venezuelan and Russian issues, but the anti-Bolivarianists also contribute to this. For instance, Guaidó spoke about the "threat to the world from global authoritarianism … embodied in the ties between Russia and Maduro" (Venezuelan National Assembly, 2022), commenting on the expulsion of Russia from the board of permanent observers of the OAS in March 2022.

However, in the long term, such an approach to "protecting democracy" regionally from Venezuela and globally from Russia seems to carry its own risks for eventual Pan-American unity. First, the policy of the United States under President Biden, which aims to further isolate and punish Russia economically, can ease pressure on Maduro. Second, its side effect is to reinforce the notion of Russia as the most powerful—albeit delegitimized and risky—source of strategic autonomy for those who want to defy the US- and Western-centric order. We must consider the latter with respect not only to the "troika of tyrannies", as the United States defines Bolivarianists in Venezuela, Cuba, and Nicaragua but also to the Latin American powers, such as Brazil or Mexico, who are trying to keep their space for action with respect to the Russia–Ukraine conflict and prevent its entering regional agendas.

2.6 Latin American security and the NATO factor

As we have already mentioned, postliberal and posthegemonic regionalism has sought to internalize the security agenda of Latin America, diminishing the US's presence. Nevertheless, since it has also been in favour of the entry of Latin America into global efforts to solve issues of war and peace and counteract terrorism and international crime, diversifiying external ties in the security domain became a priority. In this regard, many US allies, especially European ones—taking into account the value of Europe's own outstanding integration experience and its traditionally high attention to human and cooperative security—remained important and welcome to governments and multilateral fora in Latin America, from MERCOSUR to CELAC.

Moreover, the globalization of NATO, with the Lisbon Concept of 2010 as its key milestone, was approximately historically parallel to the last wave of Latin American regionalism. Both the synchronicity of these processes and the growing attention of NATO to Latin America as a part of its global strategy prompt us to tackle the issue of the attitude of Latin America towards transatlantic cooperation.

Latin American postliberal and post hegemonic integration groups are yet to define a common vision with NATO, but discussions on this topic have been implicitly embedded into national approaches concerning the agenda of regional security. On the one hand, the Bolivarinanist pole saw the potential global role of NATO as undermining regional unity and security (La Vanguardia, 2016; Bolivian Ministry of Defence, 2013). On the other hand, all the rest preferred to combine their regionalist effort with cooperation with NATO, looking at it from the broader perspective of improving the quality of work of Latin American law enforcement agencies, updating military–industrial complexes, and boosting international prestige. Thus, Brazil, with the Workers' Party in power and as the driver of UNASUR and SADC, did not object to sending its military personnel to NATO training centres in Germany and Italy. In its White Paper on National Defence (Argentine Ministry of Defence, 2015), Argentina under Cristina Fernández de Kirchner expressed dissatisfaction with the military presence of a NATO country—the UK—in the Malvinas Islands, but during the presidency of Néstor Kirchner Argentineans participated in NATO missions in Kosovo and Bosnia and Herzegovina. Colombia has always been the most consistently interested in cooperation with NATO, and it became an Alliance Global Partner in 2018, but such a gesture did not prevent Bogotá from staying in UNASUR and the SADC. Juan Manuel Santos, then the head of Colombia, spoke of his country's partnership with the Alliance as a "privilege" that would improve its image in the world (Dinero, 2018). The OECD, a prestigious club of rich countries, and the NATO are completely different in terms of their functionality, but in the rhetoric of Santos and later Bolsonaro—who spoke about the participation of Colombia and Brazil in the activities of both—they actually align in symbolic terms.

In the early 2020s, discussions about the horizons of NATO's rapprochement with Latin America intensified. This was facilitated by systemic circumstances, such as the desire of Joe Biden's administration to reverse the Trumpist split in inter-American relations and current conflicts between the West and China and Russia, which, in general, provide new incentives for NATO's global identity building. In December 2020, the NATO Secretary General Mircea Geoan raised the topic of NATO's partnership with Colombia and the prospects for its expansion to other countries at the Concordia Americas Summit (Concordia Americas Summit, 2020). In June 2021, the NATO 2030 Agenda was proclaimed, and under it Latin America fit into the overall imperative of strengthening global partnerships to improve security and effectively counter terrorism (North Atlantic Treaty Organization, 2021). Finally, the latest strategic concept, adopted at the Madrid Summit on 29–30 June 2022, focuses on perceived aggression from Russia and a perceived threat posed by China. It does not even mention Latin America, but contains an ellipsis that can be considered significant in the context of NATO's will to contain Russia and China in this region: Russia's course is perceived as reflecting "a pattern of… aggressive actions against… the *wider transatlantic community* (emphasis added by the authors)" (North Atlantic Treaty Organization, 2022), without any reservations about the Euro-Atlantic or North Atlantic zones.

In the short term, the impact of events around Ukraine on the Latin American dimension of NATO's global policy seems to be minimal. The United States is capable of forming a united diplomatic front with Latin America against Russia's actions, which are presented as a threat to international security, through both bilateral and inter-American channels. Latin American players, in turn, do not express a wish to take sides in a military conflict; this does not exclude cases of Latin American participation in the foreign legion of the Armed Forces of Ukraine and its offers to provide humanitarian aid. Nevertheless, the strategic option of interaction with NATO may become more attractive against the backdrop of growing international conflict, such as tensions between the Euro-Atlantic system and Russia and China. The lack of Latin American security communities to formulate and project the intraregional security agenda and outlook in international crises adds to the potential influence of the NATO.

To our mind, the main driver of such influence might be the NATO's self-image as the most successful global alliance of democracies that safeguards peace and upholds the rule-based world order. This idea comes both from the lips of the authorities of the bloc (Concordia Americas Summit, 2020) and from the latest conceptual documents (North Atlantic Treaty Organization, 2022). It seems important that against the backdrop of the conflict between Russia and Ukraine, not only the United States and Europe, but also the majority of Latin American governments—both right and left—at least tacitly accept such a notion. As of now, only a few leaders in the region, such as Daniel Ortega, Nicolas Maduro, Gustavo Petro, and Lula da Silva, have paid attention to Russia's argument that the NATO's eastward expansion has been a real trigger for military actions (La Nación, 2022; Semana, 2022). The general position of leaders, foreign ministries, and actors from civil societies sees Russia's behaviour as violating international law and undermining the world order. At the same time, neither Russia nor China can rely on another multilateral body with a universalist vision of international relations and international security that can compete with the NATO's moral authority. Although it is notable that the Ukrainian crisis has spurred some general interest in BRICS—for example, Argentina even applied to participate—BRICS is only an informal group.

2.7 Conclusion

Latin American integration, focused on the region's search for resources to solve internal problems and find its own way in world politics, has always developed in close connection with the logic of globalization as a heterogeneous and multidirectional process. The domain of multidimensional security seems to be quite a productive illustration of this process. On the one hand, most of the threats that Latin America is facing at present are of a transnational or intermestic nature—for example, the Venezuelan crisis, which is the largest destabilizer of regional security, COVID-19 and its impact, which forced the region to simultaneously think about sanitary sovereignty and interdependence in the sphere of health. On the other hand, the enthusiasts of the Latin American regionalism in its last—postliberal and posthegemonic—period of success sought to internalize the security agenda and, at the same time, ensure the region's participation in global multilateral structures and encourage the diversification of extraregional ties.

Currently, the Latin American region as a space of policies and ideas seems to be in the process of fragmentation. The conditions for this are created both internally, due to the uncertainty around Venezuela and Brazil and the inability of other nations to replace them as true drivers of integration momentum, and externally because of the global geopolitical situation. These circumstances echo in the area of security, creating divides there as well.

The first line of division is ideological. Electoral cycles from the late 2010s to the early 2020s contributed to the coexistence of traditional conservatives, ultra-conservatives, left-wing nationalist populists, and left–liberals in the regional context. The case of UNASUR, which integrated the Bolivarianists and deeply pro-US Colombia at the same time, showed that in the context of a common goal of creating a South American security community, ideologization was surmountable. On the one hand, PROSUR operates in conditions that are made difficult because of the aggravation of socio-economic and criminal issues and COVID-19, but on the other hand, it adheres to a minimalist integration design and does not claim to be a security community. Nevertheless, even in such a flexible format, PROSUR seems unable to embody its universalist concept and overcome the challenges which emerged as a result of right-wing ideologization. Indeed, the slowdown of the group in the 2020s and its creeping disintegration after the withdrawal of Chile in 2022 confirms this thesis. Lula da Silva, once again elected president in 2023, announced Brazil's decision to work together with Argentina on the revival of UNASUR (El País, 2023), but so far only intentions have been voiced. It would, therefore, be unrealistic to anticipate a South American security community restored by UNASUR.

The second line of division can be called "democrats versus autocrats and illiberals". Above all, it emerges in the right-wing securitization of democracy. The regional and Pan-American reaction to the Venezuelan crisis is an emblematic illustration of this.

The third line of division stems from Latin America's pulling into the bloc rivalry. The first instance of such a rivalry was during Trump's presidency. It created a split between the US as a hegemon tired of the burden of globalization as a collective good and China, which appeared as a constructive source and supporter of globalization for Latin America. The second instance is now unfolding amid Western pressure on China and especially Russia as challengers to the liberal world order. It is not in Latin America's interest to engage in this confrontation, but we argue that this is highly probable after the postliberal and post hegemonic regionalism lost its momentum. Security issues play a significant role here, including in the human dimension, which is directly related to competing attention from the US and China on the issues of political stability and development in Latin America, and in the "traditional" dimension due to the effects of political and military–technical ties between the Bolivarianist pole and Russia.

We do not consider the NATO factor in our work in order to claim that there will be some kind of "NATO-ization" of Latin America, as in the current context of NATO's goals and responsibilities, this seems impossible. At the same time, although the earlier interactions of Latin American players with NATO had a more neutral meaning in line with the diversification of external relations, the systemic context has since changed dramatically. As far as we are concerned, the moral and political significance of NATO in the global sense will only increase as the crisis in Ukraine comes to its denouement, and it might encourage Latin American players to pay more attention to this vector. At present, even the Colombia–NATO dialogue has the potential to influence the whole South American context. For example, due to its demining experience, Colombia is becoming a hub for triangular cooperation in the field of security within the South America–NATO framework (Concordia Americas Summit, 2020). Moreover, the Petro government's plan to invite NATO specialists to "guard" the Amazon area and prevent fires there not only shows the value of NATO as an exporter of security in a non-military sense but also affects the rest of the region.

While international relations are becoming less cooperative and, along with transnational threats, the factor of hard power is coming back to the fore, the creation of solid, functional multilateral structures in order to mobilize resources and jointly address the crises within and beyond the region would boost the international agency of Latin America. There have been many integration platforms in the region problematizing security through different political lenses in response to the various historical stages of regionalism. Since the end of the postliberal regionalism era, the new integration security agendas have tried to adapt to the internal and external challenges, but thus far, their strategies have appeared rather unproductive, disuniting Latin America and silencing its voice in a turbulent world.

References

Alda Mejías, S. (2010) 'Los cambios en las Fuerzas Armadas y la defensa en la "revolución democrática" de Evo Morales', in: Mathieu, H. Guarnizo, C. N. (ed.), *Anuario 2010 de la seguridad regional en América Latina y el Caribe.* Friedrich Ebert Stiftung en Colombia: Bogotá, pp. 221–242.

Argentine Ministry of Defence (2015) Libro Blanco de la Defensa. Available at: https://info.undp.org/docs/pdc/Documents/ARG/libro_blanco_2015.pdf (Accessed: 29 October 2022).

Boersner Herrera, A. and Chaguaceda, A. (2022) 'Rusia en Latinoamérica: la confluencia iliberal', *LSE Latin America and the Carribean*, 18 August. Available at: https://blogs.lse.ac.uk/latamcaribbean/ (Accessed: 29 October 2022).

Bolivian Ministry of Defence (2013) 'Bolivia pide cita de Unasur para evaluar relación Colombia-OTAN', 7 June. Available at: https://www.mindef.gob.bo/mindef/node/911 (Accessed: 29 October 2022).

Brazilian Ministry of Defence (2020) *Livro Branco de Defesa Nacional*. Available at: https://www.gov.br/defesa/pt-br/assuntos/copy_of_estado-e-defesa/livro_branco_congresso_nacional.pdf (Accessed: 20 February 2022).

Briceño Ruiz, J. (2017) '¿Un nuevo ciclo regionalista en América Latina? Debates conceptuales, modelos y realidades', *Cuadernos Americanos*, 1 (161), pp. 15–45.

Buzan, B. (1998) 'Introducción a los estudios estratégicos: tecnología militar y relaciones internacionales', *Cuadernos de Estrategia*, 99, pp. 133–166.

Colombian Ministry of Foreign Affairs (2022) 'En PROSUR, Vicepresidente—Canciller llama a defender la democracia como garantía de la seguridad de la region'. Available at: https://www.cancilleria.gov.co/newsroom/news/PROSUR-vicepresidente-canciller-llama-defender-democracia-garantia-seguridad-region&cd=19&hl=es&ct=clnk&gl=ru (Accessed: 26 October 2022).

Comini, N. (2015) 'El origen del Consejo de Defensa Suramericano. Modelos en pugna desde una perspectiva argentina', *Revista de Estudios en Seguridad Internacional*, 2 (1), pp. 109–135.

Concordia Americas Summit (2020) 'The evolving role of NATO in Latin America', Available at: https://www.concordia.net/americas/2020digital/report/the-evolving-role-of-nato-in-latin-america/ (Accessed: 29 October 2022).

Corporación Latinobarómetro (2020) *A favor o en contra de la integración de su país con los otros países de América Latina*. Available at: https://www.latinobarometro.org/ latOnline.jsp (Accessed: 21 February 2022).

Dinero (2018) 'Santos anuncia que Colombia ingresará a la OTAN como "socio global",' 26 May. Available at: https://www.dinero.com/pais/articulo/santos-anuncia-que-colombia-ingresara-a-la-otan/258855 (Accessed: 29 October 2022).

El País (2023) 'Argentina y Brasil resucitan Unasur', 22 March. Available at: https://elpais.com/argentina/2023-03-22/argentina-y-brasil-resucitan-unasur.html (Accessed: 25 March 2023).

Ellis, E. (2022) 'Russia in the Western Hemisphere: assessing Putin's malign influence in Latin America and the Caribbean'. Available at: https://www.csis.org/analysis/russia-western-hemisphere-assessing-putins-malign-influence-latin-america-and-caribbean (Accessed: 25 October 2022).

Eremin, A. (2017) 'OAS and the future of Inter-American Security in the Western Hemisphere'. *Mezhdunarodnie otnosheniya*, 3, pp. 45–53.

Examen ONU Venezuela (2019). 'Grupo de Lima: "La crisis en Venezuela constituye una amenaza a la paz y la seguridad internacionales".' Available at: https://www.examenonuvenezuela.com/democracia-estado-de-derecho/grupo-de-lima-la-crisis-en-venezuela-onstituye-una-amenaza-a-la-paz-y-la-seguridad-internacionales (Accessed: 29 October 2022).

Flemes D., Nolte D. and Wehner L. (2011) 'Una comunidad de seguridad regional en formación: la UNASUR y su Consejo de Defensa'. *Estudios Internacionales*, 170, pp. 105–127.

Frenkel, A. and Dasso-Martorell, A. (2021) 'Pandemia y desintegración regional: la COVID-19 y el retroceso de la comunidad de seguridad Sudamericana', *URVIO, Revista Latinoamericana de Estudios de Seguridad*, 31, pp. 25–42.

Fuentes, C. F. (2005) *¿Hacia una política de seguridad en el Mercosur?*, Seminario Internacional "Enfoques subregionales de la seguridad hemisférica", Quito. FLACSO-Ecuador. Available at: https://pdba.georgetown.edu/Security/citizensecurity/paraguay/documentos/fuentes.pdf (Accessed: 25 October 2022).

Fukuyama, F. (2022) 'Putin's war on the liberal order', *Financial Times*, 4 March. Available at: https://www.ft.com/content/d0331b51-5d0e-4132-9f97-c3f41c7d75b3 (Accessed: 25 October 2022).

Jeifets, V. L. (2019) *Ot bipolyarnogo k mnogopolyarnomu miru: latinoamerikanskij vektor mezhdunarodnyh otnoshenij v XXI veke [From bipolar to multipolar world: the Latin American vector of international relations in the XXI century]*. Moscow: ROSSPEN.

Jeifets, V. L. and Khadroich, L. V. (2015) 'Latinskaya Amerika mezhdu OAG i SELAK [Latin America between OAS and CELAC]', *World Economy and International Relations*, 4, pp. 90–100.

Jeifets, L. S. and Konovalova, K. A. (2019) 'Latinoamerikanskie issledovaniya integracii: ot periferijnogo kapitalizma k "Sudamekzitu" [Latin American integration studies: from peripheral realism to "Sudamexit"]', *Vestnik Rossijskogo universiteta druzhby narodov. Seriya: Mezhdunarodnye otnosheniya*, 2 (19), pp. 218–233.

Jeifets, L. S. and Konovalova, K. A. (2021) 'Latinskaya Amerika v sotrudnichestve Yug-Yug na fone protivorechij globalizacii' ['Latin America in South-South collaboration against the background of globalization's controversies'], *Mirovaya ekonomika i mezhdunarodnye otnosheniya*, 4 (65), pp. 21–29.

Jeifets, V. L., and Konovalova, K. A. (2022). 'Latin American integration against the backdrop of a conservative wave: between irrelevance and the search for new meanings', *Vestnik RUDN. International Relations*, 3 (22), pp. 447–463.

La Nación. (2022) 'Lula: Zelenski es 'tan responsable como Putin' del conflicto en Ucrania', 4 May. Available at: https://www.nacion.com/el-mundo/conflictos/lula-zelenski-es-tan-responsable-como-putin-del/XGOPJKDJGNGLRCOQQELOZK4QOE/story/ (Accessed: 29 October 2022).

La Vanguardia. (2016) 'Maduro pide a Colombia y a "pueblos de Suramérica" sacar a OTAN de la region', 27 December. Available at: https://www.lavanguardia.com/politica/20161227/412914323884/maduro-pide-a-colombia-y-a-pueblos-de-suramerica-sacar-a-otan-de-la-region.html (Accessed: 29 October 2022).

Malamud, C., Milosevich-Juaristi M., and Núñez Castellano, R. (2022) 'América Latina en la crisis de Ucrania: un convidado de piedra dentro de la estrategia de la Rusia de Putin'. Available at: https://www.realinstitutoelcano.org/analisis/america-latina-en-la-crisis-de-ucrania-un-convidado-de-piedra-dentro-de-la-estrategia-de-la-rusia-de-putin/ (Accessed: 25 October 2022).

Mijares, V. M. (2017) 'Soft balancing the Titans: Venezuelan foreign policy strategy toward the United States, China, and Russia', *Latin American Policy*, 8, pp. 201–231.

Misión de los Estados Unidos ante la Organización de los Estados Americanos (2019) 'La OEA aborda el rol desestabilizador de Rusia y Cuba en Venezuela', Declaraciones de Alexis F. Ludwig, Representante adjunto permanente de los Estados Unidos, 2 May. Available at: https://cu.usembassy.gov/es/la-oea-aborda-el-rol-desestabilizador-de-rusia-y-cuba-en-venezuela/.

North Atlantic Treaty Organization (2021) *NATO–2030*. Available at: https://www.nato.int/nato_static_fl2014/assets/pdf/2021/6/pdf/2106-factsheet-nato2030-en.pdf (Accessed: 29 October 2022).

North Atlantic Treaty Organization (2022) 'NATO 2022 Strategic Concept', Madrid, 29 June. Available at: https://www.nato.int/nato_static_fl2014/assets/pdf/2022/6/pdf/290622-strategic-concept.pdf (Accessed: 29 October 2022).

Organization of American States (2019) *La crisis en la República Bolivariana de Venezuela y sus impactos desestabilizadores para el hemisferio*. RC. 30/RES. 2/19, aprobada en la sesión plenaria, celebrada el 3 de diciembre, 3 December. Available at: https://reliefweb.int/report/venezuela-bolivarian-republic/rc-30res-219-la-crisis-en-la-rep-blica-bolivariana-de-venezuela (Accessed: 29 October 2022).

Organization of American States (2022a) *The Crisis in Ukraine*. CP/RES. 1192 (2371/22), adopted by the Permanent Council at its virtual special meeting held on March 25. Available at: https://www.google.ru/url?sa=t&rct=j&q=&esrc=s&source=web&cd=&cad=rja&uact=8&ved=2ahUKEwjZuKnFtIX7AhWolYsKHVVTAukQFnoECAsQAQ&url=https%3A%2F%2Fscm.oas.org%2Fdoc_public%2FENGLISH%2FHIST_22%2FCP45739E03.docx&usg=AOvVaw19aUjWoaP_KAjH45WUU61y (Accessed: 29 October 2022).

Organization of American States (2022b) 'Suspension of the status of the Russian Federation as a Permanent Observer to the Organization of American States', CP/RES. 1195 (2374/22), adopted by the Permanent Council at its special meeting held on April 21. Available at: https://www.oas.org/en/council/CP/documentation/res_decs/ (Accessed: 29 October 2022).

Pérez, C. (2022) 'Guatemala y otros países discuten en El Salvador propuesta del gobierno de Bukele sobre la "Unión Centroamericana",' *Prensa Libre*, 22 August. Available at: https://www.prensalibre.com/guatemala/politica/guatemala-y-otros-paises-discuten-en-el-salvador-propuesta-del-gobierno-de-bukele-sobre-la-union-centroamericana/ (Accessed: 25 October 2022).

PROSUR (2019) 'Declaración Presidencial sobre la Renovación y el Fortalecimiento de la Integración de América del Sur', Santiago de Chile, 22 March. Available at: https://foroPROSUR.org/wp-content/uploads/2020/09/DECLARACION-PRESIDENCIAL-23-3-2019.pdf (Accessed: 26 October 2022).

PROSUR (2021) 'Plan Sectorial del área temática Salud'. Available at: https://foroPROSUR.org/wp-content/uploads/2020/09/SALUD-PLAN_SECTORIAL_2021.pdf (Accessed: 26 October 2022).

PROSUR (2022) 'Declaración PROSUR sobre Seguridad Regional', Luque, 21 July. Available at: https://foroPROSUR.org/wp-content/uploads/2022/07/Declaracion-de-Presidentes-VII-Reunion-ESP.pdf (Accessed: 26 October 2022).

R4W (2021) 'OAS and R4V Platform report shows the impact of COVID-19 on specific groups of Venezuelan refugees and migrants', 27 October. Available at: https://www.r4v.info/en/news/oas-and-r4v-platform-report-shows-impact-covid-19-specific-groups-venezuelan-refugees-and (Accessed: 29 October 2022).

Riggirozzi, P. and Tussie, D. (2012) *The rise of post-hegemonic regionalism: The case of Latin America.* London: Springer.

Ripoll de Castro, A. and Quintero, S. (2016) 'Alianza del Pacifico: Nuevo regionalismo, y seguridad ampliada', VIII Congreso de relaciones internacionales, La Plata, 23–23 November, Universidad de La Plata. Available at: http://ocs.congresos.unlp.edu.ar/index.php/CRRII/CRRII-VIII/paper/viewFile/3438/845 (Accessed: 21 March 2023).

Riquelme Rivera, J. (2018) *Integración regional y comunidades de seguridad: una perspectiva desde América del Sur.* Trabajo de investigación para optar al grado académico de Doctor en Relaciones Internacionales. Universidad Nacional de La Plata, Buenos Aires. Available at: https://www.iri.edu.ar/wp-content/uploads/2018/12/tesisDoctoralRiquelme.pdf (Accessed: 25 October 2022).

Rouvinsky, V. (2019) 'El retorno ruso: la política rusa hacia América Latina y el Caribe después del fin de la Guerra Fría', *Pensamiento Propio*, 49–50, pp. 169–180.

Rouvinsky, V. and Jeifets, V. (2022) *Rethinking Russian-Latin American Relations in the Post-Cold War Era.* New York: Routledge.

Sanahuja, J. A. and López Burian, C. (2020) 'Las derechas neopatriotas en América Latina: contestación al orden liberal internacional'. *Revista CIDOB d'Afers Internacionals*, 126. pp. 41–63.

Semana. (2022) '"Irracionales": la dura crítica del presidente Gustavo Petro a la OTAN y a los poderosos del mundo', 20 September. Available at: https://www.semana.com/politica/articulo/irracionales-la-dura-critica-del-presidente-gustavo-petro-a-la-otan-y-a-los-poderosos-del-mundo/202237/ (Accessed: 29 October 2022).

SIPRI (2023) SIPRI Arms Transfers Database: Importer/exporter TIV tables – Imports to Argentina, Brazil, Colombia, Chile from 2015 to 2023. Available at: https://armstrade.sipri.org/armstrade/page/values.php (Accessed: 24 March 2023).

Stein, A. (2009) 'El concepto de seguridad multidimensional', *Bien común*, 15 (176–177), pp. 31–37.

Tusicisny, A. (2007) 'Security communities and their values: taking masses seriously'. *International Political Science Review.* 28 (4), pp. 425–449.

United Nations (2020) 'Policy brief: the impact of COVID-19 on Latin America and the Caribbean'. Available at: https://unsdg.un.org/sites/default/files/2020-07/EN_SG-Policy-Brief-COVID-LAC.pdf (Accessed: 21 October 2022).

Venezuelan National Assembly (2022) 'Presidente (e) Guaidó tras suspensión de Rusia como país observador de la OEA: "Los venezolanos ratificamos nuestro rechazo a la atroz invasión de Putin a Ucrania"'. Avaiable at: https://presidenciave.com/presidencia/presidente-e-guaido-tras-suspension-de-rusia-como-pais-observador-de-la-oea-los-venezolanos-ratificamos-nuestro-rechazo-a-la-atroz-invasion-de-putin-a-ucrania/ (Accessed: 29 October 2022).

Woods, A. (2006) 'Chavez: "Capitalism must be transcended"', *In Defence of Marxism*, 1 February. Available at: https://www.marxist.com/chavez-capitalism-transcended-socialism.htm (Accessed: 25 October 2022).

Chapter 3

Security governance in the Andean borderlands: Hybrid formations and the rising armed violence

Rafael A. Duarte Villa
University of São Paulo, Brazil

Camila de Macedo Braga
University of São Paulo, Brazil

Rafael Enrique Piñeros Ayala
Universidad Externado de Colombia, Colombia

Abstract

This chapter adopts an innovative perspective to analyse two cases of security governance in the Andean borderlands. Traditional security studies focus on examining inter-state wars, which are rare in Latin America; thus, relevant challenges in the region are better understood through other perspectives. Constructivist and reflexive frameworks reveal zones of positive and negative peace, shedding light on various non-traditional challenges to regional, national, and local security. Employing both primary (interviews and fieldwork) and secondary sources, this chapter focuses on the challenges and reality of governing the Colombia-Venezuela and Colombia-Ecuador border areas. It argues that relevant practices are best explained through the concept of hybrid security because it makes it easier to understand grey areas where territorial control, solutions to social problems and provision of basic services are determined both by the presence of the state and by various actors outside the law that sometimes play the role of the state.

Keywords: Andean region, hybrid security, armed conflict, violence, Colombia, Venezuela, Ecuador

***

3.1 Introduction

From a traditional perspective in security studies, where war constitutes the main threat to international security and peace, Latin America is seen as a region of stable peace. Nevertheless, some scholars of the constructivist bent see the region as divided into "zones of peace"—both in a negative sense as non-war zones as well as a positive sense as zones that are more integrated—even predicting the emergence of a partial security community.

It may be correct to infer that Latin America has built a historical zone of peace where peace is understood as the absence or rarity of war occurrences since the formation of the modern state system. However, through the notion of "violent peace" (Mares, 2013), academics have focused on how state actors respond to the intentions, capabilities, and actions of other regional state actors as well as the ongoing militarized disputes among them.

Hence, the presence of unresolved disputes has not automatically led to hard balancing or alliance formation. Moreover, the absence of relevant interstate wars in the region over the twentieth century and the consolidation of strong sociability ties in the security regional governance architecture accentuated the confidence in procedural and operational mechanisms to manage and resolve conflicts. As discussed elsewhere (Villa, Chagas and Braga, 2019; Villa, Braga and Ferreira, 2021), these factors led to regional states adopting an approach that is an overlap of security community and power-balancing mechanisms (see Adler and Greve, 2009). Thus, Latin American, and in particular South American, security structure and relations seem to be defined by an "unstable peace" (Braga and Romaniuk, 2022), where the balance of power and security community governance mechanisms coexist, overlap, and intertwine.

Furthermore, in addition to state-level security governance mechanisms that focus on state agency and interstate relations as the level of analysis (i.e., the security community and balance of power), we believe that another distinct level of analysis emerges when we consider transnational social violence. This third dimension refers, in particular, to the presence of non-state armed actors and their influence on regional security governance dynamics.

"Latin America currently holds 8% of the global population, nevertheless, responds [sic] for roughly 33% of the homicides reported worldwide. At the same time, the regional homicide rate (21,5 per 100,000) is more than three times the global average (7 per 100,000) and this number is expected to reach 39,6 (per 100,000) by 2030, following a growth rate of 3,7% a year" (Braga and Villa, 2022, p. 32). Therefore, in this chapter, we argue that in addition to the balance of power and security community mechanisms, a third level of analysis in security governance must be considered when studying the Latin American regional space. This analysis is related to transnational social violence and it involves both state and non-state actors in diffuse forms of interactions (vertical and horizontal, formal and informal, licit and illicit, etc.). To inform this perspective, we explore transborder security dynamics in multiple case studies pertaining to regional dynamics.

In this chapter, we will focus on the northern part of South America, especially the borders of: (i) Colombia and Venezuela; and (ii) Ecuador and Colombia, and show how violent non-state agencies are challenging and redefining regional security. We aim to provide a critical and empirical analysis of how the dimension of transnational social violence influences South America's regional security governance. Moreover, this work draws attention to the inability of traditional security governance approaches, which are state-centric, to address the current complexities in South American security governance.

3.2 Understanding theoretically the emergence of a (third) social level of security

We have reiterated in other studies that hybridity is a marked characteristic of Latin American security governance (Villa, Braga and Ferreira, 2021; Villa, Chagas and Braga, 2021, 2019). Hybridity offers, for our purposes, an alternative analytical framework by addressing systems of security governance in South America as sites of transition and change. This notion of hybridity emerges through these different (and overlapping) practices, which coexist and interrelate in a co-constitutive process (Villa, Chagas and Braga, 2019). By addressing hybridity in security governance, we ground our approach in the work of Adler and Greve (2009).

These authors focus on two overarching mechanisms of security governance: balance of power and security community. The two represent distinct sets of social practices, based on different notions of power and the role of war, alliances, and alignments in creating order and stability (Villa, Chagas and Braga, 2019). We apply the notion of hybridity to address these complex dynamics associated with the systemic interactions among actors related to security governance issues. According to Adler and Greve (2009, p. 64), security governance is "a system of rule conceived by individual and corporate actors aiming at coordinating, managing, and regulating their collective existence in response to threats to their physical and ontological security".

Therefore, security governance is characterized by order-creating mechanisms that seek to shape horizontal and vertical relations among the political and social units through which international and transnational security activities take place (Adler and Greve, 2009, p. 64). Hybridity in security governance forms through social actions and institutionalised practices, drawing on distinct security rationales and practices associated with variations in the balance of power and security community. Still, these points of overlap occur in nuances, such as hard and soft balancing or loosely and tightly coupled security communities (Villa, Chagas and Braga, 2019 and 2021).

Our theoretical contribution, however, points out that beyond the dimensions of a balance of power and security community in security governance systems, little attention has been paid to how social systems can affect the security of a region, particularly when the dynamics of violent non-state actors (VNSAs) emerge as a third interdependent dimension in the face of rising tensions in security governance. Traditionally, the focus of analysis has been on state-led governance or formal governance dynamics—considered as "governance by governments"—where authority flows vertically, merging public and private operational actors and strategies into hierarchical structures (Rosenau, 2004, 1990). Conversely, governance without government (Rosenau, 1990), which "refers to policies that may be ratified by governments but that are propelled and sustained mainly outside the halls of governments" (Rosenau, 2004, p. 43), has not been studied much.

In contrast, analysis of the role of non-state actors has focused on the overlapping and intertwining forms of governance in "weak" or "fragile" states and on the emerging "hybrid political orders" (Lawrence, 2017) resulting from hybridization processes where state and non-state modes of governance coexist, overlap and intertwine (Villa, Braga and Ferreira, 2021). One possible example emerges as we address the relationship between security and development, particularly when arguing that zones of conflict and insecurity give rise to distinct political complexes. Others argued that the so-called ungoverned spaces are actually alternatively governed (such as Clunan and Trinkunas, 2010), and more recently, authors analysing security sector reform have focused on the role of non-state providers of justice and security in societies emerging from violent conflicts (Lawrence, 2017).

However, few analysts inquire about the empirical ways in which criminal VNSAs and legal, social actors erode state authority—or vertical/formal governance, contributing to tension in regional security governance—when they aggregate horizontal/informal forms of governance, thus contesting traditional structures of control and social order. In South America, for example, global interdependence has profoundly changed the nature of illicit activities in recent decades, effectively undermining state authority in particular areas controlled by criminal organizations or disputed amongst them (Villa, Braga and Ferreira, 2021).

Therefore, following previous efforts (Villa, Braga and Ferreira, 2021; Arjona, 2016), we suggest that both parallel and interdependent dynamics may be at play, where non-state armed actors engage in horizontal modes of governance over spaces and populations to the extent that they provide alternative forms of welfare, employment, and meaning, by operating as the functional equivalents of states wherever formal state governance is perceived as weak or contested.

As such, we focus on "security beyond governments", considering the informal modes of governance that emerge in territorial spaces of limited statehood and operate "outside" government's control but may achieve a measure of legitimacy among local populations and (sometimes) the state (Villa, Braga and Ferreira, 2021).

In regions where the state does not occupy a central position in the "political framework that provides security, welfare and representation, it has to share authority, legitimacy and capacity with other actors" (Boege et al., 2008, p. 24). Hence, horizontal forms of security governance emerge, where state authority is undermined both in terms of coercion and consent, as VNSAs' control over the means of violence interacts with a resistance subculture in the face of rising levels of repressive politics. Such dynamics mobilize and consolidate spaces of hybrid governance, where the state is not absent but acts as an "other", a stakeholder or interest-party, fighting for control over a pluralistic social system (Villa, Braga and Ferreira, 2021).

By incorporating a third level of security governance analysis, in addition to the balance of power and security community, our arguments follow those of Chabat (2019). The author identifies four modes of connection between state and criminal VNSAs: varying from situations where the state has control and instrumentalizes the criminal groups to achieve its ends; situations where corruption of officials is the prevailing nexus; undisclosed alliances between the state and powerful criminal groups; and, finally, situations where the de facto control is in the hands of armed groups, who will perform some basic state functions (Chabat, 2019, pp. 17–18). Nonetheless, even if all modes of interaction are present at a certain time and space, the nexus between state and criminal organizations is difficult to map as corruption is widespread in modern states' bureaucratic structures (Villa, Braga and Ferreira, 2021).

In this chapter, in order to account for this emerging level in security analysis and analyse the interactions between all participating actors, we chose to address the nexus between the state and criminal VNSAs with reference to two particular contexts of the Andean region: the border between Colombia and Venezuela and that between Colombia and Ecuador. The qualitative research presented in the next two sections includes a triangulation between primary and secondary sources as well as fieldwork observations and key interviews conducted in December 2019 (in Bogotá and Cúcuta).

> Why work with borders? Borders are multidimensional concepts (Linares, 2019), involving territorial, political, and symbolic dimensions. For the case studies, we opt for the anthropological approach to "borderlands" or "border zones" defined by historical and contextual social dynamics. As such, "the size of borderlands depends on the extent to which cross-border transactions, including flows of people, goods or information,

reach into areas more distant to the borderline" (Mouly, Idler and Garrido, 2019, p. 56). Moreover, borderlands are not static. According to van Schendel, "the spatiality of social relations is forever taking on new shapes" (Ibid.).

Annette Idler complements this conceptualization by proposing the notion of the "border effect" (Idler, 2012a, p. 93), where two factors contribute to the borderland's dynamic nature: first, their distance from political (state) centres, and thus the relations established between the centres and peripheral areas, and second, their transnationality, pertaining to the strength of cross-border relations. Both factors act on and alter processes and outcomes of social, political or economic phenomena in borderlands (Idler, 2012b). Hence, when it comes to addressing security governance systems in border areas, we do not look at borders as "space" or "events" but as "social processes", where diverse security agencies and practices interact, overlap, and intertwine. To map this dynamic system, we start with the geopolitical structure of the countries and the historical relations between Colombia and Venezuela and Colombia and Ecuador. Next, we address the conflictive social dynamics, focusing particularly on the presence of illicit actors and their social ties across the border.

Finally, since our work involves different levels of analysis, this chapter takes a multilevel perspective, encompassing a variety of actors—VNSAs/non-state armed groups (NSAGs), individuals, organized groups, local governments, national governments, regional organizations, and international organizations—whose actions evolve in interactive processes. Of course, despite the overlapping nature of different levels of analysis, it is possible to think of them in terms of density—that is, the intensity at which each level of analysis is empirically observed in a certain space, which ultimately affects the political nature and social aspects of inter-level interaction—and the degree of emphasis on the role that the researcher assigns to each level in the analysis. Hence, by regarding the borderlands as social processes, this chapter treats them as mediated spaces between the local, national, regional, and global levels. Nevertheless, we will focus on the transnationality of the border areas by tracing the many interactions happening at the local levels and extrapolating from it.

Other studies have described the evolution of security dynamics in border areas. The coexistence of actors outside the law within a territory generates constant interactions over time that reproduce patterns of control, coexistence, and economic exploitation, which depend on the type of agreement established between the different actors involved. So, as Idler (2019) points out, hybrid governance in border areas is connected to consent, which could be voluntary or forced, between the parties involved in criminal activities. The dynamics related to forced and irregular migration, the production and distribution of narcotics, and even the consequences of the Colombian armed conflict have an effect not only on neighbouring countries (Venezuela and Ecuador), but also on others in Latin America and the Caribbean. Our case study, in this regard, provides insight into the relationship between the dynamics of legality and illegality.

3.3 Security governance in the Colombia–Venezuela borderlands

Colombia and Venezuela share a territorial border that extends for 2219 kilometres and includes seven state departments on the Colombian side of the border (La Guajira, Cesar, Norte de Santander, Boyacá, Arauca, and Vichada y Guainía), which make up 25% of the country's territory, and four state departments on the Venezuelan side (Zulia, Táchira, Apure, and Amazonas), making up around 36% of the country's territory (Linares, 2019). In contrast to other Latin American borders, this borderland is rich in both natural resources and economic activity. Historically, the economic pole was on the Venezuelan side of the border, where the push for economic development in the 1970s prompted many Colombian citizens fleeing internal armed violence to cross the border in search of a better life (Torres Aguilera, 1994).

At the time, the economic disparity between Venezuela and Colombia, where income rates were low and unemployment high, created an appropriate environment for illicit economies to prosper, in particular, the smuggling of food and fuel. The natural environment in this area favoured these activities as well as the presence of non-state armed actors (the Colombian guerrillas, Fuerzas Armadas Revolucionarias de Colombia (FARC) and Ejército de Liberación Nacional (ELN), and the drug cartels as the state forces on both sides could not access the entire border area or control illegal crossing. The dense forests still hide many paths used for illegal crossing, the so-called *trochas*. It was during the 1980s that the Colombian government started to invest more in border relations, as argued by Peña, Hoyos and Sierra-Zamora (2019, p. 778):

> According to the criteria of confidence-building mechanisms (MCM), historical in the region alongside global confrontations, since the 1980s Colombia has been strengthening the push for a border law that helps create internal coordination mechanisms with our neighbours. Said law even contemplates binational border commissions, the formation of special technical commissions for specific issues of border social problems, subsistence economy, exchange of specific information to mitigate the impact of crime, border development zones, macroeconomic cooperation, regional projects border infrastructure and even megaprojects for technology exchange and energy security. In the past, such initiatives and commitments were in force and dynamic with Venezuela, but as a result of the change in the political system there, all of these were deactivated and disappeared from the political environment.

The fluctuations in bilateral relations between Colombia and Venezuela are not new—their history has been marked by alternating periods of tension and collaboration. The period from 1830 to 1941, for example, is characterized by tensions related to the delimitation and demarcation of borders. On the other hand, from 1942 to 1970, there was a period of increasing bilateral cooperation, including the implementation of the "Estatuto Fronteirizo" (1942), on issues such as migration, environment, security, and judicial cooperation. However, again, from 1970 to 1988, cooperation was disrupted due to rising tensions with regard to maritime negotiations, which originated because of the disagreement between Colombia and Venezuela on matters related to the delimitation of marine and underwater areas. But then, from 1989 to 1998, there was a decade of cooperation, which witnessed the greatest advances in establishing a binational agenda and cooperation mechanisms. At the end of the 1990s, the members of the Andean Community of Nations (CAN) started to push for an integrated/common border policy, focusing on security and development. One important step was the definition and demarcation of the "Border Integration Zones [the Spanish acronym is ZIF] as border territorial areas adjacent to the member countries of the Andean Community for the execution of plans, programs and projects to promote joint development between the countries involved" (Linares, 2019, p. 140).

However, at the turn of the new century, the lack of integrated management for emerging security issues—such as smuggling, money laundering, vehicle theft, arms trafficking, drug trafficking and the presence of guerrillas and paramilitaries—had overshadowed all other social, political, and economic factors in the border relations between Colombia and Venezuela. In addition, the alleged nexus between the Venezuelan military and government and the Colombian guerrillas made for an explosive binational agenda.

For Venezuela, a new era of regional relations had started, with the Hugo Chávez administration distancing itself from the United States and strengthening the country's ties with other regional actors in South America and the Caribbean. In contrast, though Colombia sought regional support for peace processes from the two active guerrilla groups—FARC and ELN—at the same time, it was looking for financial and military support from the United States with Plan Colombia to combat drug trafficking and subversive activities in the region.

At the end of the 1990s and in the early 2000s, under the provision of the Andean Community border policy, Venezuela and Colombia sought to establish their ZIF, advancing economic development and commercial relations in their borders. However, border security incidents led to an increase in tensions, which prompted militarized responses from both state actors.

As indicated in Table 3.1, a number of incidents recorded from 2000 to 2010 show that interstate tensions increased in parallel with the proliferation of non-state armed actors along the border area and increased control over illicit economies. However, it was Colombia's decision to allow the United States to use its military bases that aggravated the tensions. Álvaro Uribe, Colombia's president at the time, had pushed for guerrilla groups to be considered terrorist groups and accused Chávez of protecting them. The accusations were denied by the Chávez administration; however, relations did not normalise until Juan Manuel Santos became president of Colombia. Between 2010 and 2012, Santos re-established dialogue with Venezuela and was able to address cross-border problems, such as drug trafficking, organized crime, and extortion and kidnapping, through shared information and joint operations (Linares, 2019, p. 148). However, in December 2012, Chávez left for Cuba to receive medical treatment and Nicolás Maduro Moros, who was vice president at the time, assumed power in Venezuela and was later elected as president in April 2013. With this, bilateral relations started souring once again. Throughout the next decade, relations became increasingly tense. This period was marked by a new peace process between Colombia's government and the guerrilla groups and by a deepening political and economic crisis in Venezuela.

Table 3.1 Border security incidents in Colombia and Venezuela (2002–2010)

On 13 March 2003, Venezuela announced the deployment of additional troops, arms, and aircraft to the border with Colombia, where violence between the Colombian military, the guerrilla, and paramilitary groups would sometimes spill over
On 27 March 2003, Venezuela bombed Colombian irregulars inside Venezuela but did not further establish the identity of the targeted irregulars. Venezuela denied doing so during a battle between guerrilla and paramilitary groups and also denied supporting Colombian insurgent groups. About 70 Venezuelan soldiers and a helicopter entered Colombian territory and fired on a settlement there
The dispute commenced with a border violation on 1 March 2008 or 2 March 2008 in which Colombia killed a number of FARC rebels inside Ecuador, including senior FARC member Raul Reyes (Operation Fenix). In response, Ecuador and Venezuela deployed troops to fortify their respective borders with Colombia. Venezuelan border fortifications continued through 4 March 2008
On 17 May 2008, Venezuela charged that Colombian troops had crossed the border into Venezuela
On 19 May 2008, Venezuela announced that a separate group of Colombian troops that had crossed into its territory left at the request of Venezuelan troops
On 9 August 2009, Colombia accused Venezuelan troops of an incursion into Venezuela through the Orinoco river to hunt down FARC rebels. In response to an increasing frequency of incursions into Venezuelan territory by Colombian forces, Venezuela deployed additional troops to secure its border with Colombia. This additional deployment resulted in Colombia placing its military on "maximum alert"
On 8 January 2010, Venezuela scrambled military jets to intercept a US military plane that it claimed violated Venezuelan airspace for a total of 34 minutes on two occasions
On 22 July 2010, Venezuela suspended diplomatic relations with Colombia over accusations that Venezuela harboured Colombian rebels. Venezuela charged that a Colombian military helicopter violated Venezuelan airspace on 29 July 2010. From 30 July 2010 through 2 August 2010, Venezuela deployed troops along its border with Colombia due to alleged threatening moves by Colombia

Source: Created by the authors with data from the Correlates of War (2013)

Initially, Santos and Maduro succeeded in establishing some accords related to security issues, such as sharing information and conducting joint operations against fuel, food, and medicine smuggling; narcotrafficking; and local armed violence. However, by 2015, the internal crisis in Venezuela, already at the level of a complex humanitarian crisis, spilt over into the neighbouring countries, affecting, in particular, the shared border with Colombia. A report from *Migración Colombia*, Colombian Ministry of Foreign Affairs, published in 2017, noted that around 37,000 Venezuelan citizens crossed the seven border check points daily along the border with Colombia in a pendular movement.

Between 2015 and 2017, the United Nations High Commissioner for Refugees (UNHCR) recorded 470,660 persons of concern originating from Venezuela, including refugees and asylum seekers, with most of them passing through the border into Colombia. This mixed flow, however, exacerbated the critical humanitarian situation in the destination country, where the total number of asylum seekers, refugees, internally displaced people, and returnees numbered 7,747,365 (United Nations High Commissioner for Refugees, 2017).

Therefore, from 2015 to 2020, border relations were increasingly strained because of the differential exchange rates and price systems as well as the corruption in the security forces and local institutions, which facilitated the consolidation of violent criminal structures that were competing for businesses, goods, routes, and territory on both sides of the border (Linares, 2019, p. 149).

In August 2015, after an attack on FANB (Fuerza Armada Nacional Bolivariana) officers by a Colombian armed group in San António del Táchira, Maduro announced a closure of borders and orchestrated the "Operation for the People's Liberation", which pushed for the return of 21,000 people, including Colombian illegals and undocumented immigrants, and precipitated a humanitarian crisis. Although this crisis increased tensions between the two governments, the people inhabiting border areas (*fronterizos*) had different views and acted together to push both governments towards a negotiated outcome. The "Damas de Blanco" episode is one of many instances where local society challenged the government through nonviolent means, as noted by one public authority in Cúcuta:

> … it was the Ladies in White who broke through the border. That is, pure women from different legal points … They were called the Ladies in White because they all put on a white T-shirt and crossed the border without stopping for nothing, neither for the Venezuelan nor for the Colombian guards. They broke in and, in that way … forced the

governments to sit down and come up with a solution to the border situation.[1]

Internal and regional pressures forced the neighbouring states to call for high-level talks, where regional organizations such as CELAC (Comunidad de Estados Latinoamericanos y Caribeños) and the Union of South American Nations (UNASUR) played an important role in diffusing the escalating crisis. The dialogue process was also supported by the presidents of Ecuador and Uruguay, who finally recognized the government's neglect of the region and the need to confront illegal activities in border areas, promote citizen security, and strengthen regional development in border areas. Again, border relations resumed, but by 2017, both countries were facing a deterioration in their respective internal situations, and as before, the border area was also affected (Linares, 2019).

Thus, it can be seen that in recent decades, relations between Venezuela and Colombia have tended to vary in accordance with the logic of balance of power and security community. The resulting dynamics—although occasionally escalating into militarized incidents—have not progressed to open, armed conflict. During a fieldwork interview in Cúcuta, a Colombian ministry of foreign affairs representative said that the:

> [Colombian state] has instructed its forces not to fall into a provocation. And it has been so. ... And we have pointed out, before international mechanisms, that there is an aggressive attitude on the part of Venezuela. But there is a margin of preventive action in Colombia, because we have not responded on many occasions to certain presences. Of small incidents ... We believe that regardless of a political organization, the Military Forces are aware of the inconvenient variable that an armed confrontation would be ... Let's say that, to this day, Colombia has been, institutionally, very preventive in not encouraging an armed conflict. And with Venezuela it has had incidents. But we believe that the Venezuelan Public Force also has seen and clearly sees how inconvenient a confrontation could be.

There has been a rise in criminal governance in the borderlands. Internal political and socioeconomic crises in both countries have deeply impacted their border areas, particularly because, in addition to structural neglect, there is internal violent displacement from political and economic centres to the peripheral areas. As Idler (2015) has argued, the transnationality of the borders, as well as their relative distance from political and economic centres, not only shape the lives of border populations but also make these areas more attractive

---

[1] Interview with municipal state representative, Cúcuta, December 2019.

to non-state armed actors. According to Idler (2015, p. 56), there are three facilitating conditions: (i) weak state governance systems, (ii) a low-risk, high-opportunity environment; and (iii) a proneness to impunity.

At the level of regional dialogue, starting in 2015, both the Colombian and the Venezuelan government recognized that they had historically neglected their border areas and had failed to identify possible ways in which they could cooperate to deal with emerging security issues in the region. The systemic marginalization of border areas has allowed illicit economies to flourish, particularly those related to smuggling, drug trafficking, and illegal commerce (Linares, 2019). NSAGs, operating on both sides of the border, were involved in the smuggling of fuel, food, and non-food items (i.e., medicines, sanitary products, electronics, etc.); illegal commerce; trafficking of people, arms, and drugs; and illegal migration as well as in paramilitary and insurgency activities. It was impossible to determine how many NSAGs were operating in the region at any given time point, as intra- and inter-group power dynamics were constantly changing the local structure of the illicit markets. Table 3.2, however, offers a non-exhaustive list of actors present between 2019 and 2021. The social base, in turn, remained a pool of human resources vulnerable to exploitation as unemployment rates were high and few people participated in the formal economy.

Table 3.2 NSAGs in the borderlands of Colombia and Venezuela

Name of the actor	Type of actor	Type of illegal activities
National Liberation Army (ELN)	Colombian insurgency (national)	War economy (includes large-scale drug-trafficking control, illegal mining, cooptation of public budgets, immigration control)
Popular Liberation Army (EPL) or "Pelusos"	Former leftist insurgency group that turned into a group similar to those involved in organized crime (transnational)	Large-scale drug trafficking, immigration control, gas smuggling
FARC dissidents	Member of the former Front 33 of the FARC (transnational)	Large-scale drug trafficking
Los Rastrojos	Organized criminal group rooted in former paramilitary militias (transnational)	Large-scale drug trafficking, control of illegal paths, taxation of irregular immigrants, extortion, gas smuggling
Tren de Aragua	Organized criminal group of Venezuelan origin (transnational)	Control of illegal paths, taxation of irregular immigrants
Clan del Golfo	Organized criminal group rooted in former paramilitary militias, mostly operating in the Cúcuta area (transnational)	Drug trafficking and distribution, gas smuggling
La Linea	Organized criminal group (based locally)	Control of illegal paths, taxation of irregular immigrants, human trafficking

La Frontera	Organized criminal group of Venezuelan origin (based locally)	Control of illegal paths, taxation of irregular immigrants, human trafficking
Los Diablos, Los Canelones, and Los Cebolleros	Small organized criminal groups mostly operating in the Cúcuta (based locally)	Small-scale drug distribution, extortion, contract killings
Cartel de Sinaloa, Cartel Jalisco Nueva Generación	Mexican organized criminal groups (transnational)	Large-scale drug trafficking

Source: Created by the authors; based on Pinzón and Mantilla (2021).

In the 2015 talks, both states agreed to work towards promoting higher levels of citizen security and integrated border development. Nevertheless, as internal crises took their toll in neighbouring countries, actions to promote bilateral border policies stalled once again. Informal employment became the main source of revenue for the local population. In Cúcuta, for example, the rates of informal employment were around 70% (DANE and Gobierno de Colombia, 2021). Additionally, the border closure in 2015 as well as the subsequent migratory crisis, had the double effect of providing new opportunities and sources for illegal revenues for NSAGs, which increased the exploitation of the local population and their vulnerability.

The lack of interstate cooperation over extended periods of time, such as during the border closure from 2015 to 2016, provided an opportunity for organized criminal groups to increase the exploitation of the vulnerable local population. The closure of international points of entry, for one, "spilled thousands of people to illegal paths and into the hands of those who control them, altering the current balance of power among organized crime and state authorities" (Pinzón and Mantilla, 2021 p. 272). In addition, the migration crisis also created the opportunity for NSAGs to increasingly participate in the activities associated with the transborder mobility of people and goods by making use of illegal paths (*trochas*) to cross the border. A Cúcuta municipal state representative explained this situation during an interview in December 2019:

> [O]ur border is a very dynamic border. It is said that it is the border where most people cross and have crossed in Latin America. ... Now, when the legal crossings are closed, there is another problem, which is the problem of the illegal crossings or the so-called *trochas*. It is not that people do not cross the border when the border is closed, but rather that they have to do it through the river and pay criminal organizations, which are the ones that take advantage of this management on both sides of the border.[2]

---

[2] Interview with municipal state representative, Cúcuta, December 2019.

The political and economic crises that affected both regional governments, in parallel with flourishing illicit economies, also contributed to an environment that fostered closer ties between local state actors and NSAGs. A corruption scandal emerged in 2019, when Colombian "counterintelligence and anti-corruption units captured the police intendant of Puerto Santander for being an active member of Los Rastrojos". According to the indictment, he had been an active member of this group for six years (*La Opinión* 2020, cited in Pinzón and Mantilla 2021, p. 276). In 2020, local newspapers carried an exposé on how "Venezuelan security forces captured the police chief of Táchira while she was transporting ammunition, pamphlets and war material for Los Rastrojos" (Ibid.).

For the local inhabitants, because the NSAGs have been around for more than 30 years, their presence in these borderlands has become part of their everyday lives. Although they may not legitimize these groups (Idler, 2015), they certainly normalize their existence in the area as well as the control these groups exert on informal and illicit economies from which the majority of the population derives their livelihoods. The NSAGs provide alternate forms of governance and act as providers of "protection" (sometimes negotiated with the Juntas de Acción Comunal) and "basic services" (such as "health brigades"). This is clearly recounted by a local civil society organization member, who works with victims of armed violence and forced migration, including displacement, trafficking, and other forms of illegal crossings:

> The situation in Catatumbo is still latent. The conflict is now increasing and sad to say, but, unlike other departments, *Norte de Santander*, has a great particularity that stands out for everyone, which is that here we find all the groups outside the law, all of them call themselves Rastrojos, call it the Urabeños, call it the paramilitaries, call it the ELN, call it the EPL, call it the FARC, call it now with the new dissidence. Now we also have the Mexican groups that are in the sector and that is what once again is stirring up conflict [mentions the Sinaloa Cartel].
>
> This is one of the main issues of conflict for the population rooted in these sectors and it was the very abandonment of the State that has caused these groups to be there, in these sectors ... [A]nd it is the same if the State gets involved there. The same municipal administrations of these territories oppress even more the peasantry of the territory.
>
> [This] is the law. There, they [the groups] are the law. The police may be there, but they can kill someone here half a block away, and they [the police] can't even get out of their police station. If they [the groups] do not give them the order or are not sure to go out, they cannot go out. ...

Not a leaf is moved in the territory if they do not give the endorsement. As simple as that. ...

The groups often carry out health brigades to the most remote areas of their territories ... The population has to attend this activity. That is, either they go or they go ... Just as they end up doing health brigades, they end up handling the issue of security, because sometimes the neighbors come into conflict with each other, that they invaded my farm, that this, that the other, and the armed groups end up dividing the pint. This is where it goes, period. Discord is over.

In turn, state actions to reduce the presence and curb the activities of NSAGs in the borderland area have failed to provide a long-standing solution, the main problem being the lack of transborder cooperation between institutional and armed forces on either side of the border. As noted by a Colombian state representative,

[A] criminal phenomenon in the border area does not have an exclusive nationality. You always find citizens of both countries taking part in the initiative. So, what we have managed to make neighboring countries understand is that border crime is cross-border, has no nationality, and is an object of work, cooperation, and joint operation. ... [i]n the 21st century you cannot say that the smugglers are Colombian, or they are Venezuelan, or they are Colombian and not Ecuadorian. Drug traffickers are not of a single nationality, although they always find structures that welcome the entire population that is in the area of influence... [T]he structures works sideways and requires a higher degree of cooperation ...

In summary, through fieldwork interviews and observations in the city of Cúcuta (December 2019) as well as information from secondary sources, when the border could only be crossed by people and not vehicles, we found that there were three interconnected processes: (i) in the face of structural neglect from the state, armed groups became actual providers of alternative forms of governance and social goods (Villa, Braga and Ferreira, 2021); (ii) internal conflict in Colombia and the complex humanitarian crisis in Venezuela led to ongoing waves of displacement and forced migration, opening new spaces for illicit economies and social control; (iii) as a consequence, we observed a rise in armed violence in society and increasing levels of social insecurity, related to labour and sexual exploitation, and domestic and gender-based violence; increased delinquency; and the collapse of local health systems.

3.4 Security governance in the Colombia–Ecuador borderlands

The border between Colombia and Ecuador is a unique and specific subsystem and is different from other border areas. Throughout the twenty-first century, various actors at the local level have been exposed to risk and have become vulnerable as a result of the prevalent security dynamics; this has also affected the political and diplomatic relations between both countries. The border is 568 kilometres long and includes two departments on the Colombian side (Nariño and Putumayo) and three Ecuadorian provinces (Esmeraldas, Carchi, and Sucumbíos), with remarkably varied topography: there are plateaus and coastal areas, such as in the Nariño and Esmeraldas departments, mountainous and cordillera zones, located partly in the Nariño department and partly in the province of Carchi, and finally, jungles and forests in the Putumayo department and the province of Sucumbíos (Ceballos and Ardila, 2016).

The whole subregion has historically been characterized by a fragile state presence, which has encouraged VNSAs to move in. This has created marginalization from the most important productive and business centres of both states. It has also caused interchangeable security and defence dynamics between the legal and illegal sectors, reaffirming a hybrid border structure (Ibid.).

Political, economic, and social components have all played a role in the relationship between these Andean states throughout the twenty-first century. One consequence of the implementation of Plan Colombia, which began in 1999, was the displacement of conflict dynamics and migration from the centre to the periphery of the country. This affected not only the Colombia–Venezuela border but also the border between Colombia and Ecuador (Rojas, 2013; Tickner, 2007). In addition, as the Colombian state modernized the military forces, improved its capacity to control its territories, and increased its military spending (Ramírez, 2017), perceptions of vulnerability amplified within neighbouring countries regarding US presence, especially because of the associated military actions and human rights violations committed by the troops (Isacson, 2010).

In March 2008, Colombia decided to bomb a FARC camp in Ecuadorian territory to kill one of the leaders of the group, Raúl Reyes. This generated not only a dispute between both countries, but also a diplomatic and political crisis that affected the relationship between Colombia and Venezuela and, Colombia's position in South America (Arratia, 2015).[3] In addition, after the implementation of Plan Colombia between Colombia and the United States, cooperation related

---

[3] Previously, in 2004, Simon Trinidad, a financial leader from the FARC guerrilla group was captured with the cooperation of Ecuadorian authorities in Quito.

to military and security issues progressed with Plan Patriota (2006–2010), aimed at combating VNSAs and drug trafficking (Comisión de la Verdad, 2022). This again impacted the security dynamics along the Colombian–Ecuadorian border.

These circumstances facilitated the implementation of structural programmes that had the support of Bogotá and Quito, which proposed a holistic approach to interventions in the border area. The Plan Fronteras para la Prosperidad and Plan Binacional de Integración Fronteriza (2014–2022) entailed joint initiatives to include planning schemes and national policies and pointed out that security needed to be addressed from a holistic perspective.[4] It was jointly established that security should stop being viewed from territorial and military perspectives alone so that goals of "good living" in the Ecuadorian case and "prosperity" for Colombia could also be incorporated (Departamento Nacional de Planeación, 2014).

However, new dynamics intervened, such as the signing of the peace agreement between the national government and the FARC in November 2016,[5] as well as the pandemic that began in March 2020. The violence, insecurity, and vulnerability that were inherent to the borderlands were transformed by the maintenance of strategic positions by armed dissidents, the creation of new groups, and the arrival of new actors that did not have an armed presence in the region before such as the ELN (dialogues that had been suspended with the guerrilla group since 2019 were resumed in November 2022).

On the other side of the border, political and economic instability have had a negative impact on border areas. Indeed, due to the constant political instability in Ecuador, there were eight presidents in Quito during the period 1996–2006. This led to the discrediting of political parties and a desire for change on the part of the population, as well as to the dollarization of the economy and to a deep antipathy towards the presence of elites in power and towards that of the United States military in the territory —namely, the Manta military base (Pérez, 2017). This also explains to some extent why Rafael Correa, who distanced himself from political elites, could bring stability and harmonious development through alternative and inclusive economic models that transformed the Ecuadorian political scenario.

---

[4] Other lines of work that made up the plans were the following: equity, social and cultural cohesion, productive and commercial complementarity, connectivity and infrastructure, and environmental sustainability (Departamento Nacional de Planeación, 2014).

[5] The peace agreement has five points as its basis, which were configured taking into account the causes of the conflict and its solution: ending the armed conflict; truth, justice, and reparation for the victims; solution to the problem of drug trafficking; agrarian and peasant reform; and mechanisms of political participation.

With a nationalist discourse, skilfully negotiated in relation to the US presence, the Correa government managed to ensure that the agreement for the administration of the Manta military base in Ecuador, signed in 1999, was terminated at the end of 2009. With this, both Colombia and the United States realized that the situation had become unstable with regard to the fight against drugs and terrorism (Bitar, 2016). In other words, Ecuador went from being a US ally in the region and a passive actor in the Colombian armed conflict to a state that rejected internal interference outright with respect to the former, but that was also directly affected by the dynamics of displacement and by the refugee crisis caused by conflict in the latter.

During the period 1989–2016, it is estimated that a total of 226,000 people crossed the border between Colombia and Ecuador in search of refuge, and among them, 60,524 refugees, who were directly affected by clashes between illegal groups and the Colombian military were granted refugee status in Ecuador (United Nations High Commissioner for Refugees, 2017). In addition, it was recognized that 70% of the population that arrived in Ecuador in 2012 came from Colombia, and of them, 40% came from the departments of Nariño and Putumayo, which are on the border with Ecuador (Bustamante, 2012).

With regard to border management, both Ecuador and Colombia have, historically, adopted a pragmatic perspective, avoiding possible incidents that would violate the sovereignty of each country. However, though interstate relations were stable, border areas still suffered from violence arising from the presence of the GIA (Armed Irregular Groups, the Spanish term is *grupos irregulares armados*) partly because of the lack of state institutional presence and partly due to illegal activities such as coca cultivation and cocaine processing. Such groups had an alternate view of the border—it was seen as a strategic corridor for the FARC, the ELN (guerrilla groups), and the Autodefensas Unidas de Colombia (AUC). The border provided a dividing line that authorities could not cross, whereas armed actors frequently did.

The implementation of Plan Colombia in 1999 meant the displacement of the armed conflict and trade in illicit crops from the centre to the south of Colombia and, with it, a greater presence of armed groups, who formed the rearguard. This meant that they could procure their supply and escape without direct confrontation with the Colombian armed forces. Their presence brought about the development of illicit economies that are invariably linked to armed conflict, submitting the already vulnerable populations on both sides of the border to new structures of exploitation.

This structure, however, would again be transformed with the signing of the 2016 peace agreement, when FARC abandoned an area they had historically controlled. Throughout the years of the internal conflict, the FARC had created in the municipalities of the Colombian departments bordering Ecuador a horizontal and alternative institutional framework that coexisted with the legitimate one and worked relatively well. However, the administration of justice and the processing of conflicts were done in a despotic and authoritarian manner (Valencia and Ávila, 2016).

Although before the signing of this political agreement, there was a significant decrease in armed confrontations, the progressive withdrawal of ex-combatants opened up spaces for other VNSAs to establish themselves in territories controlled by the former guerrillas, making it easier for dissidents to remain in the area and maintain military presence and control, and at the same time, stimulated disputes between other actors.

In addition, the political agreement did not eliminate the incentives for armed violence in the border area. As the Pares Foundation points out, contextual and local incentives persisted—such as the presence of other VNSAs, the persistence of illicit crop cultivation, and the maintenance of strategic corridors that contributed to the persistence of local armed violence—including in the form of dissident groups of the FARC, such as the Gentil Duarte group and the Segunda Marquetalia (Pares, 2021).

In the areas where armed actions were carried out, the FARC and other NSAGs exerted significant but fluctuating control over local dynamics. In the municipalities bordering Ecuador—Tumaco, Barbacoas, or Ricaurte—as well as those that have direct access to the Pacific Ocean—such as Pizarro, Mosquera, or La Tola—the objective of territorial control by FARC dissidents and other factions was not exclusively military. It was also related to drug-trafficking control since dissident groups needed cocaine export routes and contacts with Mexican drug cartels (Ibid.).

In turn, the powerlessness of the national government (2018–2022) to comply with the agreements regarding the substitution of illicit crops with other crops, the protection of ex-combatants, and the financing of productive projects also had a significant impact on the persistence of local violence in the departments of Nariño, Putumayo, and Cauca (Pares, 2021). In this sense, some refer to the Ecuador–Colombia borderland as a "zone of confrontation with a determined focus". This concept contains the notion of restructuring the confrontational behaviours between the VNSAs and their relationship with the civilian population and the state, which is influenced by the mutations, alliances, and reconfigurations of groups or the emergence of new armed groups and is observed in two important regions: in the departments of Nariño (Telembí, Barbacoas, and Magüi-Payan) and the lower Putumayo (Indepaz, 2021).

According to the Institute of Development and Peace Studies, certain characteristics can be identified in these regions that are common to the structures operating in conflict-affected areas, and among them, the following stand out:

First, they do not have a national scope but a local and regional effect; second, the interpretation of the armed conflict is not carried out to take political power, but to ensure income from illegal markets and strategic positioning; third, they are structures whose members are middle managers and recruits with little experience; fourth, they operate in small groups whose intention is to intimidate or collect bribes from peasants; fifth, they focus on developing strategic product exchange alliances with drug cartels and, finally, the pandemic had an accelerating effect on the emergence of these structures to the extent that it encouraged the takeover of new or reconfigured structures. (Indepaz, 2018, pp. 7–8)

The proliferation of VNSAs and NSAGs has continued after the signing of agreements and also with the emergence of the COVID-19 pandemic. As can be seen in Table 3.3, the historical structures that were present in the armed conflict have been transformed, giving way to the formation of new action fronts that make it more difficult to achieve peace and that reproduce patterns of local violence.

Table 3.3 Reconfiguration of armed conflict groups

Original name	Dissident groups	Official definition	Borderland action	Number of dissidents
Fuerzas Armadas Revolucionarias de Colombia (FARC), peace deal signed in 2016	Segunda Marquetalia Gentil Duarte Group Bloque Suroriental Oliver Sinisterra front Guerrillas Unidas del Pacífico	Grupos armados Organizados Residuales (GAOR)	Military strategic presence in the territory Value added chain in narcotics	4218
Ejército de Liberación Nacional (ELN), resumed peace process in November 2022	Frente Darío de Jesús Ramírez Frente Manuel Vásquez Castaño Frente Carlos Alberto Trocha	Grupos Armados Organizados al Margen de la Ley (GAOML)	Military presence actions Value added chain in narcotics	N/A
Autodefensas Unidas de Colombia (AUC), demobilized 2003–2006	Autodefensas Gaitanístas de Colombia Clan del Golfo Los Rastrojos Los pelusos Los Caparros Los Pachencas La Constru	Grupo delictivo organizado (GDO)	Narcotics production and distribution to Mexican cartels and other criminal groups	4030

Source: Created by the authors; based on data from Fundación Ideas para la Paz (2022), Indepaz (2021), United Nations Office on Drugs and Crime (2021)

When the pandemic started in 2020, the VNSAs took advantage of the fact that the national and local authorities were overwhelmed with COVID-19 issues to increase their criminal activities. Although the military strategy of the Iván Duque administration (2018–2022) was aimed at dismantling the structures dedicated to organized crime, the increase in the number of confrontations between dissident groups contributed to a feeling of insecurity in the population. These groups were involved in more confrontations with the civilian population than with the military; there was also less institutional impact but a greater emphasis on territorial control through mechanisms of dispute, coexistence, or dominance. Thus, local peace was put at risk (Fundación Ideas para la Paz, 2020 and 2022).

In the border departments, the dynamics reflected national patterns in the sense that trade in goods and services occurred outside the control of the authorities. The trade agreements signed by Colombia and Ecuador became an incentive for transnational transit that evaded customs controls and, in addition, aided the unauthorized daily movement of workers from one side of the border to the other (Ceballos and Ardila, 2016).

The ways in which peasants are associated with activities related to cocaine production are diverse. Some are involved in the cultivation of the coca leaf, others work in the logistics and transport sectors, and still others work in the chemical processing plants that transform the coca leaf into cocaine. Whatever the activity they are involved in, peasants face pressure to work and have to submit to the authority that is sometimes shared or disputed between groups outside the law. Thus, their options to stay away from such activities are minimal (Idler, 2019). As Pécaut (1999) points out, even in the absence of direct military confrontation, peasants cannot escape the banal violence inherent in their everyday lives caused by criminal activities and the absence of the state.

Historically, coca cultivation was based in the south of Colombia. But military activities, fumigation, and forced eradication actions carried out not only in Nariño and Putumayo, but also in other departments have generated friction with Ecuador and Venezuela.

Likewise, illegal businesses did not disappear with the signing of the peace agreement. On the contrary, the expansion of the ELN, which did not have a presence in the area, as well as the presence of dissidents from former paramilitary groups, created a situation in which, in addition to the cultivation, processing, and marketing of illicit crops, other kinds of organized crime also began to emerge. The southern border became its own subsystem, in which various businesses and criminal activities of a transnational nature thrived. Mining and logging were recently added to the list of criminal activities, in addition to the trafficking of people, weapons, and chemical supplies that had already had a presence in the area (Suárez, 2017).

Illegal mining (mainly gold), extortion, human trafficking, wood trafficking, and smuggling of goods and exotic flora and fauna were the new additions to organized crime in both Nariño and Putumayo (Fundación Ideas para la Paz, 2018). This also had implications for the Ecuadorian side of the border. At the end of 2017, the authorities discovered a gold vein in the northern province of Imbabura, which soon became one of the most important mines in the region. However, it was exploited illegally not only by the locals but also by people from Colombia, Peru, Brazil, and Venezuela (Bonilla, 2019a).

Indeed, VNSA groups used the disputed economic booty left by the FARC on the Colombian–Ecuadorian border in two ways: through extortion of mining operators and local peasants, who had to pay quotas to be able to extract the mineral, and through the smuggling of products carried out during hundreds of illegal border crossings, which became a source of resources not only for the extraction and commercialization of cocaine but also for the trafficking of arms and chemical precursors, among others (International Crisis Group, 2017).

Under these circumstances, the civilian population became a small but influential link in larger production chains with global reach. For this reason, civilians took part in drug trafficking not only for subsistence but also because of the lack of opportunities for personal growth and development. The lack of adequate infrastructure to get products out of the region inhibited participation in other activities and diluted trust in the public policies that both of the governments intended to promote (Idler, 2019).

Despite the economic and financial resources devoted to combating illicit crop cultivation, the trend in recent years has been quite worrying. By 2020, a decrease in illicit crop plantations was observed and amounted to 137,000 planted hectares, especially in the southern and Pacific zones, which reflected a trend that began in 2016, when the maximum expanse of cultivated land was 180,000 hectares (United Nations Office on Drugs and Crime, 2021). However, as can be seen in Table 3.4, the production of illicit crops in Colombia has increased rather than decreased over time.

Table 3.4 Production efficiency of coca paste and cocaine in Colombia

Coca product	2014	2020	2021
Coca leaf	308,500 tons	997,300 tons	1,134,000 tons
Coca paste	368 tons	1,228 tons	1,400 tons
Cocaine	5.6 kg/hectare	7.9 kg/hectare	7.9 kg/hectare

Source: Created by the authors based on the United Nations Office on Drugs and Crime (2021)

In the aforementioned report on illicit crops, seven productive enclaves were identified that were responsible for 40.5% of the production, two of which stand out in particular as they are situated on the border between Colombia and

Ecuador. These are the municipality of Tumaco (department of Nariño) and the municipality of Orito-Vides (Putumayo), where substantial portions of the area are dedicated to cultivation. Also, the processing laboratories are larger, which allows for the production of larger amounts of cocaine. Additionally, technological aids are used to increase the productivity of the plant (United Nations Office on Drugs and Crime, 2021).

There are certain small territorial areas where the coca leaf is produced in large quantities. The produce is then transported to large laboratories and can be easily exported because of the existence of routes that allow the product to be transported from these areas to important ports (Guayaquil and Manta) or to the Colombian Pacific, from where it can be sent to Central America and the United States through clandestine airstrips or high-speed boats (Ibid.).

Thus, it could be said that Ecuador ceased to be a passive country with respect to drug trafficking or a mere actor that helped in transit and became one more link in the production, marketing, and distribution chain due to the fact that in the five years preceding 2020 there had been a concentration of coca cultivation and processing in areas very close to the border between Colombia and Ecuador, ranging around 20 kilometres (Rivera-Rhon and Bravo-Grijalva, 2020). Similarly, the capital of Sucumbíos (Nueva Loja), which once used to clandestinely treat FARC militiamen wounded in combat, now became a sanctuary for drug traffickers, oil dealers, and chemical product dealers, who once again transformed the city and altered the dynamics of confrontation (Bonilla, 2019b).

Although the analysis carried out on the dynamics of hybrid security in the border zone between Colombia and Ecuador seems to deal exclusively with the dynamics of local security, because the relationship between the governments was fraught at various time points, regional effects also came into play. This was seen especially in the response of the UNASUR, which helped diffuse tension after the bombing that Colombia carried out in Ecuador in March 2008. In other words, the Colombia–Ecuador border has internal and regional dimensions, which was apparent during 2008 when neighbouring countries, with the help of UNASUR, made an effort to surmount the problems arising from the military bombardment of Ecuadorian territory by Colombia (Bragatti, 2019).

3.5 Conclusion

We started by reviewing the literature on Latin American security studies that call for a hybrid security governance system, where two security dynamics, or even two security subsystems, overlap—namely, the balance of power and security communities (Villa, Chagas and Braga, 2019, 2021; Braga and Villa, 2022). The argument is that, other than these overlapping systems in South

American regional security dynamics, there is a third level in security governance that is social in nature, which arises from the dynamics of social violence originating from violent non-state groups that operate in the region. The reasons for the existence of this tertiary level in regional security governance and evidence for its existence are multiple, as was shown by our case studies on the borders of Colombia and Venezuela and Ecuador and Colombia. These include crises on both sides and interstate tensions along the borderlands, occasionally involving military forces and other armed actors. Examples of such situations include border closure, low-intensity armed conflict involving intergroup competition for local turfs and trafficking routes, allocation of military forces, and militarized responses to NSAG action along the dividing line.

Furthermore, the presence of NSAGs both in the Colombian–Venezuelan and Ecuador–Colombian borderlands has grown considerably in the past decades, and state authorities on either side of the border have not addressed the problem adequately. When fieldwork was being conducted in the Venezuela–Colombia borderland, a complex humanitarian crisis was underway, and interstate relations were broken, leaving the locals and Venezuelan immigrants to try and cope on their own by establishing solidarity networks or seeking assistance from international humanitarian agencies. In contrast, on the Ecuadorian side, more intergovernmental coordination was possible, and initiatives were indeed planned. However, the current data on rising armed violence between NSAGs and the increase in the production of illegal crops demonstrates that the planned initiatives and solutions did not materialize.

Moreover, the fragmentation process resulting from criminal structures hides or hybridizes interactions with local authorities and the civilian population—on the one hand, through intervention in the local economy in the form of drug trafficking and trafficking of other products and, on the other, through the imposition of a parallel or alternative order, which interferes with the precarious institutional presence of the state and serves as a mechanism of social and territorial control over the civilian population (Fundación Ideas para la Paz, 2022). In addition, the insecurity in border territories, especially in the department of Nariño and Norte de Santander, addressed in this study, continues to be closely linked to the incentives generated by the presence of illicit crops, which contribute to the development of hybrid instruments that are neither legal nor illegal in border areas, regions that were historically marginalized by the Colombian, Venezuelan, and Ecuadorian states.

Attention to border dynamics has received increasing but insufficient attention. Since the end of the 1980s, there have been border neighbourhood commissions, constituted with the intention of binationally addressing the needs of the population, as well as initiatives such as the ZIF promoted by the CAN to facilitate cooperation. Nevertheless, because of the precarious nature of their existence, both economically and socially, peasants resort to the drug-trafficking business for sustenance and try to find employment along various stages of the production chain. In this sense, the incentives for the development of an informal and illegal economy are closely related. By 2021, the informal economy constituted 60% of the Colombian economy among the economically active population (OECD, 2022).

The formal and informal economy resulting from legal and illegal economic activities mobilizes resources in such a way that it generates dynamic income not just for criminal groups but also for some segments of the population, which contributes to strengthening criminal economic governance. The GAI, for example, tailor their techniques to take full advantage of the transnational nature of the border, thus generating higher incomes for the peasants involved in the cultivation of coca leaves and other mixed crops (e.g., coca and bananas). Such techniques also help them to smuggle chemical products using high-speed boats across the rivers (Rivera-Rhon and Bravo-Grijalva, 2020).

These strategies adopted by NSAGs create governance ties formed through social and economic relations on both sides of the border, which are consolidated over time and become more difficult to modify through state action. In this sense, the transnationality of the border enables the dynamics of marginalization, corruption, and impunity to be facilitated by the borderlands' exclusion from the main production centres. In these peripheral areas, NSAGs are capable of effectuating new forms of social governance and regional and local economy regulations through the implementation of an authoritarian system of rule. This enables them to employ force and intimidation to persuade the population to take up activities such as illicit crop production, money laundering, and trafficking of illicit goods, people, and species. Consequently, their presence has deeply impacted and shaped the security dynamics on both border area segments analysed in this study.

During the COVID-19 pandemic, the situation deteriorated as a result of increased collaboration between criminal groups that were previously in conflict. This was because their interests (i.e., economic exploitation) coincided and they needed to share the labour available for the extraction and transport of cocaine and other illicit products. Thus, the emerging third level of security governance hybridization and reconfiguration generates a dual instability. On the one hand, there is the violence unleashed by the presence or control of illegal armed groups, disputing market and territorial control—such as former militants of the FARC and the paramilitaries—as well as the presence of the ELN and criminal gangs. On the other, pandemic-related adversities and the Venezuelan humanitarian crisis have put a large number of people at risk, with the prevalence of xenophobia and rejection of newcomers as well as an increase in precarious working conditions (Idler, 2018; Idler, 2020; Idler and

Hochmüller, 2020). Those most vulnerable to NSAG activities are the local population in the surveyed borderlands, who have extensive binational social and economic ties and are also deeply impacted by the changing security relations between the neighbouring states, their socioeconomic and political marginalization, and the region's prominent role in the transnational chains of drug trafficking, which enables the rise in and entrenchment of illicit economies.

Finally, we suggest two important issues that could be explored in future studies based on the analytical framework developed in this chapter.

First, hybrid security and governance, as we understand it has an impact on the level of analysis of South American regional integration. In fact, when regional governance is established only at the state level, regional security initiatives interact more intensely in hybrid configurations. An example of this is the conflict mediation role that UNASUR played in the past in the Bolivian internal conflict at the end of the first decade of this century when there was opposition to the central government and the eastern provinces of the country in relation to the administration of the country's energy resources (especially gas and oil).

Although this hybrid security structure finds strong reception from regional governments, the same cannot be said of the way in which regional integration affects aspects of regional governance, specifically that which has to do with "criminal governance". During the UNASUR's most influential period (2008–2014), there was a debate among South American countries about whether the organization could develop some form of collective action that would tackle the problems of criminal governance related to drug trafficking. The Colombian government under President Juan Manuel Santos proposed in that forum, on different occasions, that countries should coordinate measures to fight illicit drugs and drug trafficking. However, this initiative faced resistance from most of the countries in the region because they considered this type of problem not as a "regional security" problem but as an "internal public" security problem. In fact, the idea of regional political integration encountered the fear of potential loss of boundaries between countries, both in terms of form and intensity, and the fear that the principle of non-intervention in the internal affairs of a country could be affected if collective measures were used to tackle "criminal governance". In other words, the level of regional integration does affect hybrid security governance, but the way in which each level (or actor) is affected varies greatly.

Second, the borders of Colombia and Venezuela, and Ecuador and Colombia are not "foci of security or hybrid governance", which are consummated empirically, but on the contrary, the five countries of the northern Andean region (Bolivia, Colombia, Ecuador, Peru, and Venezuela) form a regional security complex in which the security problems of a country reverberate with or are interdependent on those of other countries. This is because the actors that affect regional security in the Andean region (particularly the criminal agencies) work transnationally in networked forms of organization. Thus, the groups of drug traffickers or paramilitary groups that operate on the Colombia/Ecuador/Venezuela borders are not so different from those that operate on the borders between Peru and Bolivia or between Peru and Colombia or Ecuador. Inductively, this means that the cases analysed in this chapter can give some insight into and enable comprehension of the security issues in the rest of the Andean countries (especially Peru and Bolivia), as well as the regional security complex as a whole, which remains defined by interdependence in terms of its main security issues.

References

Adler, E. and Greve, P. (2009) 'When security community meets balance of power: overlapping regional mechanisms of security governance', *Review of International Studies*, 35 (S1), pp. 59–84.

Arjona, A. (2016) 'Institutions, civilian resistance and wartime social order: a process-driven natural experiment in the Colombian Civil War', *Latin American Politics and Society*, 58 (3), pp. 99–122.

Arratia, E. (2015) *La vía colombiana: las implicancias de la diplomacia para la seguridad en américa latina*. Santiago de Chile: Centro de estudios estratégicos ANEPE.

Bitar, S. (2016) *US military bases, quasi-bases, and domestic politics in Latin America*. New York: Palgrave Macmillan.

Boege, V., Brown, A., Clements, K. and Nolan, A. (2008) *On hybrid political orders and emerging states: state formation in the context of 'fragility'*. Available at: https://www.researchgate.net/publication/278007922_On_Hybrid_Political_Orders_and_Emerging_States_State_Formation_in_the_Context_of _'Fragility' (Accessed: 4 May 2023).

Bonilla, M. A. (2019a) *InSightCrime: Obtenido de Minería ilegal y crimen organizado se extiende al norte de Ecuador*. Available at: https://es.insightcrime.org/noticias/analisis/mineria-ilegal-y-crimen-organizado-se-extienden-al-norte-de-ecuador/ (Accessed: 4 May 2023).

Bonilla, M. A. (2019b) *InSightCrime: Obtenido de La provincia de sucumbíos en Ecuador: santuario de narcotraficantes*. Available at: https://es.insightcrime.org/noticias/analisis/la-provincia-de-sucumbios-en-ecuador-santuario-de-narcotraficantes/ (Accessed: 4 May 2023).

Braga, C. M. and Romaniuk, S. N. (2022) 'Unstable peace', in Scott, R. and Péter, M. (eds.), *The Palgrave encyclopedia of global security studies*. Cham, Switzerland: Palgrave Macmillan, pp. 1–6.

Braga, C. M. and Villa, R. A. D. (2022) 'Conflict over peace in the Southern Cone borderlands: hybrid formations of security governance from a Brazilian perspective', in Ferreira, M. A. (ed.), *Peace and violence in Brazil. Rethinking Peace and Conflict Studies*. Cham, Switzerland: Palgrave Macmillan, pp. 29–59.

Bragatti, M. C. (2019) 'Ten years of the South American Defense Council: Regional International Security Architecture', *Geopolitica(s)*, 10 (1), pp. 69–86.

Bustamante, D. M. (2012) 'Dinámicas de los flujos migratorios transfronterizos', in: Pastrana Buelvas, E. and Jost, S. (eds.), *Colombia y Ecuador: entre la integración y la fragmentación*. Bogotá: KAS, pp. 67–88.

Ceballos, M. and Ardila, G. (2016) 'The Colombia-Ecuador border region: between informal dynamics and illegal practices', *Journal of Borderlands Studies*, 30 (4), pp. 1–17.

Chabat, J. (2019) 'Criminally possessed states. A theoretical approach', in: Rosen, J. D., Bagley, B. and Chabat, J. (eds.), *The criminalization of states: the relationship between states and organized crime*. London: Lexington Books, pp. 15–29.

Clunan, A. L. and Trinkunas, H. (2010) 'Conceptualizing ungoverned spaces: territorial statehood, contested authority, and softened sovereignty', in: Clunan, A. and Trinkunas H. A. (eds.), *Ungoverned spaces: alternatives to state authority in an era of softened sovereignty*. Palo Alto: Stanford University Press, pp. 17–33.

Comisión de la Verdad (2022) *Hay futuro si hay verdad: Informe final*. Bogotá: Comisión de la Verdad.

Correlates of War (2013) Dispute Narratives, 13 December. Available at: https://bpb-us-e1.wpmucdn.com/sites.psu.edu/dist/7/104724/files/2019/05/MID_Narratives_2002-2010.pdf (Accessed: 12 May 2023).

DANE and Gobierno de Colombia (2021) *La información Del DANE en la toma de decisiones regionales. Cúcuta, Norte de Santander*. Available at: https://www.dane.gov.co/files/investigaciones/planes-departamentos-ciudades/210319-InfoDane-Cucuta-Norte-de-Santander.pdf (Accessed: 4 May 2023).

Departamento Nacional de Planeación (2014) *Plan binacional de integración fronteriza Ecuador-Colombia 2014-2022*. Bogotá: Departamento Nacional de Planeación.

Fundación Ideas para la Paz (2018) *Inseguridad, violencia y economías ilegales en las fronteras*. Bogotá: Fundación Ideas para la Paz.

Fundación Ideas para la Paz (2020) *Los impactos del Covid-19 en la seguridad y la implementación de los acuerdos de paz*. Bogotá: Fundación Ideas para la Paz.

Fundación Ideas para la Paz (2022) *Ni guerra ni paz. Escenarios híbridos de inseguridad y violencia en el gobierno de Iván Duque*. Bogotá: Fundación Ideas para la Paz.

Idler, A. (2012a) 'Arrangements of convenience in Colombia's borderlands: An invisible threat to citizen security?', *St Antony's International Review*, 7 (2), pp. 93–119.

Idler, A. (2012b). 'Exploring agreements of convenience made among violent non-state actors', *Perspectives on Terrorism*, 6 (4-5), pp. 63–84.

Idler, A. (2015) *Arrangements of convenience: Violent non-state actor relationships and citizen security in the shared borderlands of Colombia, Ecuador and Venezuela*. Unpublished doctoral thesis, University of Oxford, Oxford: UK.

Idler, A. (2018) 'Preventing conflict upstream: impunity and illicit governance across Colombia's borders', *Defence Studies*, 18 (1), pp. 58–75.

Idler, A. (2019) *Borderland battles: violence, crime, and governance at the edge of Colombia's war*. New York: Oxford University Press.

Idler, A. (2020) 'The logic of illicit flows in armed conflict', *World Politics*, 72 (3), pp. 335–389.

Idler, A. and Hochmüller, M. (2020) 'Covid-19 in Colombia's borderlands and the western hemisphere: adding instability to a double crisis', *Journal of Latin American Geography*, 19 (3), pp. 280-288.

Indepaz (2018) *Conflictos armados focalizados*. Bogotá: Indepaz.

Indepaz (2021) *Los focos del conflicto en Colombia*. Bogotá: Indepaz.

International Crisis Group (2017). *Los grupos armados de Colombia y su disputa por el botín de la paz*. Bruselas: International Crisis Group.

Isacson, A. (2010) *Don't call it a model*. Washington: Wola.

Lawrence, M. (2017) 'Security provision and political formation in hybrid orders', *Stability: International Journal of Security and Development*, 6 (1), pp. 1–17.

Linares, R. (2019) 'Seguridad y política fronteriza: una mirada a la situación de la frontera entre Venezuela y Colombia', *OPERA*, 19 February, pp. 135–156. Available at: https://doi.org/10.18601/16578651.n24.08 (Accessed: 4 May 2023).

Mares, D. (2013) *Violent peace: militarized interstate bargaining in Latin America*. New York: Columbia University Press.

Mouly, C., Idler, A. and Garrido, B. (2019) 'Zones of peace in Colombia's borderland', *International Journal of Peace Studies*, 20 (1), pp. 51–63.

OECD (2022) *Social protection and tackling informality: Building on the social and solidarity economy in Colombia*. OECD Social Economy and Innovation Unit. Available at: https://www.oecd.org/colombia/Social-Protection-and-Tackling-Informality-Colombia-workshop-highlights.pdf (Accessed: 3 March 2023).

Pares. (2021) *Grupos armados PosFarc: Una nueva espiral de violencia en Colombia*. Bogotá: Fundación paz y reconciliación.

Pécaut, D. (1999) *From the banality of violence to real terror: the case of Colombia*. London: Zed Books.

Pena-Chivata, C., Sierra-Zamora, P. A. and Hoyos Rojas, J. C. (2019) 'La política de fronteras de Colombia ante las nuevas amenazas de seguridad y defensa', *Revista Científica General José María Córdova*, 17 (28), pp. 773-795.

Pérez, D. (2017) 'Ecuador frente al proceso de paz en Colombia: reflexiones teóricas y posibles escenarios', in: Grabendorff, W. and Gudiño Pérez, D. (eds.), *Proceso de paz y posacuerdo en Colombia: Efectos en la región*. Quito: FES-Ecuador, pp. 139–162.

Pinzón, V. G. and Mantilla, J. (2021) 'Contested borders: organized crime, governance, and bordering practices in Colombia-Venezuela borderlands', *Trends in Organized Crime*, 24 (2), 265–281.

Ramírez, J. C. (2017) 'Balance de los quince años del Plan Colombia (2001–2016)', *Estudios internacionales*, 49 (186), pp. 187–206.

Rivera-Rhon, R. and Bravo-Grijalva, C. (2020) 'Crimen organizado y cadenas de valor: el ascenso estratégico del Ecuador en la economía del narcotráfico', *URVIO*, 28 (September–December), pp. 8–29.

Rojas, D. M. (2013). 'Las relaciones Colombia-Estados Unidos: ¿llegó la hora del postconflicto?', *Análisis Político*, 26 (79), pp. 121–136.

Rosenau, J. N. (1990) *Turbulence in world politics: a theory of change and continuity.* Princeton: Princeton University Press.

Rosenau, J. N. (2004) 'Strong demand, huge supply: governance in an emerging epoch', in: Bache, I. and Flinders, M. (eds.), *Multi-level governance.* Oxford: Oxford University Press, pp. 31–48.

Suárez, J. F. (2017) 'Dinámicas del subsistema fronterizo colombiano', in: Ávila, A., Suárez, J. F., Sánchez, D. and Ramírez, M. F. (eds.), *El subsistema fronterizo de Colombia: lugar estratégico de los mercados ilegales.* Quito: Flacos Ecuador, pp. 155–269.

Tickner, A. B. (2007) 'Intervención por invitación. Claves de la política exterior colombiana y de sus debilidades principales', *Colombia Internacional*, 1 (65), 90–111.

Torres Aguilera, R. F. (1994) *Venezuela and Colombia: Border security issues,* Thesis from the Naval Postgraduate School Monterey CA.

United Nations High Commissioner for Refugees (2017) *UNHCR Global Report* Available at: https://www.unhcr.org/publications/fundraising/5b4c89bf17/unhcr-global-report-2017.html?query=people%20of%20concern%20Latin%20America%202017 (Accessed: 4 May 2023).

United Nations Office on Drugs and Crime. (2021) *Colombia. Monitoreo de territorios afectaos por cultivos ilícitos.* Bogotá: United Nations Office on Drugs and Crime.

Valencia, L. and Ávila, A. (2016) *Los retos del postconflicto.* Bogotá: Ediciones B.

Villa, R. D., Braga, C. M. and Ferreira, M. A. S. V. (2021) 'Violent nonstate actors and the emergence of hybrid governance in South America', *Latin American Research Review*, 56, pp. 36–49.

Villa, R. D., Chagas, F. B. and Braga, C. M. (2019) 'Hybrid security governance in South America: an empirical assessment', *Latin American Politics & Society*, 61, pp. 72–94.

Villa, R., De Macedo Braga, C., and Ferreira, M. (2021). 'Violent nonstate actors and the emergence of hybrid governance in South America', *Latin American Research Review*, 56 (1), pp. 36-49.

Villa, R. D., Chagas, F. B. H. and Braga, C. M. (2021) 'Going beyond security community and balance of power: South America's hybrid regional security governance', *Global Studies Quarterly*, 1, pp. 1–10.

Chapter 4

Lessons from forced partnerships: The Alliance for the Prosperity of the Northern Triangle (2015–2020)[1]

Miguel Gomis
Pontificia Universidad Javeriana, Colombia

Abstract

This chapter examines the impact of the Plan of the Alliance for Prosperity of the Northern Triangle (APNT) on Guatemala, El Salvador, and Honduras from 2015 to 2020. Earlier research on the Northern Triangle (NT) has analysed the causes of its instability and the shortage of government capacity to address pressing challenges. International initiatives have sought to support state modernization; the APNT claimed to assist NT states in improving their governance, ultimately seeking to limit the incentive for locals to immigrate to the US. The chapter employs institutional documents, field interviews, and an extensive press review to analyse the effectiveness of the APNT, arguing that it benefited donors and NT elites while generating little improvement in national socio-economic conditions or institutions. The chapter concludes that the geopolitical position of the NT played a key role in the decision-making of governments, who were forced to cooperate on a common agenda.

Keywords: Northern Triangle, US, cooperation, immigration, development, geopolitics

***

---

[1] The research for this chapter was produced as part of a research project funded by Javeriana University.

4.1 Introduction

For over a decade, much research on the northern region of Central America has focused on the problems linked to its instability, including their roots (e.g., poverty and economic inequality), consequences (e.g., immigration, violence, and corruption) and desirable outcomes of potential solutions (social cohesion, and productive transformation). The Northern Triangle (NT), a sub-region of Latin America which is composed of Guatemala, El Salvador, and Honduras, often appears in the international media in connection to intense and extensive citizen security problems, caravans of immigrants trying to enter the United States of America (US), devastating hurricanes, drug trafficking routes, and even recurring controversies around leaders with autocratic tendencies. Parallel to this negative view of the NT, there is a clear debate about the states' capacity to find long-term solutions, especially given that they have been receiving all kinds of support from international partners.

The Northern Triangle (NT) is marked by a progressive maturation of its civil society, which is demanding better governance. Demonstrations in the streets have exposed the democratic deficit and questioned political leaders' lack of transparency and accountability. For example, citizens mobilized against corrupt political–economic networks in Guatemala (with two accused ex-presidents, Otto Pérez Molina and Álvaro Colom); against narco-politics (against Juan Orlando Hernández, who had a controversial re-election in 2017 and was extradited to the US in April 2022 for drug trafficking); to denounce the weakening of separation of powers (which was observed, for instance in the case of Nayib Bukele's mass dismissal of judges); or to call out authoritarian and repressive inclinations (such as Daniel Ortega's government from 2018 onwards). Evidently, when citizens' tolerance of state inefficiency decreases, it results in new political pressure on public institutions and officials.

Operating in the context of a historical economic and geopolitical dependence on the US (Collado, 2010), NT governments have responded to political pressures in three different ways: 1) repeated attempts at state modernization; 2) establishment of increasingly ambitious socio-economic policies; and 3) expansion of anti-corruption efforts. Traditional international cooperation has supported the first two approaches through bilateral projects, as well as through agreements on deepening integration. In the last category, there has been a succession of strategies over time, especially influenced by changes in the US presidency.

The Bush administration's Mérida Initiative (2007–2010, including Central American countries) and the Central America Regional Security Initiative (CARSI; 2008–2015, with a $1.2 billion budget) supported law enforcement and security forces in the fight against drug trafficking, organized crime, and gang-related activities. These two initiatives were heavily criticized by some observers (Meyer and Seelke, 2015) for inciting *mano dura* policies (a punitive approach to crime) and a lack of transparency. The US then sought to renew its cooperation under Obama's administration, which favoured a more socio-institutional perspective and involved more partners. The Plan of the Alliance for Prosperity of the Northern Triangle (APNT) was negotiated in 2015 and implemented between 2016 and 2019 through the Inter-American Development Bank (IDB), to fight the systems that generate undocumented immigration (especially of unaccompanied minors).

Research on international initiatives for NT development or change forms a limited part of the NT literature. Indeed, published works (in both peer-reviewed journals and public reports) focus on socio-economic or political issues. The first and most extensive research stream approaches violence from a wide variety of perspectives, including armed conflict legacies (Marcy, 2014), contemporary organized crime (Rodgers and Baird, 2016; Prado, 2018; Zaitch and Antonopoulos, 2019), and transnational crime (Kolb, 2012). Researchers have also sought to understand the roots of insecurity, through for example, the obstacles to reducing violence (Beeton and Watts, 2016), the education programmes and culture for peace (Acuña and Illescas, 2015), or even forced displacement (Jiménez, 2017; Knox, 2017).

The second stream of academic literature deals with immigration, including the impact of violence on immigration (Schein and Mihálycsa, 2017; Musalo and Lee, 2017); actions being taken to control immigration (Serna, 2016; Malinowski and Blaha, 2016; Medrano, 2017; Hernández, 2016); expulsion factors (Lorenzen, 2017; Portes Virginio, Garvey, and Stewart, 2017); and even xenophobic narratives (Heyer, 2018).

The third body of literature on the NT focuses more on institutional or political issues, such as corruption (Gies, 2019; Tablante and Morales Antoniazzi, 2018; Bull, 2014; Zuñiga, 2012) and other problems related to politics or public policy (Craig, 2013; Colburn and Arturo, 2016; Bull, 2016). However, between 2015 and 2021, the vast majority of researchers turned to an analysis of the International Commission against Impunity in Guatemala (Spanish: *Comisión Internacional Contra la Impunidad en Guatemala*, CICIG), including its beginnings (Villagrán Sandoval, 2016; Eguizábal, 2017), its progression (Call and Hallock, 2020), constraints and operations (Romero Alvarado, 2018), operational efficiency (Bannum, 2019), and impact or legacy (Schloss and Joanna Quinn, 2015); and the Support Mission against Corruption and Impunity in Honduras (Spanish: *Misión de Apoyo Contra la Corrupción y la Impunidad en Honduras*; MACCIH), including its resistances and obstacles (González, 2020), termination (Rodríguez and Tule, 2020), legacy and lessons (Call, 2020; Murillo Castellanos, 2020).

Academic research on the APNT is limited. Most contributions do not have a formal social scientific or research basis. Ex-president Juan Orlando Hernández published an article boasting about his support of the APNT (Hernández, 2016) and that there was enthusiasm among certain specialized sectors in Washington DC (Olson, 2016). However, the vast majority of the reviewed literature is sceptical. Orozco (2016) and Garcia (2016) analyse the APNT from a critical perspective, and Iesue (2016) and Silvina María Romano (2017, 2019) point out how the APNT favours US interests and a hegemonic vision. Thompson (2021) addresses aid effectiveness, while Villafuerte Solís (2018) emphasizes the absence of statistical improvements related to violence or immigration during the implementation of the APNT. Some make accusations of neoliberal interventionism in the formation of the alliance (Roldán Andrade, 2015; Paley, 2016), while others put forward proposals for adjustments in the format of the APNT (Oviedo Garcia, 2019) and some assessments from the perspective of civil society appeared as well (Noé Pino and Noé, 2019).

Regarding official reports, three main sources of information must be highlighted. The IDB published a fiscal pre-analysis (Instituto Centroamericano de Estudios Fiscales, 2015) and two progress reports (El Salvador, Guatemala and Honduras, 2018, 2019). Meanwhile, the US Government Accountability Office sent a report to the US Congress in September 2021 on the effects of the 2019 aid suspension decided by Donald Trump's administration (Government Accountability Office, 2021). Finally, the Washington Office on Latin America (WOLA) has exhaustively monitored US cooperation with the NT (including the APNT) using its own indicators.

Despite all this literature, an in-depth academic analysis of the flaws of cooperative initiatives is lacking, and it is necessary to make new proposals for improvement. Paradoxically, factors constraining institutional and policy reform have received little attention. Since the plans, programmes, and projects change frequently, there are few evaluations of obstacles beyond the obvious ones, such as changes in presidential approaches, scandals, or external geopolitical clashes. The true impact of initiatives with extensive, documented, and negotiated formulation processes remains unclear. For example, one of the most interesting cases of inter-state collaboration, the APNT, has received little attention from academia. Its analysis could be even more nuanced if one considers that it was created under Joe Biden's vice presidency, which seemed to influence his presidential choices—in 2022, Biden insisted that solutions go through checks for security, good governance, and the need for international investment. To understand President Biden's stance on NT, it is necessary to understand what happened to this policy when he was vice president.

To what extent has the APNT impacted Guatemala, El Salvador, and Honduras? The purpose of this chapter is to show that between 2015 and 2020, APNT benefited both the donor countries and the NT elites while having little impact on socio-economic conditions of non-elite classes and on institutions. Indeed, the national governments in question took advantage of international aid for political and geopolitical strategies to further the interests of the political elite. This paper applies the international cooperation effectiveness criteria derived from Milner (1997), Krasner (2011), and Krasner and Weinstein (2014). The research is based on a review of institutional documents, field interviews in Washington DC and Tegucigalpa, and an extensive press review.

The main finding is that the APNT has had a limited impact. On the one hand, governments instrumentalized the initiative while collaborating with each other; meanwhile, the US had a significant impact on the terms of collaboration. On the other hand, the APNT relied excessively on the capacity of local states, so it had few concrete targets and achievements but helped to create a more holistic, concerted, and structured cooperation agenda. Cooperation between NT countries was de-facto forced by donor partners through indirect means, such as providing funding to this effect and reducing international pressure on them in return. The APNT has demonstrated the ability of NT leaders to adapt cooperation rules to their geopolitical position. The rest of the text is structured as follows: theoretical and methodological framework, context, research results, and conclusion.

4.2 Theoretical framework and methodology

This chapter is based on the theoretical approach of Putnam (1988), who sees the decision-making system as manifesting through the interaction between national interests and international conditions. Putnam offers a two-level framework. There is the national (or inter-state) level where negotiators' strategies are in play, and they shape interactions. Then there are the international preferences and coalitions and international institutions. Expanding on this view, Milner (1997) proposes a theory of domestic influences on international affairs based on a structure consisting of the domestic preferences of political actors. According to him, the mutual adjustments made by actors, based on what each one seeks and receives in the cooperation process, explain the cooperation variations or coordination that occurs among states. Three dominant actors (the executive bureaucracy, legislature, and social groups) design policies that institutions implement, with electoral consequences. Since international cooperation generates domestic winners and losers, the struggle between groups shapes the possibility for international collaboration (Ibid.). For Milner, cooperation type and extent depend on four agents of power: 1) the ability to initiate and set the agenda; 2) the ability to modify any proposed policy; 3) the ability to ratify or veto the policy; and 4) the ability to propose public referendums. The probability of international cooperation also depends on the distribution of power between the executive and the legislature, the change of actors or institutions during negotiations, and the distribution and management of incomplete information (as none of the actors have full information about the decision-making process and true considerations of the others).

Krasner (2011) and Krasner and Weinstein (2014) specify that cooperation depends on the incentives for the national elite and not so much on institutional capacity or modernization. The authors explain instrumental effectiveness according to three main categories: 1) contracting has the highest rate of success, although it depends on actors' incentives to support the improvement of governance; 2) coercion has irregular results and is more prone to success if it gets the support of the political opposition elite, thus affecting status quo interests and having mobilization capacity; and 3) imposition "rarely works" (Ibid.).

For Krasner and Weinstein (Ibid.), a positive outcome of cooperation on governance (increase of institutional capacity, modification of elite incentives, and more civil society pressure) depends on the motivations of donors, as well as on the interactions between external financing and domestic authority structures. Moreover, the impact of cooperation on good governance is greater: when donors prioritize governance outcomes; when they are willing to use aid conditionality; when supported governments do not feel threatened by a liberalization of the political system or depend on aid to stay in power (Ibid.). Negative outcomes of cooperation on governance (that could be explained when donors support an autocratic or ineffective rule or are focused on their own geopolitical priorities) can be inefficient public spending, the support of bloated or corrupt bureaucracies, rent-seeking elites wanting favours, or non-tax revenues that might weaken the accountability of governments.

To understand why the APNT has had a limited impact, I apply tools derived from the theoretical frameworks discussed here and describe the factors that fostered APNT inter-state cooperation using the four criteria (ability to initiate and set the agenda, ability to modify any proposed policy, ability to ratify or veto the policy, and ability to obtain external and internal support). Then, I identify four criteria that could explain the low effectiveness of cooperation (actors' cooperation priorities, actors' incentives related to policy and institutional change, cooperation conditions, and civil society support).

The data comes from various sources. First, I examined reports from official sources and civil society. Second, I conducted semi-structured interviews with 16 negotiators, formulators, implementers, and specialists in Washington, DC (in June 2019) and Tegucigalpa (in August 2019). Third, I progressively followed the deployment of initiatives through reports in the press over three years. Our press review covered 1,240 national and international articles published between 1 July 2014 and 30 April 2021. The selected articles dealt directly or indirectly with international cooperation in the NT. They were chosen from two source streams: Google News and Central American newspapers (such as La Prensa, El Heraldo, La Tribuna, and Prensa Libre). The main media consulted were the Central American newspapers; others included Mexican newspapers and, to a lesser extent, US ones. The sample is not exhaustive, but it covers the publications that most frequently dealt with the subject. The content of the articles was used to determine the press perception of decision-making actors based on criteria proposed by Dente and Subirats (2014). The articles were categorized for analysis according to the newspapers' prioritization of problems, perception of cooperation actors, and attitude towards cooperation initiatives.

4.3 APNT context

Although current analyses tend to generalize the three NT countries as having the same characteristics, this is problematic. This is because of the issue of homogenization, while in fact, each country is characterized by demographic and socio-economic complexity.

NT countries have traditionally been partners of the US, both geopolitically and commercially, depending on the US since the nineteenth century. Since the 2000s, cooperation in the NT has focused on development and security, for instance, reducing drug trafficking and violence. Emergency and humanitarian aid have also been central because natural disasters frequently annihilate agricultural production. Immigration flows have traditionally been connected to insecurity, but evidence shows that there are three main combinations of factors which are exacerbated by climate change: family reunification; forced displacement due to physical or food-related insecurity (increased by climate change, with more coffee diseases or the destruction of banana harvests); and deficient labour income (due to high levels of informality or formal salaries not allowing people to meet their basic needs; Baker Institute Latin America Initiative, 2015).

Progression of initiatives: The APNT has promoted a US vision of cooperation with the NT. US initiatives have focused on free trade and security, with a constant watch on irregular immigration. Although the 11 September attacks led to a US foreign policy change towards the rest of the Americas, the relationship with Latin America continued to prioritize the control of populations, goods, and information flows. The Puebla-Panama Plan (PPP) was proposed in 2001 (parallel to a Smart Borders Agreement) and formally launched in September 2004, along with the creation of necessary institutional mechanisms; Colombia joined the initiative in 2006. This plan, focused on drug trafficking and insecurity, formed the basis of the Mesoamerica Project, created in July 2009.[2] The project sought to encourage development from a broad perspective, including economic and social integration (with nine priority policy areas) at a regional level (Dominican Republic and Colombia were included). While this initiative tried to project a desire for leadership coming from Latin America leadership, President Bush launched in 2007, with the support of Mexican President Felipe Calderón, a US-driven proposal: the Mérida Initiative (sometimes called Plan Mexico), designed to combat drug trafficking and organized crime.

Focused on the delivery of materials and training to the security forces of Mexico and Central America, Obama's administration split the implementation of the plan up in 2010 (Roldán Andrade, 2015). The Mérida Initiative kept working in Mexico and the Central American section became CARSI, spending $1.2 billion from 2008 to 2015 (Rosnick, Main and Jung, 2016). CARSI, which is blamed for the militarization of the fight against drugs (Kat, 2016), had five axes (two for security, two for state capacity, and one for incentives related to regional coordination and cooperation) and provided seven countries with technical assistance, equipment, and training (Meyer and Seelke, 2015).

In 2015, under pressure due to the unaccompanied teen immigration crisis, Obama agreed to negotiate a supplemental plan, the APNT, which was to be continuously implemented until 2020. However, the APNT lost support partly because of the tough and limited approach of the Trump administration, which proposed the América Crece Program, which was designed to encourage investment in the NT. Mexico withdrew from the Mérida Initiative in 2019, pleading for a new plan linking southern Mexico with Central America, so APNT proposed the Comprehensive Development Plan. This plan was formulated over three years under the leadership of Mexico and the United Nations Economic Commission for Latin America and the Caribbean (ECLAC) and very poorly implemented after its 2021 launch. It was still poorly implemented as of 2022. The latest plan was a Call for Action that Biden delegated to Kamala Harris, seeking to increase foreign direct investment and job creation in the region.

This complex succession of initiatives overlaps with more traditional international projects. Three main players in the fight against corruption must be added to the list: the CICIG (2006–2019 with the United Nations), the

---

[2] The Mesoamerica Project was created at the X Summit.

MACCIH[3] (2016–2020), and the International Commission against Impunity in El Salvador (Spanish: *Comisión Internacional Contra la Impunidad en El Salvador*, CICIES; active in 2020–2021).

International cooperation in the NT[4]: The succession of plans initiated by the US hides a complex picture. First, there is a great diversity of multilateral donors (mainly the World Bank and IDB) and bilateral ones (primarily the European Union [EU], Japan, Canada, and Taiwan), which, depending on their own priorities, have complemented or reinforced US priorities. Second, it is evident that immigration pressure and drug trafficking are the two main reasons that the US has proposed constant cooperation with the NT (Garcia, 2016).

For the present analysis, cooperation includes the amounts of official development aid, emergency aid, and loans and donations from bilateral or multilateral organizations. Having said that, issues, areas, amounts and types of international cooperation have varied with approval and execution cycles in the three NT countries. Also, net official development assistance is a fundamentally different category of economic engagement when compared to loans and investments. In El Salvador, disbursements decreased from 2014 to 2019, while they grew in Guatemala (albeit irregularly) and Honduras. The following graph shows the historical progression of net official development assistance received by countries in the NT.

Figure 4.1 Total net official development assistance and official assistance received by Guatemala, Honduras, and El Salvador (USD millions at 2020 prices)

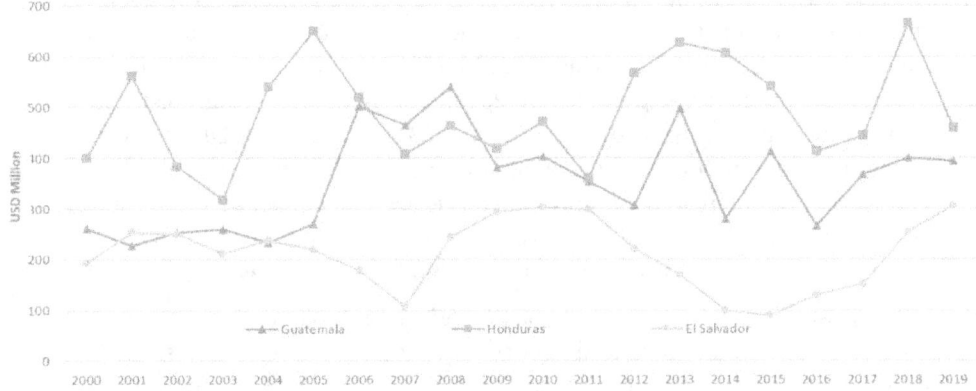

Source: Created by the author with data from the World Bank (2023a).

---

[3] The Xiomara Castro government in Honduras has requested and negotiated the establishment of a new commission hand in hand with the UN in December 2021.

[4] All the data comes from the official web pages and publications of the mentioned institutions.

Guatemala, the population of which went from 11.58 million in 2000 to 16.85 million in 2020 (World Bank, 2023b), received more aid at the beginning of the twenty-first century than El Salvador. The largest disbursements and commitment variations for Guatemala have not coincided with presidential terms, showing more cooperation stability. Most of the explanations for the overall variance cite specific changes in flows from the US, the single most important player for the NT. Between 2001 and 2017, US disbursements for projects in Guatemala increased progressively (with slight reductions in 2005, 2007, and 2012), going from $79 million to $243 million in 2017. As for commitments, there was a drastic drop in US support between 2017 and 2020, from $243 million to $108 million (it was $205 million in 2019). This progression clearly reflects, in part, the unlocked and locked APNT funds in 2016 and 2019, respectively. Nevertheless, there has been a constant: high intermediary expenses and military aid. Between 2001 and 2010, the major US disbursements went to humanitarian assistance (after disasters such as Hurricane Stan in 2005) or health-related initiatives. There has been a growing commitment to water, sanitation, and natural risk management, issues that also receive multilateral support through loans: $368 million from the IDB between 2001 and 2010 and $85 million between 2009 and 2013 from the World Bank.

Starting in 2007, US cooperation has increased, especially on issues related to governance. Here, CICIG support stands out, as well as some key institutional strengthening projects related to electoral reforms and governance. The World Bank has also implemented public sector projects, some linked to the regulation of the financial sector (a $29.73 million project from 2002 to 2013, another $5 million one from 2002 to 2018, and a $150 million loan to the government to accompany the reforms from 2002 to 2018) and others to tax administration reforms ($55 million from 2017 to 2018, and $340 million from 2014 to 2018). However, given the breadth of programmes and projects, there has also been special foreign interest in supporting various sectors: citizen security, youth, education services coverage, improvements in agricultural productivity, rural job creation, community development, and biodiversity management.

European cooperation in Guatemala (the priorities of which are food security, conflict resolution, peace and security, and competitiveness) also had a downward trend in the late 2010s. Between 2007 and 2019, Spain was the biggest donor ($712.70 million), followed by the European Commission ($355.76 million), Sweden ($332.65 million), and Germany ($247.06 million). The IDB has dedicated the highest amounts to Guatemala in the form of loans, with a strong emphasis on state modernization (2002, 2009, and 2016), the environment and natural disasters (2010), financial markets (2018 and 2020), and energy (2020). This trajectory clearly shows the increased links to the APNT, directly (via the US) or indirectly (through the IDB). The following graph shows US contributions (in donations or funding) to projects in Guatemala by sector.

Figure 4.2 US cooperation disbursements to Guatemala from 2001 to 2020 (in millions of 2020 USD)

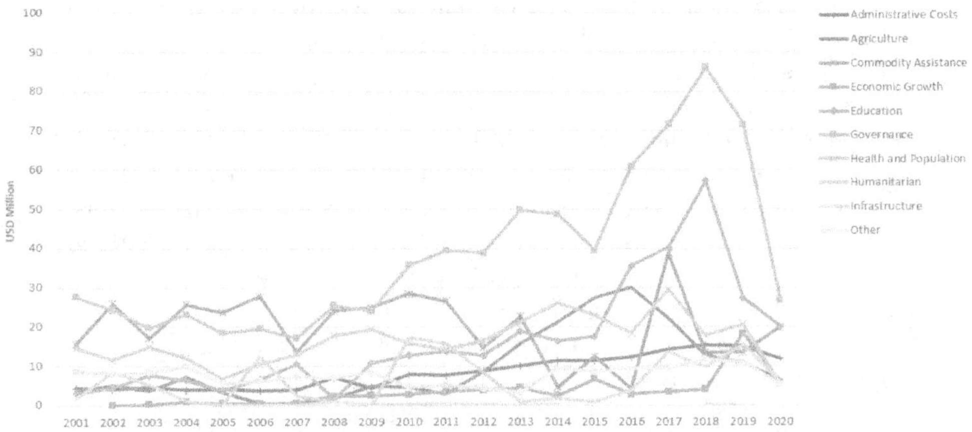

Source: Created by the author; based on data from USAID and US Department of State (2023)

The progression of US cooperation in El Salvador has differed from that in Guatemala and Honduras. By the beginning of the 2000s, the US was involved in a variety of sectors in El Salvador. Still, there were years with more project proposals: $507 million in 2007 during the Elías Antonio Saca presidency and $332 million in 2014, the hinge year between the presidencies of Mauricio Funes (2009–2014) and Salvador Sánchez Cerén (2014–2019). US disbursements increased between 2001 ($63 million) and 2004 ($137 million), after which there was a reduction in 2006 ($50 million). Cooperation disbursements recovered from 2006 to 2012 ($211 million), before they fell again in 2014 ($67 million). Contrary to what happened in Honduras or Guatemala, US disbursements increased from 2014 to 2019 ($192 million). Then, the disbursements were reduced in 2020, although in a more nuanced way than in neighbouring countries.

From the standpoint of sectors, three US cooperation cycles can be identified, all with a clear constant: high administrative costs. Between 2001 and 2008, a pressing issue was post-emergency reconstruction and rehabilitation ($144.3 million), to attend to El Salvador's needs after the two strong earthquakes of 2001. From 2001 to 2016, the World Bank also provided support towards reconstruction and health services ($142.60 million) in addition to budgetary support for the disaster prevention and management policy between 2011 and 2013 ($50 million). The IDB allocated $400 million between 2001 and 2008 to social sectors. Between 2001 and 2008, the US also strongly supported the public sector, agricultural policy ($53.7 million), basic health ($49.5 million), security sector management and reform ($50.7 million), and food ($31.4 million), among others.

Between 2009 and 2014, the US invested in infrastructure ($269.9 million, to which the IDB added $210 million for transport), basic social services ($58.1 million, plus $475 million from the IDB), rural development ($55 million, in addition to $40.20 million from the World Bank), agricultural and energy risk management ($1.83 million from the US from 2012 to 2016), the security sector ($45 million), and narcotics control ($28.9 million), among others. In line with the APNT's objectives, US cooperation increased in several prioritized sectors: international trade and competitiveness ($50.5 million between 2009 and 2019), democratic participation and civil society ($14.5 million between 2009 and 2019), and the fight against corruption ($23.3 million between 2009 and 2019). This shift was also clear among other donors. The World Bank raised its support for several public sectors (fiscal, social, financial, and public management reforms) and, between 2007 and 2015, the European Union disbursements fluctuated from $158.29 in 2009 to $58.68 million in 2015.

Between 2015 and 2019, previous trends deepened, and new priorities arose, consistent with those of the APNT. The US supported, above all, the security sector ($88.3 million between 2015 and 2019), in addition to anti-narcotics efforts ($18.5 million from 2015 to 2019) and World Bank security projects (preventing violence among young people between 2009 and 2015, and municipal security between 2014 and 2016). Between 2015 and 2019, the US dedicated more funds to education (although the projects they were intended to fund were smaller compared to those by the World Bank), the judicial and legal system, and food assistance. Meanwhile, the IDB drastically increased its funds for El Salvador in 2020 to $1.7 billion ($680 million for the modernization of the state, $221 million for financial markets, and $400 million for development and urban living). The World Bank prioritized support for economic development through two large loans ($200 million from 2005 to 2018) and a local economic resilience project ($200 million between 2019 and 2020), as well as the public response to COVID-19 in 2020. The following graph shows US contributions to projects in El Salvador by sector.

Figure 4.3 US disbursements in El Salvador from 2001 to 2020 (in millions of 2020 USD)

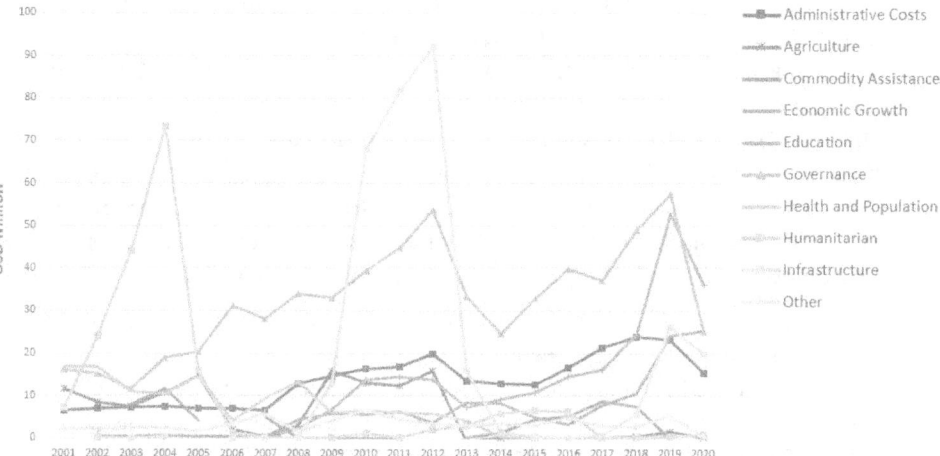

Source: Created by the author; based on data from USAID and US Department of State (2023)

Regarding the Honduran case,[5] between 2001 and 2020, international cooperation has shown a growing complementarity between donors. Three main stages of US cooperation with Honduras can be distinguished. Between 2003 and 2009, US disbursements rose to $129 million (with a drop in 2007 to $74 million, coinciding with the Ricardo Maduro presidency). Between 2002 and 2007, the US focused on two main sectors: 1) humanitarian, social, and education issues ($120.8 million post-emergency humanitarian responses, reconstruction, and rehabilitation; food assistance of $118.6 million; and $51.3 million for basic health services); 2) public sector reinforcement ($15.5 million for decentralization and sub-national governments and $47.5 million for central public management). These matters have also been prioritized by multilateral partners (the IDB and World Bank) and bilateral partners (the EU). During this period, the IDB made investments that covered almost all sectors, without major priorities standing out, except for transportation in 2007 ($70 million) and social investments ($182 million from 2001 to 2007).

Between 2009 and 2012, there was a spending reduction from $129 million down to $63 million, which was a political response to the coup d'état, which normalized during the Porfirio Lobo Sosa government. This then led to a cooperation increase from 2012 to 2018 ($160 million). Although the World

---

[5] The population of Honduras increased from 6.65 million in 2000 to 10.11 million in 2020, according to World Bank (2023b) indicators.

Bank maintained emergency management projects, the US spent money on the road sector ($117.42 million in addition to $166 million received from the IDB in 2010 alone), food assistance ($36.22 million), primary education ($31.2 million), and operating expenses, offering $32.5 million between 2008 and 2012. From 2008 to 2012, the US dedicated cooperation efforts to governance (the IDB also allocated $108 million to state modernization between 2008 and 2012), rural and agricultural matters (also a World Bank focus), family planning and national security ($9.6 million for the security system and $26.87 million for narcotics control; of this latter amount, $8.2 million was spent in 2012 alone, making it the largest expense for a single sector that year).

According to the APNT, from 2013 to 2018, the US deepened its previous orientations (especially with regard to public sector reform and civil society reinforcement) and disbursed funds to sectors that it had previously supported, among others: agricultural development ($62.1 million), primary schools ($54.2 million; $9.7 million in 2013; and $6.6 million in 2018), food aid ($57.5 million), and meals provided in schools ($55.7 million). Multilateral partners kept working on disaster prevention (especially the IDB, which invested $339 million) and public sector reform (the IDB devoted $139 million between 2013 and 2018). The US increased security sector funds ($35.2 million for related administrations and $55.4 million for anti-narcotics activity in 2013 and 2014; but almost $0 in direct support in 2018). Meanwhile, there was a similar occurrence with aid for the public security sector between 2018 and 2020 due to the mistrust of the Juan Orlando Hernández government and US security efforts being delegated to Colombia through opaque triangular cooperation amounts and projects (the Colombian police refused to provide details in 2019). Between 2018 and 2020, US cooperation dropped but IDB and World Bank funding underwent an opposite trend. The IDB invested in more central and expensive sectors, like transport (especially in 2010, 2018, and 2020), water and sanitation (particularly in 2019 and 2020), and energy (especially in 2011, 2014, and 2018). Indeed, 2018 was the year with the highest IDB investment approvals since 2001: $200 million in private development, $169 million in energy, $125 million in health, $109 million in social investments, and $90 million in transportation. The following graph shows US contributions to projects in Honduras by sector.

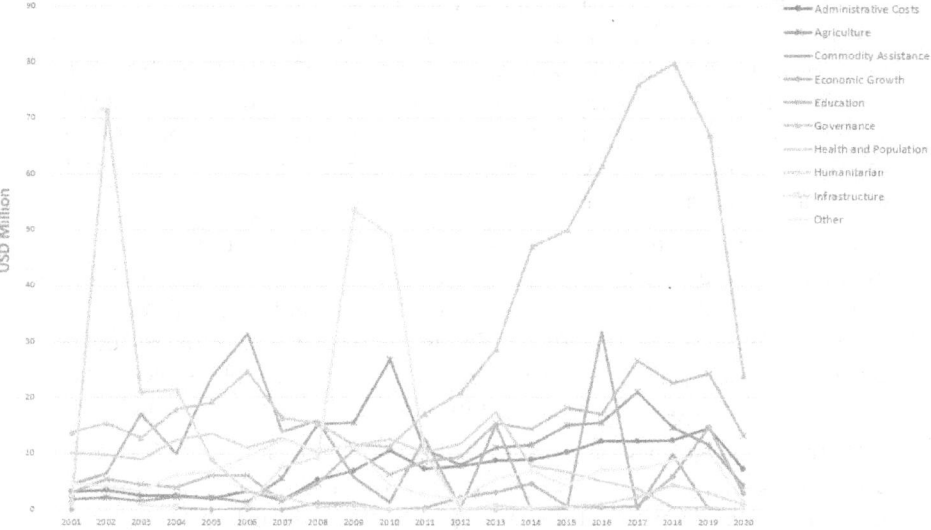

Figure 4.4 US disbursements in Honduras from 2001 to 2020 (in millions of 2020 USD)

Source: Created by the author; based on data from USAID and US Department of State (2023)

Despite all these resources, socio-economic indicators in the NT did not improve substantially during the 2010s. Indeed, NT birth, mortality, and fertility rates remained above or equal to the Latin American averages (CEPAL, 2018). Likewise, life expectancy at birth in the NT was below the average for Latin America, not including the Caribbean (CEPAL, 2018). Although some indicators improved, the impact on the population did not seem to correspond to the amounts invested. Gross domestic product (GDP) per capita had a positive progression in the three countries between 2001 and 2007; however, in 2000 and from 2008 to 2010, the GDPs underwent significant falls due to the effects of the crises experienced in the US. Unfortunately, the greatest impacts on socio-economic indicators seem to be consequences of economic expansion (linked to US cycles) rather than the effects of public programmes.

NT countries have experienced progressive improvements, although they have always stayed below the Latin American average; for instance, inequality has generally reduced, although Honduras did not reduce extreme poverty or poverty between 2008 and 2012 (CEPAL, 2018). Spending on education and health has sometimes seemed to comprise a large percentage of the GDP of each country, but unequal deployment of services across the countries and endemic corruption have resulted in poor quality public services. For example, despite literacy improvements, by 2016, less than 40% of the population between 20 and 24 years in Guatemala and Honduras had completed a secondary education (Ibid). Still, there were improvements to literacy in general—in 2017, the adult literacy rate of people 15 years and over in Honduras was 87.9%, in El Salvador 88.0%, and in Guatemala 81.3%, while the regional average for Latin America and the Caribbean (LAC) was 93.2%. However, the share of people with a tertiary education was low: in 2016, it was 18.1% in El Salvador, 18.3% in Guatemala, and only 6.4% in Honduras (Ibid). Overall, the indicators that improved the most in the 2010s were infant, neonatal, and maternal mortality, as well as child malnutrition.

Despite small improvements, because NT countries found it challenging to offer a minimum quality of life to their citizens, immigration resulted during the period of international cooperation plans, including the APNT. In fact, immigration rates from the NT were higher than in the rest of the region—the rate per 1,000 inhabitants between 2015 and 2018 during APNT implementation was −1.5 in Honduras, −6.2 in El Salvador, and −0.6 in Guatemala (Ibid).

There are two reasons that policies are not sufficiently impactful (beyond the obvious insecurity effects): 1) NT countries have bigger rural populations than the rest of Latin America (although this is true to a lesser extent in El Salvador), which means that the marginal cost of lifting a person out of poverty is higher than in other countries (in cities, the population density reduces the cost per person for the same thing); and 2) there is a great dependence on US cycles, both commercially and through received remittances (12–20% of the GDP, depending on the year and the country).

4.4 APNT's fostered cooperation from forced partnerships

The progression described thus far clearly shows that 1) the APNT has prompted an increase in the amounts allocated by the US to NT countries between 2016 and 2019; 2) the suspension of US actions concerned with the security sector were compensated by funds from the IDB; 3) the APNT modified the proportions of financing between sectors, but action areas have been the same from 2001 to 2020; and 4) allocated amounts cannot be related to notable improvements in health, education, or immigration indicators, the exception being the decrease in homicides reported between 2014 and 2020. With this in mind, I now review the factors that would help to highlight why the APNT is a successful regional cooperation scheme but deceptive when it comes to generating results.

Ability to initiate and set the agenda: In 2014, when pressure from the US increased because of immigration contention, Presidents Sánchez Cerén (El Salvador), Juan Orlando Hernández (Honduras), and Otto Pérez Molina (Guatemala) acknowledged that a common agenda would strengthen their position. According to official accounts, the NT countries contacted the IDB for assistance with formulating an ambitious, comprehensive, and medium-term initiative; indeed, many sources emphasize that the APNT was not a US creation (Paley, 2016; IDB Interviewee, 2019). Under the auspices of the IDB and the US, the deployment of technical, political, and diplomatic activities at the highest levels led to the plan formulation and negotiation between 2013 and 2014.

The agreement went ahead thanks to personal relationships between key figures (IDB Negotiator, 2019). It was presented and approved in Washington DC in December 2014, thus leaving the Central American Integration System (SICA) behind (EuropeAid Coordinator, 2019) without conducting serious consultations (Inter-American Dialogue Specialist, 2019). NT countries lobbied with their partners for rapid formulation but had no clear methodology (IDB Formulator, 2019). Although the IDB tried to adopt a different approach to previous initiatives (Ibid), there was an inherent contradiction in the process: the APNT aimed to cover long-term working issues but had funds and medium-term measures in response to an emergency (Inter-American Dialogue Specialist, 2019). According to an IDB negotiator, the NT countries' request to the IDB was based on a recognition of the bank's installed technical capacity and its closeness with the region. On the contrary, the press review shows that of the 251 articles focused on the APNT, the highest number is made up of those who estimate that the leading role was held by the US (94), while the second highest is of those who suggest that the leading role was shared by the NT governments (72); only 1 indicates that the IDB played a leading role and the remaining ones provided different responses.

One proposal offered a model for reform based on neoclassical economics; it argues that population well-being is linked to economic development, and growth is linked to foreign investment. The argument for this is that NT countries needed to lower energy costs and improve infrastructure and logistics, in addition to integrating regional markets (El Salvador, Guatemala and Honduras, 2014). The plan mixed new ideas with old solutions, with no clarity on before and after scenarios (IDB Negotiator, 2019). The APNT had four strategies: 1) boost the productive sector; 2) develop human capital; 3) improve citizen security and access to justice; and 4) strengthen institutions (El Salvador, Guatemala and Honduras, 2014). It identified 11 priority problems for a five-year action period (2016 to 2021). Barack Obama obtained Congress support of $750 million for 2016 and $750 million for 2017, but with a series of conditions, including giving priority to the fight against corruption and stricter border control. However, according to the actual allocation of funds, and as confirmed by interviewees, the axes had unequal prioritization, progress, and support (El Salvador, Guatemala and Honduras, 2019).

Ability to modify any proposed policy: The logic of APNT seemed to differ from previous plans for at least six reasons. First, the plan was made at the request of the NT countries. Second, it had an international organization as an intermediary. Third, the negotiation took place with countries acting as a subregional bloc. Fourth, most of the APNT funds came from national budgets, which resulted in the plan being viewed as a framework, with implementation rules for policies. Fifth, the US set conditionality rules against the Paris and Accra Agreements. Sixth, there was little clarity on what was and was not included in the budget, such as the place of the triangular cooperation with Colombia (involved in Honduran police reform).

NT countries proposed a plan derived through negotiations based on their contexts. To stop unchecked immigration, the US depended on joint action by NT countries as well as on maintaining a good relationship with Mexico (Inter-American Dialogue Specialist, 2019). Paradoxically, US pressure forced NT cooperation. While negotiations between NT and foreign governments were complicated (EuropeAid Coordinator, 2019), the APNT offered an unbeatable solution: it introduced a framework of priority areas and gave the countries in question a great deal of autonomy to propose or modify the policies linked to the plan. The APNT made major propositions, leaving the Technical Secretariat and its national counterparts to choose how to implement them (IDB Negotiator, 2019). The centrality of and innovation in the decision-making process was captured by think tanks and the media. Of the 251 articles reviewed that related to the APNT, the three types which characterize the majority of them are those which focused on the decision-making process, which is the most critiqued stage of policy-making (76), policy implementation (64), and formulation (22).

Ability to ratify or veto policies: Thanks to conditionality clauses, the US could easily modify its participation in some respects. The US had the capacity to modify the cooperation conditions but not the policies (and it did not want to alter the latter either). However, by delegating the coordination of the plan to the IDB, it was clear from the beginning that the US wanted to hold governments accountable for the reforms while offering support to help overcome criticism for its obvious imposition and securitization of the NT agenda.

Although the media focused on immigration, the IDB's emphasis was employment (IDB Negotiator, 2019). The focus of the US, meanwhile was security (Villafuerte Solís, 2018). At first, the APNT Technical Secretariat provided general support. Then, when implementation progressed, it tried to systematize work components through technical dialogue with each country (IDB Negotiator, 2019). The great autonomy of countries within the plan was clearly a result of the APNT's logic and structure: processes, times, and amounts did not depend on the IDB or the US but on the technical commissions in each country. As such, commitment levels fluctuated over time. However, since the APNT costs included time and diplomatic efforts, at first, the NT countries played along as it was still in their interests, and specifically in favour of the political class, to negotiate (IDB Formulator, 2019).

Cooperation with international partners continued and the only difference that the APNT brought about was greater synergy or complementarity among national initiatives. The press review revealed that the media did not always understand the particularities of the APNT's implementation; there are various reasons for this. On one hand, the APNT imposed certain issues on the national elite, such as the fight against corruption (CAN Coordinator, 2019), which was mostly well received. On the other, the APNT's restricted focus on immigration and economic development was criticized. These diverse positions existed in all three countries. But in El Salvador, the APNT generated less media attention, in Honduras, it reinforced the government's stance, and in Guatemala, it was debated among experts. The press recognized the uneven ability of the three governments of the NT to ratify or veto policies, depending on the issue. However, the media was not consistent in its coverage. Therefore, a clear conclusion cannot be drawn since changes in perspective could be explained by the ideological inclinations of media owners.

Ability to obtain external and internal support: The fact that some wanted the APNT to be an imitation of Plan Colombia conditioned their support, which was based on the Colombian experience and assessment. Yet it appears that the APNT ended up failing to satisfy both those who wanted a more ambitious plan (conservative think tanks) and those who wanted a more social plan (non-governmental organizations [NGOs], universities and civil society). However, global immigration securitization in the 2010s (especially in the EU) favoured the APNT. The UN—notably absent from discussions—openly supported the APNT in a press release stating then-Secretary General of the United Nations Ban Ki-Moon's endorsement of the initiative on 26 September 2015. Furthermore, most active NT international partners supported the plan because it provided greater clarity to the policy path, especially as some perceived a lack of cohesion among governments and administrations in terms of priorities (EuropeAid Coordinator, 2019).

Even though many local cooperation partners deemed the APNT unrealistic, most believed it would not have negative effects either (Inter-American Dialogue Specialist, 2019), especially since it was a potential source of income for NGOs. Still, a part of rural civil society was aware that boosting investments in the APNT could lead to the expansion of certain activities, such as mining, which could prompt more immigration due to violence and internal displacement (Noé Pino and Noé, 2019). Clearly, internal and external support was not homogeneous. The press review helps to unpack this heterogeneity since the stances of media publications facilitate the construction of public opinion. Of 439 press articles focused on NT cooperation initiatives, 185 had supportive positions, 91 were critical, and 163 were neutral. The critical articles most commonly dealt with the cooperation and aid processes and the conditions imposed for immigration control. This shows that, as reflected in the interviews conducted for this study, civil society actors supported anti-corruption measures, were more sceptical of or neutral towards APNT "branded" policies, and remained critical of restrictions that the APNT entailed.

4.5 APNT's limited effectiveness in mutual instrumentalization

The reviewed factors show that NT governments used a window of opportunity to launch a plan based on their negotiating positions, focusing on controlling immigration. Now, despite NT countries having common interests, APNT results did not depend on US pressure but on the political will of NT governments; indeed, US pressure was primarily intended to ensure immigration control, not the effectiveness of policies.

Cooperation priorities: The APNT was a contradictory proposal since, on the one hand, it assumed a transformation narrative and target derived from a broader diagnosis, while on the other hand, it encouraged the same mechanisms that had neither reduced immigration nor strengthened the national economies in the NT. The lack of dialogue between regional organizations (IDB, SICA, the Central American Integration System, as well as OAS, the Organization of American States) or debate on the economic model at the heart of the proposal resulted in the APNT being marked by fluctuating and contradictory intentions. Biden wanted a multidimensional proposal to complement and remove focus from the CARSI, but he also wanted to hold the NT countries accountable while promoting shared responsibility. This kind of "cognitive dissonance" (IDB Negotiator, 2019) was consistent with previous and later trajectories of the APNT.

The plan included common priorities that did not confront or call into question previous cooperation models with other partners, such as Taiwan. The APNT's purview was perhaps too broad; this led to a dilution of efforts despite the results in education and health (IDB Negotiator, 2019). As such, APNT priorities got confused with those of governments. Indeed, the governments assumed that the APNT was a backbone that would help to realize their policies. In line with APNT orientations, policies furthered the neoliberal agenda: "the centerpiece of the Alliance for Prosperity involves tax breaks for corporate investors and new pipelines, highways, and power lines to speed resource extraction and streamline the process of import, assembly, and export at low-wage maquilas" (Paley, 2016). That is why, given the lack of reduction of immigration flows, Trump suspended the APNT's US funds. The suspension of US funds was in line with the APNT's traditional agendas and reinforced the status quo (Silva Ávalos, 2014). Meanwhile, military lobbying and related economic interests kept the military aid alive: as security policies were effective, there was more need to perpetuate their continuation and to demand more positive intervention (Lindsay-Poland and Weiss, 2017).

The press review suggests that there is a hierarchy of problems within APNT. Based on the 251 articles on the APNT, the five most important problems which they appeared to focus on, in descending order, were immigration (92), economic development (70), security and violence (32), cooperation itself (27), and corruption and transparency (19); the rest of the articles focused on other issues. Analyzing only the articles on NT cooperation, of which there were 100 in total, three issues appear to be particularly contentious, namely immigration (36), economic development (24), and the mode of cooperation (19). Most critical articles focused on immigration, which is both a lever for political negotiation with the US and an escape valve (resulting in less pressure on youth in the labour market) and a means to financial stability (Kat, 2016).

Actors' incentives to effect policy and institutional change: APNT progress reports (El Salvador, Guatemala and Honduras, 2018, 2019) clearly show disparities among projects conducted in NT countries, as well as weak connections with public administration reforms. The APNT focused on policies that were "worrisome in three main dimensions: the emphasis on attracting foreign investment, the support it provides for the continuation of dubious security initiatives, and the Central American governments' lack of accountability" (Garcia, 2016). The existence of the CICIG and MACCIH was a double-edged sword, which, on the one hand, provided guidelines to reduce impunity (without building trust in the Honduras case; IDB Formulator, 2019) and, on the other, recommended a restructuring of administrative reforms to favour the fight against corruption. This means that, paradoxically, a plan that sought to promote transparency had a "lack of democratic accountability in the three recipient countries" (Garcia, 2016).

Although for some partners, public administration structures existed but were "empty" (AECID Coordinator, 2019; in Spanish, the organization is called *Agencia Española de Cooperación Internacional para el Desarrollo*), the APNT had weak public management reform targets (Inter-American Dialogue Specialist, 2019). This was to be expected since its main purpose was policy change. However, there were obstacles, including legal bottlenecks (IDB Negotiator, 2019), in addition to the fact that the APNT was to operate for the short period of four to five years (IDB Formulator, 2019). Added to this, the delay in delivering US projects (during the Obama government) and their suspension (during the Trump government) induced implementation anxiety in the NT, and pressure on the NT governments to prioritize new immigration agreements with the US, instead of focusing on implementation. Finally, change incentives were also affected by factors such as administration "paralysis" during political scandals (IDB Negotiator, 2019). The implementation period was further affected by the constant need for crisis management (AECID Coordinator, 2019).

Cooperation conditions: The NT has experienced the same contradiction Mexico faced in 1994, when the North American Free Trade Agreement (NAFTA) was established: it brought open borders for goods and finances but obstacles to human mobility (Villafuerte Solís, 2018). Two occurrences modified the APNT's negotiated cooperation conditions. First, the US wanted the NT and Mexico to act quickly on immigration control but was slow to release the necessary funds. The United States Agency for International Development (USAID) components were instituted starting in 2016, when governments had begun labelling some of their initiatives as falling under the APNT. Indeed, NT governments integrated new and old initiatives into the APNT, voluntarily mixing programmes and projects to show government action and coherence. This was consistent with APNT rules—the governments had agreed to create a policy brand. Therefore, the US delays generated higher transactional costs (IDB Negotiator, 2019), but also gave more autonomy to the NT.

The second event that altered the course of the APNT is well known: Trump suspended aid when the immigration goals were not met. His administration applied conditions in which Congress could withhold 75% of the US funds if the Secretary of State determined non-compliance with the NT. The US stopped releasing funds shortly after operations linked to the APNT were effectively launched. This was analysed in a report to the US Congress: "the 2019 suspension and reprogramming of assistance funding adversely affected 92 of USAID's 114 projects and 65 of the State's 168 projects" (Government Accountability Office, 2021). Agreements to establish a "safe third country", although this came with a breakdown of trust and discouraged the unified position of the NT countries, so encouraged before. The "tough" approach that the US sometimes adopted even included separating immigrant minors from their parents, and created the problem of unaccompanied minors. Presidential changes (e.g., taking a tougher stance under Trump) have affected the APNT's implementation and shifted the focus from development to geopolitical issues. More recently, immigration was only truly stopped by the restrictions linked to the COVID-19 pandemic.

Despite all these ups and downs, the media remained quite optimistic. Of the 251 articles on the APNT, 187 determined that there was a collaborative relationship between the main actors, 12 a negotiating one, 45 did not take a stance, 6 saw confrontation, and 1 saw opposition. Out of 100 articles on NT cooperation, 81 envisioned a collaborative relationship and only 3 a confrontational one, while the rest envisioned a negotiating or a neutral stance. The press did not hold the US accountable for suspending its support and presented the situation as it was normal.

Civil society support: The Trump administration's position on various issues went against public opinion, including when it came to the APNT. In the APNT's initial phase, civil society organizations sent an open letter warning of APNT's probable failure due to its "militarization of citizen security" and "harmful, private- and foreign-investor-led development policies" (Kat, 2016). This position, widely shared among civil society organizations in the US and NT countries, had different motivations. First, some activists and think tanks expressed concern about the APNT formulation process, which assumed that the governments had the credibility and legitimacy to establish a development path backed by the neoliberal vision. In fact, as Villafuerte Solís (2019, p. 109) recalls, the very idea of "prosperity" was associated from the beginning with "free trade, the opening of markets, mining concessions and the exploitation of strategic resources owned by the underdeveloped countries, all this seasoned with security policies against any social movement or group that opposes such policies".[6] The plan "stresses the promotion of infrastructure projects and foreign investment as opposed to the development of social inclusion programs" (Garcia, 2016), leaving aside the most vulnerable populations, precisely ones that tend to immigrate to the US, thus perpetuating the very problem that needs to be fixed.

Second, many civil society actors mistrusted the processes and actors involved, as the formulation process side-lined civil society by assuming a technocratic character. Moreover, the APNT had little institutional credibility, low expectations, little publicly available information, and low citizen interest (Universidad Nacional Autónoma de Honduras Professor, 2019). As NGOs do state work at local levels (Friedrich-Ebert-Stiftung Expert, 2019), when it was clear that the APNT was using public resources, civil society organizations demobilized (Ibid., 2019), knowing that would result in a opaque fund attribution would result. Although the APNT tried to standardize its communications and actions (IDB Negotiator, 2019), in addition to creating a common framework (IDB Implementer, 2019), civil society organizations saw a lack of transparency (Inter-American Dialogue Specialist, 2019). The media took a less homogeneous stance on this issue and presented different viewpoints.

---

[6] The translation from Spanish to English is done by the author.

4.6 Conclusion

The APNT was successful in reinforcing cooperation among NT countries but failed to generate real changes to socio-economic conditions and institutions. During the cooperation process, the NT had a window of opportunity, promoting an agenda that strengthened its means and legitimacy while the US simplified its involvement. The arrangement included a rather holistic framework aimed at improving the synergy between public actions. This gave NT countries the ability to modify any proposed policy within the APNT since the framework was more about cooperation branding than about making new policy proposals. Simultaneously, NT countries had a high degree of implementation autonomy and priorities that depended on intersectoral dialogue; the IDB, which had formulated the plan, held the role of an intermediary and facilitator while complying with specified requirements. The plan had strong support from the economic and political elite in each NT country as well as from the international community, which had little confidence in the APNT's ability to bring about real change. With regard to cooperation effectiveness, the US prioritized drug trafficking and immigration reduction while NT countries prioritized increasing their income and government legitimacy, which resulted in limited efficiency on both matters. Due to the relatively loose way that the APNT was structured, actors' incentives to effect policy and bring about real institutional change were low.

Although the US applied pressure, the traditional interests of the NT elite were never in danger. The NT countries achieved some political coherence while promoting cooperation through traditional schemes. The APNT addressed US and NT interests derived from the securitization of immigration and the fight against drugs but cannot be linked to a reduction in immigration flows. A favourable APNT outcome for the US did not depend on NT state reforms (Mexican collaboration with the US limited immigrant transit, and APNT medium-term policies did not impact climate change, only increasing NT immigration). Therefore, the APNT was more of a narrative and political instrument that served government purposes. Although NT countries negotiated as a bloc in forced partnership, lessons from the APNT have still not been applied. As long as the development model is not discussed with civil society organizations, and governments lack credibility and efficiency when it comes to public spending, innovations in project formulation will not really matter for most people as they do not feel a tangible difference in their everyday lives.

References

Acuña, J. and Illescas, R. (2015) 'Educación cultura de paz y los partidos políticos en Centroamérica', *Orbis: Revista Científica Ciencias Humanas*, 11 (31), pp. 35–57.

AECID Coordinator (2019) Personal interview. Conducted by Miguel Gomis.
Baker Institute Latin America Initiative (2015) *Co-responsibility and reform: foreign and domestic perspectives on immigration immigration.* Houston: James A. Baker III Institute for Public Policy of Rice University.
Bannum, K. (2019) 'Guatemala 2018: facing a constitutional crossroad', *Revista de Ciencia Politica*, 39 (2), pp. 265–284.
Beeton, D. and Watts, R. (2016) 'No, Honduras isn't necessarily getting safer', *NACLA Report on the Americas*, 48 (4), pp. 315–318.
Bull, B. (2014) 'Towards a political economy of weak institutions and strong elites in Central America', *European Review of Latin American and Caribbean Studies*, 97, pp. 117–128.
Bull, B. (2016) 'Governance in the aftermath of neoliberalism: aid, elites and state capacity in Central America', *Forum for Development Studies*, 43 (1), pp. 89–111.
Call, C. (2020) 'Un éxito fugaz: el legado de la misión internacional contra la corrupción en Honduras (Fleeting success: the legacy of Honduras' international anti-corruption mission)', *SSRN Electronic Journal*, 27. Available at: https://papers.ssrn.com/sol3/papers.cfm?abstract_id=3645114 (Accessed: 23 June 2023).
Call, C. and Hallock, J. (2020) '¿Una iniciativa demasiado exitosa? El legado y las lecciones de la comisión internacional contra la impunidad en Guatemala (Too much success? The legacy and lessons of the international commission against impunity in Guatemala)', *SSRN Electronic Journal*, 24. Available at: https://papers.ssrn.com/sol3/papers.cfm?abstract_id=3516775 (Accessed: 23 June 2023).
CAN Coordinator (2019) Personal interview. Conducted by Miguel Gomis.
CEPAL (2018) *Anuario estadístico de América Latina y el Caribe 2018 (Statistical yearbook for Latin America and the Caribbean 2018).* United Nations Publications.
Colburn, F. D. and Arturo, C. S. (2016) 'Latin America's new turbulence: trouble in the "Northern Triangle"', *Journal of Democracy*, 27 (2), pp. 79–85.
Collado, C. (2010) 'México y Centroamérica en la formación de la política de la buena vecindad', *The Latin Americanist*, 54 (1), pp. 51–70.
Craig, K. (2013) 'Public policy in Central America: an empirical analysis', *Public Administration Research*, 2 (2), pp. 105–124.
Dente, B. and Subirats, J. (2014) *Decisiones públicas. Análisis y estudio de los procesos de decisión en políticas públicas.* Barcelona: Editorial Planeta.
Eguizábal, C. (2017) *Logros-y limitaciones-de la comisión internacional contra la impunidad en Guatemala (CICIG).* Fundación nacional para el Desarrollo (FUNDE). Available at: https://repo.funde.org/1089/ (Accessed: 23 June 2023).
EuropeAid Coordinator (2019) Personal interview. Conducted by Miguel Gomis.
El Salvador, Guatemala and Honduras (2014) *Plan of the alliance for prosperity in the Northern Triangle: a road map.* Available at: https://pdf.usaid.gov/pdf_docs/PA00T969.pdf (Accessed: 23 June 2023).
El Salvador, Guatemala and Honduras (2018) *Principales avances y logros 2017–2018.* Available at: https://www.iadb.org/es/alianzaparalaprosperidad (Accessed: 23 June 2023).

El Salvador, Guatemala and Honduras (2019) *Informe de avances y logros 2018–2019*. Available at: https://www.iadb.org/es/alianzaparalaprosperidad (Accessed: 23 June 2023).

EuropeAid Coordinator (2019) Personal interview. Conducted by Miguel Gomis.

Friedrich-Ebert-Stiftung Expert (2019) Personal interview. Conducted by Miguel Gomis.

Garcia, M. (2016) *Alliance for prosperity plan in the Northern Triangle: not a likely final solution for the Central American migration crisis*. Available at: http://www.coha.org/alliance-for-prosperity-plan-in-the-northern-triangle-not-a-likely-final-solution-for-the-central-american-migration-crisis/ (Accessed: 23 June 2023).

Gies, H. (2019) 'Will AMLO respond to the Central American exodus With compassion—or militarization?', Nacla, 1 February. Available from: https://nacla.org/news/2021/09/20/will-amlo-respond-central-american-exodus-compassion%E2%80%94or-militarization (Accessed: 2 April 2023).

González, J. A. (2020) 'Honduras: entre la corrupción y el espanto', *Realidad: Revista De Ciencias Sociales y Humanidades*, 75, pp. 219–236.

Government Accountability Office (2021) *Northern Triangle of Central America. The 2019 suspension and reprogramming of U.S. funding adversely affected assistance projects*. Available at: https://www.gao.gov/products/gao-21-104366 (Accessed: 23 June 2023).

Hernández, J. O. (2016) 'Alliance for prosperity in the Northern Triangle: a leap towards ensuring regional security', *Prism*, 5 (4), pp. 11–19.

Heyer, K. E. (2018) 'Internalized borders: immigration ethics in the age of Trump', *Theological Studies*, 79 (1), pp. 146–164.

IDB Formulator (2019) Personal interview. Conducted by Miguel Gomis.

IDB Implementer (2019) Personal interview. Conducted by Miguel Gomis.

IDB Interviewee (2019) Personal interview. Conducted by Miguel Gomis.

IDB Negotiator (2019) Personal interview. Conducted by Miguel Gomis.

Iesue, L. (2016) *The alliance for prosperity plan: a failed effort for stemming migration*. Available at: https://coha.org/the-alliance-for-prosperity-plan-a-failed-effort-for-stemming-migration/ (Accessed: 23 June 2023).

Instituto Centroamericano de Estudios Fiscales (2015) *Position regarding the "plan of the alliance for prosperity in the Northern Triangle"*. Available at: http://idbdocs.iadb.org/wsdocs/getdocument.aspx?docnum=39224238 (Accessed: 23 June 2023).

Inter-American Dialogue Specialist (2019) Personal interview. Conducted by Miguel Gomis.

Jiménez, E. V. (2017) 'La violencia en el triángulo norte de Centroamérica: una realidad que genera desplazamiento', *Papel Político*, 21 (1), pp. 167–196.

Kat, Q. (2016) 'Toward real prosperity', *Nacla*, 7 November. Available at: https://nacla.org/news/2016/11/07/toward-real-prosperity (Accessed: 10 December 2022).

Knox, V. (2017) 'Factors influencing decision making by people fleeing Central America', *FM Review*, 56 (October).

Kolb, A. C. (2012) 'Outgunned: the Honduran fight against transnational cocaine traffickers', *Journal of International Affairs*, 66 (1), pp. 213–224.

Krasner, S. D. (2011) 'Changing state structures: outside in', *Proceedings of the National Academy of Sciences of the United States of America*, 108 (4), pp. 21302–21307.

Krasner, S. D., and Weinstein, J. M. (2014) 'Improving governance from the outside in', *Annual Review of Political Science*, 17 (1), pp. 123–145.

Lindsay-Poland, J. and Weiss, L. (2017) 'Re-arming the drug war in Mexico and Central America', *NACLA Report on the Americas*, 49 (2), pp. 182–185.

Lorenzen, M. (2017) 'The mixed motives of unaccompanied child migrants from Central America's Northern Triangle', *Journal on Migration and Human Security*, 5 (4), pp. 744–767.

Malinowski, T. and Blaha, C. O. (2016) 'De-militarizing civilian security in Mexico and the Northern Triangle', *Prism*, 5 (4), pp. 27–34.

Marcy, W. L. (2014) 'The end of civil war, the rise of narcotrafficking and the implementation of the Mérida initiative in Central America', *International Social Science Review*, 89 (1), pp. 1–36.

Medrano, C. (2017) 'Securing protection for de facto refugees: the case of Central America's Northern Triangle', *Ethics and International Affairs*, 31 (2), pp. 129–142.

Meyer, P. J. and Seelke, C. R. (2015) *Central America regional security initiative: background and policy issues for congress*. Congressional Research Service. Available at: https://sgp.fas.org/crs/row/R41731.pdf (Accessed: 23 June 2023).

Milner, H. V. (1997) *Interests, institutions, and information: domestic politics and international relations*. Princeton: Princeton University Press.

Murillo Castellanos, J. C. (2020) 'La macro-comparación entre la CICIG y la MACCIH, una necesidad compartida y diferenciada', *La Revista de Derecho*, 41 (1), pp. 37–54.

Musalo, K. and Lee, E. (2017) 'Seeking a Rational Approach to a Regional Refugee Crisis: Lessons from the Summer 2014 "Surge" of Central American Women and Children at the US-Mexico Border', *Journal on Migration and Human Security*, 5 (1), pp. 137–179.

Noé Pino, H. and Noé, E. M. (2019) *Plan alianza para la prosperidad: Resultados e incidencia en las causas estructurales que generan las migraciones en Honduras*. Fundación Panamericana para el Desarrollo. Available at: https://ciprodeh.org.hn/wp-content/uploads/2021/08/Investigacion_PAP_Resultados_Incidencia_PADF_CIPRODEH.pdf (Accessed: 23 June 2023).

Olson, E. L. (2016) *A glimmer of hope in Central America*. Available at: https://www.wilsoncenter.org/sites/default/files/media/documents/article/a_glimmer_of_hope_in_central_america.pdf (Accessed: 23 June 2023).

Orozco, M. (2016) *¿Qué ofrece el plan alianza para la prosperidad?* Available at: https://www.thedialogue.org/wp-content/uploads/2016/03/AlianzaParalaProsperidad_Final_3.16.16.pdf (Accessed: 23 June 2023).

Oviedo Garcia, A. J. (2019) 'El triángulo norte y el benelux: dos modelos de libertad y prosperidad economica', *Revista de Investigacion En Humanidades UFM – RIHU*, 6, pp. 1–26.

Paley, D. (2016) 'The alliance for prosperity will intensify the Central American refugee crisis', *The Nation*, 21 December. Available at: https://www.thenation.

com/article/archive/the-alliance-for-prosperity-will-intensify-the-central-american-refugee-crisis/ (Accessed: 23 June 2023).

Portes Virginio, F. V., Garvey, B. and Stewart, P. (2017) 'The perforated borders of labour migration and the formal state: meta-state and para-state regulation', *Employee Relations*, 39 (3), pp. 391–407.

Prado, R. (2018) 'El entramado de violencias en el triángulo norte Centroamericano y las maras', *Sociológica (México)*, 33 (93), pp. 213–246.

Putnam, R. D. (1988) 'Diplomacy and domestic politics: the logic of two-level games,' *International Organization*, 42 (3), pp. 427–460.

Rodgers, D. D. and Baird, A. A. (2016) 'Entender a las pandillas de América Latina: una revisión de la literatura', *Estudios Socio-Jurídicos*, 18 (1), pp. 13–53.

Rodríguez, C. G. and Tule, L. G. (2020) 'Honduras 2019: Persistent economic and social instability and institutional weakness', *Revista de Ciencia Politica*, 40 (2), pp. 379–400.

Roldán Andrade, Ú. (2015) *Notes on the alliance for prosperity plan for the Northern Triangle*. Envio, 406, May. Available at: https://www.envio.org.ni/articulo/5027 (Accessed: 23 June 2023).

Romano, S. M. (2017) '¿Alianza para la prosperidad de quién? La integración centroamericana bajo la supervisión estadounidense', *Cartografías Del Sur. Revista de Ciencias, Artes y Tecnología*, 3, pp. 72–91.

Romano, S. M. (2019) 'Alianza para la Prosperidad y la consolidación de la dependencia en Centroamérica', *Revista Interdisciplinaria De Estudios Sociales*, 11, pp. 39-57.

Romero Alvarado, W. (2018) *Las élites económicas y la captura de las instituciones de la política fiscal en Guatemala*. CLASCO and Oxfam. Available at: http://biblioteca.clacso.edu.ar/clacso/becas/20190516060215/Informe_Guatemala_vf.pdf (Accessed: 23 June 2023).

Rosnick, D., Main, A. and Jung, L. (2016) *¿Se han reducido el crimen y la violencia en Centroamérica con los programas CARSI financiados por estados unidos?* Center for Economic and Policy Research. Available at: https://cepr.net/images/stories/reports/carsi-2016-09-spanish.pdf (Accessed: 23 June 2023).

Schein, G. and Mihálycsa, E. (2017) 'Invisible war', *World Literature Today*, 91 (1), p. 23.

Schloss, D. W. and Joanna Quinn, S. R. (2015) *Elusive peace, security, and justice in post-conflict Guatemala: an exploration of transitional justice and the international commission against impunity in Guatemala (CICIG)*. Master's thesis. Western University, London. Available at: https://ir.lib.uwo.ca/etd/3037/ (Accessed: 23 June 2023).

Serna, N. R. (2016) 'Fleeing cartels and maras: international protection considerations and profiles from the Northern Triangle', *International Journal of Refugee Law*, 28 (1), pp. 25–54.

Silva Ávalos, H. (2014) *The United States and northern tier: Central America's the ongoing disconnect*. Available at: https://www.thedialogue.org/wp-content/uploads/2015/04/IAD9433_Silva_FINAL.pdf (Accessed: 23 June 2023).

Tablante, C. and Morales Antoniazzi, M. (2018) *Impacto de la corrupción en los derechos humanos*. México: Instituto de Estudios Constitucionales del Estado de Querétano.

Thompson, T. (2021) *Determining the effectiveness of conditionalities for international development by analyzing DR-CAFTA and the alliance for prosperity in the Northern Triangle*. Master's thesis. Texas State University, San Marcos. Available at: https://digital.library.txstate.edu/bitstream/handle/10877/14934/THOMPSON-THESIS-2021.pdf?sequence=1&isAllowed=y (Accessed: 23 June 2023).

Universidad Nacional Autónoma de Honduras Professor (2019) Personal interview. Conducted by Miguel Gomis.

USAID and US Department of State (2023) *Complete Dataset*. Available on: https://www.foreignassistance.gov/data (Accessed: 25 April 2023).

Villafuerte Solís, D. (2018) 'Seguridad y control geopolítico: crónica de la iniciativa para la prosperidad del triángulo norte de Centroamérica', *Revista CS*, 24, pp. 91–118.

Villagrán Sandoval, C. A. (2016) 'Soberanía y Legitimidad de Actores Internacionales en la Reforma Constitucional Guatemalteca: El Rol de la CICIG', *Política Internacional*, 1 (1), pp. 36–57.

World Bank (2023a) *Net official development assistance received*. Available at: https://data.worldbank.org/indicator/DT.ODA.ODAT.CD (Accessed: 18 April 2023).

World Bank (2023b) *World development indicators*. Available at: https://databank.worldbank.org/source/world-development-indicators (Accessed: 23 June 2023).

Zaitch, D. and Antonopoulos, G. A. (2019) 'Organised crime in Latin America: an introduction to the special issue', *Trends in Organized Crime*, 22 (2), pp. 141–147.

Zuñiga, L. (2012) 'Desafíos institucionales de la colaboración policial–militar: el triángulo norte', *Revista Latinoamericana de Seguridad*, 12 (12), pp. 83–96.

PART II:
REGIONAL RESPONSES TO COLLECTIVE HEALTH CHALLENGES

Chapter 5

Institutional factors influencing the success of Latin American organizations confronting epidemics[1]

Octavio González Segovia
National Autonomous University of Mexico, Mexico

Alfonso Sánchez Mugica
National Autonomous University of Mexico, Mexico

Abstract

This chapter aims to identify the type of institutions that have performed relatively well to help addressing epidemic outbreaks in Latin America, and to explain the reasons for their success. It entails analysis of key institutional factors that enable international organizations to learn, adapt and ultimately be effective. The chapter relies on a variety of sources, including semi-structured interviews with health and foreign affairs senior officials and international bureaucrats who have worked for regional organizations such as the Panamerican Health Organization (PAHO) and the Amazon Cooperation Treaty Organization (ACTO). The central argument is that transgovernmental networks (TGNs) are more effective than intergovernmental organizations (IGOs) when speed is a priority for several reasons. Two key ones are that the values and interests of TGN members are homogeneous and that it is easier to coordinate decision-making between them due to the relatively smaller number of states in a single network.

---

[1] This research was supported by the Dirección General de Asuntos del Personal Académico (DGAPA). The authors are grateful to Programa de Becas Posdoctorales en la UNAM for the awarding of a postdoctoral scholarship to Octavio González Segovia for conducting research at the Faculty of Social and Political Sciences, National Autonomous University of Mexico (UNAM).

Keywords: epidemics, transgovernmental networks, intergovernmental networks, institutional design, PAHO, GHSI, biosecurity threats

**

5.1 Introduction

In the aftermath of every major epidemic, studies are conducted by experts to identify concerns and propose a series of corrective measures (Ringe and Rennó, 2023; Popic and Moise, 2022; Rajan and Topp, 2022; Marchiori Buss and Tobar, 2021; Phelan, Katz and Gostin, 2020; Peeri et al., 2020; Ravi, Snyder and Rivers, 2019; Hoffman and Silverberg, 2018; Youde, 2018; Bastug and Bodur, 2015; Heymann et al., 2015; Fineberg, 2014; Kalra et al., 2014; Fidler and Gostin, 2008). International organizations, both intergovernmental organizations (IGOs) and transgovernmental networks (TGNs),[2] have embarked on comprehensive assessments of their performance, with member states contributing case studies of lessons learnt, conducting workshops, and submitting official reports (World Health Organization, 2021; Kahler, 2009).

For instance, the Review Committee on the Functioning of the International Health Regulations (World Health Organization, 2021) during the COVID-19 Response determined in April 2021 that "while there has been progress on implementing the recommendations of the three previous IHR Review Committees (i.e. in relation to the AH1N1 Pandemic; on second extensions for establishing National Public Health Capacities, and on the role of the IHR in the Ebola outbreak), implementation has been uneven and the overall pace of change since 2011 has been too slow" (Ibid., p. 55). Furthermore, the Review Committee (Ibid.) concluded that had the international community acted on the recommendations made in 2011, 2015, and 2016, states, parties, and the WHO would have been better prepared to deal with COVID-19.

Indeed, the 2009 influenza pandemic and the Ebola virus disease (EVD) epidemic in Western Africa revealed several institutional shortcomings and challenges (Ravi, Snyder and Rivers, 2019; Hoffman and Silverberg, 2018; Vetter et al., 2016; Bastug and Bodur, 2015; Dallatomasina et al., 2015; Grépin, 2015; Heymann et al., 2015; Fineberg, 2014; Enserink and Cohen, 2009). As regards the influenza pandemic, the Review Committee on the functioning of the new

---

[2] In line with Kahler's (2009) networks-as-actors approach and Podolny's (1998) definition of networks, we regard TGNs in the biosecurity domain as networks of consciously coordinated action, which are composed of at least two states, lack a legitimate authority to resolve and arbitrate coordination problems, and seek to change international outcomes and national policies.

IHR identified the 2005 version[3] (World Health Organization, 2015) as insufficient, citing "vulnerabilities in global, national and local public-health capacities, limitations of scientific knowledge, difficulties in decision-making under conditions of uncertainty, complexities in international cooperation and challenges in communication among experts, policymakers and the public" (World Health Organization, 2021, p. 6). In their evaluation of the EVD epidemic, the independent panel of experts called by the WHO concluded that the Ebola crisis not only exposed organizational failings in the functioning of the WHO but also demonstrated shortcomings in the application of the IHR from 2005. The panel even asserted that the "Ebola outbreak might have looked very different had the 2011 recommendations of the Review Committee on the functioning of the IHR from 2005 in relation to the pandemic been fully implemented" (González Segovia and Ébodé, 2020).

From the above examples, it is clear that we have not learnt any lessons from earlier outbreaks of diseases or, rather, that we have not learnt the right lessons. Although there are important similarities in the handling of the three most important and recent public health emergencies of international concern[4] (PHEICs)—that is, the 2009 A (H1N1) influenza pandemic, the EVD epidemic in West Africa, and the COVID-19 pandemic—there are also important differences that call into question the priorities of some global and regional health actors as well as the effectiveness of their actions. The questions we are interested in are whether successful management—understood as effectiveness in international outcomes—is related to the institutional design (e.g., in terms of legalization, flexibility) of health-related organizations, and if so, to what extent? Additionally, we also aim to determine which international/regional organization acting in Latin America learns faster from its failures and, hence, is more successful than others?

---

[3] The IHR from 2005 have two main functions: first, "to establish a regime for routine public-health protection and provide for the ongoing management of disease threats both within countries and at their borders"; second, "to provide a framework for coordinated and proportionate responses to significant and urgent disease threats, ranging from national public-health events to events of regional or global public-health significance" (World Health Organization, 2021, pp. 30–31).

[4] As explained in the IHR from 2005, a "PHEIC refers to an extraordinary event, including those of unknown causes or sources, which constitutes a public health risk to other states through the international spread of disease, and which requires a coordinated international response" (World Health Organization, 2016, p. 43).

5.2 Theoretical framework

Academics have proposed many mechanisms for interrogating experience. These mechanisms are generally called "lessons-learnt" processes. They comprise tools such as in-progress reviews, retrospective reviewing and reporting, and various kinds of debriefings. While the tools vary, they have the common objective of sharing performance information to help deal with similar situations (and the ensuing problems) in the future and prevent the recurrence of adverse events. Most of these processes involve some version of three core components: evaluating an incident by systematically analysing what occurred as well as its causes; identifying strengths to be sustained and weaknesses to be corrected; and finally, learning—that is, specifying and inculcating behavioural changes consistent with the lessons (González Segovia and Ébodé, 2020). In the biosecurity[5] field, an international organization is successful when it reacts fast, communicates in a timely manner, prevents the dissemination of pathogenic microbes, and learns from past mistakes.

We learn when we allow new evidence to change our beliefs. One can learn directly from one's own experiences or indirectly from others' experiences. Organizations learn by encoding inferences from history into routines that guide behaviour. Routines comprise forms, rules, procedures, conventions, strategies, a structure of beliefs, frameworks, paradigms, and so on. In this sense, "the lessons of history are captured by routines in a way that makes the lessons, but not the history, accessible to organizations and organizational members who have not themselves experienced the history" (Levitt and March 1988, p. 320).

The lessons learnt are not always the right lessons: civil servants can draw wrong conclusions from observations of past events, or they may select unsuitable analogies to help decide on a course of action to address a similar problem. For instance, despite the critical geographical differences between Uganda and Iran, most of the American senior civil servants involved in the 1980 Iranian rescue mission used the Entebbe rescue raid carried out by the Israel Defence Forces in Uganda as the operative analogy.

In the realm of public policy, actors may be learning both at the simple tactical level—that is, how to better achieve a particular objective—and at a deeper level—that is, what goals they should pursue. Therefore, "learning does

---

[5] Borrowing the definition from Fidler and Gostin (2008, pp. 4–5), we define biosecurity as a society's collective responsibility to safeguard the population from dangers presented by pathogenic microbes, whether intentionally released, as in the case of biological weapons or biological terrorist attacks (e.g., 2001 Anthrax mail attacks in the US), or naturally occurring, as with infectious diseases such as influenza, Ebola, or COVID-19.

not occur when policymakers simply adapt to the policy shifts of others, but only when their beliefs about cause-and-effect change" (Dobbin, Simmons and Garrett, 2007, p. 460). In this regard, because of lessons-learnt workshops, actors dealing with HIV-AIDS in countries such as Liberia and Sierra Leone predicted that the health system would fail due to prolonged civil war. They also identified structural adjustments to be made, among other recommendations. However, the international community did not act in a timely manner. Thus, we may well ask whether any fundamental change in the beliefs of responsible actors have occurred in recent years, including those in IGOs and TGNs.

Drawing on the literature dealing with legalization, biosecurity, rational choice, and network studies, we developed a theoretical framework for establishing the conditions under which we can expect governments to choose a TGN instead of an IGO for effectively dealing with epidemics and biological terrorism. The theoretical framework consists of seven hypotheses—that is, conditions—which represent the external and domestic factors (ideological, rational, etc.) that would prompt governments to select a TGN.

To operationalize the theoretical framework, we conducted elite interviews and online surveys with senior civil servants affiliated either with American health-related IGOs (e.g., South American Institute of Government in Health (ISAGS), the Pan American Health Organization (PAHO), the Andean Health Organization, the Amazon Cooperation Treaty Organization) or with the Ministries of Health/Foreign Relations of Argentina, Bolivia, Brazil, Canada, Chile, Colombia, Ecuador, Italy, Mexico, Peru, the United States, or Uruguay. Some of the questions put to senior civil servants were the following: How effective are organizations operating in the biosecurity field? Under what circumstances are TGNs more effective than IGOs? Which organization learns faster? By examining the answers to these questions, policymakers can obtain data for designing, modifying, or joining a certain organization in the biosecurity field. This is not a minor issue, as is evident from the long process of modifying the IHR from 2005 and the numerous lessons-learnt workshops and official reports issued after every PHEIC.

We start with the four broad assumptions that underlie the hypotheses framing this research: first, states act self-interestedly and thus deliberately choose and design international institutions [6] to further their own goals; second, the value of expected gains from cooperation is strong enough to support an institutional arrangement; third, establishing and participating in international organizations is costly; and finally, states are risk-averse when

---

[6] We use the terms "institution", "organization", and "institutional arrangement" interchangeably.

creating or modifying international institutions (Koremenos, Lipson and Snidal, 2001, pp. 781–782). In line with the definition by Koremenos, Lipson and Snidal (Ibid., p. 762), we broadly define international institutions as explicit arrangements negotiated among international actors which prescribe, proscribe, and/or authorize behaviour.

Our argument to substantiate these assumptions is twofold. First, in the event of an epidemic, a government's choice is restricted to IGOs and TGNs, and second, governments will opt for TGNs, which are regarded as a superior institutional arrangement, because they are capable of reacting quickly to prevent the dissemination of pathogenic microbes. Hence, success is linked to institutional design. In other words, governments choose or design a TGN because they regard it as more effective for dealing with the threat posed by pathogenic microbes (i.e., viruses/bacteria) regardless of their source (i.e., naturally occurring or man-made, as in the case of biological terrorism).

Koremenos, Lipson and Snidal (2001) argue that many institutional arrangements are best understood through the "rational design" approach involving multiple participants. According to them, states use diplomacy and conferences to select institutional features that will further their individual and collective goals. They do so by creating new institutions and modifying existing ones, and this is often the case in Latin America. The difficulty of creating or modifying institutions is evidence that institutional design is deliberate—for instance, the evolution of the GATT into the WTO or the Rio Group, which in 2011 became the Community of Latin American and Caribbean States (CELAC). Most institutions evolve as members learn, new difficulties arise, and international structures change. Furthermore, even institutional evolution involves "deliberate choices made in response to changing circumstances" (Ibid., p. 767), as recently witnessed with the international debate to update the IHR from 2005.

Previous results and evolutionary forces lay down the conditions for institutional development. Thus, as institutions evolve, rational design choices can arise in two ways. First, members may modify institutions progressively, either by making purposeful decisions subject to new circumstances, by adopting features from other institutions that work well, or by designing explicit institutions to strengthen informal cooperation. Second, institutions may change over time as a consequence of states and other actors favouring some institutions over others. Furthermore, Koremenos, Lipson and Snidal (Ibid., p. 767) contend that "even institutions that are not highly formalized and arise through informal and evolutionary processes may embody significant rational design principles". According to them, states favour certain institutions because they regard them as being more suited for dealing with new situations or new problems and reject those that are not compatible (Ibid.).

5.3 Cooperation, transgovernmental networks and international organizations

In their seminal work, Keohane and Nye (1974) differentiated between transgovernmental policy coordination and transgovernmental coalition building. The former refers to activities designed to facilitate smooth implementation or adjustment of policy, whereas the latter occurs when substate officials of a government ally with like-minded peers from other governments against officials of their own administrative structures. For example, Avery (2010) points out that Canadian officials were aware that three US departments—namely, agriculture, health, and state—were supportive of the North American Plan for Avian and Pandemic Influenza (NAPAPI), the cornerstone of the North American Coordinating Body for Pandemic Influenza (NACOBPI), whereas the Department of Homeland Security was against it.

Intergovernmental cooperation, in contrast, refers to diplomatic relations between unitary states headed by chiefs of government or foreign affairs ministries and involves multilateral treaties often linked with international organizations. Hence, the main differences between TGNs and IGOs pertain to membership (i.e., conception and representation of the state), structure (i.e., degree of centralization and level of hierarchy), and degree of formality (i.e., legalization, obligation, and irreversibility; González Segovia and Ébodé, 2020). For further clarification, see Table 5.1.

Table 5.1 Main features of TGNs and IGOs

Variable	TGNs	IGOs
1. Membership	Substate agencies / Officials	Unitary states
2. Structure	Decentralized / Flat	Centralized / Hierarchial
3. Political visibility	Low	High
4. Legalization	Low	High
5. Obligation	Low	High
6. Irreversibility	Low	High
7. Unit relations	Trust-based	Rule-based
8. Scope	Narrow	Broad
9. Decision mode	Consensus Only	Consensus or Qualified majority vote
10. Support for implementation / compliance	Low (self-enforced principles / voluntary compliance)	High

Source: González Segovia and Ébodé (2020), based on Eilstrup-Sangiovanni (2009, p. 201)

Some authors, including Eilstrup-Sangiovanni (2009, p. 205), Slaughter (2004), and Pollack (2005, pp. 911–912), argue that in the security domain, chiefs of government can elect to form or prevent the formation of TGNs and set parameters for their activities. Although we mostly adhere to this view, we also argue that in the biosecurity domain, sub-state officials (e.g., ministers/secretaries of health) may occasionally select/design TGNs (e.g., according to various sources, former US Secretary of Health and Human Services Tommy G. Thompson created the GHSI). Slaughter herself recognizes that depending on the issue area, sub-state officials frequently play a role in the lead-up to the creation of the institution (Slaughter, 2003, p. 1049). Thus, in keeping with Slaughter's typology of TGNs, we consider the NACOBPI as a TGN within the framework of an executive agreement—that is, of the second type—but would categorize the GHSI—integrated by the G7 and Mexico—as a "spontaneous" TGN of the first subtype, like the BRICS Health Network.

According to Koremenos, Lipson and Snidal (2001), the factors influencing international cooperation are of various kinds: cooperation problems (distributional or enforcement-related), uncertainty (about behaviour, the state of the world, and others' preferences), and others, such as the number of actors and the asymmetries among them (including differences in capabilities). "Distribution problems" arise when more than one cooperative agreement is possible. Its magnitude is contingent on how each actor compares their preferred alternative to other actors' preferred alternatives (González Segovia and Ébodé, 2020). "Enforcement problems" emerge either if incentives to defect are greater than the "shadow of the future" or if interactions between the actors are not frequent enough (Koremenos, Lipson and Snidal, 2001, p. 776). This is because frequent interactions enable the actors to reward and punish each other.

However, we do not expect to observe enforcement problems in TGNs or in other forms of soft law because of the "generalized trust" that exists among their members (Rathbun, 2011, pp. 247–248; Podolny and Page, 1998, pp. 60–62; Scharpf, 1997, pp. 137–138).[7] As pointed out by Scharpf (1997, p. 138), "membership in a network allows access to a larger number of potential partners of trustworthy interactions and thus increases the value of social capital". Transgovernmentalists contend that regulatory agreements between states are "pledges of good faith" that are self-enforcing because each state will be better able to enforce its national law by implementing the agreement, provided that the other members of the network do likewise (Raustiala, 2002, p. 24; Slaughter, 1997, p. 192).

Uncertainty arises from the fact that actors lack complete information about the state of the world or about others' behaviour or others' preferences. In the

---

[7] According to Podolny and Page (1998, p. 60), "[t]he network forms of organization can be characterized by a distinct ethic or value orientation on the part of exchange partners." They underline that in this kind of relationship, there exists a "spirit of goodwill", namely a commitment to use "voice" rather than "exit" to solve conflicts, as well as a high level of mutual trust.

case of the former, states do not possess knowledge about the consequences of their own actions, the actions of other states, or the actions of international institutions. The knowledge referred to could be scientific, technical, political, or economic. "Uncertainty about behaviour" means that states may be unsure about the actions taken by others, whereas in the case of "uncertainty about preferences", states may be unsure about what their counterparts really want. However, we do not expect to see these kinds of uncertainties in TGNs. Since TGNs are based on trust and frequent contact and because its members have relatively homogeneous values and interests, we assume that information would not be a problem. Finally, "number" refers to the number of relevant actors who are potentially eligible to join the organization, either because their actions affect others or vice versa. In "number", we also include asymmetries arising from differences in the capabilities of various actors (Koremenos, Lipson and Snidal, 2001, pp. 773–779).

5.4 Factors for joining a TGN

We grouped rational choice conditions according to the origin of the stimuli (i.e., external or domestic) and related them to certain factors (e.g., cooperation problems, perceptions, capacities, interests, group size). We may thus hypothesize that governments are likely to select a TGN for dealing with biosecurity threats under the conditions enumerated in Table 5.2 (and described in detail later).

Table 5.2 External and internal factors for joining a TGN

External factors
1) When they foresee distributional problems and thus aim to reduce bargaining costs.
2) When the other prospective members are capable and strongly committed.
3) When they share interests and values with other governments and when the group is small (i.e., from 3 to 10 members).
4) When they are uncertain about the "state of the world" and hence have doubts regarding the future implications of agreements.
5) When speed is a priority and time horizons are short.
6) When they aim to reconceptualize their responsibilities and interests with respect to biosecurity threats.
Domestic factors
7a) When they anticipate high sovereignty costs and react to domestic opposition (within either the government's structure or society).
7b) When sub-state officials wish to build coalitions with like-minded peers from other governments against elements within their own administrative structures.

Source: Created by the author based on data from González Segovia (2020).

Condition 1. Distributional problems: Governments are more likely to choose a TGN when they expect distributional problems from cooperation. Koremenos, Lipson and Snidal (2001, p. 794) posit that "[s]tates may reduce distributional problems and bargaining costs by adopting a more flexible agreement structure". A distribution problem occurs when governments must select one outcome from a range of known possible outcomes. As a rule, where the distributional implications of a choice are minor—such as when the shadow of the future[8] is short—bargaining costs will be proportionately small. In contrast, where the distributional implications are significant—that is, when the shadow of the future is long—bargaining costs will likely be high (Koremenos, Lipson and Snidal, 2001, p. 775). Nonetheless, network relations can reduce the risk of opportunism by extending the shadow of the future and by increasing the visibility of transactions. Thus, the existence of a network will ultimately determine the interactions that take place among its members in various ways: by enabling some interactions that would not otherwise have arisen, by making some of them more likely than others, and by altering the outcomes of some in favour of one or another of the members (Scharpf, 1997, p. 137).

Condition 2. Commitment, capabilities, and the exclusion of spoilers: TGNs are more likely to form among strongly committed and capable states that wish to exclude spoilers from cooperation. In contrast to IGOs, which often strive for universality, TGNs enable a few committed states to initiate an agreement without consulting others (Eilstrup-Sangiovanni, 2009, p. 209). Consequently, we argue that by setting the rules for membership, members can prevent spoilers from being admitted into the group. However, the opposite could also work—that is, by not setting any rules for membership, members may be in an even better position to refuse requests for membership. By limiting an initiative to a small group of highly influential states, "insiders" can set standards that "outsiders" are later compelled to accept, which Raustiala calls "regulatory export" (Raustiala, 2002, p. 7; Slaughter, 1997, p. 192). This is particularly the case when the initial group includes many powerful states in an issue area. Non-members may find themselves forced to accept the rules set by the group, not because of their binding nature but because networked members would be able to deny them important privileges if they refused to comply (Eilstrup-Sangiovanni, 2009, pp. 209–210).

Condition 3. Small size and homogeneous interests and values: According to Eilstrup-Sangiovanni (2009), we should expect governments to favour TGNs for two reasons. First, small groups are more likely to benefit from the speed and flexibility associated with network cooperation. Second, for reasons of credibility, networks are more likely among small homogeneous groups because cheating within such groups is less likely, and the small numbers make it easier to achieve effective peer-to-peer monitoring. Eilstrup-Sangiovanni

---

[8] As stated by Koremonos, Lipson and Snidal (2001, p. 781) the "shadow of the future" implies that the value of future gains is strong enough to support a cooperative arrangement.

(2009, p. 205) describes "homogeneous groups" as those who have "harmonious preferences" in terms of interests and values. Slaughter (1997) also contends that judges participating in judicial TGNs share values and interests, which are acknowledged and reinforced through their interactions (pp. 186–189). TGNs depend on expectations of generalized reciprocity. Thus, like other networks, they usually rely on higher levels of trust than is expected in other institutional arrangements (Eilstrup-Sangiovanni, 2009, p. 200).

Condition 4. Uncertainty: Governments are more likely to opt for a TGN when they are uncertain regarding the state of the world because, then, the longer-term implications of agreements come into play. According to Koremenos, Lipson and Snidal (2001, p. 773), "uncertainty is the linchpin of traditional security problems". Eilstrup-Sangiovanni (2009) argues that there may be situations in which states' interests are uncertain due to either inadequate information about the situation at hand or doubts about the likely outcomes of different courses of action. Uncertainty about the state of the world refers specifically to states' lack of knowledge about the consequences of their own actions or those of other states. According to Eilstrup-Sangiovanni (Ibid.), this kind of uncertainty favours more flexible arrangements. Under uncertainty, actors will opt for institutional flexibility as a way of protecting themselves against unanticipated costs or adverse distributional consequences (Ibid., pp. 207–208).

Condition 5. Speed and short time horizons: Governments are more likely to favour TGNs when speed is a priority and time horizons are short. TGNs are generally faster to set up than IGOs (Raustiala, 2002, p. 24). Consequently, "reliance on TGNs should shorten the time between when a problem is identified, and some form of collective action can be taken" (Eilstrup-Sangiovanni, 2009, pp. 206–207). Slaughter contends that the network form of TGNs is ideal for providing the speed and flexibility required for functioning effectively in the information age (Slaughter, 2004, p. 162; Slaughter, 1997, p. 193). Likewise, Lipson (1991) argues that "less formal" instruments will be chosen when security issues must be resolved quickly or quietly to avoid serious conflict. Since these kinds of instruments do not require elaborate ratification, they could be concluded and implemented rapidly (Ibid., pp. 500–501). We argue that this is particularly the case in complex, rapidly changing circumstances, such as that prevailing in the biosecurity domain, where speed is clearly an advantage.

Condition 6. Reconceptualization of responsibilities and interests: Governments are more likely to select a TGN to reconceptualize their responsibilities and interests with respect to biosecurity threats. Fidler and Gostin argue that the reconceptualization of state responsibilities and interests in biosecurity makes states hesitant to accept binding schemes of international governance as envisioned by the Biological Weapons Convention (BWC) protocol or various proposals for new treaties. They claim that "partnering arrangements" enable states to engage in cooperation without contracting the high transaction costs of negotiating and implementing formally binding rules. Due to the prevailing disagreement about which biosecurity policies are more appropriate, "flexible, cooperative relationships have advantages (vis-à-vis treaties) in allowing states to navigate uncertainties present in the new worlds of biological weapons and public health governance" (Fidler and Gostin, 2008, p. 231).

Condition 7a. High sovereignty costs and domestic opposition: Governments are more likely to favour TGNs rather than treaties linked to an IGO when they anticipate high sovereignty costs and expect key domestic groups (e.g., legislatures, interest groups, and the public) to oppose an international agreement. For various reasons related to their nature, TGNs are likely to enable governments to evade various domestic constraints to a greater extent than IGOs. First, cooperation through TGNs reduces the significance of public debate. Second, TGNs may reduce incentives for domestic groups to mobilize and pressure their governments to adopt specific policies that favour their interests. Finally, the narrow technical scope of many TGNs could allow members to claim special scientific and technical expertise and avoid scrutiny or intrusion by other agencies (Eilstrup-Sangiovanni, 2009, pp. 208–209; Slaughter, 2003, p. 1056; Raustiala, 2002, p. 24; Lipson, 1991, p. 535).

Condition 7b, Coalition building: Sub-officials are more likely to choose a networked form of cooperation when they wish to build coalitions with like-minded peers from other governments against elements in their own administrative structures (Slaughter, 2003, pp. 1054–1056; Pollack and Shaffer, 2001, pp. 287, 295; Keohane and Nye, 1974, p. 44). Transgovernmental coalitions are more likely when the following conditions are present: first, when there are broad and intensive contacts among sub-state officials; second, when the degree of executive control is low; and finally when there is a severe conflict of interests within governments. However, they are not enough to guarantee the formation of a coalition. In other words, they are necessary but not sufficient conditions. For coalitions to be feasible, networked actors with common interests also need to combine their resources effectively. This implies that the political resources of actors outside a government must be attractive and useful for some actors within it. Such resources comprise funds, prestige, information, and consent (Keohane and Nye, 1974, pp. 48–49). When coalitions succeed, the outcomes will be different from what would have been obtained in the absence of a coalition (Ibid.).

5.5 Research design and methods

To prove that some of the main premises of rational design and network theories contributed to the performance (i.e., success) of nine organizations dealing with PHEICs, we conducted elite, semi-structured interviews with 41 ministers, vice ministers, and senior civil servants (e.g., general directors or GDs of international relations) of 12 nationalities working either for the ministries of health and foreign relations or for health-related IGOs.[9]

To offset some of the disadvantages associated with interviews, we also conducted an analysis of relevant documents, including TGN ministerial statements, action plans, and WHO reports of the review committee on the functioning of the IHR (e.g., WHO, 2021).

The interviewees in this study reflect a greater or lesser extent, the high level of technical expertise of the personnel in the biosecurity issue area as well as the mobility within the area—that is, some of them had been in varied roles in different kinds of organizations (IGOs, governments, research institutes, and pharmaceuticals). For instance, two former health ministers of two South American countries had recently occupied leading positions in two regional IGOs dealing with health. Their cases were not unique, and it should be pointed out that mobility goes the other way around—that is, from IGOs to the national government. Furthermore, there were interviewees who had occupied positions within the MoH but now worked as researchers for the National Institute of Health. In addition, one interviewee had occupied a position at a National Institute of Health and, some years ago, had become a vice minister in the MoH of a Latin American country. As expected, some of them had held a high-ranking governmental position, then joined a well-known pharmaceutical company before finally returning to government service. This was the case with a health minister of the GHSI. Finally, the same representatives of the state frequently attended meetings of different TGNs and IGOs; hence, they were acquainted with each other, which helped them forge strong ties.

Of the 41 interviewees, 9 had served as international relations GDs at the MoH in Argentina, Canada, Chile, Colombia, Italy, Mexico, the United States, and Uruguay. Among other duties, international relations GDs oversee the organization of meetings of senior officials and health ministers. Thus, they integrate the agendas, know how the different institutional arrangements operate, and have access to all relevant information. Since GDs are not the ones who make the final decisions, it made sense to integrate the viewpoints of those who, according to Keohane and Nye's (1974) definition of transgovernmentalism, represent the state and hence make decisions on its behalf. These include ministers and vice ministers of ministries other than the MoFA (e.g. health). In this study, the former account for 11.76% of all interviewees (i.e., four people),

---

[9] Some relevant IGOs which have a key role in health-related matters include the WHO, PAHO, UNASUR-ISAGS, the Andean Health Organization (the Hipólito Unánue Agreement), and the Amazon Cooperation Treaty Organization.

while the latter account for 14.71% (i.e., five people). Considering that health, foreign affairs, and, to a lesser extent, defence are interconnected in the biosecurity realm, we included the answers of two ambassadors, one former minister who at different times led the Ministry of Foreign Relations and the Ministry of Defence, and five senior foreign relations civil servants.

Questionnaire design: We designed and hosted a questionnaire on the Zoho platform,[10] which enables designing and distributing surveys via email. Responses were securely stored, classified, and analysed on the same platform, accessible only by the researcher through a password. The questionnaire included 18 questions, of which 4 were open-ended, 3 were closed-ended, and the remaining 11 were multiple choice, Likert-type scale and rank order questions. These mixed-method questions served two purposes: on the one hand, they enabled respondents to add information they felt may have been missed in the structure of the question or provide any other information they deemed necessary, and on the other, they allowed us to estimate the degree of influence/importance and effectiveness of the selected organizations. The 11 multiple-choice questions served to detect the strengths, weaknesses, and degree of flexibility of TGNs and IGOs working in the biosecurity field.

5.6 Research results

Effectiveness of organizations operating in the biosecurity field: In question number eight of the questionnaire, we asked respondents to rate the degree of effectiveness of the nine organizations under study on a Likert scale (from 1 to 5), with 5 being very effective. Although only 15 respondents answered this question, it gives us clues concerning the perceived degree of effectiveness, and thus, it enables us to compare TGNs and IGOs.

At first glance, it might seem surprising that respondents rated the biggest IGO operating in the biosecurity field (i.e., the WHO) as very effective (26.67%), particularly given the severe criticism it received for its handling of the SARS outbreak in 2003 and EVD in West Africa during 2014–2016. Although a similar percentage (25%) of respondents rated the GHSI as very effective, the result changes when we combine the two highest values (effective and very effective—4 and 5, respectively). In this scenario, the percentage for the GHSI is 62.5%, whereas for the WHO, it is 60%. However, none of these was rated as the most effective organization; rather, the PAHO, with 71.43%, was the most effective (50% regarded it as effective and 21.43% as very effective).

---

[10] See online questionnaire at https://survey.zoho.com/survey/newui#/preview/314970 000000002007?portalid=655920406&zsgid=hSCumC

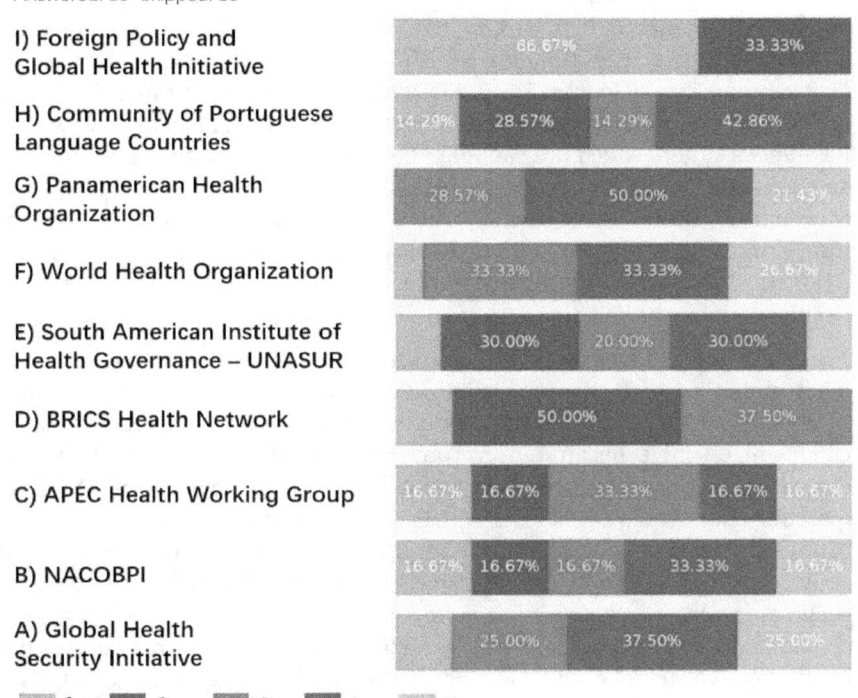

Figure 5.1 Effectiveness of organizations

Source: Created by the author using Zoho software; based on data from González Segovia (2020).

In contrast, 66.67% of respondents rated the Foreign Policy and Global Health Initiative (FPGHI) as the most ineffective (see Figure 5.1). Although important, this information does not tell us why respondents assessed TGNs and IGOs as effective or ineffective. To complement question eight, we asked the interviewees to give reasons to support their choices. For instance, a health specialist from Chile considered that the WHO and PAHO are effective because "they have global/regional scope, country-offices, regional action plans, resources (human, financial and material) and convening power" (face-to-face anonymous interview, O3 MoH).

An international bureaucrat from Peru who also assessed both IGOs as effective reasoned that "they have clear mandates and receive backing from countries to face threats; moreover, they have technical and financial resources and experience". Besides, he noted the importance of having links to other organizations: "[b]oth PAHO and the WHO are effective because they have links with other organizations competent in health (e.g., animal health, agriculture, education) and with institutions that conduct research on health" (Beingolea, 2018).

A former health minister from Bolivia, who is currently an international bureaucrat, answered, "PAHO and the WHO are effective because of their technical capacity, whereas the UNASUR is effective due to its technical and political capacities" (Heredia, 2018). An international bureaucrat from Colombia added that the PAHO is very effective because "the organization counts with Reference Centers which are capable of assuming the management in group and because it has implemented network actions at the country level in coordination with IGOs" (Sánchez Otero, 2018). A senior health civil servant from Uruguay considered that the WHO is very effective, and the PAHO and the GHSI are also effective "because of the success they have had when addressing health emergencies and biosecurity threats" (Rigoli, 2017).

Information sharing seems to be another factor that plays a role in determining how effective an organization can be. In this respect, a senior health civil servant from Argentina pointed out that "UNASUR, PAHO and the CPLP are effective because they can socialize information and have the capacity to negotiate and reach joint solutions (e.g., in the case of UNASUR, member countries were able to buy in block the vaccine against AH1N1)" (Tobar, 2017). A Mexican ambassador agreed with other interviewees and considered "the NACOBPI, the WHO and PAHO to be effective because they are legitimate and can exchange information rapidly" (Roldán, 2017). An Argentinian senior health civil servant concurred with the Mexican ambassador concerning legitimacy as a factor behind effectiveness but limited its assessment to IGOs—that is, the Union of South American Nations (UNASUR), the WHO, PAHO, and the Community of Portuguese Language Countries (Tobar, 2017).

Flexibility: According to the literature on networks, flexibility is one of the strengths of the network form. Thus, we deemed it important to ask the respondents to assess the degree of flexibility of not only the five TGNs, but also the four IGOs under study (see Figure 5.2). As for previous questions, we asked participants to use a Likert scale (from 1 to 5) for rating. We assigned the lowest value of 1 to "not flexible", 2 to "slightly flexible", 3 to "flexible", 4 to "fairly flexible", and the highest value of 5 to "very flexible".

Institutional factors influencing the success of health organizations 139

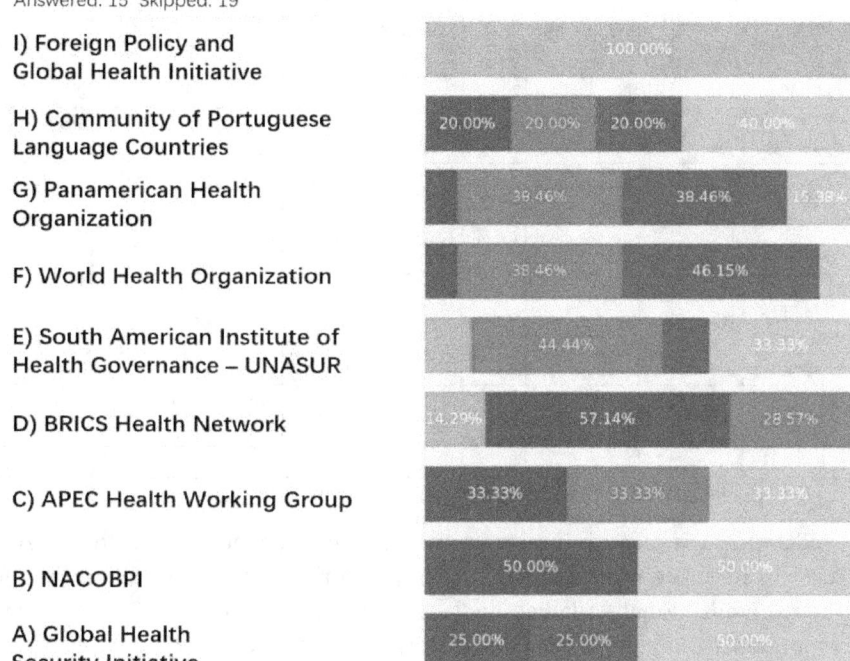

Figure 5.2 Flexibility of organizations in dealing with PHEICs

Source: Created by the author using Zoho software; based on data from González Segovia (2020).

As for previous questions, respondents predominantly opted to assess the WHO and PAHO. Indeed, 13 respondents assessed both IGOs, whereas only 1 did the same with the apparently less popular TGN—the FPGHI. In contrast, seven respondents decided to evaluate the BRICS Health Network in passing, which, when it comes to flexibility, is by far the most assessed network. However, the number of mentions does not translate into high levels of flexibility. In fact, despite receiving few mentions, 50% of respondents considered the GHSI and the NACOBPI to be very flexible, whereas even though the BRICS Health Network received seven mentions—the highest number of mentions for a TGN—not even one respondent considered it to be very flexible. Overall, the most flexible organization is the GHSI, with an average rating of 4

(1 denoting "not flexible" and 5 denoting "very flexible"), with the CPLP in second place with an average rating of 3.8 and PAHO in third place with an average rating of 3.62 (see Table 5.3).

Table 5.3 Flexibility of various organizations

	Range		Less Frequent		More Frequent		Mean	Median	Standard Deviation	Variance
	From	To	Frequency	Value	Frequency	Value				
A) GHSI	2	5	1	2, 4	2	5	4	1.41	2	
B) NACOBPI	2	5	-	-	1	2, 5	3.5	2.12	4.5	
C) APEC HWG	2	5	-	-	1	2, 3, 5	3.33	1.53	2.33	
D) BRICS HN	1	5	1	1	4	2	2.14	0.69	0.48	
E) UNASUR-ISAGS	1	5	1	1, 4	4	3	3.56	1.33	1.78	
F) WHO	2	5	1	2, 5	6	4	3.54	0.78	0.6	
G) PAHO	2	5	1	2	5	3, 4	3.62	0.87	0.76	
H) CPLP	2	5	1	2, 3, 4	2	3	3.8	1.3	1.7	
I) FPGHI	-	-	-	-	1	1	1	0	0	

Source: Created by the author based on data from González Segovia (2020).

Judging by the mean values, we cannot arrive at a conclusion as to whether TGNs or IGOs are more flexible in the biosecurity field. We need to consider other organizational variables, such as learning and capacity. On analysing respondents' replies to the question "Why are selected organizations flexible?", we find that some respondents correlated flexibility with capability—to adjust processes and proceedings, to reallocate resources, or to create working groups and networks. Interestingly, a vice minister of health (see answer 3 in Table 5.3) associated flexibility with the ease of entering or exiting from a TGN. He also noted that unlike IGOs, which are dependent on the MoFA, TGNs enable participants to enjoy a higher degree of freedom: "When you participate in IGOs you are not the Boss" (see Table 5.4; Ruocco, 2012).

Table 5.4 Respondents' replies to "Why are selected organizations flexible?"

#	Respondents' Replies
1	When a threat is identified, they are capable of responding almost immediately and can reallocate human and financial resources
2	Because the members of these organizations know that each situation requires different responses and respect that decision of each country, trusting its commitment with public health
3	"TGNs imply resources to participate (travels, meetings). The choice to participate in one organization is not a possible choice, because a government cannot avoid to participate in an official agency as the WHO is, but it can decide to exit from a TGN for instance for economic reasons, because you have to spend time to do this activity. In times of a crisis, it might not be easy to have available money. It is a voluntary activity." (Interviewer: Then, please correct me if I'm wrong, but it seems you would see TGNs as more flexible than IGOs?) "Yes." (Interviewer: Because you may exit if the TGN is not effective…?) "Yes. Because when you participate in IGOs, you are not the boss, the Ministry og Foreign Affairs is. They make a lot of diplomatic consultations before deciding whether to exit this kind of organizations. In this case [referring to the GHSI], it is a technical… network. The health minister can decide if it is beneficial for society. You can enter, exit… Obviously, you try to remain [in a stable position] in the organization. Anyway, you are still free to decide, on a case by case basis, what could be the best way [to cooperate]."
4	I selected three organizations because I do not think they are particularly flexible, understanding flexibility as the capacity to adjust processes and proceedings rapidly.
5	I focused on the case of UNASUR-ISAGS because it is closely related to member countries.
6	Because they have the capacity to form networks and working groups. Besides, they even have the ability to modify guiding actions without dealing with extensive bureaucratic mechanisms.
7	Consensus enables members to adapt their decisions.
8	International support and legitimacy.
9	The proximity and liaisons among the countries.

Source: Created by the author based on data from González Segovia (2020).

Fast learning: In contrast to previous questions, for this one respondents had to simultaneously compare and rank all the organizations studied from 1 to 9, with 1 being the highest rank—for the organization that learns faster than the other eight—and 9, the lowest rank—for the slowest organization. It is important to note that, owing to the software we employed to construct the questionnaire, respondents could not assign the same number to two organizations. The only alternative to allotting different numbers to different organizations was the possibility of not ranking a certain organization (i.e., ranking as "N/A"). See Figure 5.3.

Figure 5.3 Which organization learns faster?

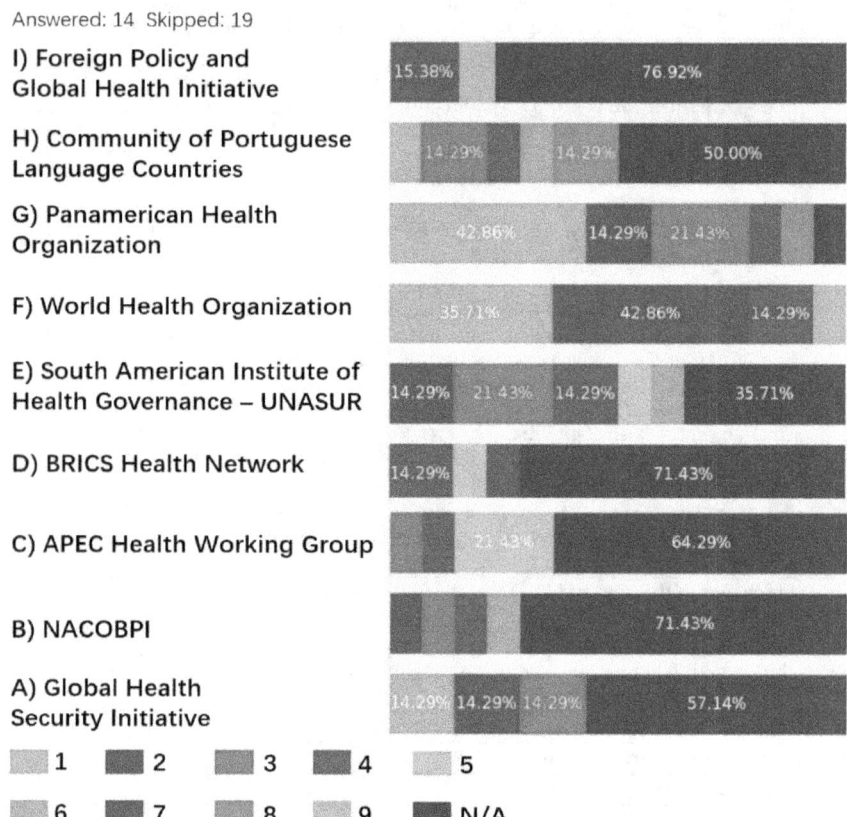

Source: Created by the author using Zoho software; based on data from González Segovia (2020).

As can be seen in Figure 5.3, respondents preferred to rank IGOs, with the WHO ("F") being the most assessed organization, followed by the PAHO ("G") and the ISAGS-UNASUR ("E"). Once more, the most assessed TGN was the GHSI ("A"). As previously discussed, fast learning is one of the most important characteristics of the network form—irrespective of whether they are advocacy networks, TGNs, or even dark networks. Hence, in regard to flexibility, it made sense to ask respondents to rank all organizations to see if this characteristic was also true of the biosecurity field (see Table 5.5).

Table 5.5 Which organization learns faster (rank from 1 to 9)?

	Range		Less Frequent		More Frequent		Rank	Mean	Median	Standard Deviation	Variance
	From	To	Frequency	Value	Frequency	Value					
A) GHSI	1	N/A	2	1, 2, 3	8	N/A	4	6.57	10	4.15	17.19
B) NACOBPI	2	N/A	1	2, 3, 4, 6	10	N/A	7	8.21	10	3.04	9.26
C) APEC HWG	3	N/A	1	3, 4	9	N/A	6	8	10	2.83	8
D) BRICS HN	4	N/A	1	5, 7	10	N/A	8	8.57	10	2,44	5.96
E) UNASUR-ISAGS	2	N/A	1	5, 6	5	N/A	3	5.86	4.5	3,37	11.36
F) WHO	1	9	1	9	6	2	1	2.43	2	2.14	4.57
G) PAHO	1	N/A	1	4, 8, N/A	6	1	2	2.93	2	2.79	7.76
H) CPLP	1	N/A	1	1, 4, 6	7	N/A	5	7.36	9	3.3	10.86
I) FPGHI	7	N/A	1	9	10	N/A	9	9.46	10	1.13	1.27

Source: Created by the author based on data from González Segovia (2020).

Contrary to what network theories would predict, respondents ranked three IGOs as the organizations that learn faster—the WHO (first), the PAHO (second), and the ISAGS-UNASUR (third). In this respect, of 14 respondents who answered this question, 6 (42.86%) ranked PAHO as number one, 5 (35.71%) ranked the WHO as number one, 2 (14.29%) ranked the GHSI as the fastest, and only 1 (7.14%) assigned that place to the CPLP (see Figure 5.3). Nonetheless, we should be cautious about these results because, as shown in Figure 5.3, most respondents decided not to rank the TGNs (fluctuating from 57.14% to 76.92%), instead selecting the option "N/A" shown in dark grey.

Capabilities: As the responses in previous sections show, irrespective of the kind of institutional arrangement, capabilities do matter. In order to better understand this, we asked informants to rate the nine organizations on a Likert scale (from 1 to 5; see Figure 5.4). We assigned the lowest value 1 to "incapable", 2 to "slightly capable", 3 to "capable", 4 to "fairly capable", and 5 to "very capable".

Figure 5.4 Capability of organizations (most assessed organizations)

Source: Created by the author using Zoho software; based on data from González Segovia (2020).

For other questions, we offered respondents the option of not assessing a certain organization. Despite receiving only 15 responses—from a total of 34—informants also provided comments that enabled us to make some inferences concerning the role of capabilities when selecting a certain institutional design. For different reasons, when asked, "How capable are the following organizations?", respondents predominantly decided to assess IGOs. Indeed, in descending order, respondents selected the PAHO (14 mentions, representing 23%), the WHO (13 mentions, representing 21%), the ISAGS-UNASUR (9 mentions, representing 15%), and the CPLP (7 mentions, representing 11%). The five TGNs accounted for the remaining 30%. The bar chart in Figure 5.4 shows these values.

As Figure 5.5 and Table 5.5 show, respondents ranked the WHO and the PAHO as the most capable organizations in the biosecurity field. The former received an average rating of 4.23, and the latter an average rating of 4.07 (5 denotes "very capable"). At the other extreme, the FPGHI received the lowest average rating of 2.33 (2 denotes "slightly capable").

The GHSI, in third place, was ranked as the most capable TGN, with respondents giving it an average rating of 3.67 (4 denoted "fairly capable"). The NACOBPI had a slightly lower rating, with an average of 3.67. The ratings for the rest of the organizations were far lower and were between 2.33 and 2.86. Among these, the organization that received the highest average rating was the CPLP (2.86), whereas the FPGHI had the lowest average value (2.33). Finally, the BRICS Health Network had an average rating of 2.75, the APEC Health Working Group 2.5, and the ISAGS-UNASUR, 2.44.

Figure 5.5 Capability of Organizations

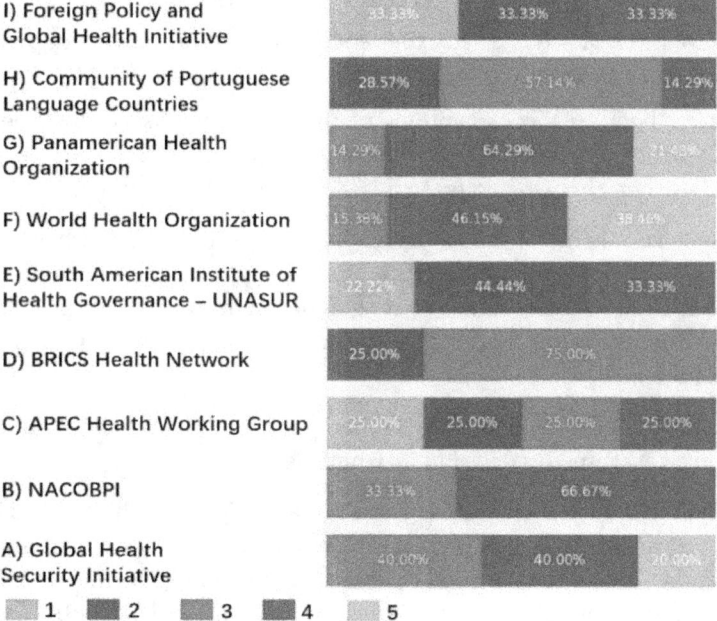

Source: Created by the author using Zoho software; based on data from González Segovia (2020).

Why are health-related organizations capable? To elucidate the rationale behind the ratings, we included a follow-up question in the questionnaire: Why are the selected organizations capable? In general, respondents cited technical and financial resources but, interestingly, also underlined the importance of having other sorts of resources, such as institutional and ideational (e.g., trust, commitment, learning). For example, an international bureaucrat from an Andean country noted,

> The WHO and PAHO have the capacity of convening technicians in different subjects. Moreover, these technicians have representativeness before the ministries of health. Besides, both have the capacity of providing technical advice in the form of documents (e.g., guides); finally, they have financing as well as contacts with health-related institutions. (Beingolea, 2018)

A former South American health minister pointed out that "technically the WHO, PAHO and the ISAGS-UNASUR have the duty to be capable" (Vance, 2017). Another former senior health civil servant from the same region also mentioned technical capacities, but in addition, noted that learning was also an important asset: "The ISAGS-UNASUR and PAHO have technical capacities and have internalized learned experiences that enable them to cooperate with its partners" (Hague, 2017).

Coming back to the capabilities of the actors, we asked an experienced Brazilian health civil servant to enumerate the factors that governments consider when choosing between a TGN and an IGO? He replied,

> I believe it is institutional capacity and governance. Brazil has a very well-established power structure. Historically we have had a ministry of health that was substantially strengthened in the democratic period due to an intense popular participation. (face-to-face anonymous interview, P8 MoH)

We then asked the interviewee whether capabilities would be the only factor behind a government's decision, to which he answered,

> I think it would also be the legal delimitation. The structure of Brazilian governance is very organized; we depend very little on international and national NGOs. The Brazilian public power is very large, that applies to its three levels. For example, Doctors without Borders (MSF) has no expression in Brazil (Marchiori Buss, 2017).

The above response is indicative of the role of capabilities. Despite "legal delimitation" being cited as an additional explicative variable, it is important to note that the answer also emphasizes "public power" as well as "local and national capabilities". The example provided demonstrates this well if we recall that Médecins Sans Frontières (MSF) played an important role during the Ebola epidemic in West Africa and in other countries whose medical capacities were insufficient or limited.

A Canadian senior civil servant also underlined the importance of having high capacities and like-mindedness as prerequisites for collaborating in a TGN. Moreover, she linked high capacities with a low prevalence of diseases and stressed how one institutional arrangement can reinforce the other when it comes to strengthening health capacities:

> Within a country's decision making there are certain benefits to these affiliations of like-minded countries to get together, to have a shared strategy and shared objectives to work collectively towards something and you tend to gather not only with likeminded but people that are or groups that are within the same ... "Low prevalence/high resources". Gatherings of "Low prevalence/high resource" countries that help together to move things forward. Like-mindedness helps stimulate activity. Moving forward together and not taking a scattered approach. High resource countries help to move things forward. For us, we don't look at one being better than the other in terms of legally binding treaties vs affiliations of like-minded countries we look at how the two can support each other. So, for instance with the GHSI, one of our conversations has been around IHR Regulations and how we might help WHO help its member states meet IHR capacity requirements (Engelhardt, 2012).

Besides capabilities, according to a secretary of health from the United States, there are two important factors for collaborating in a TGN: a long history of interactions and transparency. He said that it is more probable to witness the appearance of TGNs in the biosecurity field "among strongly committed and capable states who have worked together for a long time (i.e., history course of action), and when there is transparency among them" (Azar II, 2012). According to Eilstrup-Sangiovanni (2009, p. 209), "TGNs are useful for forming clubs of strongly committed states and for excluding spoilers. By confining an initiative to a small group of highly committed states, 'insiders' can set standards to which 'outsiders' are later compelled to accede".

A South American senior foreign relations civil servant reasoned that the WHO and the PAHO are capable because of their "proven track-record" (Da Nobrega, 2017). Concerning the GHSI, a former North American health vice minister noted that "[a]t the GHSI, differences related to the budget, in other words to members' capacities" (López Gatell, 2012). Another former health civil servant from the same region added that "at the WHO and the GHSI the commitment and trust of each country allows a fast resolution and facilitates the communication within established meetings" (Lawlley, 2012). In this respect, it is remarkable that respondents not only equated material resources with capabilities, but also broadened the range of options to include other resources, such as learning, commitment, and trust, which have also been mentioned by other authors as being relevant (Rathbun, 2011; Eilstrup-Sangiovanni, 2009; Koremenos, Lipson and Snidal, 2001; Levitt and March, 1988).

Under what circumstances are TGNs more effective than IGOs? Overall, we tried to substantiate this main question by incorporating other variables deemed relevant in the literature. Consequently, we combined the conditions proposed by rationalists and network theorists with some insights from the biosecurity area. We included 12 conditions and left a blank space in case respondents wished to add other(s). For this question, respondents could select more than one condition. In contrast to what was seen with other questions, 29 respondents answered or provided information related to the question, and only 5 skipped it. Thus, the degree of reliability is high. Additionally, 10 respondents included other conditions that they thought were relevant (see Figure 5.6 and Table 5.6).

As Figure 5.6 shows, TGNs in the biosecurity field are more effective than IGOs when the network is small (48.28%), when speed is a priority (37.93%), when TGNs collaborate with the WHO (34.48%), and when its members have similar interests and values (31.03%). According to respondents, the specific nature of the biosecurity threat also plays a role when considering the institutional arrangement to select. For example, respondents maintained that TGNs are more effective than IGOs when fighting regional threats (24.14%); dealing with a specific threat such as influenza (17.24%); and confronting biological terrorism (13.79%).

Institutional factors influencing the success of health organizations 149

Figure 5.6 Under what circumstances are TGNs more effective than IGOs?

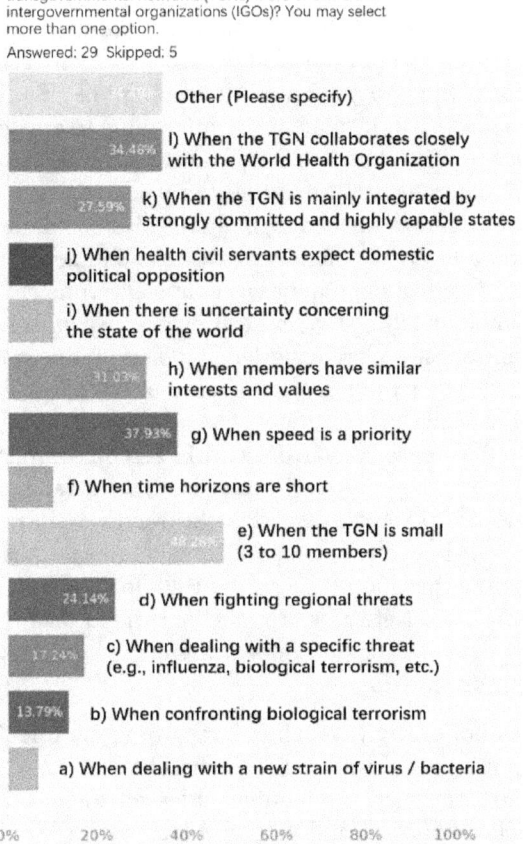

Source: Created by the author using Zoho software; based on data from González Segovia (2020).

The findings are consistent with condition 3 of the theoretical framework (i.e., small group size and relatively homogeneous interests) for networked cooperation laid out by Eilstrup-Sangiovanni (2009); according to her, these characteristics lessen the need for central arbitration and sanctioning. As noted, small groups are more likely to take advantage of the speed and flexibility associated with networked cooperation. Furthermore, due to credibility issues, networks are more likely to form among small, homogeneous groups. The rationale behind this is that it is easy to achieve peer-to-peer monitoring when the numbers are small, and this will act as a substitute for central arbitration and sanctioning (Eilstrup-Sangiovanni, 2009, p. 205). A former foreign affairs and defence minister from South America affirmed this reasoning concerning the relationship between effectiveness and the small size of international organizations:

> Each organization has its role. If you take an initiative, let us say to create a fund for fighting Zika, in general it is easier to act in a smaller group. For example, at the G20 you could do a thing like that, and whoever wants to join can do it. Instead, if you are willing to create standards it must be done at WHO. In other words, to create longer-term plans, you must do it preferably at the WHO, because it is the international organization. Organizations have different roles. Ideally, at some point in the future, a topic like standards creation should be treated in an international organization that has rules and everyone participates. It is the most democratic thing that exists. However, we must recognize that in the current phase we are experiencing, certain decisions—whether due to the need to act quickly, or because of the obstacles that might exist in a more formal organization—can be taken in transgovernmental networks. In that sense, I believe networks can be complementary and not exclusionary. These networks can also have a catalytic effect as it happened in the G20. You can discuss Ebola inside the G20, or tuberculosis inside the BRICS but you are not going to create a rule that is applicable to everyone in either the BRICS or the G20, for that you must go to a larger organization. Networks are mechanisms to take initiatives that later can be extended or not, depending on the case (epidemics, for example) (Amorim, 2018).

These remarks not only give us clues concerning the role that size plays in each of the organizations but also validate what Raustiala (2002) calls "regulatory export"—that is, when highly influential states set standards that "outsiders" are later compelled to accept and that ultimately serves the purpose of TGNs, namely to change international outcomes. Furthermore, we asked a vice minister of health from Mexico about the strengths of TGNs, and he agreed with the South American former minister of foreign affairs that small size is important. However, additionally, he emphasized homogeneity among members—in terms of interests, capacities, and political features—as an important factor in determining the effectiveness of TGNs vis-à-vis IGOs:

> The GHSI is a trust-based organization; it has a wide margin of freedom to discuss in a safe environment; the group of countries is small and homogeneous to help maintaining a dynamic group. In that respect, in various GHSI meetings colleagues remarked that if the group grows bigger it could impinge upon the groups' effectiveness. The NACOBPI is like the GHSI. An important strength of the NACOBPI is its cross-sectoral perspective. I think TGNs are indeed complementary to IGOs. I would

expect TGNs to be more effective than IGOs in smaller groups of countries who have common political features, similar capacities or clearly identified regional interests. TGNs require a higher level of implicit understanding to work without binding rules. I would expect TGNs to be more effective than IGOs in matters that require quick responses: global (or regional) health security, food safety, environmental security, public safety, etc. (López Gatell, 2012).

A foreign affairs and defence minister from South America stressed the importance of institutional experiences, similar interests, and, at times, ideological affinities as prerequisites for the emergence of TGNs. According to him, this even applied to cases where, in principle, experiences had nothing to do with a new issue or conditions:

It is not necessarily ideological affinities what is behind a decision [to create a certain organization]. Every story is a different story. The India, Brazil, South Africa Dialogue Forum (IBSA) for example, there was clearly a coincidence of interests and worldviews. In the case of the BRICS, affinities were less important, but not interests, particularly from an economic point of view. It arises from the opportunity to create a group of countries that could influence global economic issues. However, the BRIC group began as a forum for exchanging ideas at the UN, between Brazil and Russia, which were the ones that provoked the idea. Together with Minister Lavrov, I participated from the beginning—and then it evolved to address other issues including health. I believe these groups [TGNs] arise when there is a perception of either affinities or interests. Some are, so to say, functional for certain issues but dysfunctional for others. Health, for example, can be treated within the BRICS. Two cases that illustrate the previous point are antimicrobial resistance or tuberculosis. The 40% of the world's population lives within the BRICS, but those countries account for the 60% of patients infected with tuberculosis, so there is obviously a common interest in dealing with this issue. The BRICS already existed, i.e., it was not created for that purpose, but once you create an *ad hoc* group, you discover other points in common. I do not think they are exclusive of other treatments. When it comes to normative issues, the BRICS for example does not serve to regulate. In that case, the only thing you can do is exchanging experiences, but these countries cannot create rules, either for biosecurity or against epidemics. That you must do it at the WHO because it is the only organization that has legal weight and can be followed by everyone (Amorim, 2018).

The above argument supports the main assumption of Keohane's functional regime theory—that is, institutions exist to perform specific functions. Therefore, it is essential to elucidate the function an institution serves to explain its creation (Keohane, 1984, pp. 80–82). As noted earlier, in the case of the WHO, the function would be to regulate, whereas, in the case of the BRICS, the main function would be to influence international outcomes in the financial area. Moreover, we can relate the statements of the BRICS and IBSA to Abbott and Snidal's (2000, p. 423) arguments concerning soft law instruments[11]—namely, that specific forms of soft law chosen by states, in their varying combinations of obligation (O), precision (P), and delegation (D), reflect the particular problems they are trying to solve. According to previous statements, in the case of the G20 group of developing countries,[12] the BRICS, and IBSA, the problems that would help us explain their institutional dimensions (i.e., O + P + D) would be agricultural subsidies; the reform of international institutions, including the UN Security Council; antimicrobial resistance; tuberculosis; and drug patents.

A variable that plays an even more prominent role than the ones associated with the biosecurity field relates to the capabilities and commitment of TGN members. In other words, if the majority of TGN members are strongly committed and highly capable states, the TGN will be more effective than IGOs (27.59%). Some of the conditions that received less support derive from the rational choice framework (e.g., when time horizons are short), are related to a domestic variable (i.e., when health civil servants expect domestic political opposition), or pertain to a particularity of the biosecurity realm (i.e., when dealing with a new strain of virus/bacteria). For instance, three respondents (10.34%) pointed out that TGNs are more effective than IGOs when time horizons are short ("f" in Figure 5.6), when there is uncertainty concerning the state of the world ("i"), and when health civil servants expect domestic political opposition ("j").

As stated, 10 respondents (34.48%) mentioned other circumstances in which TGNs are more effective than IGOs (see Table 5.6). This represents the same number of people who selected the third most chosen option—that is, TGNs collaborating with the WHO ("l"). Although respondents mentioned a variety of conditions, we can group them into three categories: trust, the technicality of the issue, and the need for better communication. With respect to the first

---

[11] Namely, an informal organization not linked to a treaty or international convention.

[12] For a detailed explanation concerning the origins of the G20 Group of Developing Countries, see da Motta Veiga (no date). Among others, da Motta Veiga argues that the "political trust" built up among IBSA countries gave rise to the G20 group of developing countries.

category, a health vice minister from a North American country who had actively participated in several GHSI meetings mentioned that TGNs are more effective than IGOs "when members trust each other …" (López Gatell, 2012). A former health vice minister from the same region who also participated in the GHSI meetings underlined the importance of "building a circle of trust among the top-level people and getting decisions made faster in a short period of time" (Troy, 2012). Finally, three North American senior health civil servants asserted that TGNs are more effective than IGOs "when members trust each other" (López Gatell, 2012; Troy, 2012; Engelhardt, 2012).

Table 5.6 When are TGNs more effective than IGOs?

Choices	Response percentage	Response count
1. When dealing with a new strain of virus/bacteria	6.90%	2
2. When confronting biological territorism	13.79%	4
3. When dealing with a specific threat (e.g., influenza, biological terrorism, etc.)	17.24%	5
4. When fighting regional threats	24.24%	7
5. When the TGN is small (3 to 10 members)	48.28%	14
6. When time horizons are short	10.34%	3
7. When speed is a priority	37.93%	11
8. When TGN members have similar interests and values	31.03%	9
9. When there is uncertainty concerning the state of the world	10.34%	3
10. When health civil servants expect domestic political opposition	10.34%	3
11. When the TGN is mainly integrated by strongly committed and capable states	27.59%	8
12. When the TGN collaborates closely with the World Health Organization (WTO)	34.48%	10
13. Other (Please specify)	34.48%	10

Source: Created by the author using Zoho software; based on data from González Segovia (2020).

It is worth highlighting that trust could be used an explanatory variable for a condition as important as "c"—dealing with a specific threat such as influenza, biological terrorism, and so on—which accounted for 17.24% of responses. Alternatively, the fact that five respondents mentioned trust validates the decision made to combine the fundamentals of the rational design project with insights from network theories, where generalized trust appears as a prominent explanatory variable behind the decision to select TGNs. However, this also demonstrates one of the limitations of the rational design project, where the preferences of the actors are not considered and are assigned a secondary role, subsumed under the uncertainty about others' preferences. It should be noted that these findings are in line with those from network research (Podolny and Page, 1998, pp. 60–62; Scharpf, 1997, pp. 137–138).

Concerning the second category related to the technicality of the issue, a former health minister from a North American country asserted that TGNs are more effective "when the nature of the problem is very technical (push and pull factors) and when there is a very clear objective that involves affected countries" (Azar II, 2012). A scholar from the same region stated that TGNs are more effective when the situation is complex and "expertise intensive but where the expertise substantially lies within the State apparatus" (Avery, 2012). A health vice minister from North America mentioned that TGNs are more effective than IGOs "…[w]hen the threat has technical and political connotations" (Troy, 2012).

With regard to the third category (i.e., need for better communication), an experienced senior health civil servant who worked for a North American country and for the PAHO stated that TGNs are more effective than IGOs "when there is a need for better communication between the countries" (St. John, 2012). A former health vice minister from the same region who participated in the GHSI meetings underlined the importance of "getting the high-level decision makers to have face-to-face conversations" (Troy, 2012). Furthermore, a former health minister from North America maintained that TGNs are more effective than IGOs when there is a "[n]eed of secrecy (e.g., for dealing with terrorist information, national security information)" (Azar II, 2012). These remarks serve to illustrate condition 7a—that is, governments prefer to opt for a TGN when they fear high sovereignty costs and domestic opposition in order to escape public scrutiny.

The remaining informants pointed out other conditions, despite receiving few mentions, are nonetheless relevant for network theories and rational choices, such as membership, flexibility, and obligation. In this respect, a South American senior foreign relations civil servant who participated in the G20 meetings pointed out that TGNs are more effective than IGOs "when they are flexible, i.e., when there are no pre-established rules" (Soares Damico, 2017). Furthermore, a European health vice minister considered that TGNs are more effective "when countries are directly involved and when there is not broad involvement of other countries" (Ruocco, 2012). These arguments reinforce the need to prevent the admission of spoilers (condition 2).

5.7 Conclusion

Institutional design is deliberate, and TGNs in the biosecurity field are not an exception. Governments consciously select certain institutional features to achieve objectives that range from reacting rapidly to new problems (e.g., dealing with a new strain of a virus) to influencing international outcomes (e.g., modifying other institutions such as the IHR from 2005). They are, however, not homogeneous in their preferences, and senior health civil servants are aware of the alternatives they can employ when confronting epidemics. The selection of a particular institutional arrangement will depend on various factors, including a country's location, interests, values, capabilities, and scientific knowledge.

Although it is not possible to make generalizations with this sample, we can nonetheless make some inferences concerning the Americas. Within the biosecurity issue-area, North American governments will more likely opt for a TGN as a way of dealing with both epidemics (especially influenza) and biological terrorism (e.g., weaponized anthrax). A TGN is the ideal institutional arrangement for influencing international outcomes (e.g., reforming IGOs), evading domestic scrutiny, reacting rapidly, communicating freely and directly with peers, and excluding spoilers. In contrast, South American governments have a predilection for intergovernmental cooperation, adamantly refuse to securitize health, and are willing to knock on all doors to achieve their objectives. In North America, common interests, values, and geography drive cooperation in biosecurity, whereas in South America—at least when there is a confluence of left parties in power—ideology also plays a role in the formation of institutional arrangements (e.g., ISAGS-UNASUR). In South America, biological terrorism is neither a priority nor an area of concern. Rather, South American countries create organizations to increase universal health coverage, strengthen capacities, exchange knowledge, and deal with communicable and non-communicable diseases. Epidemics also play a role in their decisions regarding how to cooperate. This is particularly the case when it comes to tropical diseases such as cholera, yellow fever, dengue, chikungunya, or Zika virus disease, and this was evident recently during the Zika virus outbreak.

Despite regional preferences, when is transgovernmental cooperation better? In other words, under what conditions are TGNs more effective than IGOs for dealing with biosecurity threats? Almost one in two respondents (48.28%) considered that TGNs are more effective than IGOs when the network is small—consisting of 3 to 10 members. This helps us to understand why the GHSI, ranked as one of the most effective, has not expanded its membership. Besides small size, speed is another factor that policymakers consider when making decisions. Indeed, 37.93% of respondents regarded TGNs as more effective when speed is a priority. These results come as no surprise. Irrespective of the policy field, small size and speed are two of the most prominent characteristics associated with effective networks.

What is new is that despite their previous failures and drawbacks (e.g., the EVD epidemic in West Africa), policymakers considered TGNs to be more effective than IGOs when they collaborated with the WHO. In other words, respondents selected collaboration with the WHO as the third most important condition (34.48%) for TGNs to be effective. In this respect, ties between the GHSI, the BRICS Health Network, the FPGHI, and the WHO are particularly strong. The fourth condition respondents associated with effectiveness is common interests and values. In fact, almost one out of three respondents (31.03%) considered that TGNs are more effective when members have similar interests and values. According to the qualitative content analysis, common interests and values played a crucial role in the creation of the GHSI, whereas in the case of the BRICS Health Network, what cemented cooperation was not values but common interests. A fifth condition behind the effectiveness of networks is related to strong commitment and high capabilities (27.59%). Hence, if, as suggested by Fidler and Gostin (2008) we aim to replicate the design of the GHSI, we need to include some powerful and strongly committed states. The A(H1N1) pandemic and the NACOPBI are indicative in that respect (Avery, 2010).

In other respects, contrary to what rationalism would predict, and in line with other perspectives such as constructivism, we were surprised to find that for different reasons, policymakers from the north and the south of the continent alluded to trust and ideology, respectively, as reasons for creating or modifying institutional arrangements. Concerning trust, GHSI members frequently mentioned it as a characteristic of the network form and believed that it led to a high degree of compliance. Due to frequent and direct interactions, TGN members know their peers well and know they can count on them whatever the circumstance because, over the years, they have cultivated strong ties. Although their governments may change due to the technicalities of their field, they usually remain in office. Therefore, it would not be surprising if, over time, a convergence of interests transcends into a collective identity.

What is not so clear is whether, as Wendt (2001) and Bull (1977) claim, this scenario should be viewed the other way around—that is, the attainment of a certain level of collective identity precedes the rational design of institutions. Although, seemingly, ideology was not a factor influencing the design of TGNs in the biosecurity field, it was an important condition behind the creation of several IGOs in South America, irrespective of the issue area. A prominent example is UNASUR, which almost ceased to exist due to the accession of Bolsonaro to power but was reinvigorated in 2023 by Lula's and Fernandez's decisions to re-incorporate Brazil and Argentina into the regional organization. What this may imply is that although the institutional design is rational, there may be other variables contingent on the time or site that may explain the choice made by a government.

Although the focus of the study was on TGNs, we nonetheless decided to ask respondents to assess all organizations operating in the biosecurity field, irrespective of whether they were governmental or non-governmental. Since most interviewees were civil servants—except for two scholars—it was reasonable to expect them to align with the governmental view, which was what happened. Surprisingly, despite all criticism directed in the past years towards the WHO, almost 60% of respondents were of the view that IGOs are more effective for dealing with epidemics. The PAHO was rated as the most effective organization operating in Latin America. The reasons given by respondents for its effectiveness included its technical capacity, clear mandates, experience, financial resources, speed at exchanging information, linkages with other organizations, legitimacy, support from member countries, and negotiation capacity for reaching joint solutions. It was also ranked as the third most flexible organization and the second (after the WHO) in terms of learning speed. Thus, we can consider the PAHO to be successful because it reacts fast, communicates in a timely manner, prevents the dissemination of pathogenic microbes, and learns from past mistakes.

However, despite the fact that a significant majority support organizations such as the WHO, the World Bank, UNASUR, and so on, there are also voices that call for coordination between different organizations (29.17% of respondents) and those who suggest that TGNs such as the GHSI or the BRICS Health Network are more effective than IGOs (16.67%). Nevertheless, what is striking is that despite the leading role played by MSF during the Ebola epidemic in West Africa, only 1 out of 25 interviewees regarded NGOs as an integral part of a coordinated answer to epidemics. Finally, it is worth mentioning that as claimed by scholars such as Raustiala (2002), some of the interviewees regarded IGOs and TGNs as complementary.

References

Abbott, K. W. and Snidal, D. (2000) 'Hard and soft law in international governance', *International Organization*, 54 (3), pp. 421–456.

Amorim, C. (2018) Personal interview. Conducted by Octavio González Segovia on 3 March at Rio de Janeiro, Brazil.

Avery, D. (2010) 'The North American Plan for Avian and Pandemic Influenza: a case study of regional health security in the 21st century', *Global Health Governance*, 3 (2). Available at: https://www.ghgj.org/Avery_the%20North%20America%20plan%20for%20influenza.pdf (Accessed: 10 May 2023).

Avery, D. (2012) Personal interview. Conducted by Octavio González Segovia on 12 April at Toronto, Canada.

Azar II, A. (2012) Personal interview. Conducted by Octavio González Segovia on 10 April via Skype.

Bastug, A. and Bodur, H. (2015) 'Ebola viral disease: what should be done to combat the epidemic in 2014?', *Turkish Journal of Medical Sciences*, 45 (1), pp. 1–5.

Beingolea, L. (2018) Personal interview. Conducted by Octavio González Segovia on 7 February via Skype.

Bull, H. (1977) *The anarchical society: a study of order in world politics*. London: Macmillan.

Da Nobrega, F. (2017) Personal Interview. Conducted by Octavio González Segovia on 12 November at the Ministry of Foreign Affairs, Brasilia, Brazil.

Dallatomasina, S., Crestani, R., Sylvester Squire, J., Declerk, H., Caleo, G. M., Wolz, A. and Spreicher, A. (2015) 'Ebola outbreak in rural West Africa: epidemiology, clinical features and outcomes', *Tropical Medicine & International Health*, 20 (4), pp. 448–454.

Dobbin, F., Simmons, B. and Garrett, G. (2007) The Global Diffusion of Public Policies: Social Construction, Coercion, Competition, or Learning? *Annual Review of Sociology*, 33 (1), pp. 449–472.

Eilstrup-Sangiovanni, M. (2009) 'Varieties of cooperation. Government networks in international security', in: Kahler, M. (ed.), *Networked politics: agency, power, and governance*. Ithaca: Cornell University Press, pp. 194–227.

Engelhardt, R. (2012) Personal interview. Conducted by Octavio González Segovia on 15 April at the Ministry of Health, Ottawa, Canada.

Enserink, M. and Cohen, J. (2009) 'Virus of the year. The novel H1N1 influenza', *Science*, 326 (5960). Available at: https://pubmed.ncbi.nlm.nih.gov/20019257/ (Accessed: 10 May 2023).

Fidler, D. and Gostin, L. (2008) *Biosecurity in the global age: biological weapons, public health, and the rule of law*. Stanford: Stanford University Press.

Fineberg, H. (2014) 'Pandemic preparedness and response—lessons from the H1N1 influenza of 2009', *New England Journal of Medicine*, 370 (14), 1335–1342.

González, S. O. and Ébodé, A. (2020) 'A comparison of the institutional management of the H1N1 influenza pandemic and the Ebola virus disease epidemic in West Africa. Why we have not learned the lesson when preparing and responding to Public Health Emergency of International Concern?', *Face à face: Regards sur la santé*. Available at: https://journals.openedition.org/faceaface/1787?lang=en (Accessed: 10 May 2023).

Grépin, K. A. (2015) 'International donations to the Ebola virus outbreak: too little, too late?', *BMJ: British Medical Journal*, 350, pp. 1–5.

Hague, E. (2017) Personal interview. Conducted by Octavio González Segovia on 4 October at ISAGS, Rio de Janeiro, Brazil.

Heredia, N. (2018) Personal interview. Conducted by Octavio González Segovia on 7 February via Skype.

Heymann, D. L., Chen, L., Takemi, K., Fidler, D. P., Tappero, J. W., Thomas, M. J. and Kalache, A. (2015) 'Global health security: the wider lessons from the west African Ebola virus disease epidemic', *The Lancet*, 385 (9980), pp. 1884–1901.

Hoffman, S. J. and Silverberg, S. L. (2018) 'Delays in global disease outbreak responses: lessons from H1N1, Ebola, and Zika', *American Journal of Public Health*, 108 (3), pp. 329–333.

Kahler, M. (2009) 'Networked politics. Agency, power, and governance', in Kahler, M. (ed.), *Networked politics: agency, power, and governance*. Ithaca: Cornell University Press, pp. 1–20.

Kalra, S., Kelkar, D., Galwankar, S. C., Papadimos, T. J., Stawicki, S. P., Arquilla, B., Hoey, B. A., Sharpe, R. P., Sabol, D. and Jahre, J. A. (2014) 'The emergence of Ebola as a global health security threat: from "Lessons Learned" to coordinated multilateral containment efforts', *Journal of Global Infectious Diseases*, 6 (4), pp. 164–177.

Keohane, R. O. (1984) *After hegemony: Cooperation and discord in the world political economy*. Princeton: Princeton University Press.

Keohane, R. O. and Nye, J. (1974) 'Transgovernmental relations and international organizations', *World Politics: A Quarterly Journal of International Relations*, 27 (1), p. 39–62.

Koremenos, B., Lipson, C. and Snidal, D. (2001) 'The rational design of international institutions', *International Organization*, 55 (4), pp. 761–799.

Lawlley, S. (2012) Personal interview. Conducted by Octavio González Segovia on 15 April at the Ministry of Health, Ottawa, Canada.

López Gatell, H. (2012) Personal interview. Conducted by Octavio González Segovia on 16 May via Skype.

Levitt, B. and March, J. G. (1988) 'Organizational learning', *Annual Review of Sociology*, 14 (1), pp. 319–338.

Lipson, C. (1991) 'Why are some international agreements informal?', *International Organization*, 45 (4), pp. 495–538.

Marchiori Buss, P. (2017) Personal interview. Conducted by Octavio González Segovia on 13 November at the Oswaldo Cruz Foundation (Fio Cruz), Rio de Janeiro, Brazil.

Marchiori Buss, P. and Tobar, S. (2021) *Salud global y diplomacia de la salud. Una visión desde América Latina y el Caribe*. Brussels: Ediciones Alasag. Available at: https://www.orasconhu.org/sites/default/files/Salud%20Global%20y%20Diplomacia%20en%20Salud.pdf (Accessed: 10 May 2023).

Peeri, N. C., Shrestha, N., Rahman, M. S., Zaki, R., Tan, Z., Bibi, S., Baghbanzadeh, M., Aghamohammadi, N., Zhang, W. and Haque, U. (2020) 'The SARS, MERS and novel coronavirus (COVID-19) epidemics, the newest and biggest global health threats: what lessons have we learned?', *International Journal of Epidemiology*, 49 (3), pp. 717–726.

Phelan, A. L., Katz, R. and Gostin, L.O. (2020) 'The novel coronavirus originating in Wuhan, China: challenges for global health governance', *Journal of the American Medical Association*, 323 (8), pp. 709–710.

Podolny, J. and Page, K. L. (1998) 'Network forms of organization', *Annual Review of Sociology*, 24, pp. 57–76.

Pollack, M. (2005) 'The New Transatlantic Agenda at Ten: reflections on an experiment in international governance', *Journal of Common Market Studies*, 43 (5), pp. 899–919.

Pollack, M. and Shaffer, G. (2001) *Transatlantic governance in the global economy*. Lanham: Rowman & Littlefield.

Popic, T. and Moise, A. D. (2022) 'Government responses to the COVID-19 pandemic in eastern and Western Europe: the role of health, political and economic factors', *East European Politics*, 38 (4), pp. 507–528.

Rajan, R. and Topp, S. M. (2022) 'Accountability mechanisms of inquiries and investigations into Australian governments' responses to the COVID-19 pandemic', *Australian and New Zealand Journal of Public Health*, 46 (4), pp. 488–494.

Rathbun, B. (2011) 'Before hegemony: generalized trust and the creation and design of international security organizations', *International Organization*, 65 (2), pp. 243–273.

Raustiala, K. (2002) 'The architecture of international cooperation: transgovernmental networks and the future of international law', *Virginia Journal of International Law*, 43 (1), pp. 1–92.

Ravi, S. J., Snyder, M. R. and Rivers, C. (2019) 'Review of international efforts to strengthen the global outbreak response system since the 2014–16 West Africa Ebola Epidemic', *Health Policy and Planning*, 34 (1), pp. 47–54.

Rigoli, F. (2017) Personal interview. Conducted by Octavio González Segovia on 4 October at ISAGS, Rio de Janeiro, Brazil.

Ringe, N. and Rennó, L. (2023) *Populists and the pandemic: how populists around the world responded to COVID-19*. New York: Routledge.

Roldán, E. (2017) Personal interview. Conducted by Octavio González Segovia on 17 May via Skype.

Ruocco, G. (2012) Personal interview. Conducted by Octavio González Segovia on 17 September via Skype.

Sánchez Otero, L. (2018) Personal interview. Conducted by Octavio González Segovia on 15 March via Skype.

Scharpf, F. (1997) *Games real actors play: actor-centered institutionalism in policy research*. Boulder: Westview Press.

González Segovia, O. M. (2020) *When can we expect States to select a transgovernmental network instead of an intergovernmental organization to effectively deal with biosecurity threats?*, June 5, PhD Thesis at the Autonomous University of Baja California. Available at: https://repositorioinstitucional.uabc.mx/server/api/core/bitstreams/cba7c3ab-075f-406c-9526-4abdc419854d/content (Accessed 20 May 2023).

Slaughter, A. M. (1997) 'The real new world order', *Foreign Affairs*, 76 (5), pp. 183–193.

Slaughter, A. M. (2003) 'Global government networks, global information agencies and disaggregated democracy', *Michigan Journal of International Law*, 24 (4), pp. 1041–1076.

Slaughter, A. M. (2004) 'Disaggregated sovereignty: towards the public accountability of global government networks', *Government and Opposition*, 39 (2), pp. 159–190.

Soares Damico, F. (2017) Personal interview. Conducted by Octavio González Segovia on 15 November via Skype.

St. John, R. (2012) Personal interview. Conducted by Octavio González Segovia on 13 April at Toronto, Canada.

Tobar, S. (2017) Personal interview. Conducted by Octavio González Segovia on 13 November at the Oswaldo Cruz Foundation (Fio Cruz), Rio de Janeiro, Brazil.

Troy, T. (2012) Personal interview. Conducted by Octavio González Segovia on 6 April at Washington, D.C.

Vance, K. (2017) Personal interview. Conducted by Octavio González Segovia on 4 October at ISAGS, Rio de Janeiro, Brazil.

Vetter, P., Dayer, J., Schibler, M., Allegranzi, B., Brown, D., Calmy, A., Christie, D., Eremin, S., Hagon, O., Henderson, D., Iten, A., Kelley, E., Marais, F., Ndoye, B., Pugin, J., Robert-Nicoud, H., Sterk, E., Tapper, M., Siegrist, C. A., Kaiser, L. and Pittet, D. (2016) 'The 2014–2015 Ebola outbreak in West Africa: hands on', *Antimicrobial Resistance & Infection Control*, 5, pp. 1–17.

Wendt, A. (2001) 'Driving with the rearview mirror: on the rational science of institutional design', *International Organization*, 55 (4), pp. 1019–1049.

World Health Organization (2016) *International health regulations*. Available at: https://www.who.int/publications/i/item/9789241580496 (Accessed: 14 May 2023).

World Health Organization (2021) *Report of the review committee on the functioning of the international health regulations (2005) during the COVID-19 response*. Available at: https://www.who.int/publications/m/item/a74-9-who-s-work-in-health-emergencies (Accessed: 10 May 2023).

Youde, J. (2018) *Global health governance in international society*. Oxford: Oxford University Press.

Chapter 6

The impact of COVID-19 on the national power of Latin American countries

Daniel Morales Ruvalcaba
Sun Yat-sen University, China

Abstract

This chapter provides comprehensive analysis of the impact that the COVID-19 pandemic had on the national power of Latin American countries, accounting for a wide range of factors. It employs the World Power Index (WPI), which measures the national power of a country based on 18 indicators, organized along 3 dimensions: material, semi-material, and immaterial. The chapter compares 2020 WPI values with those from the pre-pandemic years to measure the impact of COVID-19 on the 14 best-positioned Latin American countries in the international geostructure. It categorizes them according to the extent that their national power changed, arguing that some countries, such as Guatemala and Ecuador, were less affected, others such as Argentina, Brazil, and Venezuela, saw a significant decrease in their national power. The analysis highlights not only the multidimensionality of the crisis caused by COVID-19 and its heterogeneous impact on Latin American countries but also underscores the resilience and effective government responses of some nations in the face of the region's most significant crisis in the last decades.

Keywords: Latin America, COVID-19, national power, World Power Index, multidimensional impact, international geostructure

***

6.1 Introduction

Between 12 and 29 December 2019, China reported several cases of a new and rare flu that was spreading through its population. Then, in January 2020, China announced that the pneumonia cases were 'atypical', as the symptoms did not correspond with any known type of Severe Acute Respiratory Syndrome (SARS) or Middle East Respiratory Syndrome (MERS). This quickly alerted not only the

World Health Organization (WHO), but also the health authorities of various national governments.

Later in January 2020, the new virus was identified as COVID-19. But throughout the month, there was a lack of consensus among WHO specialists about the magnitude of the virus. Despite all the actions taken, the virus multiplied and spread across the globe. During the last week of February and the first days of March 2020, COVID-19 reached Latin America:

- On 26 February, Brazilian authorities reported the presence of COVID-19 in a 61-year-old man;
- On 29 February, Mexico announced the infection of a 35-year-old man who had recently been in Italy; meanwhile, Ecuador reported its first case in a woman who had returned from Spain;
- On 1 March, the Dominican Republic confirmed its first case of COVID-19 in a 62-year-old Italian tourist;
- On 3 March, Argentina and Chile reported their first cases of COVID-19: for the former, it was a man who had returned from a stay in Italy and, for the latter, a 33-year-old man who had travelled through Southeast Asia, especially Singapore;
- On 6 March, the virus was detected in several countries in the region: in Peru, it was a 25-year-old man who had been travelling in Europe; in Colombia, it was a 19-year-old student who had returned from Italy; and in Costa Rica, it was a 49-year-old American tourist.

When it reached Haiti on 20 March, the virus was present in every country in the region. Under the recommendation of the WHO, all countries implemented physical distancing and isolation measures; this time has been called the Great Lockdown. Thus, 2020 is a milestone in recent history, not only because of the millions of COVID-19 infections and the loss of millions of lives but also because of the economic consequences and shifts in human activity.

There is no doubt that the COVID-19 pandemic impacted the entire Latin American region. But what effect did it have on the national power of Latin American countries? Which national capacities were most affected in the region? Did COVID-19 decrease the relevance of Latin America within the international geostructure of power?

This chapter will argue that COVID-19 had profound effects on all human activities. It is, therefore, impossible to observe its impact using only the number of deaths and illnesses or the drop in gross domestic product (GDP). These indicators are important but insufficient. To better understand the impact of COVID-19 on national power, I use the World Power Index (WPI). This index measures the national power of a country based on 18 indicators that are organized along 3 dimensions—material, semi-material, and immaterial. In this research, the effects of COVID-19 in Latin America are analysed using each of these dimensions of national power, comparing the 2020 WPI values with those from the pre-pandemic years. The results of this research will facilitate an understanding of the multidimensional impact of COVID-19 on the region and the development of public policies that help reduce the negative effects on the national power of Latin American countries.

This chapter is organized into two parts. First, the impact of COVID-19 on the different dimensions of national power (material, semi-material, and immaterial) is analysed to determine which national capacities were most affected. In the second part, using the WPI, I review the evolution of national power in 14 Latin American countries during the pandemic.

6.2 Impact of COVID-19 on the material capacities of Latin American countries

The COVID-19 pandemic caused a crisis in Latin America, with repercussions in at least three important areas: health, economy, and society. Therefore, evaluating the impact of the pandemic on the national power of states requires a broad and comprehensive approach. Consequently, national power is observed as a multivariate and multidimensional phenomenon. To proceed methodically, the guidelines provided by the WPI were followed.

The WPI is the numerical expression of the accumulation of national capacities that a state possesses to exercise its power in the international system (Rocha Valencia and Morales Ruvalcaba, 2018, pp. 159–163). The WPI is an integration of three sub-indexes—the Material Capacities Index (MCI), Semi-material Capacities Index (SMCI), and Immaterial Capacities Index (IMCI)—which measure specific dimensions of national power.

Although some critics argue that the WPI considers a relatively small number of indicators, which may limit its accuracy, the strength of the index lies in that it provides measurements for more than 180 countries and accumulates data from almost 5 decades (from 1975 to 2021). Compared to other national power measurement tools, such as the Composite Indicator of National Capability (CINC) and Asia Power Index (API), the WPI is useful for analysing states at the bottom of the international geostructure. In summary, the WPI will help provide a comprehensive and multidimensional understanding of the impact of COVID-19 on the national power of states in Latin America.

In the realist paradigm, national power is directly related to the state's ability to attack, defend, or prevent its internal disintegration by force (Morgenthau, 1960; Waltz, 1979; Del Arenal, 1983; Rocha Valencia and Morales Ruvalcaba, 2018). Historically, the elements necessary to exercise coercion are economic, militaristic, financial, industrial, and technological in nature; these are material capacities. In other words, military-economic power, also called "hard power", is a material capability which can be measured using the MCI, which is part of the WPI. The impact of COVID-19 on the material capacities of Latin American countries is considered here through the six indicators that make up the MCI: national production, territory, trade, finance, defence, and research. Of these indicators, only five will be analysed because there were no alterations to territorial borders during the pandemic.

National production: The repercussions of COVID-19 on national production in Latin American countries were the worst worldwide. As can be seen in Table 1.1, the 2020 drop in GDP in Latin America was not only twice the average world, but also the largest among developing economies.

Table 6.1. Real gross domestic product (percentage change from the previous year)

Region	2019	2020	2021
World	+2.6%	−3.3%	+5.7%
Advanced economies	+1.7%	−4.6%	+5.1%
Emerging and developing economies	+3.8%	−1.6%	+6.6%
- East Asia and the Pacific	+5.8%	1.2%	+7.2%
- Europe and Central Asia	+2.7%	−1.9%	+6.5%
- Latin America and the Caribbean	+0.8%	−6.4%	+6.7%
- Middle East and North Africa	+0.9%	−3.7%	+3.4%
- South Asia	+4.1%	−4.5%	+7.6%
- Sub-Saharan Africa	+2.6%	−2.0%	+4.2%

Source: Created by the author; based on data from the World Bank, 2022b, p. 4.

From a historical point of view, it is important to note that the largest falls in Latin American regional GDP were −4.5% in 1983 because of the debt crisis and −3.0% in 2009 due to the United States subprime mortgage crisis. Evidently, the contraction of −6.4% in 2020 due to COVID-19 is by far the largest drop in the economic activity in Latin America since The World Bank has been keeping track. However, the impact of the crises in the region has been heterogeneous, as Table 6.2 shows. In some countries, the economic repercussions of the Great Lockdown were relatively minor; these included Paraguay, Guatemala, Nicaragua, St Vincent and the Grenadines, and Haiti. However, some nations were more severely affected, reporting economic contractions greater than 10% of the GDP; these include most members of the Caribbean Community (CARICOM) members, Panama, Peru, and Cuba.

Table 6.2. Annual growth rate of the total GDP in 2020

Region	Country	Percentage
South America	Venezuela	−30.0
	Peru	−11.0
	Argentina	−9.9
	Bolivia	−8.8
	Ecuador	−7.8
	Colombia	−6.8
	Uruguay	−5.9
	Chile	−5.8
	Brazil	−3.9
	Paraguay	−0.6
Mesoamerica, Cuba, and the Dominican Republic	Panama	−17.9
	Cuba	−10.9
	Honduras	−9.0
	Mexico	−8.2
	El Salvador	−7.9
	Dominican Republic	−6.7
	Costa Rica	−4.1
	Nicaragua	−2.0
	Guatemala	−1.5
CARICOM members	St Lucia	−20.4
	Antigua and Barbuda	−20.2
	Belize	−16.7
	Dominica	−16.6
	Suriname	−15.9
	The Bahamas	−14.5
	St Kitts and Nevis	−14.4
	Barbados	−14.0
	Grenada	−13.8
	Trinidad and Tobago	−7.4
	Jamaica	−5.3
	St Vincent and the Grenadines	−3.3
	Haiti	−3.3
	Guyana	+43.5
	Montserrat	0.0
Latin America and the Caribbean		−6.4

Source: Created by the author; based on data from CEPAL (2022a, p. 32) and the IMF (2022).

The COVID-19 pandemic revealed the enormous vulnerability of the region, made up of peripheral and semi-peripheral countries, in the face of a complex global crisis. It should be noted that, by the end of 2022, half the countries in the region had still not managed to raise their GDPs to pre-pandemic levels.

Trade: Although world trade had already begun slowing down in 2018, as a result of the trade war between China and the USA, initiated by then-President Donald Trump, the COVID-19 crisis had a more negative impact on it. In 2020, the pandemic caused a contraction of –5.3% of commercial activity worldwide (WTO, 2021). However, the consequences in Latin America were different for each country, depending on its export matrix.

The products least affected by the pandemic were those from the agricultural sector: "the prices of soybeans, corn, and wheat fell by up to 4%, and the prices of beef and chicken decreased by 6%" (CEPAL, 2020a, p. 12). However, the prices of minerals (such as iron ore, copper ore, zinc, and aluminium, among others) were greatly impacted. These minerals ceased to be globally consumed once their supply chain flows were interrupted; however, the prices of these products rapidly rebounded when supply chains were reactivated in the second half of 2020. Finally, the prices of hydrocarbons fell to historic levels as the implementation of quarantines around the world caused a contraction in their demand of 30%. This sparked a "price war" in March 2020 between Saudi Arabia and Russia due to their disagreements about reducing production and adjusting prices. As a consequence, during the Great Lockdown, the price of a barrel of oil fell to such an extent that West Texas Intermediate (WTI) reached, on 20 April, a value of –$36. In the case of Latin America, Mexican oil closed at –$2.37 on 19 April 2020 (Banco de México, 2022) and averaged $12.23 in April 2020, the lowest in the last decade (CEFP, 2022).

According to an index of exports of goods prepared by CEPAL (2022b, p. 239), countries that did not experience decreases in 2020 were Guatemala, Nicaragua, and Costa Rica. This is because their economies mainly focus on the export of agricultural products. Countries with moderate falls included Chile, the Dominican Republic, Ecuador, Mexico, Argentina, Brazil, and Peru since these ones export large quantities of minerals as well as agricultural products (and oil in the case of Ecuador). Lastly, countries with the greatest drops in exports were Paraguay, Haiti, Bolivia, Panama, and Colombia, where oil or gas features significantly in the country's trade.

Reserves: As a result of the abrupt and widespread interruption of global production, many companies were hit hard, reporting losses that impacted the stock markets. In March 2020, some of the biggest falls were recorded in the Latin American and world stock markets.

Stock market crashes and an increase in volatility which reached historic levels produced massive capital outflows and, correspondingly, a devaluation of the main Latin American currencies. As can be seen in Figure 1.1, the currency that was least affected by the COVID-19 pandemic was the Chilean peso—at the end of 2020, it had a higher value against the dollar than at the beginning. The currencies of Colombia, Mexico, Costa Rica, Peru, the Dominican

Republic, Paraguay, and Uruguay were moderately affected, having experienced strong devaluations between March and May 2020. But their values stabilized in the following months. Finally, the Brazilian real and Argentine peso underwent the steepest falls in 2020.

Figure 6.1 Variation of the currencies of Latin America and the Caribbean against the US dollar, December 2019–December 2020

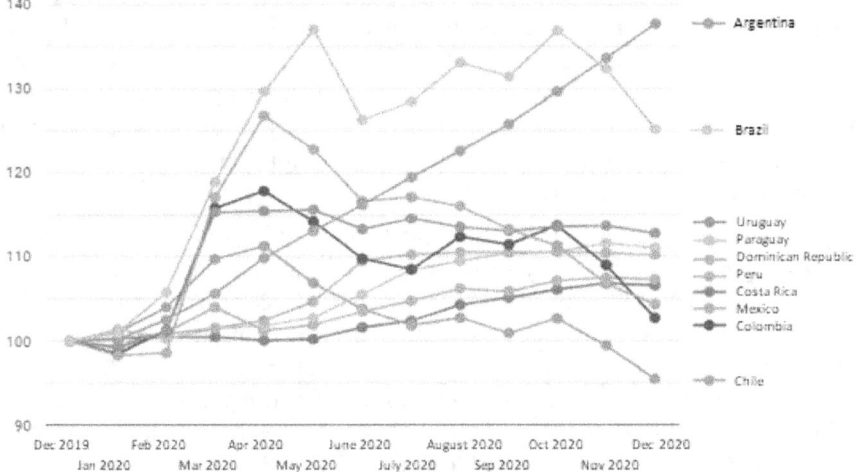

Source: Created by the author; based on Arias and Salazar (2021)

Due to the threat that COVID-19 posed to national finances, CEPAL warned that:

> expansive monetary policies will not be enough; central banks will need to intervene directly to provide the liquidity needed by the financial and private non-financial sectors, in particular to ensure full liquidity of the overnight bank lending market and to avoid disruption of payment chains. (CEPAL, 2020a, p. 14)

Indeed, Latin American governments had to increase their public spending to avoid a further drop in the economy and, although this caused the international reserves of some countries—such as Argentina, Costa Rica, Chile, El Salvador, Brazil, and Bolivia—to fall, the region as a whole achieved an increase. Between 2019 and 2020, reserves rose from $852.2 to $891.6 billion (CEPAL, 2020a, p. 3).

Military: The need to maintain physical distancing led various governments to impose curfews and states of exception, with Ecuador, Costa Rica, Honduras, Panama, Paraguay, Peru, and the Dominican Republic being some of the most striking cases in Latin America. In fact, various academics have observed militaristic responses to COVID-19 and, in some cases, a tendency for governments to violate certain human rights (Passos and Acácio, 2021; Passos, 2021; Robledo,

2022). However, they also found it unlikely that such activities would damage the democratic relations between civil society and the military once the pandemic was over (Herrera and Croissant, 2022; Acácio et al., 2022). But did the military spending of the countries undergo changes?

In one of its first assessments of the issue, the Stockholm International Peace Research Institute (SIPRI) declared that, although the impact of the COVID-19 pandemic on military spending would become clearer in the coming years, four major trends can already be formulated: 1) there was a reduction or diversion of military spending to deal with the pandemic; 2) military spending was linked to economic recovery and, therefore, increasing it became a part of financial stimulus packages; 3) most states increased their military spending in 2020; and 4) military personnel were deployed to support COVID-19 responses and containment efforts (SIPRI, 2021a, p. 12).

Although the participation of the military in containing the spread of COVID-19 was highly visible, "military spending in South America fell by 2.1% in 2020, to $43.5 billion" (SIPRI, 2021b, p. 7). Meanwhile, in Central America and the Caribbean it "was almost unchanged in 2020, with a minor 0.2% decrease to $8.6 billion, [and] Mexico's military spending was stable in 2020, at $6.1 billion" (SIPRI, 2021b, p. 7). However, the greatest impact of the pandemic on military spending was recorded in 2021—compared to the previous year, most countries made significant cuts, the most notable being Peru, Brazil, Argentina, and Chile.

Research: Despite the strong heterogeneity in the number of resources allocated to research and development (R&D) in Latin American countries, according to UNESCO, "since 2015, there has been little change of note in the governance of national innovation systems. New institutions designed to consolidate these systems have not managed to thrive in the face of political instability. Research budgets have been shrinking" (Dutrénit et al., 2021, p. 230). Indeed, Latin America and the Caribbean is a region that not only has difficulties in the management and promotion of R&D activities but that is also weighed down by a historic lag in financing; since 2000, spending in this area has remained in the range of 0.5–0.8% of the regional GDP (World Bank, 2022c).

In recent years, investments in R&D have been declining in several countries in the region. For instance, in 2020, Brazil allocated the smallest budget in more than a decade to its Ministry of Science, Technology and Innovation. Mexico reduced its CONACYT budget by 9% in 2019. And Chile, where although R&D investment has remained steady at around 0.3% for a decade, reduced the degree of its participation during 2019 and 2020. Given this adverse outlook, a gradual increase in R&D in the region is urgently needed and, above all, as Alicia Bárcena said, it is necessary to "bring science, technology and innovation closer to the productive sectors" (De Oliveira and Marques, 2020, p. 36). That is, countries must bring R&D closer to the real and urgent health needs of their populations.

6.3 Impact on the semi-material capacities of Latin American countries

In the neo-Marxist paradigm, national power is related to a state's ability to distribute wealth to the entire population, extend welfare to all social groups, and promote collective well-being (Callinicos, 2007; Bidet, 2011; Rocha Valencia and Morales Ruvalcaba, 2018). Traditionally, some of the elements that reflect the quality of life and well-being of a national society are related to individual production and consumption capacity, the educational level of the population, and access to basic services such as healthcare, energy, and water, among others. However, in capitalist or communist societies alike, ensuring general welfare requires solid and functioning institutions. This is why welfare can be called "socio-institutional power" or "boost power" since it encompasses hard power and soft power, promoting society as a whole. The boost power thus exists in semi-material capacities, which can be measured through the SMCI, a part of the WPI. The impact of COVID-19 on the semi-material capacities of Latin American countries is presented here through the six elements that make up the SMCI: population size, individual productivity, levels of product and service consumption, energy consumption, education, and health. For this study, the energy consumption variable has been discarded, as research suggests that, although there was a drastic decrease in consumption between April and June 2020 due to the Great Lockdown, by September of the same year, there was a recovery to pre-pandemic levels, (Buechler et al., 2022; Xu et al., 2021; IEA, 2021).

Population: Despite its huge impact on the economy and people's health, COVID-19 fortunately did not have much higher lethality than other pandemics such as the Black Death in the mid-fourteenth century (the most devastating in history), the Justinianic plague in the sixth century, smallpox in the first half of the sixteenth century, the influenza pandemic between 1918–1920 (commonly known as the Spanish flu), and even the global epidemic of HIV-AIDS, ongoing since the 1980s. Still, the human losses have been enormous. According to the WHO, which has been monitoring COVID-19 infections, by the end of 2022, there had been 6.6 million deaths from the disease (WHO, 2022).

When breaking down the figure by region, it is clear that, from the start of the pandemic to 31 December 2021, "Latin America and the Caribbean ha[d] the highest number of reported COVID-19 deaths of any region in the world" (CEPAL, 2022c, p. 18), with 1.5 million deaths. This figure is extremely alarming since this region accounted for 28.8% of the deaths worldwide. Meanwhile, the population of Latin America and the Caribbean represents only 8.4% of the world's population. Furthermore, according to the Johns Hopkins Coronavirus

Resource Center, Brazil was, until December 2022, the second country (after the USA) with the highest number of deaths from COVID-19, with just over 691,000 deaths. Mexico stood in fifth place with 330,000 deaths, while Peru recorded the highest number of deaths per 100,000 inhabitants worldwide—660.73 (Johns Hopkins University & Medicine, 2022).

Although the number of deaths fell significantly in 2022, the impact of COVID-19 on the general well-being of the Latin American population will be long-lasting. According to the United Nations Economic Commission for Latin America and the Caribbean (ECLAC); the life expectancy at birth in Latin America has decreased by almost three years as a result of the pandemic (CEPAL, 2022d).

GDP per capita: In terms of per capita production, the consequences of the pandemic for Latin America were dismal in 2020 as GDP per capita declined by 16.28% from 2019; according to 2021 and 2022 data, the level of GDP per capita is still below USD 9,000, which means that the level of economic development continues to remain at pre-2010 levels (World Bank, 2022a; 2022b). Moreover, growth and productivity growth are projected to decline, with an impact in terms of lower potential growth" (OECD, 2021, p. 27). The risk of a new lost decade like the 1980s is latent.

Nevertheless, it is necessary to point out the variable impact of the COVID-19 pandemic on per capita production. Some activities were directly affected, especially those "related to tourism (airlines, accommodation, restaurants and hotels), trade and the manufacturing industry, as well as real estate and administrative activities" (CEPAL and OIT, 2020, p. 8). Others continued with a relatively low impact, especially those that could dispense with the physical presence of employees and make use of information and communication technologies (ICT)

Consumption: The drop in global production had a negative impact on household consumption. In some countries, this was further aggravated by labour informality in which workers are two times more likely to enter non-contractual employment relations, which means they lack benefits or social protection. In the case of Latin America and the Caribbean, "in 2019, one in two employed people was in informal conditions. At the beginning of the crisis, the informality rate fell since the loss of this type of job was enormous" (OIT, 2021, p. 7). This has been unprecedented in the recent history of the region.

Faced with the impossibility of working to generate income in an ordinary way due to the restrictions imposed by the Great Lockdown, Latin American people struggled. Therefore, the governments had to make economic interventions—they made emergency transfers that benefited 326 million people (CEPAL, 2021a, p. 24). However, this did not prevent the number of people living in poverty from increasing by 22 million at the regional level to 209 million (33.7% of the population), and the number living in extreme poverty from growing by 8 million to 78 million (12.5% of the population) (CEPAL, 2021a, p. 20).

Education: As part of the strategies to contain the spread of COVID-19, the governments of many countries decided to temporarily close educational institutions starting in the second quarter of 2020. According to UNESCO data, 1.5 billion students were affected in the world (UNESCO, 2020), and the impact was disproportionately large in developing regions, where the availability of technology and the internet connection speed lag behind. In the case of Latin American countries, "face-to-face classes were totally or partially interrupted for 70 school weeks in the period from February 2020 to March 2022. [...] This represents a fairly extended period, even more so considering that the global average was 41 weeks" (Huepe et al., 2002, p. 13). The impact of this interruption was enormous, with huge economic costs, losses in learning, and increases in school dropouts.

Regarding the resources allocated to education, according to CEPAL and UNESCO, spending in this area would have increased by 3.9% from 2019 to 2020. However, due to the pandemic, the opposite occurred, with the expenditure contracting by approximately 9% in 2020 (CEPAL and UNESCO, 2020, p. 17).

Health: According to estimates, public spending on health in Latin America was 7.9% of the region's GDP in 2019 (World Bank, 2022c). This coincides with the 6% recommended by the WHO. However, the pandemic revealed weak health systems, with little universal coverage for the population.

After the waves of infections in Europe and the USA, the new global epicentre of the pandemic became Latin America, which registered the largest number of cases in the world between June and August 2020. By the end of 2022, Latin American countries had recorded more than 80 million cases of COVID-19 and, above all, the highest number of deaths by region (WHO, 2022). Evidently, the health systems in the region need to be strengthened in the rest of the 2020s. However, governments might continue to limit their spending due to the increase in public debt in 2020.

6.4 Impact of COVID-19 on the immaterial capacities of Latin American countries

For liberals, national power is related to a country's ability to generate adherents, shape the international agenda, and influence international organizations (Keohane and Nye, 1989; Lake, 2009; Rocha Valencia and Morales Ruvalcaba, 2018). Commonly, the elements that allow for this are related to the image of a national government, the export of cultural values, and cultural appeal, among others. Thus, the communication and cultural power, also called "soft power", reflects immaterial capacities. This power can be measured using the ICI, which is part of the WPI. This section examines the impact of COVID-19 using the six elements that make up the ICI: public expenditure, tourism, official development assistance, telecommunications, international immigrants, and academic production. Of these, the migration variable has been omitted since the restrictions on international mobility imposed by the Great Lockdown prevented significant changes to this indicator.

Public expenditure: The emergency transfers made by Latin American governments not only helped prevent poverty and extreme poverty rates from growing further in 2020, rising by 3.5% and 2.3%, respectively but also contributed to the Gini Index growing by only 2.9% (OECD, 2021, p. 70). However, to achieve this, the public spending of all the countries in the region increased significantly: according to estimates, "the level of spending reached 24.7% of GDP in 2020 compared to 21.4% of GDP in 2019" (CEPAL, 2021a, p. 16). The increase in public spending was aimed at boosting two factors corresponding to semi-material capacities: household consumption and production and national health systems. However, along with the increase in spending, most countries in the region experienced historic contractions in their tax revenues in 2020. All this contributed to an increase in public debt, from "68.9% to 79.3% of [the] GDP between 2019 and 2020 at the regional level, making Latin America and the Caribbean the most indebted region in the developing world" (CEPAL, 2021b, p. 3). For this reason, despite the fact that public spending was able to cushion the effects of the pandemic during 2020, the countries of Latin America and the Caribbean will have to deal, in the first five years of the 2020s, with the complicated challenge of indebtedness.

Tourism: Tourism not only contributes to spreading the image of the region throughout the world but is also one of the key economic sectors for the generation of foreign exchange in Latin America. However, the COVID-19 pandemic caused a drastic drop, both in the arrival of international tourists and in the income generated. Some of the most affected countries were in the Caribbean, where the share of tourism in the GDP before the pandemic was more than 25% for the majority of nations. Meanwhile, in the cases of Antigua and Barbuda, St Lucia, the Bahamas, and Grenada, tourism accounted for more than 40% of the GDP (CEPAL, 2020b, p. 2). The interruption of tourism activity in 2020 helps explain the abrupt drop of more than 10% in the GDP of most CARICOM members (Table 6.2). In addition to these, other countries whose tourist income was strongly affected by the pandemic were Panama, Colombia, Peru, and Argentina. However, Mexico was positioned as a preferred destination for international tourists in 2020 due to the laxity of its measures to deal with COVID-19.

Official development assistance: As part of collective efforts to deal with the COVID-19 pandemic, many countries increased their official development assistance (ODA) grants. In recent years, the ODA received by Latin American countries has represented around 7% of the total; in per capita terms, the average during the 2010s fluctuated between $40 and $90. However, during the pandemic, the ODA in Latin America rose significantly, from $88 per capita in 2019 to $132 in 2020, which represented an increase of 50%. The pandemic has revealed the enormous vulnerability and dependence of some countries on foreign aid, especially Caribbean and Central American countries, which reported the largest increases in the region.

Telecommunications: Telecommunications played a fundamental role in mitigating the impact of the Great Lockdown on the daily activities of society, especially in work and education. However, although globally speaking, Latin America is at an intermediate level (compared to other countries) in terms of the development of telecommunications, the pandemic brought to light the inequalities within the countries of the region. Indeed, approximately 33% of the population lacks internet or has limited access. The main lag is observed in rural areas and among the elderly—"67% of urban households are connected to the Internet, in contrast to 23% in rural areas. The very young (5 to 12 years old) and adults over 65 are the ones with the least connectivity" (Finquelievich, 2020).

Academic production: According to the SCImago Lab databases, in 2019, 4.34 million scientific documents were produced worldwide (SCImago, 2022a). Of these, 185,232 documents, representing 4.2% of the total, were prepared in the countries of Latin America and the Caribbean. Despite the limitations imposed by the pandemic, the production of scientific documents in 2020 increased to 4.59 million worldwide (SCImago, 2022b). Latin American countries also increased their production and contribution—they published 202,981 documents, which represented 4.4% of the total. The main countries invested in scientific production in the region continued to be Brazil, Mexico, Chile, Argentina, and Colombia, in that order.

6.5 Effects on the national power of Latin American countries in 2020

In a preliminary assessment of the impact of the COVID-19 pandemic, José Antonio Ocampo (2020, p. 61) predicted that "Brazil and Chile would be the least affected countries among the medium and large ones in the region, but [that] there are several smaller economies that would have fewer contractions in their activity economic". But can these economic conclusions be extrapolated to national capacities? The objective of this section is to measure how the COVID-19 pandemic affected the national power of Latin American countries.

Table 6.3 below presents an overview of the geostructure of all 33 countries that make up Latin America and the Caribbean, listing the ranking of each one. However, for reasons of space, the following discussion is further narrowed down only to the 14 states which have the greatest power in the region according to the WPI for 2021.

Table 6.3. Geostructure of Latin America, with categories and positions of states as of 2021

State categorization	Country	Regional ranking*
Regional powers	Brazil	1
	Mexico	2
	Argentina	3
Secondary semi-peripheral states	Chile	4
	Uruguay	7
Subregional powers	Colombia	5
	Venezuela	14
Middle peripheral states	Peru	6
	Cuba	8
	Ecuador	9
	Costa Rica	10
	Dominican Republic	11
	Panama	12
	Guatemala	13
Minor peripheral states	Trinidad and Tobago	15
	Paraguay	16
	Bolivia	17
	El Salvador	18
	Bahamas	19
	Honduras	20
	Jamaica	21
	Nicaragua	22
Subperipheral states	Guyana	23
	Barbados	24
	Haiti	25
	Suriname	26
	Antigua and Barbuda	27
	Belize	28
	St Lucia	29
	St Kitts and Nevis	30
	Grenada	31
	St Vincent and the Grenadines	32
	Dominica	33

Source: Created by the author; based on data from the WPI (2023).

This section includes an analysis of the 14 Latin American countries that occupy the best position in the international geostructure (Morales Ruvalcaba and Rocha Valencia, 2022). These include the regional powers (Brazil, Mexico, and Argentina), the secondary semi-peripheral states (Chile and Uruguay), the subregional nations (Colombia and Venezuela), and the middle peripheral states (Peru, Cuba, Ecuador, Costa Rica, Dominican Republic, Panama, and Guatemala). All these countries reported reductions in their WPI ranking in 2020 compared to the previous year; that is, they all experienced reductions in their national power. However, the changes were diverse. Therefore, the following analysis will be conducted for three groups, categorized according to the impact of the pandemic.

Minor impact on national power: The countries least affected in their national power are those that, from 2019 to 2020, did not have WPI reductions greater than –0.005. These countries were Guatemala and Ecuador (–0.001), Uruguay (–0.002), and Colombia (–0.004).

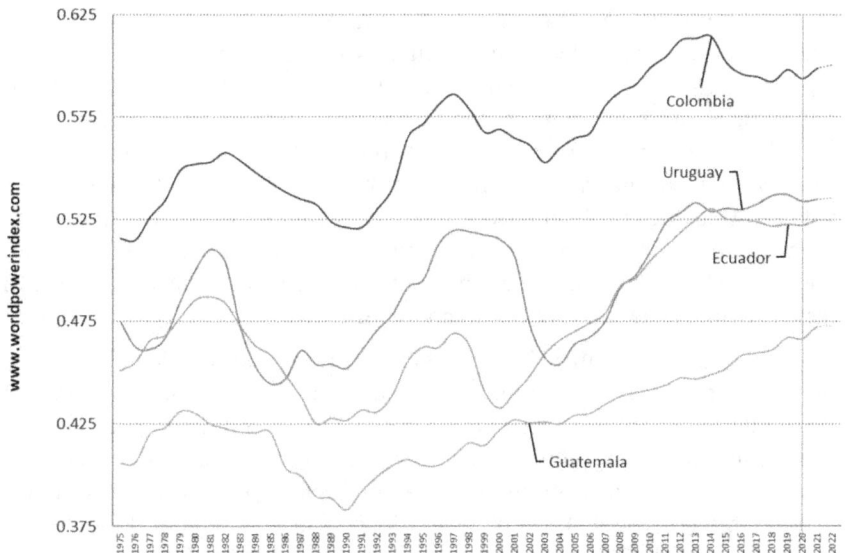

Figure 6.2 Latin American countries least affected in terms of national power by the COVID-19 pandemic, according to the WPI

Source: Created by the author; based on data from Morales Ruvalcaba (2023)

Historically, Guatemala has been immersed in an exhausting and bloody civil war that lasted for 36 years, from November 1960 until the signing of the peace accords in December 1996. The social effects of this large-scale civil war during the 1980s, coupled with the consequences of the "lost decade" for the Latin American economy, caused the country's greatest drop in its national capacities, which reached its lowest level in 1990. However, progress in the peace process, achieved with Esquipulas II (1987) and the Oslo Agreement (1990), generated the social, political, and economic conditions necessary for Guatemala to begin to develop its national capacities. Since then, the country has gradually been increasing its national power. Although Guatemala also suffered due to the pandemic, in 2020, it reported a moderate drop of −1.5% in its national production thanks to the large-scale expansion of social protection networks. This helped, to a certain extent, to keep other elements of its national power stable. As such, it has recorded the lowest impact on its national power in the region. Further, it has since shown its resilience in the process of deploying and increasing its national capacities in the post-pandemic era.

Next, it is necessary to acknowledge the "Ecuadorian miracle" because few countries in the region have managed to increase their material capacities with such vehemence as Ecuador. After a period of crisis in the second half of the 1990s, Ecuador accelerated and sustained an increase in its national power between 2000 and 2014. However, this momentum stopped when international prices oil prices plummeted by around 50% in 2014. From then until 2021, which corresponds to the last years of the government of Rafael Correa (2007–2017) and the entire government of Lenín Moreno (2017–2021), Ecuador's national power gradually reduced. In this context, despite the fact that it reported a drop of −7.8% in its GDP in 2020 and COVID-19 caused a high fatality rate of 3.5% of its population (Johns Hopkins University & Medicine, 2022), Ecuador practically kept other components of its national power stable. However, its external and internal debt rose by 8.5% and 11%, respectively, between December 2019 and December 2020 (Torres, 2021). Undoubtedly, one of the main challenges for the government of Guillermo Lasso, which came to power on 24 May 2021, has been to boost Ecuadorian national capacities while restructuring its debt, especially in cooperation with China, its main lender.

Uruguay has modernized its national institutions and significantly improved the living conditions of its population. This is visible in its high semi-material capacities, as its middle class, which represents 60% of its population, is, in relative terms, the largest in the region. Regarding the evolution of its national power, Uruguay had a serious setback in the last years of its civic-military dictatorship (1973–1985). Then, it experienced accelerated development of its national capacities during the governments of Luis Alberto Lacalle (1990–1995) and Julio María Sanguinetti (1995–2000). However, the 2001 crisis in Argentina—its second economic partner at the time—had a direct impact on Uruguay, dragging its national power down to the level of the mid-1980s. Although a new phase of geostructural ascent began in 2004 and was maintained during the presidencies of Tabaré Vázquez (2005–2010) and José Mujica (2010–2015), since the end of the latter government, Uruguayan national capacities have remained practically stagnant. However, COVID-19 did not have a significant impact on the national power of Uruguay. This was largely thanks to the early manoeuvres of the government of Luis Alberto Lacalle, which rose to power in March 2020, at the same time as the pandemic in South America.

Colombia is the most powerful country in the Andean Community and it also ranks fifth in Latin America. For this reason, it has been seen as a secondary regional power (Ardila, 2022) or subregional power (Morales Ruvalcaba, 2020; Souza, 2021). After facing social difficulties—due to guerrilla warfare and drug trafficking—and economic issues in the 1980s, the governments of César Gaviria (1990–1994) and Ernesto Samper (1994–1998) stabilized the country and accelerated the development of Colombian national power. Then, due to the economic crisis of the late 1990s, by the end of the decade, the national power of Colombia regressed to 1994 levels. Finally, it started a new phase of geostructural ascent and reached its highest point at the end of the first term of Juan Manuel Santos (2010–2018). But despite the pacification it achieved in 2016, Colombia has not been able to further enhance its national capacities since then. In this sense, even though the COVID-19 pandemic has caused a slight setback for Colombia, it has ultimately accentuated the country's trend of geostructural stagnation that has been ongoing for half a decade.

Medium impact on national power: Countries that experienced, from 2019 to 2020, variations in the WPI ranking between –0.005 and –0.010 are considered moderately affected in their national power. These countries were Cuba, Costa Rica, and Peru (–0.006), Mexico (–0.008), and Chile (–0.009).

Figure 6.3 Latin American countries moderately affected in terms of national power by the COVID-19 pandemic, according to the WPI

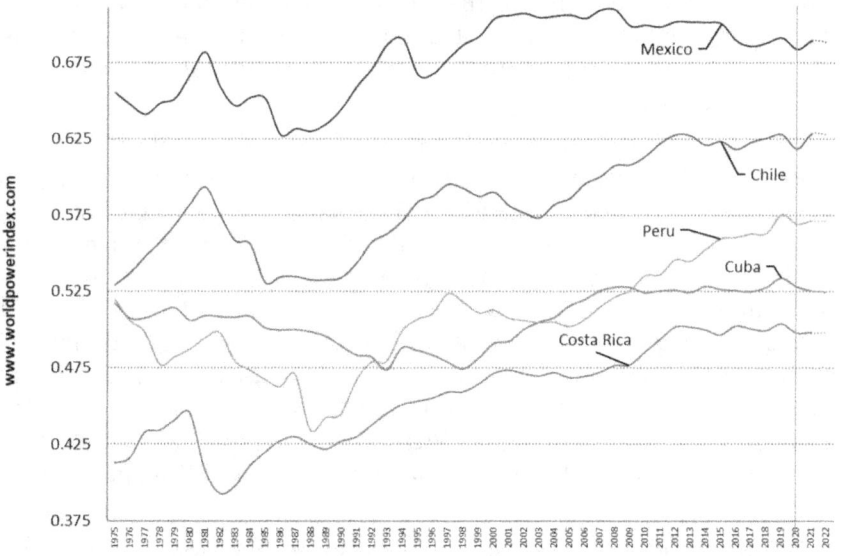

Source: Created by the author; based on data from Morales Ruvalcaba (2023)

The case of Cuba is relatively different from that of the other Latin American countries because it is the only one whose development, economic relations, and ties with the world are affected by an embargo that the USA has maintained on the island for more than six decades. Cuba experienced a gradual deterioration of its national power during the 1970s and 1980s, largely due to the knock-on effect caused by the decline of the Soviet Union, its main economic and political partner during the Cold War. After the lowest level, observed during the "special" period in times of peace in the 1990s, Cuba enhanced its national capacities between 1998 and 2008. This coincided with the last phase of the government of Fidel Castro (1976–2008). The following decade, however, corresponding with the government of Raúl Castro (2008–2018), was one of stagnation. The generational change with Miguel Díaz-Canel in 2018 and the implementation of the new laws derived from the 2019 Constitution gave a favourable boost to the country's national power. However, this success was relatively brief for various reasons. The year 2020 brought new setbacks due to 1) the strong financial, social, and immigration restrictions imposed by the Trump administration; 2) the drop in demand for Cuban doctors in allied countries due to changes in the governments in Brazil (as Bolsonaro had broken medical agreements in November 2018), Ecuador (Lenín Moreno had cancelled health agreements in November 2019), and Bolivia (because Jeanine Áñez suspended relations with Cuba in January 2020); 3) the downturn in the tourism sector due to the COVID-19 pandemic; 4) reduced aid from Venezuela, its main partner in the post–Cold War era; and 5) low agricultural production because of mismanagement and the impact of climate change. Hence, the consequences of these problems have prolonged the stagnation in Cuba.

In Central America, Costa Rica has held the highest levels of national power since the early 1990s, although this position has begun to be challenged by Panama in recent years. Costa Rica stands out for not only its relatively high levels of well-being but also for the stability of its political system and the quality of its institutions. Regarding its national power, Costa Rica experienced a significant drop in the early 1980s as a result of the debt crisis and the recession that affected all of Latin America in those years. Then, in the following three decades, this Central American country increased its national power by 27%. However, since 2013, Costa Rica has failed to further develop its national capacities. In this context, the COVID-19 pandemic was not so hard on the country, but it has prolonged the stagnation in Costa Rica's geostructural position.

Peru is second in the hierarchy of power of the Andean Community (after Colombia) and has enormous geopolitical potential derived from its "position in the South American context and its access to the Pacific, its rich historiography that gives it a particular identity, the multiethnicity of its population, the great number of its natural resources and the diversity of its territory" (Lauriani, 2016, p. 23). After experiencing some of the most complicated moments in its modern history, with the Revolutionary Government of the Armed Forces (1968–1980), the era of terrorism (1980–2000), and the economic crisis of the 1980s, starting in the last years of the twentieth century, Peru underwent one of the most outstanding geostructural ascent processes in the region. Between 1998 and 2018, its WPI increased by 32%. However, the last significant advance in the development of its national power was registered in 2018–2019. Since then, Peru has had a setback, due partly to the pandemic in 2020 but also to the political crisis that the country has been going through. Indeed, the country has appointed five presidents in three years (from Martín Vizcarra in March 2018 to Dina Boluarte in December 2022). In addition to dealing with the economic and social consequences of COVID-19, the challenge for Peru lies in achieving stability in its political system to help lay the foundations for a new phase of geostructural ascent.

Mexico has stagnated in terms of developing its national power since the turn of the century. The country experienced its greatest geostructural ascent between 1986 and 2000 when the presidential hegemony of the Institutional Revolutionary Party (PRI) ended and the democratic alternation with the National Action Party (PAN) began. However, the PAN presidencies, led by Vicente Fox (2000–2006) and Felipe Calderón (2006–2012), resulted in stagnation; Mexico's national power was practically unchanged in these years. Later, with the new PRI government, which had Enrique Peña Nieto (2012–2018) at the helm, the country began to experience a gradual decline. Then, there was a new political alternation in 2018 with the appointment of President Andrés Manuel López Obrador, leader of the National Regeneration Movement (Morena) party. López Obrador's ambitious project has been to lead Mexico through its fourth transformation (4T), that is, to induce radical changes in Mexico—similar to the processes of Independence (1810–1821), Reform (1856–1861), and Revolution (1910–1917)—that would facilitate an outburst of social and economic development. Although the first reforms of the López Obrador government contributed to Mexico slightly increasing its power in 2019, the pandemic had a negative impact and halted what appeared to be a trend towards geostructural ascent. Although 2021 and 2022 have come with a moderate recovery for Mexico, the pandemic subtracted practically an entire year from López Obrador's project. This could possibly determine the legacy of his administration, which ends in 2024.

After a period of geostructural stagnation during the last five years of the Augusto Pinochet regime (1973–1990), Chile experienced a highly visible increase in its national power until 1997, when the country was swept up in the

Asian financial crisis. However, after the setback between 1997 and 2003, Chile embarked on a new journey of increasing its national power that lasted a decade. Since the last two years of the first government of Sebastián Piñera (2010–2014) and the entire second government of Michelle Bachelet (2014–2018), Chile's national capacities have stagnated. Despite this, it is important to highlight the historical rise of the country—from the mid-1980s to 2010, the South American country increased its national power by 18%. Although Chile has immense potential to continue on its geostructural ascent, the COVID-19 pandemic has been a serious obstacle.

Strong impact on national power: The countries most affected in their national power are those that had WPI variations greater than –0.010, from 2019 to 2020. From least to most affected, these countries were the Dominican Republic (–0.011), Panama (–0.012), Argentina and Brazil (–0.017), and Venezuela (–0.019).

Figure 6.4 Latin American countries strongly affected in terms of national power by the COVID-19 pandemic, according to the WPI

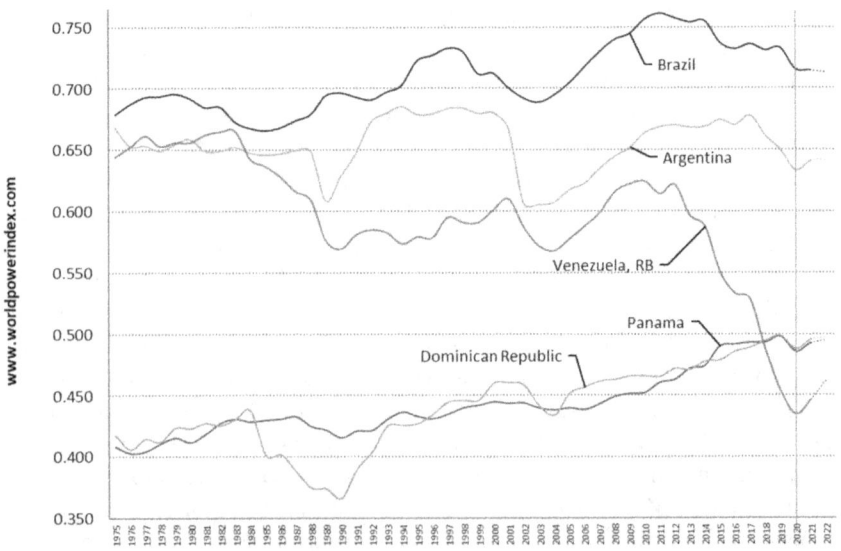

Source: Created by the author; based on data from Morales Ruvalcaba (2023)

Although the Dominican Republic is not a member of CARICOM, in the Caribbean context, it is one of the countries that has increased its national power the most. After a sharp decline in its national capacities in the second half of the 1990s, the Dominican Republic maintained a remarkable upward geostructural trend from 1990 to 2019, raising its national power by 36% over these three decades. Even though the impact of the pandemic was as strong on the national capacities of the Dominican Republic as the financial crisis of 2003, indicators suggest a speedy recovery thanks to the increase in remittances, the attraction of foreign investment, and growth during the Luis Abinader government, which began in August 2020, when the pandemic was still raging.

As mentioned earlier, Panama is another of the countries with the greatest national power in Central America. Like Costa Rica, it also stands out for its relatively high levels of well-being and the quality of its institutions. In the evolution of its national power, Panama achieved certain advances during the military government of Omar Torrijos (1968–1981), but these vanished under the dictatorship of Manuel Antonio Noriega (1983–1989) due to the economic sanctions of the USA against that regime (which caused a drop of –13.4% in the GDP in 1988), and the subsequent US military invasion in December 1989. However, once the military governance ended in 1990, Panama established the basis for a gradual increase in its national capacities. These have been maintained since then, albeit with a phase of stagnation between 2000 and 2006. In this sense, the COVID-19 pandemic has had the greatest impact on the national power of Panama since the US invasion, as it caused the strongest contraction in the economy in recorded history (a drop of –17.9% in the GDP in 2020). The pandemic not only necessitated the cancellation of international flights between March and October 2020 and consequently prohibited the arrival of foreign tourists but also slowed down the construction sector and caused the temporary closure of some mines. For all these reasons, Panama was the Central American country most affected in its national power by COVID-19.

In the case of Argentina, after the historical crisis of 2001—in which the country lost around 10% of its national power—and a subsequent period of stabilization, starting in 2004, Argentina began an important and accelerated recovery of its national capacities that lasted until 2011. These years coincided with the government of Néstor Kirchner (2003–2007) and the first government of Cristina Fernández de Kirchner (2007–2011). Subsequently, this growth slowed down, although it did not stop, during the second government of Cristina Fernández (2011–2015) and the first half of the government of Mauricio Macri (2015–2019). However, during the second half of the Macri government, the country experienced a significant reduction in its national power that took it back almost a decade. In other words, between 2017 and 2019, Argentina declined in its geostructural position to 2008 levels. On 10 December 2019, there was a change of government when Alberto Fernández assumed the presidency. Unfortunately, he had to face the COVID-19 emergency just three months after being appointed. In 2020, the deterioration of Argentine national power deepened further; Argentina was the second most affected country in the group analysed. However, the most recent WPI figures suggest that the Fernández government managed to reverse the trend in 2021 and might possibly reinvigorate Argentina's national capacities in the remainder of its term.

Brazil has experienced a gradual reduction in its national power since 2011, that is since Lula da Silva finished his second term. Despite the continuation of the government project of the Partido dos Trabalhadores by Dilma Rousseff (2011–2016), the rise of Brazil as a regional power in the previous decade could not be maintained. Furthermore, the main fall in national power in Brazil occurred from 2014 to 2015. This helps explain the discontentment in Brazilian society in those years and, some of the motivation that drove the case for Dilma Rousseff's impeachment, which was realised on 31 August 2016. The transitional government of Michel Temer (2016–2018), however, did not contribute to Brazil increasing its national power either, but only to stagnation. During the Jair Bolsonaro government (2019–2022), Brazil continued its decline and, in 2020, suffered the second-largest reduction in national capacities among the Latin American countries analysed here (after Argentina). Lula da Silva was elected president in 2022, once more taking charge of Brazil at a time of decline in its national power, just as it was in 2002 when he took over from Fernando Henrique Cardoso (1995–2002). However, unlike in 2002, the new government has to deal with greater and more complex constraints that have resulted from the pandemic.

The decline of Venezuela has been extraordinary. After achieving a significant increase in its national power between 2004 and 2010, Venezuela entered a phase of stagnation in the last three years of Hugo Chávez's government (1999–2013) to begin, in 2012, a geostructural decline, unprecedented in the recent history of Latin America. There are multiple factors that have contributed to the Venezuelan crisis, but the main ones are internal political instability, excessive dependence on oil revenue (82% of the exports were petroleum oils in 2019), the sharp drop in the price of oil between 2012 and 2016, the effective collapse of PDVSA, and the economic–financial sanctions imposed by the USA and some of its European allies against Venezuela. All this has caused Venezuela to lose national capacities year after year, amounting to a contraction of –27% of its national power between 2010 and 2020. The COVID-19 pandemic accentuated the pre-existing crisis, collapsing the country's basic services, deteriorating people's purchasing power, and increasing poverty and inequality. Although the country did rebound in 2021, the geostructural repositioning of Venezuela as a subregional power will possibly take the entirety of the 2020s.

6.6 Conclusion

The former executive secretary of ECLAC, José Antonio Ocampo, has confirmed that "the COVID-19 crisis will go down in history as the worst in Latin American economic history" (Ocampo, 2020, p. 48). However, this crisis has not been exclusively economic, but also permeated many different spheres of society and even the collective psyche. For this reason, it is necessary to assess its impact from a broader and more comprehensive perspective.

The COVID-19 pandemic has had a significant impact on various dimensions of human activities. Understanding its effects requires a thorough evaluation, which calls for analytical tools that capture its multidimensionality. The WPI is an excellent tool for assessing the impact of COVID-19. Methodologically, the assessment of national power has followed the WPI guidelines by breaking down the impact of the COVID-19 pandemic into the material, semi-material, and immaterial dimensions of national power. Although numerical variations in the WPI from 2019 to 2020 may seem relatively small, they are critical in a broader historical context.

This study reveals that all the selected Latin American and Caribbean countries experienced reductions in their national capacities and, therefore, in their national power in 2020. However, it also shows heterogeneity in the pandemic's impact on the region, which has led to the categorization of countries into three groups according to the level of impact: low, medium, and high.

It is still too soon to say whether the problems caused by the pandemic have been fully resolved. The analysis presented in this chapter suggests that government responses, such as economic and fiscal stimuli, have helped diminish the effects of the crisis. However, in the medium term, all countries in the region will have to confront the pandemic's consequences. This could negatively impact the region's development prospects.

The COVID-19 pandemic has been the most recent and complex stumbling block in the efforts of Latin American countries to increase their national capacities and achieve more favourable positions in the international geostructure. Conducting this analysis of the pandemic's impact on the national power of Latin American and Caribbean countries might facilitate the design of internal socio-economic policies and international insertion strategies that help strengthen autonomy in the region. Variations in the WPI shed light on the pandemic's impact on the power dynamics of nations and can provide policymakers with insights into developing effective strategies to deal with future crises.

References

Acácio, I., Passos, A. and Pion-Berlin, D. (2022) 'Military responses to the COVID-19 pandemic crisis in Latin America: military presence, autonomy, and human rights violations', *Armed Forces & Society*, 49 (2), pp. 372–394.

Ardila, M. (2022) 'Potencias regionales latinoamericanas: debilitamiento y acomodamiento en su inserción internacional', *Estudos Internacionais*, 10 (1), pp. 7–24.

Arias, J. and Salazar, E. (2021) 'Monitoreando los tipos de cambio y sus efectos sobre sector agroalimentario durante el COVID-19', *Blog del IICA*, 19 March. Available at: https://blog.iica.int/blog/monitoreando-los-tipos-cambio-sus-efectos-sobre-sector-agroalimentario-durante-covid-19 (Accessed: 1 November 2022).

Banco de México (2022) *Precio de la mezcla mexicana de petróleo*. Available at: https://www.banxico.org.mx/apps/gc/precios-spot-del-petroleo-gra.html (Accessed: 1 November 2022).

Bidet, J. (2011) *L'état-monde: libéralisme, socialisme et communisme à l'échelle globale – Refondation du marxisme*. Paris: PUF.

Buechler, E., Powell, S., Sun, T., Astier, N., Zanocco, C., Bolorinos, J., Flora, J., Boudet, H. and Rajagopal, R. (2022) 'Global changes in electricity consumption during COVID-19', *iScience*, 25 (1), pp. 1–18.

Callinicos, A. (2007) 'Does capitalism need the state system?', *Cambridge Review of International Affairs*, 20 (4), pp. 533–549.

CEFP (2022) *Precio de la mezcla Mexicana de exportación de petróleo*. Available at: https://www.cefp.gob.mx/new/graficas_interactivas.php (Accessed: 15 May 2023).

CEPAL (2020a) *Informe especial COVID-19 no. 12: Informe sobre el impacto económico en América Latina y el Caribe de la enfermedad por coronavirus (COVID-19)*. Available at: https://hdl.handle.net/11362/47489 (Accessed: 15 May 2023).

CEPAL (2020b) *Medidas de recuperación del sector turístico en América Latina y el Caribe: una oportunidad para promover la sostenibilidad y la resiliencia*. Available at: http://hdl.handle.net/11362/45770 (Accessed: 1 November 2022).

CEPAL (2021a) *Informe especial COVID-19 no. 11: la paradoja de la recuperación en América Latina y el Caribe*. Available at: http://hdl.handle.net/11362/47043 (Accessed: 15 May 2023).

CEPAL (2021b) *Informe especial COVID-19 no. 10: financiamiento para el desarrollo en la era de la pandemia de COVID-19 y después*. Available at: http://hdl.handle.net/11362/46710 (Accessed: 1 November 2022).

CEPAL (2022a) *Anuario estadístico de América Latina y el Caribe, 2021*. Available at: https://hdl.handle.net/11362/47827 (Accessed: 15 May 2023).

CEPAL (2022b) *Estudio económico de América Latina y el Caribe, 2022*. Available at: https://repositorio.cepal.org/bitstream/handle/11362/48077/S2201058_es.pdf?sequence=4&isAllowed=y (Accessed: 1 November 2022).

CEPAL (2022c) *Social panorama of Latin America 2021*. Santiago: United Nations.

CEPAL (2022d) 'Latin America and the Caribbean lost nearly 3 years of life expectancy at birth between 2019 and 2021 as a result of the COVID-19 pandemic', *ECLAC – United Nations*, 22 August. Available at: https://www.cepal.org/en/notes/latin-america-and-caribbean-lost-nearly-3-years-life-expectancy-birth-between-2019-and-2021 (Accessed: 1 November 2022).

CEPAL and OIT (2020) *Coyuntura laboral en América Latina y el Caribe. El trabajo en tiempos de pandemia: desafíos frente a la enfermedad por coronavirus (COVID-19)*. Available at: http://hdl.handle.net/11362/45557 (Accessed: 15 May 2023).

CEPAL and UNESCO (2020) *La educación en tiempos de la pandemia de COVID-19*. Available at: http://hdl.handle.net/11362/45904 (Accessed: 1 November 2022).

De Oliveira, R. and Marques, F. (2020) 'O tamanho da aposta na ciência', *Pesquisa*, 294, pp. 34–37.

Del Arenal, C. (1983) 'Poder y relaciones internacionales. Un análisis conceptual', *Revista de Estudios Internacionales*, 4 (3), pp. 501–524.

Dutrénit, G., Aguirre-Bastos, C., Puchet, M. and Salazar, M. (2021) 'Latin America', in Scheneegans, S., Lewis, J. and Straza, T. (eds.), *UNESCO science report: the race against time for smarter development*. Paris: UNESCO Publishing, pp. 200–233.

Finquelievich, S. (2020) 'La COVID-19 saca a la luz las desigualdades en el uso de Internet en América Latina', *The Conversation*, 22 October. Available at: https://theconversation.com/la-covid-19-saca-a-la-luz-las-desigualdades-en-el-uso-de-internet-en-america-latina-148603 (Accessed: 1 November 2022).

Herrera, A. M. and Croissant, A. (2022) *Mapping military roles in COVID-19 responses in Latin America: contours, causes and consequences*. Available at: https://journals.ub.uni-heidelberg.de/index.php/hciaswp/article/view/84516/79158 (Accessed: 1 November 2022).

Huepe, M., Palma, A. and Trucco, D. (2002) *Educación en tiempos de pandemia: una oportunidad para transformar los sistemas educativos en América Latina y el Caribe*. Santiago: CEPAL.

IEA (2021) *Covid-19 impact on electricity*. Available at: https://www.iea.org/reports/covid-19-impact-on-electricity (Accessed: 1 November 2022).

IMF (2022) Countering the cost-of-living crisis. October. Available at: https://www.imf.org/en/Publications/WEO/Issues/2022/10/11/world-economic-outlook-october-2022 (Accessed: 6 November 2022).

Johns Hopkins University & Medicine (2022) *Mortality analyses*. Available at: https://coronavirus.jhu.edu/data/mortality (Accessed: 1 November 2022).

Keohane, R. and Nye, J. (1989) *Power and interdependence*. Reprint, New York: HarperCollins, 1977.

Lake, D. (2009) *Hierarchy in international relations*. New York: Cornell University.

Lauriani, C. (2016) 'Objetivos del Perú: una aproximación a partir de su potencial geopolítico', *Revista de Marina* (5), pp. 22–25.

Morales Ruvalcaba, D. (2020) 'Subregional powers of Latin America: Colombia and Venezuela', *The Oxford Encyclopedia of Latin American Politics*. Available at: https://doi.org/10.1093/acrefore/9780190228637.013.1707 (Accessed: 20 May 2023).

Morales Ruvalcaba, D. (2023) *World power index database*. Available at: https://www.worldpowerindex.com/data-world-power-index/ (Accessed: 1 January 2023).

Morales Ruvalcaba, D. and Rocha Valencia, A. (2022) 'Geoestructura de poder en el sistema político internacional: un enfoque trans-estructural', *Geopolítica(s)*, 13 (1), pp. 41–81.

Morgenthau, H. (1960) *Politics among nations*. Calcutta: Scientific Book Agency.

Ocampo, J. A. (2020) 'La crisis del COVID-19 de América Latina con una perspectiva histórica', *Revista CEPAL* (132), pp. 47–65. Available at: http://hdl.handle.net/11362/46838 (Accessed: 15 May 2023).

OECD (2021) *Latin American economic outlook 2021: Working together for a better recovery*. OECD iLibrary. Available at: https://doi.org/10.1787/5fedabe5-en (Accessed: 15 May 2023).

OIT (2021) *Panorama laboral 2021 América Latina y el Caribe*. Available at: https://www.oitcinterfor.org/panorama-laboral-2021-am%C3%A9rica-latina-caribe-oit-0 (Accessed: 15 May 2023).

Passos, A. (2021) 'La militarización en América Latina en tiempos de Covid-19', *The Conversation*, 6 February. Available at: https://theconversation.com/la-militarizacion-en-america-latina-en-tiempos-de-covid-19-154781 (Accessed: 15 May 2023).

Passos, A. and Acácio, I. (2021) 'The militarization of responses to COVID-19 in Democratic Latin America', *Revista de Administração Pública*, 55 (1), pp. 261–272.

Robledo, M. (2022) *Militarización, emergencia del militarismo civil y erosión democrática en América Latina*. Available at: https://www.fundacioncarolina.es/militarizacion-emergencia-del-militarismo-civil-y-erosion-democratica-en-america-latina/ (Accessed: 1 November 2022).

Rocha Valencia, A. and Morales Ruvalcaba, D. (2018) 'El poder nacional-internacional de los estados. Una propuesta trans-estructural', *Geopolítica(s)*, 9 (1), pp. 137–169.

SCImago (2022a) *SCImago journal & country rank 2019*. Available at: https://www.SCImagojr.com/countryrank.php?year=2019 (Accessed: 1 November 2022).

SCImago (2022b) *SCImago journal & country rank 2020*. Available at: https://www.SCImagojr.com/countryrank.php?year=2020 (Accessed: 1 November 2022).

SIPRI (2021a) *SIPRI yearbook 2021*. Available at: https://www.sipri.org/sites/default/files/2021-06/sipri_yb21_summary_en_v2_0.pdf (Accessed: 1 November 2022).

SIPRI (2021b) *Trends in world military expenditure, 2020*. Available at: https://www.sipri.org/sites/default/files/2021-04/fs_2104_milex_0.pdf (Accessed: 1 November 2022).

Souza, T. (2021) 'Rethinking the regional security complex theory: a South American view between 2008–2016', *Revista de Estudios en Seguridad Internacional*, 7 (1), pp. 83–103.

Torres, W. (2021) 'En un año la deuda pública de Ecuador aumentó USD 5,847 millones', *Primicias*, 22 January. Available at: https://www.primicias.ec/noticias/economia/deuda-publica-ecuador-sigue-aumentando/ (Accessed: 1 November 2022).

UNESCO (2020) *COVID-19 educational disruption and response*. Available at: https://www.unesco.org/en/covid-19/education-response (Accessed: 1 May 2020).

Waltz, K. (1979) *Theory of international politics*. London: Addison-Wesley Publishing Co.

WHO (2022) *WHO coronavirus (COVID-19) dashboard*. Available at: https://covid19.who.int/ (Accessed: 1 December 2022).

World Bank (2022a) *Global economics prospects.* Available at: https://doi.org/10.1596/978-1-4648-1843-1 (Accessed: 15 May 2023).

World Bank (2022b) GDP per capita (current US$) - Latin America & Caribbean. Available at: https://data.worldbank.org/indicator/NY.GDP.PCAP.CD?locations=ZJ (Accessed: 1 May 2023).

World Bank (2022c) *Current health expenditure (% of GDP) – Latin America & Caribbean.* Available at: https://data.worldbank.org/indicator/SH.XPD.CHEX.GD.ZS?locations=ZJ (Accessed: 1 November 2022).

WPI (2023) *World power index.* Available at: www.worldpowerindex.com (Accessed: 15 May 2023).

WTO (2021) *World trade primed for strong but uneven recovery after COVID-19 pandemic shock.* Available at: https://www.wto.org/english/news_e/pres21_e/pr876_e.htm (Accessed: 1 November 2022).

Xu, T., Gao, W., Li, Y. and Qian, F. (2021) 'Impact of the COVID-19 pandemic on the reduction of electricity demand and the integration of renewable energy into the power grid', *Journal of Renewable and Sustainable Energy* (13), pp. 1–12.

Chapter 7

Regional integration and presidential elections in Latin America in the context of COVID-19

Ignacio Medina Núñez
El Colegio de Jalisco, México

Abstract

This chapter analyses the impact of the COVID-19 pandemic on the results of elections and on the integration process in Latin America. During 2020 and 2021, healthcare systems across the region faced a critical situation; this affected national elections because they involved concentration of crowds in assemblies and rallies, and also directly impacted social behaviour on the day of the vote. This subsequently impacted the political landscape against which regional integration develops in Latin America, causing adjustments to the ongoing process. The chapter employs a framework rooted in historical sociology and it argues that the impact of COVID-19 was to create a specific context of political trends which are favourable towards the deepening of regional integration. First, it explores the impact of COVID-19 on presidential elections in Ecuador, Peru, Nicaragua, Chile and Honduras; and then, it analyses broader effects at the regional level in the context of CELAC's Sixth Summit.

Keywords: Latin American politics, COVID-19, presidential elections, regional integration, historical sociology, CELAC

***

"It is a great idea to try to form a single nation from the entire New World... Diverse situations, opposing interests, dissimilar characters, divide America" (Bolívar, 1815, p. 29).

7.1 Introduction

The COVID-19 pandemic that affected the entire world, especially in 2020–2021, had severe consequences on many aspects of the economic, political, and cultural life of all nations. In developing countries, the situation was critical as our weak public health systems could not face the high demands of the affected population. In this chapter, I will focus on the political and electoral developments in some Latin American countries, placing special emphasis on the implications of this situation for the regional integration processes and on the Sixth Summit of Latin American States (CELAC) on September 2021 in Mexico City.

I will apply a method of historical sociology[1] to the context of presidential elections in Latin American countries across different times as *Revista Internacional de Ciencias Sociales* did some decades ago: "About 25 years ago, sociology and political science rediscovered history, thus recovering one of the greatest traditions of their past, the one recreated in the past by Max Weber and Otto Hintze" (Makison, 1992, p. 339). It compares historical contexts at different points in time across regions to "interpret the behaviour and strategy of the social actors" (Tilly, 1992, p. 335).

In this chapter, I will first outline the critical situation of healthcare systems that were not prepared to face the magnitude of the effects of COVID-19. But due to the great risks of contagion during 2020–21—and given that electoral processes involve the concentration of crowds in assemblies and rallies, especially when casting their votes—certain voting dates were postponed. Finally, in 2021, countries such as Ecuador, Peru, Honduras, Nicaragua, and Chile conducted elections after considering how they were affected by the pandemic. After discussing the critical years of the pandemic, I will focus on how CELAC's Sixth Summit in Mexico in 2021 reactivated expectations of Latin American integration with the impetus of President Andrés Manuel López Obrador, then president *pro tempore* of this community.

I will develop two sections. The first will describe the context of the pandemic in several countries in the subcontinent that held electoral processes for the presidency during 2020–2021; the second will discuss the reactivation of the idea of Latin American integration in the CELAC Summit in Mexico City in September 2021. Thus I illustrate that the COVID-19 pandemic influenced, in

---

[1] Many authors discuss historical sociology (Lachmann, 2013; Lo and Lawson, 2017, etc.) but I refer specifically to the book edited by T. Skocpol (1984), *Vision and Method in Historical Sociology*, where she and others analyse the academic works of Bloch, Anderson, Tilly, Polanyi, Bendix, Thompson, and Wallerstein.

lesser or greater measure, the electoral results and especially the integration process.

7.2 COVID-19 and presidential elections in Latin America

In January 2020, the World Health Organization (WHO) took the matter of COVID-19—discovered in December 2019 in Wuhan in the Hubei province of China— seriously and announced on January 30, 2020 that a total of 7,818 people caught the virus. Almost all of them were in China, but 82 infected people were detected in 18 other countries, which showed a very high global risk. By February 2020, the WHO described the situation as alarming, given the notable increase in the number of infected people and the inaction of governments, and finally officially declared COVID-19 a pandemic on March 11, 2020. By April 4 of that year, the WHO declared more than a million people in the world infected, with Europe the epicentre. It made a detailed statement in June 2020, offering a chronology of the main events since the emergence of the virus.[2]

One year later, at the 148th meeting of its executive committee (January 18–26, 2021), the General Director of the WHO pointed out in his opening address that the world was already "on the verge of a catastrophic moral failure" because all countries did not have equitable access to vaccines as "some countries and companies continue to prioritize bilateral agreements, bypassing COVAX (COVID-19 Vaccines Global Access), driving up prices and trying to get to the front of the queue" (WHO, 2021). The lack of group agreements forced governments to seek bilateral solutions.

The great number of infections and deaths cannot be attributed to a single cause because even highly developed countries—such as the United States or those of the European Union—faced more serious consequences than countries with weak health institutions. This is especially apparent in the specific case of Latin American countries, as we can see in Table 7.1.

---

[2] This document is available at: https://www.who.int/es/news/item/29-06-2020-covidtimeline

Table 7.1 COVID-19 deaths in Latin American countries

Brazil	678,376
México	330,279
Peru	216,877
Colombia	141,820
Argentina	129,970
Chile	61,455
Ecuador	35,904
Bolivia	22,237
Guatemala	19,859
Paraguay	19,596
Honduras	11,007
Costa Rica	8,974
Cuba	8,530
Panama	8,506
Uruguay	7,510
Venezuela	5,820
Dominican Republic	4,384
El Salvador	4,230
Haiti	857
Nicaragua	225

Source: Created by the author; based on data from Statista (2022).

There is no doubt that the pandemic had devastating social effects across the world. According to the Economic Commission for Latin America and the Caribbean (ECLAC, 2021a)[3], on June 30, 2021, the Latin American region suffered 1.26 million deaths from the virus, with great inequality in the levels of vaccination among the population. Thirty countries in Latin America and the Caribbean had vaccinated 13.6% of their populations, while vaccination efforts in the European Union had reached 34.9%, and in North America, 46.3%. Along with the decline in employment levels, the most dramatic effect was evident in the increase in poverty levels: "in 2020, it went from 189 million in 2019 to 209 million, which could have been 230 million, and 70 million in 2019 to 78 million, which could have been 98 million in the case of extreme poverty" (ECLAC, 2021a).[4]

In this region, nations with strong economies, large health institutions, and governments with different ideologies (left- and right-wing and centrist), such

---

[3] CEPAL is the Comisión Económica para América Latina y el Caribe. It was created by the UN in 1948 to discuss and propose better models for economic development.

[4] Specific data about this situation is available in this ECLAC (Economic Comission for Latin America and the Caribbean) document: https://www.cepal.org/es/comunicados/crecimiento-america-latina-caribe-2021-alcanzara-revertir-efectos-adversos-la-pandemia

as Brazil, Mexico, Argentina, and Colombia, were tremendously affected by infections and deaths. However, it is surprising to note that the poorest countries in Latin America, such as Haiti and Nicaragua, saw the lowest number of deaths. This trend also arose in Africa, where many countries with low levels of development also had the lowest number of infections and deaths from the virus.

I present further analyses of some political processes that took place during the pandemic in Latin American countries. All governments had to apply greater security measures, health protocols, quarantines, and curfews. This necessarily affected electoral campaigns, meetings, rallies, and the exercise of the vote itself as people feared contagion. However, it is clear that public policy that aimed to treat COVID-19, regardless of success, was one of the main influences on electoral results. In these countries, the people's perception of their governments' public policy responses to the pandemic was also one of many elements that influenced their votes in favor of or against the incumbent rulers.

Although these elections were very important for each country, in some cases, events had to be postponed for several months because of the pandemic. In addition, levels of abstention from voting were high in some countries, but we cannot directly attribute this to the virus even in a population fearful of contagion because in general citizen participation in voting has always been around the range of 50–70%, except for the countries where voting is mandatory and abstaining is penalized with a fine.

The year 2020–2021 in Latin America saw seven presidential electoral processes—in the Dominican Republic, Bolivia, Chile, Peru, Nicaragua, Ecuador, and Honduras—and some legislative elections.[5] Although the people's imagination of their governments' responses to the pandemic influenced their vote, it is still necessary to pay attention to the particularity of ideological battles and broader domestic political dynamics in each country.

---

[5] Venezuela, for example, was in the process of electing a National Assembly. The conflict with a discredited opposition continued as the United States promoted Juan Guaido against the Nicolas Maduro government. The situation was complicated, with many right- and left-wing political forces facing each other. The pandemic did not change the situation. There were also legislative elections in El Salvador, where President Nayib Bukele won a triumphant majority in Congress. Mexico also had midterm legislative elections where Morena lost some seats but retained a relative majority along with his allies. Bolivia had regional elections where the MAS (Movement for Socialism) political party dominated, but in Argentina the ruling party lost the congressional midterm elections.

In this chapter, I will make some general considerations about the 2021 electoral processes for the presidency in Ecuador, Peru, Nicaragua, Chile, and Honduras to show certain political effects of COVID-19, which reflected support for or opposition to the incumbent leaders and the candidates. The dates of these elections are shown in Table 7.2 below, within the context of other Latin American political elections. These processes occurred as the region experienced the consequences of the economic contraction due to strikes in productivity and services, which led to an average decrease in GDP of 6.8% (ECLAC, 2021a) and pushed about 40 million people into poverty—all with fear of widespread contagion.

Table 7.2 Electoral processes in 2021 in Latin America

Country	Date	Election
Ecuador	February 7	**Presidential election** (first round)
	April 11	Presidential election (runoff)
El Salvador	February 28	Congressional midterms
Bolivia	March 7	Sub-national elections
Peru	April 11	**Presidential election** (first round)
	June 6	Presidential runoff
Mexico	June 6	Congressional midterms
Argentina	October 24	Congressional midterms
Nicaragua	November 7	**Presidential election**
Chile	November 21	**Presidential election** (first round)
	December 19	Presidential runoff
Honduras	November 28	**Presidential election**
Venezuela	December 6	Congressional election

Source: Created by the author; based on data from UC San Diego (2023)

Each case deserves a more profound analysis because some of them are very complex, but for the purpose of this chapter, I will consider the presidential electoral processes only for 2021—one year after the declaration of COVID-19 as a pandemic. This was a period when citizens chose, in several cases, new political options, opposing several governments that had not attended to the consequences of the virus in a serious manner.

In Ecuador, President Lenin Moreno's party (2017–2021) suffered a terrible electoral defeat in 2021 due to his lack of attention to those affected by the pandemic (there were many images of people killed by the virus lying on the streets) and his bad performance in government. The Alianza País, Moreno's political party, nominated Ximena Peña as the next candidate, but she only obtained 1.54% of the votes in the first round on February 7, 2021. It is also necessary to see the broader context with other elements, such as the fact that former Ecuadorian President from Alianza País, Rafael Correa's supporters were not consolidated and that the Ecuadorian political left faced a rising indigenous movement opposing both the Moreno and Correa currents. For example, according to the Social Observatory of Ecuador (Observatorio Social del Ecuador, 2022), the government recognized that a total of 35,884 people died from COVID-19 during March 2020–August 2022. However, the Observatory claims that deaths in this period amounted to 89,165. We must also take into account the decrease in the GDP of the previous year, which had fallen by 7.8% (Expansión, 2021).[6] For instance, considering the mismanagement of the health crisis and the repression of people on the streets in October 2019, the presidential election in Ecuador exhibited a tendency towards a punitive vote against Lenin Moreno, who succeeded Rafael Correa in 2017 and adopted a neoliberal perspective, disregarding public affairs to further emphasize the business-friendly, free trade model. The results of the first round of votes on February 7, 2021, were overwhelming, placing the candidate Andres Arauz in the lead with 32.72% of the vote. In contrast, the then president's party, Alianza País, with its candidate Ximena Peña, received only 1.54% of the vote.

Chile saw a presidential election and a plebiscite. In 2022, the plebiscite would decide whether to change the constitution imposed by General Augusto Pinochet in 1988. This process was also affected by the presidential elections in November–December 2021. In the first electoral round in November 2021, candidate José Antonio Kast won 27.9% of the vote; he was a right-wing candidate who wanted to maintain the 1998 Pinochet constitution. Gabriel Boric came second with 25.8% of the votes and a proposal for a new political direction focused on gender equality and the satisfaction of social demands. In this context, the state carried out the process of elaborating on the text of the new constitution. In the runoff of December 2021, Gabriel Boric won 55.9% of votes with his proposals for education as a social right, a feminist perspective, a social and ecological transformation, territorial decentralization, and an economic approach that the state must have a key role in the free market. The September 2022 referendum ended with the rejection of the proposal of the text for a new constitution. But against these political events—the big movement against President Piñera in October 2019, the election of the constituent assembly to write a proposal for a new constitution, the first and second rounds of the presidential elections, and the voting for the approval or rejection of the proposal for the constitution—the pandemic had minor importance, with citizens divided on the legacy of Pinochet constitution.

Peru had congressional and presidential elections in 2021: Pedro Castillo became president in a political fight between the executive and legislative powers. On October 2, 2022, there were regional and municipal elections before

---

[6] Data about the year-wise GDP of Latin American countries is available at: https://datosmacro.expansion.com/pib/ecuador

Congress removed President Castillo from office on December 7, 2022. In 2020, Peru had three presidents: Martín Vizcarra, Manuel Merino, and Francisco Sagasti. After the congressional elections in January 2020 following the dissolution of Congress in 2021, Peru finally witnessed the triumph of President Pedro Castillo, who was then taken to prison in December 2022 by the congress of legislators promoting Dina Boluarte as the new president for 2022–23 in an unstable political situation. The new Boluarte government repressed and detained some of the demonstrators who protested the impeachment of the then ex-president Castillo. The impact of COVID-19 was considerable during the presidential elections and the political clash. People went to polls in Peru because voting was obligatory and came with a financial penalty; there was still an abstention of 17% despite the penalties. As Corvetto Salinas (2022, p. 6) writes, "[t]he health crisis was added to a period of political crisis and a vulnerable management of this context…, which ended up revealing the existing deficiencies in the Peruvian health system. This made Peru the country with the highest mortality rate per million inhabitants worldwide and the one with the worst performance in the face of the pandemic". The period of intense political instability during 2020–2021 and the government's poor response to the virus had a great influence on the dissatisfaction of Peruvians with the traditional political system, which led them to vote for an outsider like Castillo, although it did not happen in an overwhelming way.

In Nicaragua, where there were few consequences of the pandemic, the presidential election was held on November 7, 2021. Daniel Ortega, who had returned to rule the country in 2006, sought re-election against five party candidates. In June–July 2021, the government arrested seven possible candidates while other opponents chose to leave the country. Ortega of FSLN (Sandinista National Liberation Front) won the November elections and achieved his fourth consecutive re-election with 75% of the votes. The Liberal Constitutionalist Party was second with 14% of the vote. Of the 91 deputies in the National Assembly, the FSLN achieved an absolute majority with 60 legislative seats. At first, the government minimized the effects of the pandemic. Although infections and deaths occurred in a fragile health system despite government action, compared to other Latin American countries, COVID-19 did not have devastating effects on the population of Nicaragua. Many aspects of the country's political system are questionable due to the repression of social movements and the arrest of possible opposition candidates, but there is no doubt that from the point of view of electoral democracy, the government achieved a clear victory in the Ortega re-election—although its legitimacy has been questioned by the internal opposition and other international organizations. The FSLN's social programs to improve the standard of living of the population in the midst of the pandemic acted as a determining factor in their continued internal support. "The government reported a total of 17,442 cases and 215 deaths and said 40.9% of Nicaragua´s population has been fully vaccinated" (Congressional Research Service, 2021, p. 5). Like other Latin American economies, the Nicaraguan one contracted in 2020–2021, and the situation was aggravated by hurricane damage. However, even though Nicaragua continues to be one of the poorest countries in Latin America with an authoritarian regime, the electoral processes went on with massive attendance at meetings and rallies throughout the pandemic.

> During a difficult year caused by the coronavirus disease (COVID-19) pandemic, the Nicaraguan economy contracted by 2.0% in 2020, one of the least marked declines in the region... the economy suffered the effects of both the complicated global economic environment and the difficult domestic sociopolitical situation. Towards the last quarter of 2020, the economy was also hit by Hurricanes Eta and Iota... the immediate economic impact was slight... ECLAC expects the Nicaraguan economy to grow 2.5% in 2021 (ECLAC, 2021b, p. 1).

On November 28, 2021, Honduras had presidential and legislative elections after three terms of the National Party of Honduras. They ruled for 12 years—with Porfirio Lobo and Orlando Hernández at the helm twice, even though the constitution prohibited re-election—after the military and legislative coup in 2009. The traditional parties announced their candidates for the 2021 elections: the mayor of Tegucigalpa Nasry "Tito" Asfura for the National Party and the businesswoman Yani Rosenthal for the Liberal Party. However, Xiomara Castro, wife of the ousted president Manuel Zelaya in 2009, from the Party of Liberty and Refoundation (LIBRE), emerged victorious as an alternative to these traditional parties when both Porfirio Lobo and Orlando Hernández were accused of drug trafficking in the United States. Honduras—along with Haiti—is one of the poorest countries in Latin America, and therefore the most discussed issues among the population in the 2021 elections were poverty, unemployment, migration, violence and homicides, corruption and, above all, the effects of the pandemic and hurricanes. All of these actions were, in the imagination of many, the result of the actions of the National Party government. Although many Hondurans had lost confidence in the electoral system (both due to the 2009 coup and the electoral fraud of Orlando Hernández in 2017 and his attempt to be re-elected with the authorization of the Supreme Court), the result was the triumph of LIBRE and Xiomara Castro with 51% of the votes, followed by Nasry Astura of the National Party with almost 36% of the votes. They proposed changes such as the creation of an anti-corruption commission supported by the UN; the legalization of abortion; the creation of a constituent assembly for a new constitution; and the change in diplomatic relations from allyship with Taiwan to support for mainland China. The pandemic was certainly a concern for Hondurans—in October 2022, there were 11,007 deaths from COVID—but the most urgent need was for a change in the government that could offer better solutions to other, more serious economic and social problems.

Although it did not have a presidential election in 2021, Brazil has a key role in Latin American regional politics; hence, I will also make some brief comments about its situation. President Jair Bolsonaro's mismanagement of the pandemic remained in the imagination of the Brazilian people during the 2022 election. The influence of the pandemic on his defeat in 2022 is clearer because the government minimized the effects of COVID-19 at a time when the country suffered its highest number of infections and deaths only when Lula da Silva regained strength. For example, one year before the election and a year into the pandemic, in November 2021, the *Times* said about Bolsonaro:

> His approval ratings slipped to a record low of 19% in late November, with 60% of the population saying he is doing a bad job. In the past two years, Bolsonaro has made headlines around the world, criticized for destructive environmental policies in the Amazon rainforest and a denialist stance on the COVID-19 pandemic. By discouraging social distancing and rejecting offers from vaccine manufacturers to buy badly-needed doses, the president has helped Brazil's official COVID-19 death toll reach more than 600,000—second only to that of the U.S.[7]

Against the backdrop of the many presidential elections during 2021, specifically with the pandemic and Brazil's political context, several analysts took into consideration:

a) the way in which the Brazilian government managed the health crisis;
b) the government's management of the vaccination process at the national level;
c) the capacities and proposals presented by the presidential candidates;
d) allegations of corruption against politicians and/or public officials. Several situations that have implied a state response, especially when such measures are perceived as deficient, with high mistrust or that have deepened the problems associated with the crisis,

---

[7] This was written in *Time* magazine on December 28, 2021, by Clara Nugent: https://time.com/6130308/bolsonaro-brazil-2022-election/. The newspaper *El País* had also shown, in November 2021, the drop in approval for Bolsonaro to 29.3%. Explicitly, 59% of those interviewed reported poor performance of the government in terms of the treatment of COVID-19, corruption, unemployment, inflation, inequality, and poverty: https://brasil.elpais.com/brasil/2021-11-29/aprovacao-a-bolsonaro-cai-para-29-nivel-mais-baixo-desde-o-inicio-do-governo.html

favourably stimulate, as a positive indirect effect, the involvement of people in the political-electoral debate and the taking of actions focused on politically mobilizing other people (Zumárraga et al., 2022, p. 207, 213).

The pandemic was an occasion—though not the only one—that aroused greater interest among citizens in how their governments dealt directly with COVID-19 and the way in which it affected them. I emphasize that it was not the only element that determined the citizens' political behaviour because other factors triggered moments of political crisis, as was the case in Ecuador in October 2019, when President Moreno decreed an increase in fuel prices, or when in 2020 President Piñera in Chile authorized a slight increase in the price of public transport in Santiago. In both cases, triggered large mobilizations that questioned government policy at the root. In Ecuador, the government of Lenin Moreno fell into total disrepute to such an extent that in the 2021 elections, so his party faced a resounding defeat in the race for the country's presidency. In Chile, something similar happened with the Piñera government, but with a radical questioning of a bipartisan political system that had governed for many years. The presidential elections of November 21 (the first electoral round) and December 19, 2021 (the runoff) led to the triumph of a new rising political current with ruling President Gabriel Boric.

In a context of political crisis and distrust in the institutions management, added to the uncertainty generated by the effects of the pandemic, it is understood that the concern for the election of State representatives is highly relevant, especially in regard to how this can form responses to the present crises (Zumárraga, et al., 2022, pp. 2012–2013).

In the presidential elections in Peru, whose first round was on April 11 and the runoff on June 6, 2021, a different option from the traditional political parties emerged with the triumph of Pedro Castillo. This is a similar occurrence to Ollanta Humala's victory in 2011. There was also a similar trend in the presidential elections in Honduras on November 28, 2021, when the National Party, whose leaders Porfirio Lobo and Juan Orlando Hernández had governed since the 2009 coup, was defeated. This led to the rise of a new progressive political candidate—the current leader, Xiomara Castro from the LIBRE political party.

Let us now consider the citizens' electoral participation. If we look at the years 2000–2018, on average, we find high levels of participation: "Between 1978 and 2000, the average participation in presidential elections in the 18 regional countries was 73.2%" (Espí Hernández, 2019, p. 19). However, two important elements explain this. First, there is greater reliability in electoral processes in the twenty-first century, which enabled effective alternation in governments with triumphant political tendencies not previously imagined in traditional political systems. Second, it included necessary to consider how, in several countries—such as Argentina, Bolivia, Brazil, Ecuador, Peru and Uruguay (Chile until 2012)—a failure to vote was met with a penalty, which necessarily raised the level of voting. In this way,

> When there is no sanction, participation is slightly higher in countries where it is mandatory (65% on average) compared to those countries where voting is not mandatory (55%). On the other hand, in those countries where it is mandatory and there is a sanction, participation reached 82% on average (CELAG, 2022).

Thus, despite the average, there are countries where participation is traditionally low, such as Colombia (47.43%), Guatemala (53.02%), Mexico (62.27%), Honduras (59.59%), and Paraguay (63.45%), specifically in the years 2000–2018 (Espí Hernández, 2019, pp. 24–25). In Chile, it is surprising that participation was high with the mandatory vote and sanctions (86.94% in 2010), but when the vote was free, it decreased to 41.98% in 2013.[8]

I argue that although some may assume that COVID-19, social distancing, and the fear of contagion could have alienated citizens during the 2020–2021 polls, this did not occur in a significant way because, although elections were postponed in some cases, the voting trends remained unchanged because many citizens were still interested in determining their governments.

Thus, Ecuador saw the participation of more than 80% of voters; in Peru, 74% of the population went to vote; in Chile, 56% of the voters participated; in Nicaragua, 65% of the population participated; and in Honduras, 68% of registered citizens voted. So in relation to the general trends of Latin American voting, COVID-19 did not limit participation since citizens continued voting in a similar way to previous years. The people's interest in trying to politically influence the election of their rulers was more important, according to Zumárraga et al. (2022, pp. 2012–2013).

---

[8] It is very interesting to analyse the abrupt decrease in the electoral participation of Chileans before and after the mandatory vote with sanctions in 2012. The significant drop from 87% to 42% posed a fundamental question: which is better: a compulsory vote or a free vote? The former meant greater participation; the latter, a marked lack of interest in casting the vote. This contrast was clear when the government—which proposed the text for a new constitution in September 2022, decreed that—in this exceptional case, voting would again be mandatory; then, there were 85.82% of the voters participating. The obligatory nature of the vote remains a matter of debate.

7.3 Reactivation of integration processes in 2021

The pandemic in 2020–2021 taught the world one significant lesson: nation-states were more concerned with improving health systems and acquiring vaccines for the people than with cooperation among groups of countries. The only exception to this tendency was the European Union, which made an effort to negotiate with the pharmaceutical companies. The governments negotiating with pharmaceuticals achieved better prices and more vaccines. Although the African Union has 55 member states, it had little influence compared to individual governments when it came to negotiating during the pandemic. This was also the case in the Latin American region, where the capacity of each government was more than that of any regional integration group. There were no negotiations with CELAC (Community of Latin American and Caribbean States), MERCOSUR (Southern Common Market), UNASUR (Union of South American Nations), SICA (System of Central American Integration), ALADI (Latin American Integration Association), or ALBA (Bolivarian Alliance for the Peoples of Our America). The pandemic could have been an opportunity for Latin America to re-activate its integration processes to face future crises better. Maybe, as it happened with the European Union, we can achieve better development and better responses to a crisis as a group of nations.

In particular, the meeting of the CELAC in September 2021 was a great re-activation of the integration process of the Latin American region. Representatives or heads of state of 33 nations attended in answer to the call of the Mexican president Andrés Manuel López Obrador (AMLO), who held the pro tempore presidency. Thus, we can consider the Sixth Summit of the CELAC on September 18, 2021 in Mexico City to be the product of a progressive government that envisioned better solutions through joint negotiations because the virus was global.

The idea of one great American homeland, or a union of republics, arose during the independence of the Latin American countries at the beginning of the nineteenth century with the liberator Simon Bolivar, who wrote, "I want more than any other to see the formation of the greatest nation in the world in America for its freedom and glory" (Bolívar, 1815, p. 27).

However, the tragedy of failed Latin American unity was the product of local geographic projects and local leaders. The Creole economic elites believed they could exercise absolute power without any influence or pressure beyond their borders. The independence of Latin American nation-states (Mexico, Venezuela, Colombia, Ecuador, Chile, and Argentina) in the nineteenth century was the result of the pulverization of local interests, a situation that immediately benefited the project of President James Monroe, who governed the United States of America during 1817–1825 and enunciated his idea of "America for

Americans" in his annual message to the American Congress on December 2, 1823.

Contrary to Bolívar's aspirations, unification projects persisted strongly in the twentieth century but under the model of Pan-Americanism and as a legacy of the Monroe Doctrine. They were expressed through two institutional instruments. The first was the elaboration and signing of the TIAR (Treaty for Inter-American Reciprocal Assistance) or Treaty of Rio in 1947 as a defensive agreement, where the USA promised to be the police of the continent against any attempts at subversion or insurrection against its national interests. The second was the creation of the OAS in 1948, after the Second World War; its mission for fulfilment in the twenty-first century has continued through the current Secretary General of the OAS, Luis Almagro, since 2015, despite functions of subordination to North America and undue interference in the internal affairs of many countries.

Established with ambitious aims in 1959–60, the Latin American Free Trade Association (ALALC), which became the Latin American Integration Association (ALADI) in 1980, currently has 13 countries as members: Argentina, Bolivia, Brazil, Chile, Colombia, Cuba, Ecuador, Mexico, Panama, Paraguay, Peru, Uruguay, and Venezuela. It still wants a common Latin American market. Other regional associations and more specific projects have been the Andean Pact (Pacto Andino) and MERCOSUR.

At the beginning of the twenty-first century, the Alianza Bolivariana (ALBA), which was founded initially by Cuba and Venezuela in 2004, largely under the initiative of the latter and personally promoted by Hugo Chavez, focused primarily on the fight against poverty and social inequality. We can appreciate that at the time, the progressive governments of Venezuela, Cuba, Bolivia, Ecuador, Nicaragua, and Honduras coordinated their public policies. In addition, it is also important to highlight the project of the UNASUR in 2008, which explicitly tried to create programs beyond horizontal free trade agreements among Latin American nations through social development and cooperation projects. It was initially made up of 12 countries: Argentina, Bolivia, Brazil, Colombia, Chile, Ecuador, Guyana, Paraguay, Peru, Suriname, Uruguay, and Venezuela. ALBA and UNASUR not only proposed an integration model based solely on free trade under the principles of the Washington Consensus,[9] but were also inspired by

---

[9] The economist John Williamson invented the term 'Washington consensus' in 1989 to synthesize a series of recommendations or impositions of the United States together with the International Monetary Fund and the World Bank to implement the Free Trade model. These institutions had met in Washington to express the measures that countries

the public policies of the progressive governments that emerged at the beginning of the twenty-first century in the framework of electoral democracies with a clearer social development agenda.

These regional integration projects were very important between the end of the twentieth century and the beginning of the twenty-first. However, we must note that they coincided with the rise of many progressive governments in the region, especially during 1998–2010,[10] parallel to the broader desire of governments for greater economic and social collaboration in order to go beyond simple free-trade agreements which benefit mostly the elites, while also searching for greater autonomy against the dominant neoliberalism of the United States.

In the second decade of the twenty-first century, when Venezuela began to suffer a serious economic and political crisis, ALBA lost strength as its member countries were unable to agree with each other. UNASUR also began to lose unity when new governments—Argentina's Mauricio Macri, Uruguay's Luis Lacalle Pou, and Paraguay's Mario Abdo Benitez—opposed the aim of the institution. In 2017, in Ecuador, the government of Lenin Moreno abandoned the ideals of Correa's citizen revolution, and along with other governments, it shelved both integration models. Lenin Moreno even closed down the UNASUR headquarters, and a coup d'état took place in Bolivia in 2019 with a new government led by interim president Jeanine Áñez, abandoning progressive integration projects.

We also saw the dismemberment of MERCOSUR when the right and extreme right took over power in the government of Paraguay in 2012 (after the coup d'état that brought down President Fernando Lugo), Brazil in 2016 (in the legislative coup d'état the same year against Dilma Rousseff), and Uruguay in 2020 (after Tabare Vazquez). For a few years, Argentina also came under right-wing leadership with President Mauricio Macri from 2015 to 2019.

The Andean community lost its initial impulse from the late 1990s to pursue a relatively proactive agenda when Venezuela left the organization and moved to MERCOSUR in 2000. In addition, the right-wing governments in Colombia, Ecuador, and Chile and the Bolivian interim president Jeanine Áñez strengthened the promotion of the Forum for the Progress and Integration of South America

---

had to implement: free trade, deregulation, sale of state companies, and tax reforms to favor business investment.

[10] For details on the processes by which these progressive governments reached the executive power in several countries through electoral democracy during the first decade of the twenty-first century, see a book by Medina Núñez (2009), *Presidential elections in Latin America: the ascent of the left*.

(PROSUR). This new initiative which would promote free trade, and create room for initial development at a time when UNASUR and CAN (the Andean Community) were weakened. PROSUR was a symbol of the neoliberal model promoted by the right-wing governments of Colombia and Chile in 2019; its main purpose was to oppose UNASUR. It managed to bring together Brazil, Argentina, Ecuador, Paraguay, and Peru in order to deepen the neoliberal model and the economic power of business owners.

Complementary to PROSUR, and in an attempt to fortify the political offensive against progressive governments—especially that of Nicolás Maduro in Venezuela—the Lima Group was created in 2017, initially integrating 12 countries. They signed the Declaration of Lima, supported by the OAS and the European Union, giving their explicit recognition to the artificial Venezuelan opposition represented by Juan Guaido, who was supported by the United States. However, the political situation in each country reduced the power of The Lima Group. The new progressive government of Mexico in 2018 and the victory of Luis Arce of the MAS (Movement for Socialism) Party in Bolivia in 2020 were sharp shifts which differed from what some states in the region expected and further undermined the authority of Lima Group. After coming to power, the new Argentinian government, led by Alberto Fernández, left the right-wing movement as well, and finally, the triumph of Pedro Castillo in Peru in 2021 made the political weight of Lima Group completely insignificant.

Regional integration saw variations over the years because governments took positions regardless of their stances on the right or the left. Right-wing governments are willing to follow the US neoliberal model and the Washington consensus, while the heterogeneous left demands greater autonomy in relation to the United States and greater coordination between Latin American governments in order to achieve better development. One can consider that in the first decade of the twenty-first century, the rise of the heterogeneous left was clearly marked in many countries (Medina Núñez, 2009), but in the second decade, some of them, like Honduras, Paraguay, Uruguay, Brazil, and Argentina, saw a regression. As Schuster and Stefanoni point out:

> In the mid-2010s, the governments of the so-called Latin American left turn began to show signs of exhaustion. These were explained by various reasons: wear and tear due to the years in power, difficulties in renewing leadership, global economic changes, insistent reformist agendas, etc. (Schuster and Stefanoni, 2021, p. 2).

But the third decade of the twenty-first century represents a new global political situation for the region, with the leadership of progressive governments such as Mexico, Bolivia, Argentina, Chile, and Colombia and the return of Lula as president in Brazil.

The coming to power of Andres Manuel Lopez Obrador in Mexico and the return of Peronism in Argentina were added to the fall and return to government of the Movimiento al Socialismo (MAS) in Bolivia, the electoral rise of the Chilean left and the triumph of Pedro Castillo in Peru and, more recently, the recovery of the Brazilian left... From the institutions as from the streets, the road seems to be paving for a kind of second turn to the left. The victories of the left take place, in any case, in a different climate (Schuster and Stefanoni, 2021, pp. 2–3).

We can see then that in the Latin American governments of the twenty-first century, electoral struggles placed both progressive and neoliberal governments in a regional context where different visions of integration models collided.

For its part, the USA continued supporting the FTAA (Free Trade Alliance for the Americas) with a Pan-American vision subordinated to the economic power of the North while also promoting the formation of regional blocs such as NAFTA (North America Free Trade Agreement between Mexico, United States, and Canada) in 1994; the Pacific Alliance (Colombia, Chile, Mexico, and Peru) in 2011; the Central American treaty, CAFTA (Central America Free Trade Agreement), which also included the Dominican Republic; and many bilateral treaties (USA–Chile, USA–Colombia, USA–Peru, etc.). At the same time, with the vision of integration and the awareness of its repercussions on the social development of the people, the region proposed the project of ALBA and the South American Community of Nations. This later became UNASUR, which emphasized significant autonomy from the United States.

At the continental level, ALADI in 1980 was certainly the first attempt to cover the entire continent with a common market. It is made up of 13 countries, and its membership is open to others. Without getting involved in ideological disputes, this Montevideo-based institution has retained its objectives of removing obstacles to trade and promoting the economic development of the region. However, the CELAC stands out—it has a large, declarative, autonomous integration project for all the countries of the continent to which the governments of the United States and Canada are not invited.

The so-called Rio Group, which emerged in 1986, was an important precedent formulated as a permanent consultation and agreement mechanism for all the countries of this region. But it was the government of Brazil, led by President Lula da Silva, who proposed to 33 countries a Summit of Latin America and the Caribbean (CALC), which was held in 2008 in Salvador de Bahía. The final declaration of this meeting, with commitments to strengthen cooperation and negotiation among governments, specifically in the context of facing the international financial crisis that year, was well received by all governmental powers. The meeting of the Ministers of Foreign Affairs of all the CALC governments that took place in Montego Bay, Jamaica, in 2009 was a follow-up to this summit. This process culminated in the XXI Summit of the Rio Group and the second CALC that occurred in February 2010 in southeastern Mexico. The Summit established the CELAC in its final declaration with the objective of

> making efforts with our peoples, that allow us to advance in unity and in political, economic, social and cultural integration, advance in social well-being, quality of life, economic growth and promote our independent and sustainable development, on the basis of democracy, equity and the broadest social justice (CELAC, 2010).

It is very interesting to note the enthusiasm for this new, almost continental instance where the Latin American and Caribbean governments felt represented—despite the ideological and programmatic diversity in their national spheres—without the presence of the United States among them. For this reason, in 2011, the Declaration of Caracas recognized that CELAC was the "only mechanism for dialogue and agreement that brings together the 33 countries of Latin America and the Caribbean" and was

> the highest expression of our desire for unity in diversity, where henceforth our political, economic, social and cultural ties will be strengthened on the basis of a common agenda of well-being, peace and security for our peoples, in order to consolidate ourselves as a regional community (CELAC, 2011).

The Rio Group and CALC held summits to follow up on member states' progress with the declarations of the CELAC. Table 7.3 provides the schedule for the summits.

Table 7.3 Schedule of CELAC summits

#	City	Date	Hosting President
1	Santiago de Chile	January 27–28, 2013	Sebastián Piñera
2	La Habana, Cuba	January 28–29, 2014	Raúl Castro
3	San Jose, Costa Rica	January 28–29, 2015	Luis Guillermo Solís
4	Quito, Ecuador	January 27, 2016	Rafael Correa
5	Punta Cana, Dominican Republic	January 24–25, 2017	Danilo Medina
6	CDMX, Mexico	September 18, 2021	Andres Manuel Lopez Obrador

Source: Created by the author; based on data from UC San Diego (2023).

The final declarations of the CELAC Summits emerged from the consensus of all participating governments despite the diversity of their ideological tendencies—all of them promote dialogue, negotiation, and the search for common agreements. However, it is precisely the fact that the declaration depends on the positions of member governments—and the contradictions among them—that constitutes its Achilles' heel. Since in the second decade of the twenty-first century, there has been a strengthening of conservative-leaning governments, and it has become more difficult to reach agreements on the final declarations. During their tenure, the governments of Iván Duque (Colombia), Abdo Benitez (Paraguay), Mauricio Macri (Argentina), Jeanine Añez (Bolivia), Lenin Moreno and now Guillermo Lasso (Ecuador), Jair Bolsonaro (Brazil), and Luis Lacalle Pou (Uruguay), leaned strongly towards neoliberalism and have strong ties of subordination towards the United States. This makes it very difficult for CELAC to adopt, for example, a strong position of autonomy in relation to the power of the North. There are few other instances of horizontal integration that can be extended beyond free-trade agreements to other areas of social development. For this reason, we can consider that having held summits year after year since its inception in 2013, CELAC's meetings were suspended in 2017 and could only be resumed with the pro tempore presidency of Mexico under the AMLO government to achieve the Sixth Summit in Mexico City in September 2021.

After two years of the pandemic, the Sixth CELAC Summit was held. We can consider it successful due to its great impact on the reactivation of integration processes, but some results were also controversial because the final declaration did not carry a clear call for a reform of the OAS[11] and there was an open discussion about the representation of Cuba and Nicaragua in democracy and human rights. Still, some parts of the meeting were very successful and overall, it had a high level of legitimacy due to the attendance of most of the heads of state, who once again discussed the need for Latin American unity or integration. All agreed that CELAC should continue as a mechanism for consultation and political dialogue with 33 countries in Latin America and the Caribbean. This summit

> reiterates its commitment to political, economic, social and cultural unity and integration, and the decision to continue working together to address the health, social, economic and environmental crisis caused by the COVID-19 pandemic, climate change, natural disasters and the degradation of the planet's biodiversity, among others (CELAC, 2021).

The various representatives discussed the effects of COVID-19 and stressed the need for better coordination and integration in order to strengthen health

---

[11] The OAS's attempt not to be an instrument of interventionism in the internal affairs of other countries, based on the guidelines of the United States, was the subject of great discussion among the heads of state and in public opinion, but the text of the final declaration did not reflect an agreement. It was a success to have opened the subject to public debate, but the divergent positions of the Latin American governments meant that there was no consensus on this point.

systems and have greater bargaining power when it comes to acquiring vaccines or other forms of health care for the benefit of the population.

However, the internal contradictions and obstacles to this project in the near future remain very explicit because transnational negative instruments to the detriment of the participating nation-states are very strong. Perhaps we could consider that, at the end of the twentieth century, the power of the nation-states declined in favour of globalization, but this would be too easy a conclusion. We also have to look at the nations where one of the constitutive elements of the state, the executive branch, has enormous influence in defining the course of each country during the period of time that it has to exercise its mandate. The state still has great power to decide the course of the nation in many public policies, whether in favour of the economic elites or among the majority of the population.

> Current efforts to relocate the State through theories of transnationality or globalization tend to recover the traditional nation-state, often as part of a notion of internationalism, as its basis, and therefore reassess the State form as the indispensable horizon of any political question, either to upset it or to accept it. It is as if the State form had the same influence on politics that metaphysics has on philosophy: the very moment that a project frees itself from the State is the moment that it falls most firmly into its clutches (Levinson, 2004, p. 123).

The economic situation in Latin American countries is very unequal: strong nations see GDP growth while others see its decline; wealth is concentrated among a few inhabitants while a large part of the population survives in moderate to extreme poverty. In this context, can integration mechanisms be more efficient in promoting social development and better responses to future economic and health crises than the national efforts of isolated countries? Logic indicates that the first is easy to sustain, but many governments continue to get closer to the USA, thinking that it would be a better engine for development than the effort of better coordination among Latin American countries themselves.

The economic inequality among Latin American countries greatly influences their relationship with the United States: the strength of large economies,[12] such as Mexico, Brazil, Argentina, Chile, and Colombia, for example, can give them more autonomy and bargaining power with other governments from

---

[12] Even Venezuela could be considered a great economy due to its abundant natural resources, but the position of the United States and the internal opposition during the governments of Hugo Chávez and Nicolás Maduro have led to a painful confrontation and a prolonged economic crisis with a multitude of Venezuelan migrants abroad. The complex case of Venezuela needs to be analysed in more depth.

more developed countries. However, economies such as those of Haiti and Central American countries are more vulnerable when they face pressure from the US government, which has large amounts of aid that it can provide or take away. However, there can be space for political manoeuvring when a party takes charge of a government with broad popular support for more autonomous and independent socioeconomic development. Many integration mechanisms will continue to depend, to a large extent, on the will of the goverments in power. Analysing the project of the European Union shows an original agreement that has been institutionalized beyond changes in each government's economic and political orientation, but in Latin America, each government in its constitutional period (four, five, or six years) has the power to guide the nation along the economic or political path of its choosing. We can see, then, for example, that integration processes have been easily accepted or promoted by progressive governments as it happened during the first decade of the twenty-first century. When right-wing political forces returned to power during the second decade of this century, integration processes decayed (Ecuador closed the UNASUR headquarters, ALBA almost disappeared, and there were no CELAC Summits for some years after 2017). Additionally, in the third decade of the twenty-first century, with more progressive governments in México, Argentina, Chile, Bolivia, and Colombia, and against the backdrop of the pandemic, CELAC had its rebirth.

In Latin America, the strength of CELAC will always be subject to political changes within each country. Its political orientation will affect the emphasis it gives to two integration models: one that is based more on facilitating free trade between the economic elites of each nation with a subordinate link to North American interests and another that is more focused on economic growth along with the social well-being of its population—which reflects greater autonomy in relation to the power of the North. In any case, the fact that it is an exclusive space for dialogue among Latin Americans without the USA and Canada is already a positive sign in recognizing a historical, cultural identity that could move towards a better economic and political project. In both cases, if Latin American countries achieve greater horizontal economic exchange, it will be an advancement compared to the previous scenario, where they only sought to penetrate the US market. This is why it is in the interest of all governments, regardless of their ideology, to maintain and increase collaboration among Latin Americans.

AMLO's call for a CELAC summit in Mexico in 2021 was successful; however, the Bolsonaro government did not send any representatives at all; Iván Duque, the head of government of Colombia, did not want to attend in person but sent a representative. Uruguay's Lacalle and Ecuador's Lasso were present and signed the final declaration but did not favour autonomous integration; they defended the discredited OAS and made direct attacks on the governments of Cuba, Nicaragua, and Venezuela. In any case, the 44 points of the CDMX (acronym from Spanish, Ciudad de México) Declaration of September 18, 2021, are essential for this complex project of Latin American integration. Some of its points are the call to democratize the production of anti-COVID-19 vaccines, its emphasis on multilateralism, the fight against corruption, its commitment to eradicate poverty, the rejection of unilateral coercive measures against certain countries; the promotion of gender equality and respect for human rights; the rejection of the criminalization of migration; the fight against climate change; and the condemnation of terrorism and all kinds of interference in the internal affairs of other countries.

7.4 Conclusion

In this chapter, I have focused on the behaviours and strategies of social actors using some mechanisms of historical sociology and comparing political trends across several Latin American countries, especially during the COVID-19 pandemic. For this reason, I conclude on several important points. The increase in the number of progressive governments—despite their diversity—at the end of the second decade of the twenty-first century demonstrates an intensification in the integration processes. They seem to be seeking more autonomy in relation to the imperial will of the United States, and this became more evident during the pandemic when these governments were forced to negotiate directly with pharmaceutical companies and industrialized countries for vaccines and other health instruments.

In the context of the pandemic in 2021, the UN tried to implement the COVAX program because industrialized countries had monopolized the purchase of vaccines for the benefit of their own populations while leaving their distribution to developing countries. COVAX was a useful intervention at a time when fighting COVID depended on bilateral negotiations determined by the strengths or weaknesses of the governments in power. The results would have been different if the governments had not acted alone but instead coordinated or integrated to negotiate to obtain the vaccine. The bilateral collaboration between Mexico and Argentina, with the support of the Slim Foundation, was an example of greater effectiveness in dealing with the virus. The CELAC summit in Mexico in 2021 recommended mechanisms to face future crises in a more coordinated manner, with a proposal for health, self-sufficiency, and a regional vaccine purchase mechanism that included, above all, the flexibility for states to produce their own vaccines in the subcontinent. The crises are now global and, therefore, require coordinated responses from governments and heads of state.

I recall the vision that some Argentinian researchers had in 2017 that gained more strength in 2021 despite the difficulties of the pandemic:

CELAC finds it difficult to become a true regional integration mechanism that can lead to a superior form of institutionality and prevents it, in some way, from becoming an international organization with precise objectives. Among the obstacles that exist for this, one of a historical nature undoubtedly stands out: Latin America and the Caribbean have traditionally been reluctant to integrate into supranational legal bodies and have usually opted for more flexible integration formulas. In addition, integration schemes, whose remote origins we must place in the positions that Bolivar adopted in connection with the convocation of the Panama Congress in 1826, they have been hindered by multiple factors. This is due to the region's own historical development in relation to the hegemonic claims of the United States over the continent since the 19th century (Díaz Galán and Bertot Triana, 2017, p. 58).

In the twenty-first century, we are no longer under the Monroe Doctrine of the nineteenth century because the old Pan-Americanism under North American rule has been substituted by the neoliberal model and free trade. Latin American autonomy has been growing but with a great heterogeneity of national positions that now depend on electoral democracy. We have come a long way in the world of globalization and the power of supranational forces, but it is evident that the power of the nation-state continues to be dominant, as it is determined by the orientation and project of each government.

Hegemony has yet to be won or lost at the nation state and/or local state level. In other words: hegemony must still pass through the nation state at some point or another (Beverley, 1999, p. 152).

We must be aware that the revitalization of the integration process with the realization of CELAC in 2021 does not erase the pre-existing struggles and contradictions in regional schemes. SICA will continue to stagnate as long as the Central American governments do not come together in basic consensus for their economic development. MERCOSUR also remains stagnant because the conservative governments of Brazil, Paraguay, and Uruguay are not interested in constituting a unified bloc to promote the region. PROSUR, proposed in 2019 by the conservative governments of Chile and Colombia to replace the more progressive UNASUR, was successful at first because it seemed to hold a conservative position, but it has now radically changed along with the political situation in these two countries. We also see that with Alberto Fernández in Argentina, Luis Arce in Bolivia, and formerly Pedro Castillo in Peru, the region arrived at more progressive positions. PROSUR is declining as a conservative group, as is the Lima Group.

COVID-19 led to a difficult economic situation with negative effects on the population, but it created a specific context of favourable political trends towards integration processes, as we can see from the new positions of Peru (when Castillo was president), Chile, Colombia, and Honduras—although in Ecuador, in 2021, by a small margin, the progressive candidate Andres Arauz did not win the presidency. In 2022, President Jair Bolsonaro lost the October elections, which highlights that after his government minimized the threat of the virus, it did not make an effort to implement a public policy of effective support for the population to better confront the pandemic.

It is clear that COVID-19 had severe effects on the Latin American population and revealed the weakness of health systems, with most nations having institutions that were privatized. On the one hand, this situation had political effects on most citizens, who voted against the unfavourable public policies of some rulers to enable a transition towards other political tendencies. On the other hand, in the midst of the same health crisis, many rulers met at CELAC 2021 to reactivate the momentum for regional integration—something that the conservative governments seemed to have forgotten for years. In 2021, Paraguay, Ecuador, Chile, Colombia, and Brazil remained opposed to the processes of the Bolivarian Project, but in 2023, the political situation has changed in Chile, Colombia, and Brazil, who are now in favour of integration processes and better coordination in order to solve common problems.

I believe that in the first years of the third decade of the twenty-first century, Latin American nations have shown great enthusiasm in reopening the path towards autonomous Latin American integration with social development projects for the well-being of the people. However, this is still a very uncertain and conflicted path with different possibilities for the way forward. We hope that in the aftermath of COVID-19, CELAC can become one of the best mechanisms to reactivate the Bolivarian dream of a union of republics, which will have a greater capacity to face the social problems that affect us.

References

Beverley, J. (1999) *Subalternity and representation: arguments in cultural theory*. Durham: Duke University Press.

Bolívar, S. (1815) *Carta de Jamaica*. Centro de Estudios Latinoamericanos. Faculta de Filosofía y Letras. México: National Autonomous University of Mexico.

CELAC (2010) 'Declaración de la Cumbre de la Unidad de América Latina y el Caribe'. Riviera Maya, México. 23 February 2010. Available at: https://ppt-celac.sre.gob.mx (Accessed: 18 April 2023).

CELAC (2011) 'Declaración de Caracas 'En el bicentenario de la lucha por la Independencia. Hacia el Camino de Nuestros Libertadores'', CELAC Summit 2011, 3 December in Caracas, Venezuela.

CELAC. (2021) 'Declaración de la Ciudad de México', VI Cumbre de Jefas y Jefes de Estado y de Gobierno de la Comunidad de Estados Latinoamericanos y

Caribeños (CELAC). 18 September 2021. Available at: https://www.gob.mx/presidencia/documentos/declaracion-de-la-ciudad-de-mexico-celac-2021 (Accessed: 25 March 2023).

CELAG (2022) 'Voto obligatorio y participacion electoral en América latina'. Centro Estratégico Latinoamericano de Geopolítica (CELAG). 11 November 2022. Available at: https://www.celag.org/voto-obligatorio-y-participacion-electoral-en-america-latina/ (Accessed: 3 May 2023).

Congressional Research Service (2021) 'Nicaragua in brief: political developments in 2021, U.S. policy, and issues for congresss'. Updated December 28, 2021. Available at: https://crsreports.congress.gov/product/pdf/R/R46860/5 (Accessed: 4 April 2023).

Corvetto Salinas, P. A. (2022) 'Los efectos de la pandemia en el sistema democrático peruano: la organización de las Elecciones Bicentenario', *Revista Elecciones*, 20 (22), pp. 15–49.

Díaz Galán, E. C. and Bertot Triana, H. (2017) 'La Comunidad de Estados Latinoamericanos y Caribeños (CELAC)', *Cuadernos de política exterior argentina*, 126, pp. 47-66.

ECLAC (2021a) 'Documento de la CEPAL': Crecimiento de América Latina y el Caribe no alcanzará a revertir los efectos adversos de la pandemia. Available at: https://www.cepal.org/es/comunicados/crecimiento-america-latina-caribe-2021-alcanzara-revertir-efectos-adversos-la-pandemia (Accessed: 12 May 2023).

ECLAC (2021b) 'Nicaragua: Economic survey of Latin America and the Caribbean'. Economic Comission for Latin America and the Caribean (ECLAC). Available at: https://repositorio.cepal.org/bitstream/handle/11362/48575/19/PO2022_Nicaragua_en.pdf (Accessed: 8 April 2023).

Espí Hernández, A. (2019) 'Participación electoral en América Latina: Un análisis comparado desde la simultaneidad de las elecciones 2000–2018', *Apuntes Electorales*, 28 (61), pp. 11–38.

Expansión (2021) *Mejora el PIB en Ecuador*. Available at: https://datosmacro.expansion.com/pib/ecuador (Accessed: 3 May 2023).

Lachmann, R. (2013) *What is historical sociology?* Cambridge: Polity Press.

Levinson, B. (2004) *Market and thought: meditations on the political and biopolitical*. New York: Fordham University Press.

Lo, J. and Lawson, G. (2017) *Global historical sociology*. Cambridge: Cambridge University Press.

Makison, D. (1992) 'Editorial', *La sociología histórica*, 44 (3), pp. 339-341.

Medina Núñez, I. (2009) *Presidential elections in Latin America: The ascent of the left*. Buenos Aires: Elaleph.

Observatorio social del Ecuador (2022) *Exceso de fallecidos por todas las causas: Decesos diarios desde mayo de 2021*. Available at: https://www.covid19ecuador.org/fallecidos#:~:text=Registro%20Civil&text=El%20Estado%20Ecuatoriano%20reconoce%20oficialmente,204.9%20por%20cada%20100%2C000%20habitantes (Accessed: 27 March 2023).

Tilly, C. (1992) 'Prisoners of the state', *International Social Science Journal*, 44 (3), pp. 329–342.

Schuster, M. and Stefanoni, P. (2021) ¿Un segundo "giro a la izquierda" en América Latina? *Revista Nueva Sociedad.* 15 October. https://nuso.org/articulo/un-segundo-giro-a-la-izquierda-en-america-latina/

Skocpol, T. (1984) *Vision and method in historical sociology.* Cambridge: Cambridge University Press.

Statista (2022) Available at: https://es.statista.com/ (Accessed: 19 October 2022).

UC San Diego (2023) Latin American Studies Online: Elections. https://ucsd.libguides.com/c.php?g=1020872&p=7407087 (Accessed: 22 November 2022).

WHO (2021) 'NCD Alliance Advocacy Briefing for World Health Organization 148th Executive Board 2021 (EB148)', NCD Alliance, 18–26 January 2021. Available at: https://ncdalliance.org/resources/ncd-alliance-advocacy-briefing-for-world-health-organization-148th-executive-board-2021-eb148 (Accessed: 5 May 2023).

Zumárraga-Espinosa, M., Egas-Balseca, S. and Reyes-Valenzuela, C. (2022) 'La preocupación por el COVID-19 y sus efectos en la participación política online de la ciudadanía en el contexto ecuatoriano', *Revista de Ciencias Sociales y Humanas,* 36, pp. 195–219.

Chapter 8

Interactions of Brazil, Peru, PAHO and ACTO in overcoming the effects of COVID-19

Alla Yurievna Borzova

Peoples' Friendship University of Russia, Russia

Abstract

The Pan American Health Organisation (PAHO) has a long history of helping to tackle health issues and combat the spread of infectious diseases. However, the effect of the COVID-19 pandemic was too sudden and too impactful to be curbed through top-down action by the organization alone, so its member states also began to collaborate through various other channels simultaneously. They include bilateral cooperation and engagement through other mechanisms such as the Amazon Cooperation Treaty Organisation (ACTO). This chapter argues that a deepening of interactions between Brazil and Peru took place during the COVID-19 pandemic, spilling over from healthcare to other areas, often through ACTO. These areas include the protection of indigenous rights, the formation of an integrated management system of the Amazon River Basin and ensuring control over the extraction of natural resources, among others. As a result, this ultimately helped to deepen the process of regional integration in Latin America.

Keywords: COVID-19, health governance, Brazil, Peru, PAHO, ACTO

***

8.1 PAHO in Latin America

The main task of the Pan American Health Organization (PAHO), when it was founded in 1902, was to control the spread of infectious diseases. Later it began to promote the development of healthcare systems and ensure the well-being of populations in Latin American and Caribbean (LAC) countries. Today, the PAHO also provides recommendations to member states on how to manage communicable and noncommunicable diseases; offers information on the causes of the diseases; provides support in responding to emergencies and disasters throughout the LAC; and stimulates cooperation between countries.

According to the UN (United Nations, 2022), universal health coverage in the LAC averaged 75% in 2017. PAHO experts add that 30% of the population of the Americas does not have access to essential healthcare due to financial, geographical, institutional, social, and cultural factors. Countries in the LAC invest an average of 4.2% of their gross domestic product (GDP) in health—less than the World Health Organization (WHO) recommended minimum of 6%—and allocate an average of 26% of their health budget to primary care (PAHO, 2022b).

In 2020, the outbreak of the coronavirus disease in Latin America had devastating health, social, and economic impacts, highlighting and exacerbating existing inequities among and within countries. It also suspended progress in the field of healthcare and had serious, aggravating effects on the problems of hunger and food security (OECD, 2020). However, the differences between individual countries were significant. This was reflected in the pace of the spread of the disease. As of 8 June 2021, 1,184,233 deaths due to COVID-19 were registered in Latin America.

Table 8.1 Data on COVID-19 in selected Latin American countries, as of 21 December 2022

Country	Population in 2022 (millions)	Confirmed COVID-19 cases (% of the population)	Fatalities (% of the confirmed COVID-19 cases)
Brazil	218.4	3,599,262 (16.5%)	692,210 (1.90%)
Colombia	52.1	6,330,409 (12.1%)	141,996 (2.20%)
Argentina	46.4	9,829,236 (21.1%)	130,080 (1.30%)
Peru	34.0	4,424,906 (12.9%)	217,941 (4.90%)
Chile	18.4	4,987,847 (27.1%)	62,905 (1.26%)

Source: Created by the author; based on data from Statista (2022).

According to this data, two countries in South America—Brazil and Argentina—were the most affected by the pandemic, based on confirmed cases of COVID-19. The number of fatal outcomes was high in Brazil, Peru, and Colombia; meanwhile, Argentina and Chile seemed to have dealt with the problem more successfully, recording a smaller percentage of deaths. To avoid such disastrous outcomes in future, it is necessary to identify the reasons for the dire situations in Brazil and Peru, taking into account the total loss of life. Additionally, there are several factors that distinguish these two states from the others, and contribute to their rapprochement.

8.2 Background of the rapprochement

Peru and Brazil are separated by a border of almost 3,000 kilometres, which runs through the vast territory of the Amazon. The wealth of the Amazon is of particular importance to the development of both countries because about

63.4% of the Amazonia is located in Brazil, and 8.3% in Peru. Peru and Brazil face similar challenges and threats associated with the development of the Amazon, including the spread of terrorism, cross-border crime and drug trafficking, environmental crimes, and violations of the legal status of indigenous territories associated with the illegal extraction of natural resources. About 900,000 indigenous people live in the Brazilian territory and lead a tribal lifestyle. In the Peruvian *selva* (jungle), more than 4 million indigenous people live in voluntary isolation. They have established initial contacts with other communities but are extremely vulnerable to various infections.

A white paper on the Ministry of Defence of Peru notes that:

> The Amazon River enters the Orinoco watershed, which projects into the Atlantic Basin. The Amazon, in addition to being navigable from the Peruvian territory all the way to the Atlantic Ocean, [...] turns Peruvian and Brazilian territory into a platform of access to two large oceans that calls to exploit the advantages of strategic access to huge markets located in both basins (Peru Ministerio de Defensa, 2005, p. 50).

So it is possible to export goods from Peru to Brazil. Indeed, this transportation artery is vital to the supply of goods to the city of Manaus, the capital of the Amazonas state, which imports about 80% of its food.

Awareness of the need to jointly search for solutions to complex problems has led these two states, which did not show interest in deepening ties for a long time, to become strategic partners. Today, Brazil and Peru are active members of the Amazon Cooperation Treaty Organization (ACTO), which was founded in 1995 to protect the Amazon and promote joint action between countries in the region to overcome shared challenges.

Before commencing full-scale multilateral interactions, however, Brazil and Peru entered into bilateral cooperation. On 16 October 1979 Brazil and Peru signed the Friendship and Cooperation Treaty, which states that both sides give priority to the fulfillment of obligations that bind them to the Amazonian area (OAS, 1979). Later, in July 1987, the then presidents of Brazil and Peru signed the Rio Branco Declaration and the Puerto Maldonado Action Program. Subsequently, the two sides also established a Mixed Brazilian–Peruvian Commission for Amazonian Cooperation to carry out studies of common interest.

In 1993, the two countries signed the Treaty on Economic Interdependence, and in 1996, established the Good Neighborhood Commission, which became a mechanism for the development of bilateral relations. In 1999, during an official visit to Peru, the Brazilian President Fernando E. Cardoso signed the Lima Action Plan for the development of bilateral relations. Then, in 2003, the Agreement on Strategic Partnership between Brazil and Peru was finalized to promote the development of trade and investment, as well as cooperation in different areas. In 2010, the construction of a transoceanic highway from the Peruvian port of San Juan de Marcon across the Andes and to the city of Madre de Dios on the border with Brazil was completed. It connected with roads leading to the Atlantic coast, further strengthening the ties between the two countries. In 2011, Lima and Brasilia signed the Agreement on Strategic Military Cooperation, aimed at improving the operational capabilities of the armed forces, industry, and scientific and technological development to counter organized crime, drug trafficking, smuggling, and illegal extraction of natural resources using the SIVAM/SIPAM (Amazon Surveillance System).

Over the past three decades, Peru has made significant progress in economic development, while Brazil has emerged as Peru's first trading partner in the region. Trade between the countries amounted to $4 billion in 2021 (up by 62% from pre-pandemic levels), Brazil's foreign direct investment (FDI) in Peru was $9.184 million, and Peruvian investment in the Brazilian economy totalled $878 million (UN Comtrade Database, 2021). Evidently, cooperation between the two countries is becoming mutually beneficial and comprehensive.

The COVID-19 pandemic has had catastrophic effects on Brazil and Peru. It has brought the transition of the countries to a sustainable development model under threat, also slowing down the implementation of sustainable development goals (SDGs).

Table 8.2 Comparative data on sustainable development in Peru and Brazil

Country	Sustainability Index			Submission of voluntary national report on SDGs	Human Development Index		
	2019 (162 countries)	2020 (166 countries)	2022 (163 countries)		2014–2018	2020	2021
Brazil	57	79	53	2017	79	86	87
Peru	51	61	58	2016, 2020	82 (+7)	83	84

Source: Created by the author; based on data from CEPAL (2018) and Sustainable Development Solutions Network (2020).

The presented factors indicate that the pandemic has exacerbated existing problems in Brazil and Peru. It has also led the previously observed positive direction in social well-being to acquire a negative trend. This is primarily reflected in a decrease in the population health indices, and an increase in problems in the healthcare systems of the two countries.

8.3 PAHO in Brazil and Peru

PAHO and Brazil have developed a system of technical cooperation to achieve the strategic goals established by the Brazilian government: to ensure the universal right to healthcare through the Unified Health System (SUS/ Sistema

Único de Saúde); to establish partnerships with the Ministry of Health, councils, and institutions of the SUS; and to strengthen international cooperation in the field of health (PAHO, 2020b). For Peru, PAHO developed a cooperation strategy— Estrategia de Cooperación con el País: Perú 2014–2019 (PAHO, 2020a); the main achievements and problems associated with the spread of COVID-19 are presented in the 2021 Annual Report (PAHO, 2021b).

Brazil, unlike Peru, provides technical assistance in the development of healthcare to other countries. In 2005, PAHO, WHO, and Brazil made an important commitment (O Termo de Cooperação Internacional em Saúde, TC 41), with the participation of the Ministry of Health and the Oswaldo Cruz Foundation (Fiocruz), to strengthen international cooperation in the field of health. The aim was to accomplish this through the exchange of experience, knowledge, and technologies available in public health institutions between Brazil and PAHO/WHO member countries through south–south cooperation. Priority was to be given to South American and Portuguese-speaking African countries. In subsequent years, within the framework of TC 41, 51 projects, including more than 680 activities, have been implemented (PAHO, 2015).

The Center for International Relations in Health (CRIS) of the Brazilian Fiocruz is a specialized unit dealing with health diplomacy. It works on advancing health negotiations in the international context and on arranging technical and financial resources for projects. It also oversees four facets of the WHO: leptospirosis, health and environment, the technical school of health, and pharmaceutical policy.

Since 2009, Fiocruz has been promoting a new approach called "health collaboration structuring". This method includes strategic planning, with a focus on the realities of each country or institution. Participating bodies are understood as partners and, therefore, the traditional dynamic of donors and recipients is abandoned. Instead of a vertical care programme (with interventions for specific diseases or problems), a horizontal approach is adopted, aimed at the holistic development of health systems.

Previously, the South American Health Council (SHC) which had operated under the Union of South American Nations (UNASUR), had overseen the activities of the South American Network of National Institutes of Health (RINS-UNASUR). However, as a result of the suspension of UNASUR activities in 2018, this network of institutions ceased to function. However, with the assistance of CRIS/Fiocruz, in 2019, a new network of schools and training centres for public health in Latin America was founded (Rede de Escolas e Centros Formadores em Saúde Pública da América Latina [RESP-AL]), by 11 countries in the region (Souza and Costa, 2019). RESP-AL addresses the challenges associated with public health education in the countries, proposes approaches to sharing experiences and knowledge, and works to strengthen learning strategies in each country (Pereira et al., 2020). The member states of RESL-AL have made joint declarations, expressing concerns about the rise of infections and the fact that some governments were advocating the resumption of production at the expense of the health of their citizens.

To understand the gaps in the development of the healthcare system in Brazil and Peru, we consider some primary indicators.

Table 8.3 The main indicators of the health system in Brazil and Peru

Country	Year	Health expenditure per capita ($)	GDP per capita ($)	Government health expenditure (%)	Out-of-pocket expenditure (%)	Health expenditure (% of GDP)	Health system type	Population covered by health insurance (%)	Physicians per 1,000 people
Peru	2010	240	5,091	51.9%	39.5%	4.72%	Mixed: public and private	100%	1.3
	2015	310	6,228	60.9%	29.4%	4.99%			
	2020	389	6,163	67.9%	22.8%	6.30%			
Brazil	2010	894	11,249	45.0%	29.4%	7.79%	Public	80%	1.8
	2015	783	8,783	43.3%	24.7%	8.91%			
	2020	701	6,795	44.8%	22.4%	10.31%			

Source: Created by the author; based on data from the WHO (2021) and Benítez et al. (2020).

At the same time, other efforts have been made to set up new initiatives or adapt existing ones. For instance, a Regional Network for Latin America and the Caribbean was created under Fiocruz. This network has risen in prominence since the advent of the pandemic, with members analysing and discussing the role of national institutions in combating COVID-19 (Tobar et al., 2017). Along with Fiocruz, Agência Nacional de Vigilância Sanitária (Anvisa) is promoting international development and cooperation in the field of health. This collaboration takes into consideration the Brazilian experience of regulating the pharmaceutical industry and vaccines and of producing other vital products (e.g., protective equipment) for the health sector. The National Health Foundation (Funasa) and the Ministry of Health of Brazil, through its Office of International Affairs, coordinate international health cooperation between relevant departments and structures; governments and organizations in developed countries; and international and regional organizations (Buss, 2018).

As follows from the table, both countries recorded an increase in the percentage of the GDP allocated to the health system. However, government spending in Peru was higher, which is also noticeable in the growth in per capita income and healthcare costs. The population covered by health insurance in Peru was 100%, and in Brazil, 80%. Brazil's health workforce ratio appears to be higher than Peru's, but in practice, this advantage has not been properly utilized in Brazil.

The actions of both governments impacted the spread of COVID-19. In Peru, early in the pandemic, resource allocation was rigorous among various healthcare institutions, and strict movement restrictions were implemented. Still, the massive exodus of workers from Lima to the peripheries likely spread the virus to the rest of the country (Yacila and Turkewitz, 2020). Unlike Peru, however, Brazil was an example of mismanagement. The public health response was not coordinated and there was no federal policy to enforce social distancing and physical isolation (Phillips and Briso, 2020). Further, no guidance was given to states as the central government was unable to decide on a strategy. This reduced the country's ability to contain the spread of the virus. But although at the beginning of the pandemic, Brazil had allocated less than $1 per capita for actions related to stopping the spread of COVID-19, and only significantly increased its medical services package. This helped the situation to stabilize. Evidently, the effects of the COVID-19 pandemic on the populations of Brazil and Peru were different. Moreover, they depended on each country's health system capacity, preparedness for health-related risks, and several other uncontrollable factors.

The Global Health Security Index, which was first compiled in 2019, takes into account 37 indicators that mark the readiness of a country's healthcare system to withstand epidemics and pandemics. According to this measure, compared to 2019, Peru improved its index in 2021 to 54.9 (+1.1) and ranked 32 among 195 countries. During the same time period, Brazil advanced as well, with a score of 51.2 (+0.2) and ranked 43rd. Both countries fell within the 'above average' range, from 40.1 to 60.0 (GHS Index, 2021). As for the COVID Economic Recovery Index (2020), which assesses health system capacity and access, pandemic preparedness, and health risk factors, Brazil ranked 51st (72.84) and Peru 64th (66.75) out of 122 countries.

After the outbreak of COVID-19, the Brazilian Ministry of Health supported a joint project for the simultaneous vaccination of populations in the territories of countries adjacent to the Southern Common Market (MERCOSUR), to strengthen control over the spread of viral diseases, including measles, rubella, and yellow fever (Cobradi and IPEA, 2022). In February 2020, experts from Fiocruz, the Brazilian Ministry of Health, and PAHO conducted training sessions on laboratory diagnosis of the novel coronavirus for specialists from Argentina, Bolivia, Chile, Colombia, Ecuador, Panama, Paraguay, Peru, and Uruguay. They reviewed and discussed the main available tests and protocols (PAHO, 2022a).

Later, in February 2022, the presidents of Peru and Brazil signed an agreement in the field of healthcare, which includes a memorandum of understanding to promote cooperation between the Social Health Insurance System of Peru (EsSalud) and the Ministry of Health of Brazil. The agreement has a series of joint actions designed to improve the health services provided by both countries. Indeed, the EsSalud and Brazilian Ministry of Health will exchange information on social health security policy; decentralization of health management; medicine policy and the functioning of information systems at health facilities; financial regulation of health services and human resource training in health; and information and experiences on strategies to promote vaccinations for diseases such as COVID-19 (Andina, 2022).

Moreover, Peru and Brazil have set up a bilateral border working group to report on experiences with combating COVID-19 and malaria; share information on the prevention of drug and alcohol abuse; prioritize health education and services to improve the quality of their citizens' lives; and bring the presence of the state to the most remote areas in the nations (El Peruano, 2022).

8.4 Brazil and Peru in ACTO

On 14 December 1998, after approval of the amendments by all member countries, the Amazon Cooperation Treaty was transformed into the Amazon Cooperation Treaty Organization (ACTO; the Spanish acronym is OTCA). Subsequently, a Special Commission on Health was established to develop a dialogue between ACTO member countries on issues of social integration and the quality of healthcare systems, monitoring the epidemiological situation in the region (ACTO, 2021a). Then a Special Commission on the Environment in the region and a Special Commission on Indigenous Affairs were set up (ACTO, 2021b). There are more than 30 million people in the Amazon, many of whom belong to indigenous groups and live in voluntary isolation, which makes them particularly vulnerable to new infections. Brazil and Peru have expanded their cooperation within the framework of ACTO to implement the necessary measures to prevent the further spread of COVID-19 (ACTO, 2021e).

Issues related to the lives of the indigenous population of ACTO member countries are being implemented jointly with the relevant confederations of indigenous people of each of the member countries within the framework of the new Strategic Cooperation Program for 2019 to 2030, adopted in 2018 (ACTO, 2019). In accordance with this strategy, the cooperation includes epidemiological surveillance, environmental health measures, health protection, and the exchange of technologies for conducting health measures. The permanent secretariat of ACTO serves as a link between the healthcare structures of the member countries. Responsibilities include processing requests, arranging additional funds for the implementation of programmes in the field of healthcare, and distributing the material assistance received.

As far back as 2011, ACTO, PAHO, and Banco Interamericano de Desarrollo (IADB) began to implement the Program for the Protection of Indigenous Peoples in Voluntary Isolation (ACTO, 2021c). This programme was carried out in two stages:

1. Definition of joint actions of ACTO member countries in order to protect the indigenous population;
2. Continuing and strengthening preventive and community health protection activities as well as incorporating traditional knowledge and practices into territorial management.

Within the framework of this programme, five countries—Bolivia, Brazil, Colombia, Peru, and Ecuador—prepared reference materials on the problems of indigenous peoples living in their countries. This made it possible to direct joint actions of ACTO member countries to protect the indigenous population, develop a regional health strategy, and establish the Secretaria de Vigilância en Saúde (SVS) to control the spread of the zika virus, chikungunya virus, and dengue fever. A system of monitoring the epidemiological situations in the region was established, and measures were adopted to improve the sanitary conditions in the area. Research institutes were created under ACTO, which coordinated the activities of medical institutions. An important act was the creation of the Rede Amazônica de Vigilância da Resistência as Drogas Antimaláricas, which works to combat malaria, and the adaptation of strategic documents to monitor the efficacy and resistance of antimalarial drugs in the current epidemiological context.

The spread of COVID-19 in the Amazon area has shown that problems with access to healthcare for indigenous populations have greatly increased. The main strategy being used to fight the pandemic is vaccinations. However, its dissemination among indigenous communities of the Amazon has been complicated due to low population densities, the need to travel long distances to reach communities, the responsibilities of countries being poorly defined, and cultural barriers.

In October 2020, a cooperation agreement was signed between ACTO and the Fund for the Development of the Indigenous Peoples of Latin America and the Caribbean (FILAC) (ACTO, 2021d). It emphasizes the importance of joint action for protecting the rights of indigenous peoples and other tribal communities in the Amazon region. In March 2021, IADB created the Fund for Sustainable Development for the Amazon. The bank allocated $20 million and highlighted the following areas: biodiversity, agriculture, bioeconomy, infrastructure projects, and human capital (IADB, 2021).

In 2021, PAHO launched the Programa Subregional de la Organización Panamericana de la Salud (OPS). Its aim is to support the efforts of Brazil, Peru, and Colombia in analysing the health status of indigenous peoples in the tri-border zone of the Amazon basin (PAHO, 2021a). The subregional programme also supports the la Ruta de la Salud Indígena Amazónica Hivos (Amazon Indigenous Health Route, AIR). This initiative aims to promote structural change; reduce the impact of COVID-19 on the Amazon indigenous peoples in Brazil, Ecuador, and Peru; improve access to care, prevention, and protection measures; and position the rights and cultures of indigenous peoples at the heart of public health systems. The AIR project is an innovative healthcare model based on intercultural dialogue and the promotion of multilateral processes. It brings together public health professionals, indigenous organizations, academia, and civil society organizations to combat COVID-19 in the Amazon. The implementation of AIR is organized around four main strategies (Hivos, 2022):

- Strategy 1: Place the needs and rights of indigenous peoples at the centre of diagnostics and primary healthcare, including telemedicine networks;
- Strategy 2: Adapt health promotion interventions using an intercultural approach;
- Strategy 3: Develop the capacity of indigenous health advocates;
- Strategy 4: Increase early warning and contact tracing capabilities through a digital application.

This project covers more than 7 million indigenous peoples in Brazil, 270,000 in the Amazonian area of Ecuador, and 173,811 in Peru. The governments of these countries work closely with the Center for Indigenous Work (CTI) in Brazil, the Confederation of Indigenous Nationalities of the Ecuadorian Amazon (CONFENIAE) in Ecuador, and the Native Federation of the Madre de Dios River and Tributaries (FENAMAD) in Peru. There is an integrated healthcare network in Maranhão (Brazil), the Ecuadorian Amazon, and Madre de Dios (Peru). Moreover, 18 maps have been created, with routes to health centres to facilitate access for indigenous populations from the three countries. Training courses for more than 50 community health promoters in Brazil, 15 in Ecuador, and 14 in Peru have also been organized.

In May 2022, Brazil, Peru, and representatives of ACTO member countries, together with PAHO and IADB, drafted the Indigenous Peoples' Health Emergency Response Plan (ACTO, 2022c). The plan intends to consolidate regional cooperative actions of ACTO member countries in the border areas of the Amazon Basin. This would strengthen local health services and help to reduce the impacts of COVID-19 as well as threats of emerging and endemic tropical diseases among highly vulnerable indigenous peoples, with a special emphasis on those in isolation. The consultants and collaborators highlight their expertise in terms of their participation and skills to work in the following territories: Ecuador/ Peru border, Napo-Tigre territory; Bolivia/Peru border, Madidi and

Bahuaja-Sonene National Parks; Brazil/Colombia/Peru, a territory of the Putumayo and Içá Rivers; Brazil/Peru border, Madre de Dios region and the Mamoadate indigenous land; Brazil/Peru, Valle del Javari and Loreto regions; and the tri-border region between Brazil, Guyana, and Suriname (ACTO, 2022b).

One recent notable development was that Peru and ACTO hosted an international forum on the main problems associated with vaccinating indigenous peoples in the Amazon region (ACTO, 2022a). O Conselho Nacional das Fundações de Amparo à Pesquisa (CONFAP/Brazilian National Council of Research Support Funds) published on 17 November 2022 a list of 39 research proposals approved for the Amazon+10 Initiative, with a budget of R$42 million. There are 137 affiliated research groups from 19 Brazilian states collaborating on research on the territories and peoples of the Amazon (Governo do Estado de São Paulo, 2022).

8.5 Conclusion

PAHO has been dealing with health issues and combating the spread of infectious diseases in Latin America for more than 120 years. The organization assists in the development of the healthcare system of each member country, makes recommendations, and offers practical assistance in the improvement of the health system. This has allowed members to progress towards in achieving their SDGs. However, the COVID-19 pandemic has had serious impacts on socio-economic development in the region, and revealed grave problems in the strategies of PAHO both in organizing the healthcare systems in individual countries and in ensuring universal access to healthcare.

For a more detailed analysis, the most affected countries in the region—Brazil and Peru—were selected. These two countries began developing their relations when they signed the Friendship and Cooperation Treaty in 1979; with the Agreement on Strategic Partnership, signed in 2003, the nations deepened their political, trade, and economic cooperation. Within the framework of the Amazon Cooperation Treaty, these countries continue to face challenges and threats related to drug trafficking, organized crime, the illegal extraction of natural resources, environmental problems, and the protection of the legal status of indigenous peoples in the Amazon.

The activities of Brazil and PAHO, which aim to address healthcare problems, can help in terms of providing technical assistance for similar issues in Latin America and Africa within the framework of health diplomacy. The Ministry of Health of Brazil and Fiocruz has implemented a number of programmes to train doctors in Peru, conduct joint research, develop a system for managing medical institutions, and share technologies for the production of medicines.

The effects of the COVID-19 pandemic in Brazil and Peru have highlighted the need to revise the basics of healthcare and reconsider relevant areas of cooperation. Brazil and Peru have thus begun expanding their bilateral collaboration to improve health systems, develop new projects, strengthen cross-border cooperation, and increase participation in indigenous peoples' protection issues through their ACTO engagements.

The spread of COVID-19 in the Amazon area has exacerbated problems of access to healthcare among indigenous populations. Still, countries in the region have been able to learn from the mistakes they made during the pandemic. This has given them a new impetus to enhance and expand cooperation in the field of healthcare, set up a bilateral border working group, and collaborate under ACTO. Indeed, ACTO members started the Program for the Protection of Indigenous Peoples in Voluntary Isolation. Peru and Brazil joined forces to protect their indigenous populations, develop a regional health strategy, and establish the SVS. The IADB created the Fund for Sustainable Development for the Amazon, allocating $20 million and highlighting biodiversity, agriculture, bioeconomy, infrastructure projects, and human capital.

Brazil and Peru support the subregional AIR project and the Indigenous Peoples' Health Emergency Response Plan. These initiatives aim to: promote structural change and reduce the impact of COVID-19 on Amazon indigenous peoples in Brazil, Ecuador, and Peru; improve access to care, prevention, and protection measures; and place the rights and cultures of indigenous peoples at the heart of public health systems. Such a deepening of interactions between these two leading countries, not only in healthcare but also in other sectors, has contributed to the process of regional integration in Latin America.

References

ACTO (2019) 'Agenda estratégica de cooperación Amazónica 2019–2030 es validada a nivel técnico', 9 November. Available at: http://otca.org/agenda-estrategica-de-cooperacion-amazonica-2019-2030-es-validada-a-nivel-tecnico (Accessed: 22 December 2022).

ACTO (2021a) *Comisión especial de salud de la Amazonia (CESAM) acta constitutiva.* Available at: http://otca.org/wp-content/uploads/2021/02/Comision-Especial-de-Salud-de-la-Amazonia-%E2%80%93-CESAM.pdf (Accessed: 22 December 2022).

ACTO (2021b) *Comisión especial de medio ambiente de la Amazonía (CEMAA).* Available at: http://otca.org/project/comision-especial-de-medio-ambiente-de-la-amazonia-cemaa/ (Accessed: 22 December 2022).

ACTO (2021c) *Marco estratégico para la protección de los pueblos indígenas en aislamiento voluntario y contacto inicial.* Available at: http://otca.org/en/project/strategic-framework-for-protecting-indigenous-peoples-in-voluntary-isolation-and-initial-contact/ (Accessed: 22 December 2022).

ACTO (2021d) *Acuerdo marco de colaboración entre el fondo para el desarrollo de los pueblos indígenas de America Latina y el Caribe (FILAC) y La Organización del Tratado de Cooperación Amazónica (OTCA)*. Available at: http://otca.org/eventos/acuerdo-marco-de-colaboracion-entre-la-otca-y-filac (Accessed: 22 December 2022).

ACTO (2021e) 'Principios y directrices para la protección de los pueblos indígenas amozónicos frente a la pandemia del coronavirus (COVID-19)', 16 October. Available at: http://otca.org/principios-y-directrices-para-la-proteccion-de-los-pueblos-indigenas-amazonicos-frente-a-la-pandemia-del-coronavirus-COVID-19-2 (Accessed: 22 December 2022).

ACTO (2022a) 'Ministerio de Cultura del Perú y la OTCA realizan foro internacional sobre principales retos para la vacunación de los pueblos indígenas en la región Amazónica', 19 April. Available at: http://otca.org/ministerio-de-cultura-y-otca-realizan-foro-internacional-sobre-principales-retos-para-la-vacunacion-de-los-pueblos-indigenas-en-region-amazonica/ (Accessed: 22 December 2022).

ACTO (2022b) 'Contratación de consultoría para la elaboración de informes de análisis de situación de salud de pueblos indígenas en Frontera Perú y Brasil, región del "javari"', 3 May. Available at: http://otca.org/contratacion-de-consultoria-para-la-elaboracion-de-informes-de-analisis-de-situacion-de-salud-de-pueblos-indigenas-en-la-frontera-la-frontera-peru-y-brasil-region-del-javari/ (Accessed: 22 December 2022).

ACTO (2022c) 'Puntos focales de los países miembros participan de reunión del proyecto plan de contingencia para la protección de la salud en pueblos indígenas', 6 May. Available at: http://otca.org/puntos-focales-de-los-paises-miembros-participan-de-reunion-del-proyecto-plan-de-contingencia-para-la-proteccion-de-la-salud-en-pueblos-indigenas/ (Accessed: 22 December 2022).

Andina (2022) 'Brazilian presidents sign health agreements', 3 February. Available at: https://andina.pe/ingles/noticia-peruvian-brazilian-presidents-sign-health-agreements-879629.aspx (Accessed: 22 December 2022).

Benítez, M. A., Velasco, C., Sequeira, A. R., Henríquez, J., Menezes, F. M. and Paolucci, F. (2020) 'Responses to COVID-19 in five Latin American countries', *Health Policy Technology*, 9 (4), pp. 525–559. Available at: https://www.ncbi.nlm.nih.gov/pmc/articles/PMC7451099/#bib0042 (Accessed: 22 December 2022).

Buss, P. M. (2018) 'Cooperação internacional em saúde do Brasil na era do SUS', *Ciência & Saúde Coletiva*, 23 (6). Available at: https://doi.org/10.1590/1413-81232018236.05172018 (Accessed: 22 December 2022).

CEPAL (2018) *La región Amazónica en cifras*. Available at: https://foroalc2030.cepal.org/2018/sites/default/files/presentations/otca-presentacion_ods_cepal_sela-17abril2018.pdf (Accessed: 22 December 2022).

Cobradi and IPEA (2022) *Cooperação internacional em tempos de pandemia: relatório Cobradi 2019–2020*. Available at: http://cdi.mecon.gov.ar/bases/docelec/az5609.pdf (Accessed: 22 December 2022).

COVID Economic Recovery Index (2020) Available at: https://www.COVIDrecoveryindex.org/ranking (Accessed: 22 December 2022).

El Peruano (2022) 'Peru and Brazil agree to optimize education and health', 2 April. Available at: https://elperuano.pe/noticia/138691-peru-y-brasil-acuerdan-optimizar-educacion-y-salud (Accessed: 22 December 2022).

GHS Index (2021) Available at: https://www.ghsindex.org/#l-section--countryranksect (Accessed: 22 December 2022).

Governo do Estado de São Paulo (2022) 'Iniciativa Amazônia +10 seleciona 39 projetos de pesquisa', *São Paulo Governo do Estado*, 17 November. Available at: https://www.saopaulo.sp.gov.br/spnoticias/iniciativa-amazonia-10-seleciona-39-projetos-de-pesquisa (Accessed: 22 December 2022).

Hivos (2022) *Ruta de la salud indígena Amazónica*. Available at: https://america-latina.hivos.org/program/rutadesaludindigenaamazonica/#:~:text=El%20proyecto%20Ruta%20de%20Salud,de%20la%20sociedad%20civil%20en (Accessed: 22 December 2022).

IADB (2021) *Desarrollo sostenible de la región Amazónica*. Available at: https://www.youtube.com/watch?v=Ua_XJFAbuEs (Accessed: 22 December 2022).

OAS (1979) *El tratado de amistad y cooperación entre la República del Perú y la República Federativa del Brasil*. Available at: http://www.oas.org/OSDE/publications/Unit/oea09s/ch05.htm (Accessed: 22 December 2022).

OECD (2020) 'COVID-19 in Latin America and the Caribbean: Regional socio-economic implications and policy priorities', *OECD Policies Responses to Coronavirus (COVID-19)*, 8 December. Available at: http://www.oecd.org/coronavirus/policy-responses/COVID-19-in-latin-america-and-the-caribbean-regional-socio-economic-implications-and-policy-priorities-93a64fde/ (Accessed: 22 December 2022).

PAHO (2015) *Relatório de avaliação final do termo de cooperação nº 41 – cooperação internacional em saúde*. Available at: https://www.paho.org/pt/documentos/relatorio-avaliacao-final-do-termo-cooperacao-no-41-cooperacao-internacional-em-saude (Accessed: 22 December 2022).

PAHO (2020a) *Estrategia de cooperación con el país: Perú 2014–2019*. Available at: https://iris.paho.org/handle/10665.2/7664 (Accessed: 22 December 2022).

PAHO (2020b) *Cooperação técnica da OPAS/OMS no Brasil*. Available at: https://www.paho.org/pt/cooperacao-tecnica-no-brasil (Accessed: 22 December 2022).

PAHO (2021a) *Informe anual 2021. Programa subregional para América del Sur: Respuesta a la COVID-19 y preparación para el futuro*. Available at: https://iris.paho.org/handle/10665.2/56362 (Accessed: 22 December 2022).

PAHO (2021b) *Informe anual 2021. Perú: Respuesta a la COVID-19 y preparación para el futuro*. Available at: https://iris.paho.org/handle/10665.2/56355 (Accessed: 22 December 2022).

PAHO (2022a) *New coronavirus: Fiocruz, Ministry of Health of Brazil and PAHO provide training in laboratory diagnosis in nine countries*. Available at: https://www3.paho.org/hq/index.php?option=com_content&view=article&id=15719:nuevo-coronavirus-fiocruz-ministerio-de-salud-de-brasil-y-la-ops-capacitan-a-nueve-paises-en-diagnostico-de-laboratorio&Itemid=0&lang=en#gsc.tab=0 (Accessed: 22 December 2022).

PAHO (2022b) *Quinquennial report 2018–2022 of the director of the Pan American sanitary bureau*. Available at: https://www.paho.org/sites/default/files/od366-e-quinquennial-report-director-paho-2018-2022-rep1_0.pdf (Accessed: 22 December 2022).

Pereira I. D. F., Corbo A. D., Paula T. S. G., Mendonça R. C. R., Carvalho P. R. and Bottino F. O. (2020) *Manual sobre biossegurança para reabertura de escolas no contexto da COVID-19*. Rio de Janeiro: Escola Politécnica de Saúde Joaquim

Venâncio/Fundação Oswaldo Cruz. Available at: https://www.epsjv.fiocruz. br/publicacao/livro/manual-sobre-biosseguranca-para-reabertura-de-escolas-no-contexto-da-covid-19-2a (Accessed: 22 December 2022).

Peru Ministerio de Defensa (2005) *Libro blanco de la defensa nacional del Perú*. Available at: https://cdn.www.gob.pe/uploads/document/file/397073/Libro _blanco.pdf (Accessed: 22 December 2022).

Phillips, T. and Briso, C. B. (2020) 'Judge orders Bolsonaro to resume publishing Brazil COVID-19 data', *The Guardian*, 9 June. Available at: https://www.the guardian.com/world/2020/jun/09/judge-orders-bolsonaro-to-resume-publishing-brazil-covid-19-data (Accessed: 22 December 2022).

Souza, P. R. M. and Costa, P. P. (2019) 'Educação permanente em saúde na formação da rede Brasileira de escolas de saúde pública', *Saúde Debate*, 43 (1): 116–129. Available at: https://www.scielo.br/pdf/sdeb/v43nspe1/0103-1104-sdeb-43-spe01-0116.pdf (Accessed: 22 December 2022).

Statista (2022) *COVID-19 cases worldwide as of December 21, by country or territory*. Available at: https://www.statista.com/statistics/1043366/novel-coronavirus-2019ncov-cases-worldwide-by-country/ (Accessed: 22 December 2022).

Sustainable Development Solutions Network (2020) *Sustainable development report 2020: sustainable development goals and COVID-19*. Available at: https://sdgindex.org/reports/sustainable-development-report-2020 (Accessed: 22 December 2022).

Tobar, S., Buss, P., Coitiño, A., Kleiman, A., Fonseca, L.E., Rigoli, F., Sealey, K. and Victoria, V. (2017) 'Diplomacia de la salud: fortalecimiento de las oficinas de relaciones internacionales de los ministerios de salud en las Américas', *Rev Panam Salud Publica*, 41 (e145). https://pubmed.ncbi.nlm.nih.gov/31391834/ (Accessed: 22 December 2022).

UN Comtrade Database (2021) Available at: https://comtrade.un.org/data (Accessed: 22 December 2022).

United Nations (2022) *The sustainable development goals report* [Online]. Available at: https://unstats.un.org/sdgs/report/2022/The-Sustainable-Development-Goals-Report-2022.pdf (Accessed: 22 December 2022).

WHO (2021) *Global health expenditure database*. Available at: https://apps.who. int/nha/database/country_profile/Index/ru (Accessed: 22 December 2022).

Yacila, R.C. and Turkewitz, J. (2020) 'Highways of Peru swell with families fleeing virus', *The New York Times*, 30 April. Available at: https://www.nytimes.com/ 2020/04/30/world/americas/20virus-peru-migration.html (Accessed: 22 December 2022).

PART III:
REGIONAL RESPONSES TO COLLECTIVE ENVIRONMENTAL CHALLENGES

Chapter 9

MERCOSUR's environmental policy: Institutional evolution and limitations

Tatiana de Souza Leite Garcia

University of São Paulo and Inter-American Institute for Cooperation on Agriculture, Brazil

Abstract

This chapter explores how environmental policy is negotiated in the Southern Common Market (MERCOSUR). The member states of the organization have abundant natural resources, and this makes environmental negotiations particularly important for them. This chapter explores the extent of institutional advances that MERCOSUR has made in terms of environmental regulations; it also analyses their limitations and the difficulties which emerged in the negotiation process. The research methodology employed in this study includes an extensive literature review and detailed analysis of MERCOSUR documents published between 2009 and 2019; the discussion explores domestic, regional, and international variables in the negotiation process. The chapter argues that MERCOSUR has contributed significantly to the formulation of environmental governance frameworks in Latin America in several ways such as facilitating further harmonisation of environmental legislation between states. Nevertheless, the negotiation process is characterised by severe limitations such as insufficient input from non-state actors.

Keywords: MERCOSUR, environmental policy, sustainability, institutional evolution, negotiation, legislation

***

9.1 Introduction

MERCOSUR's founding states—Argentina, Brazil, Paraguay, and Uruguay—have many natural resources. They share the international waters of the Río de la Plata Basin (also referred to as the La Plata Basin) and the Guaraní Aquifer, which were previously exploited by European colonizers and are now essential to the economic and social development of these countries. During the eighteenth and nineteenth centuries, independence struggles and civil conflicts took place in the La Plata Basin region, along with parallel disputes to expand borders and defend strategic territories.

Between 1960 and 1980, several South American countries were under military rule and wherever political alignment was possible, regional cooperation was favoured. However, at times, tensions between governments would arise due to mistrust and historical hostilities. To a certain extent, cooperation on matters related to the La Plata Basin allowed countries in the region to identify common issues and to consider possible joint solutions.

In 1967, the La Plata Basin nations created the Intergovernmental Coordinating Committee of the La Plata Basin Countries (CIC Plata). Its aims were to promote, coordinate, and jointly monitor the use of the waters; facilitate the integrated development of the Platine countries; provide support on decisions approved by the ministers of foreign affairs; and manage technical and financial assistance from international organizations. In 1969, the Treaty on the Rio de la Plata Basin was signed in Brasilia, Brazil, by Argentina, Bolivia, Brazil, Paraguay, and Uruguay. It is considered the legal instrument for cooperation in the Platine hydrographic system.

In 1974, the Financial Development Fund of the La Plata Basin (FONPLATA) was created. Its aim was to reduce socio-economic disparities and physically integrate the La Plata Basin through financial cooperation for studies, projects and works focusing on physical infrastructure, social investment in education and health, basic sanitation, productivity, promotion of export, creation of employment opportunities, environmental impact mitigation, and nature conservation.

The La Plata Basin region epitomizes environmental geopolitics. Even though there are already cooperation agreements between the states in this region, tensions (political, economic, and social) have persisted between the actors. This is because they have different interests and capacities to exert influence at different levels of power and, consequently, act under asymmetric conditions to use natural resources, especially water. There is clear evidence for the existence of regional hydro-politics. Even though the border strips between Brazil and Paraguay have water in abundance, disputes occur between the agricultural and energy sectors, relating to access to and control over water to meet their respective purposes; this reinforces the asymmetries between them (Ribeiro, 2017; Garcia, 2019).

The hydro-politics situation in the La Plata Basin reached a crossroads when Brazil and Paraguay signed the Itaipú Treaty (1973). The construction of the hydroelectric plant then began in 1975. The regional balance of power favoured Brazil to the point where Argentina felt aggrieved and briefly claimed the rights to use the Platine waters. Tensions decreased after negotiations that resulted in the Itaipú-Corpus Tripartite Agreement (1979), which settled issues regarding the use of water resources for river circulation and energy production, including an agreement between Argentina and Paraguay to start the construction of the Yacyretá hydroelectric power plant. This enabled new paths for the relationship between Brazil and Argentina (Mello, 1997; Simões and Garcia, 2022).

In 1989, during the XIX Meeting of Foreign Affairs Ministers of the La Plata River Basin, the Paraguay-Paraná Waterway System was included in the La Plata River Treaty system. Subsequently, the Intergovernmental Committee of the Paraguay-Paraná Waterway System (CIH) was formed. Its aim was to improve navigability in the Paraguay and Paraná rivers, reduce transportation costs, and minimize the risks of navigating the La Plata Basin rivers (Garcia and Jesus, 2019).

In the 1980s, with the end of military governments and the return of democracy, the regional conjuncture became favourable. There was, at this point, a need to ensure economic stability, control inflation, and settle public and foreign debts. These issues demanded domestic plans and international cooperation projects. Open regionalism was presented as a complementary and necessary mechanism for Latin American economies, which needed to strengthen regionally in order to enhance their participation in the international trade regime.

Thus, from 1985 onwards, a series of joint declarations and multi-sector cooperation agreements between Argentina and Brazil were established for the gradual opening and expansion of trade, industrial and technological development, nuclear energy, aeronautics, land and maritime transport, automobile industry, culture, communications, public administration, food supply, binational companies, financial cooperation, and investment funds, among others. These cooperative relations heralded the reduction of rivalries in the La Plata Basin, and were consolidated with the invitations extended to Paraguay and Uruguay to form a group and establish the Southern Common Market (MERCOSUR).

MERCOSUR was made official in 1991, with the Treaty of Asunción, to include the founding states of Argentina, Brazil, Paraguay, and Uruguay. The treaty aims to expand regional trade and accelerate economic growth and social development through the efficient use of available resources, considering the preservation of the environment, improvement of physical connections, coordination of macroeconomic policies, and collaboration among productive sectors. The bloc acquired legal personality in 1994 with the Protocol of Ouro Preto. MERCOSUR is open to the accession of other member states of the Latin American Integration Association (ALADI).

Venezuela applied to become a full member of MERCOSUR in 2006 and Bolivia did the same in 2015. As of 2023, Venezuela is still suspended from all rights and obligations inherent to its status as a member state for failing to comply with some fundamental commitments, especially those related to the Ushuaia Protocol, concerning the issues of political freedom and democracy. Bolivia, meanwhile, had its Accession Protocol signed by all member states in 2015 and is in the process of incorporating all agreements and protocols and harmonizing laws and regulations. The bloc also has associated states—Chile, Colombia, Ecuador, Guyana, Peru, and Suriname—which are authorized to participate in meetings on matters of common interest but have no voting rights. As of 2023, MERCOSUR currently has 12 South American countries as full and associate members.

In the first phase, the bloc's aim was to deepen intraregional trade relations and gradually move from the most superficial level of integration to become a free trade zone, thus eliminating customs and non-tariff barriers. In the second phase, the bloc aimed to establish a unified external trade policy, with common external tariffs (CET), reaching the conditions for a customs union. The ultimate goal was to become a regional common market, with the free movement of goods, capital, people, labour, and knowledge, and to establish common macroeconomic and sectoral policies. Members of the bloc have already managed to make many advances in various sectors, including in the circulation of goods, people, and labour. However, they have not yet been able to fully achieve their established objectives and have been classified as an incomplete customs union.

MERCOSUR is not restricted to economic and trade issues; its organizational structure incorporates institutions to deal with border and technical issues of interest to the member states, in line with the transformations occurring at domestic and international levels. Indeed, the main objective established in MERCOSUR's Constitutive Treaty has not yet been achieved, and it has not always managed to integrate other fundamental topics on regional trade and the promotion of wellbeing. However, the bloc has become the main South American arena for the identification and discussion of social pressures of the countries in the region and challenges related to globalization (Mariano, 2007). This is despite institutional crises which have reflected changes in the member states' governments as well as political and ideological misalignments, international pressures, and unfavourable conjunctures.

MERCOSUR is a consolidation of the overcoming of rivalries in the La Plata Basin. Through it, Brazil and Argentina, regional powers of the subcontinent, decided to converge their foreign policies around bilateral cooperation projects and recognized that their neighbours had historically been in unfavourable conditions but that they could work together to overcome common and cross-border challenges, including solving environmental issues.

Over the 30 years of MERCOSUR's existence, various negotiations, norms, and actions have been established that have gradually facilitated the movement of goods, people, labour, capital, and knowledge among member states. To this end, the institutional structure of the organization was expanded to include technical and political frameworks, where issues can be negotiated by country representatives, who provide support during the decision-making processes for high-level issues. Environmental issues are also part of MERCOSUR's negotiation agenda, although the academic community, and society in general, knows about this aspect.

To investigate how issues related to the environment are negotiated in this regional arena, the guiding questions in this text are as follows:

a) Why and to what extent is the environment important to MERCOSUR member states?

b) What environmental topics are negotiated in MERCOSUR?

c) Which institutional advances have been made in this regional arena regarding environmental topics?

d) Are there limitations and difficulties in MERCOSUR's environmental policy?

The methodology used for this study includes a literature review and analysis of MERCOSUR documents published between 2009 and 2019. The research showed that MERCOSUR negotiations and documents, resulting from technical and political bodies specializing in the environment, deal with various topics which are influenced by the interests of central governments. In addition, decision-making processes often prioritize issues that have a correlation with trade. Furthermore, specific actors and conjunctures in the domestic and international arenas influence negotiations on certain environmental topics in the bloc, especially those in vogue in global environmental governance. This text presents MERCOSUR's institutional evolution in terms of its environmental policy, identifying and analysing the domestic, regional, and international variables that resulted in advances and limitations.

9.2 MERCOSUR and its specialized environmental bodies

In the late 1980s and the 1990s, several events led to major changes in international relations that impacted all regions in the world; for instance, the collapse of the USSR and the end of the Cold War, and the multidimensional advances in globalization, neo-liberalism, and global capitalism. The decline in international security concerns created space for environmental and human rights issues on the agendas of multilateral negotiations and countries' public policies.

In the realm of international relations, the United Nations has organized a series of conferences on global social and environmental issues. These have included the World Summit for Children (1990), the Conference on Environment and Development (1992), the World Conference on Human Rights (1993), the International Conference on Population and Development (1994), the World Summit for Social Development (1995), the World Conference on Women (1995), the Conference on Human Settlements: Habitat II (1996), and the World Food Summit (1996). These conferences have produced conventions, declarations, cooperation programmes, commitment agendas, and documents that constitute the normative basis at the international level. At the same time as these conferences were occurring, these themes were also gaining prevalence in national policies and were introduced into some regional integration processes.

Signed in 1991, MERCOSUR's Constitutive Treaty stated that the bloc's objective was to promote integration by expanding national markets and by accelerating member countries' economic development and social justice through the efficient use of available resources, environmental preservation, improvement of physical interconnections (e.g., transport and infrastructure), and coordination of macroeconomic policies to complement other sectors of the economy, based on the principles of gradualness, flexibility, and balance (MERCOSUR, 1991). MERCOSUR's organizational structure was expanded to include specialized bodies composed of representatives from the member states to discuss the sectoral agendas using a technical and political lens. In this context, frameworks were also created for the purpose of discussing environmental issues pertinent to the bloc.

The recognition among MERCOSUR members of the importance of the environment was not merely coincidental to what was happening in the international arena because of the United Nations. In the same year the bloc was created, Brazil applied and was accepted to host the United Nations Conference on Environment and Development, known as Rio-92 or Eco-92, which took place in June 1992. In support of the Brazilian proposal, in February 1992, MERCOSUR member states met in the city of Canela in Brazil to discuss the environmental issues that would be dealt with at Rio-92. At this meeting, they signed the Canela Declaration, in which they acknowledged the environmental crisis and the importance of balanced ecosystems. The member states are committed to promoting environmental conservation through education, research funding, clean technologies, and the codification of international environmental law (MERCOSUR, 2006). In this declaration, no principles or goals were established to guide MERCOSUR's joint Environmental Policy (Reboratti, 2007).

During the second meeting of MERCOSUR presidents, held in 1992 in Las Leñas, Argentina, the Common Market Group (GMC), the bloc's decision-making and executive body, created the Specialized Environment Meeting (REMA) through Resolution nº22/92. The purpose of this group was to analyse the legislation of member states; propose environmental protection measures through recommendations to the GMC; advise the technical subgroups (SGT) for agricultural policy, industrial and technological policy, and energy policy; and address aspects related to the environment and sustainability. Despite the importance of environmental issues, REMA was not granted the status of a technical body and was not a decision-making body, but rather a mechanism that worked in parallel to other bodies (Irachande, Almeida and Vieira, 2010).

In the following two years, the REMA and Technical Subgroups SGT nº7 (Industrial and Technological Policy), SGT nº8 (Agricultural Policy), and SGT nº9 (Energy Policy) analysed the national environmental legislation in the respective sectors of the member states, conducted studies, and proposed harmonizing these legislations, while respecting the specificities of each sector and country. Environmental harmonization did not mean creating a universal legislation to be adopted by all countries but rather establishing common criteria that considered environmental aspects (Irachande, Almeida and Vieira, 2010).

In 1995, the first Meeting of MERCOSUR's Environment Ministers (RMMA) took place in Montevideo, Uruguay. The RMMA is a subsidiary of the Common Market Council (CMC), the highest body responsible for the political aspects of the regional integration process and for ensuring that decision-making complies with the objectives established in the Treaty of Asunción. The Declaration of Taranco was produced in this first RMMA; it expressed recognition of the efforts of the REMA and recommended its transformation into a technical subgroup linked to the GMC. This declaration also pointed out aspects related to ISO 14000 standards, the importance of cooperation between states for the implementation of Agenda 21 at national levels, the environmental impact studies of the Paraguay-Paraná Waterway System, environmental costs of production processes, and coordination of the positions of MERCOSUR members in international environmental agreements (Garcia, 2019). This declaration reinforced the need to create organizations dedicated to environmental issues in the bloc and for the environmental agenda to be aligned with commercial and production issues.

Through Resolution nº20/95, the GMC accepted the recommendations of the Declaration of Taranco, abolished the REMA, and created the Technical Subgroup nº6 Environment (SGT nº6), a technical organization specialized in environmental issues. In general terms, the aim of SGT nº6 is to formulate and propose strategies and guidelines for environmental issues that are important to the regional integration process. It aims to promote sustainable development through the protection of the environment of the member states, considering the interests of free trade and of consolidating the customs union, with competition conditions remaining equal (Garcia, 2019). Thus, the GMC defined the following obligations of SGT nº6 (Torres, 2012):

- Analyse restrictions and non-tariff measures related to the environment;
- Conduct studies and implement actions that value and include environmental costs for adequate competitiveness among bloc and extra-bloc countries;
- Accompany the elaboration, discussion, and implementation process of the ISO 14000 environmental management series and outline possible impacts on MERCOSUR;
- Assist other SGTs in implementing environmental issues and costs;
- Provide technical assistance for the establishment of MERCOSUR's legal environmental instrument and national legal frameworks on specific environmental issues;
- Create MERCOSUR's environmental information system; and
- Propose the creation of a regional seal for environmentally sustainable products.

SGT nº6 also has the responsibility of assisting in the definition of export and import quotas for certain products, such as wood and fertilizers; phytosanitary measures; and packaging regulations. It can receive complaints related to environmental crimes, but the responsibility for inspection and punishment lies with the national environmental bodies (Braga, 2014). The national bodies, whose officials are responsible for the dialogue in SGT nº6, are as follows: Argentina's Ministry of Social Development, Secretary of Environment and Sustainable Development (SayDS); Brazil's Ministry of Environment (MMA); Paraguay's Secretariat of the Environment (SEAM); and Uruguay's Ministry of Housing, Land Management and Environment (MVOTMA) (Garcia, 2019).

To cater to the demand for specific environmental studies, SGT nº6 created ad-hoc groups that produced reports, which were then forwarded to the GMC, the executive decision-making body of the bloc. The study groups created and incorporated into the internal structure of SGT nº6 were for the following areas: 1) competitiveness and the environment; 2) MERCOSUR's environmental information system; 3) environmental goods and services; 4) biodiversity; 5) adequate management of the hunting of migratory and common species in transboundary areas; 6) environmental management of chemical substances and products; 7) ballast water; 8) environmental emergencies; 9) the fight against desertification and drought; 10) air quality; 11) and environmental management of waste and post-consumption responsibility (MERCOSUR, 2008).

The RMMA became responsible for politically analysing sensitive environmental issues, which cannot always be discussed within the scope of SGT n°6. The RMMA also had the potential to conduct dialogue with the CMC, the highest decision-making body in the organizational structure of the bloc. The RMMA created the following ad-hoc groups: 1) waste and post-consumption responsibility, 2) water resources, 3) air quality, and 4) desertification (MERCOSUR, 2008).

The RMMA and SGT n°6 work together to strengthen the region's response to environmental issues with the other bodies within the bloc. They work on the implementation and development of various cooperation projects, identifying priority issues for MERCOSUR's environmental agenda, submitting recommendations to higher organizations, and simplifying decision-making processes, according to the competencies of relevant actors.

Other organizations linked to the bloc are also concerned with environmental issues. They include the MERCOSUR Parliament (Parlasur) and the International Network of MERCOSUR Cities (Mercocidades). These bodies are not directly linked to the bloc's decision-making structures and do not have deliberative powers but act as advisory institutions. Parlasur has commissions that directly and indirectly deal with environmental issues. For instance, the Commission on Sustainable Regional Development, Territorial Planning, Housing, Health, Environment and Tourism and the Commission on Infrastructure, Transportation, Energy Resources, Agriculture, Livestock and Fisheries. The growing politicization of the environmental issue and Parlasur's role as a forum to represent the member states allowed it to submit recommendations to the CMC; its aim is to promote the exchange of information and experiences and enable broader and more democratic environmental legislation within countries (Leite, 2018). Meanwhile, since Mercocidades' establishment in 1995, it has addressed the environmental issue by inspiring the creation of Thematic Unit of Urban and Environmental Planning, which was later transformed into the Thematic Unit of Environment and Sustainable Development (Torres, 2012).

9.3 The evolution of MERCOSUR's environmental policy

MERCOSUR's environmental policy has been built over 30 years of the regional bloc's operation and maturation. In the Constitutive Treaty signed in 1991, the mention of the need to preserve the environment was superficial because the bloc's main purpose was related to trade integration and economic development of the member states until they reached the common market level.

As previously mentioned, institutions were created in MERCOSUR's organizational structure to deal with issues that became part of broad thematic agendas, such as sanitary standards, environment, transportation, human rights, education, and labour, among others. This was demanded by specific internal actors or conjunctures arising from within the member states. Besides these, external actors and conjunctures, whether regional or international, were (and continue to be) influential on the introduction of issues into MERCOSUR's negotiations and decisions. There are currently over 300 negotiation forums for different areas, composed of representatives from each member state.

The first step in the construction of MERCOSUR's environmental policy took place in 1994 when the Specialized Environment Meeting (former REMA) prepared Recommendation nº1/94. The GMC approved it in Resolution nº10/94 with the Basic Guidelines on Environmental Policy, which contained 11 general guidelines for the harmonization of environmental legislation, the joint management of natural resources, and the lines of action for the environmental treaties of member states, and for ensuring equitable conditions of competitiveness, with the inclusion of the environmental costs of production processes (Garcia, 2019). From this moment, the first guidelines of MERCOSUR's environmental policy were established, but commercial and economic issues still needed to be prioritized to avoid generating advantages or disadvantages for a particular country or productive segment.

In December 1995, MERCOSUR members and the European Economic Community signed the Cooperation Agreement for the Protection of the Environment. The purpose of this was to exchange information and experiences, including those related to regulations and standards, training on environmental education, and technical assistance for the execution of projects and research (MERCOSUR, 2006).

In 1996, SGT nº6 created the Ad-hoc Group Environmental Information System with the objective of setting up a database of technical and political decisions related to the environment. The construction of MERCOSUR's database on environmental issues was possible thanks to financial assistance provided by the Spanish Association for Cooperation and Development (AECID). MERCOSUR's Environmental Information System (SIAM) website was created in 2004. Although it has been inoperative during some stages, it now provides a series of documents and information related to the meetings of SGT nº6 and RMMA. It also includes environmental agreements and projects, environmental standards, and a digital library (Garcia, 2019).

In 1997, SGT nº6 prepared the Additional Protocol on Environment to the Asunción Treaty, presented to the GMC through Recommendation nº04/97. This protocol was distinct in its inclusion of issues related to environmental damage, environmental emergencies, and environmental impact assessments. But despite having been discussed in several meetings, it was not initially approved by Argentina because its content was deemed insufficient. However, Brazil strongly defended this protocol and after reformulations, it was accepted by all member states (Irachande, Almeida and Vieira, 2010; Torres, 2012).

At the ordinary meeting of SGT nº6 in December 2000, MERCOSUR's Environment Framework Agreement was approved. On 22 June 2001, through Decision nº02/01 of the CMC, the respective document was approved. Moreover, member countries reaffirmed their commitments to the principles established during the United Nations Conference on Environment and Development (1992)—to promote sustainable development in the region, encourage cooperation between member states in research, information exchange, and formal and non-formal education; and give special attention to border areas, with a focus on the legal and political aspects of environmental issues. In addition, they recognized the participation of competent national bodies and civil society organizations specialized in the environment (MERCOSUR, 2001; Brazilian Chamber of Deputies, 2003).

Member states had to ratify the agreement in their domestic political organizations, with effect from 2004. This agreement represented a significant advance for environmental public policies at the regional level, as it reinforced the need to continue the process of harmonizing national environmental legislation, consolidate the exchange of information on environmental issues, establish the shared management of environmental resources, encourage scientific production, develop clean technologies, and promote environmental education (Garcia, 2019). Despite this agreement's normative leap with regard to the environment, it was not binding, and the operational tools for forming concrete procedures were not defined (Torres, 2012).

In 2002, after the World Summit on Sustainable Development, held in Johannesburg, South Africa, the GMC approved the negotiating agendas of SGT nº6, through Resolution nº45/02. The aim was to adapt them to the new reality of the demands and instruments adopted in the national and international spheres. The negotiating agendas incorporated into the schedule of SGT nº6 were the following: 1) non-tariff measures; 2) competitiveness and the environment; 3) sectoral issues; 4) implementation of MERCOSUR's environment framework agreement; 5) instruments and mechanisms for improving environmental management; 6) MERCOSUR's SIAM; 7) the environment as a generator of opportunities for the promotion of sustainable development; 8) protection and management of natural resources for economic and social development; 9) environmentally sound management of hazardous chemical substances and products; and 10) follow-up of the international environmental agenda (MERCOSUR, 2006).

These negotiating agendas follow the mandate established by SGT nº6 in 1995, in line with the technical work developed by the linked ad-hoc groups.

This work included topics and commitments made at other international conferences, such as the Basel Convention on the Control of Transboundary Movements of Hazardous Wastes and their Disposal (1989) (Garcia, 2019). Clearly, environmental issues should be addressed jointly with trade-related issues.

In June 2004, the CMC approved, with Decision nº14/04, the Additional Protocol to the Framework Agreement on the MERCOSUR's Environment on Cooperation and Assistance in the Face of Environmental Emergencies. This enables collaboration during natural disasters among member countries. This document was internally ratified by member states, and laws or legislative decrees were created and adapted to harmonize environmental legislation at the regional level (MERCOSUR, 2006; Brazilian Chamber of Deputies, 2003; Presidency of Brazil, 2013).

At the same time, the Agreement between MERCOSUR and the Federal Republic of Germany to Promote Environmental Management and Cleaner Production for Small and Medium-sized Enterprises was also signed. The aim of this was to formalize the technical and financial cooperation project and reflect on the studies conducted by the Ad-hoc Group on Competitiveness and the Environment of SGT nº6. The following year, the Agreement on Sustainable Production Project and Competitiveness and Environment was negotiated with Germany. It was to be coordinated by the German Cooperation Agency (GTZ), and had the aim of improving the performance and compatibility of sustainability standards in the public and private sectors of MERCOSUR's member states (MERCOSUR, 2006; Garcia, 2019).

Torres (2012) argues that by 2007, many advances were made in relation to environmental issues in MERCOSUR's member states, with an emphasis on the following:

- The insertion of an environmental dimension in all levels of government and in parts of productive sectors and organized civil society;
- MERCOSUR's Strategy against Desertification;
- The Declaration on Climate Change in MERCOSUR;
- The Strategy for the Conservation of Biodiversity in MERCOSUR; and
- MERCOSUR's Policy for Promotion and Cooperation in Sustainable Production and Consumption.

9.4 Discussion of the research methodology and results

During the search for and analysis of available studies in Portuguese and Spanish, whose objectives included tracing the institutional and political evolution related to environmental issues in MERCOSUR, I found no surveys of the bloc's documents from 2008 onwards. To try to fill this gap and contribute to the academic debate, and to compare this debate with the political and bureaucratic reality, I conducted an extensive search of the databases of the MERCOSUR Secretariat, the Ministry of Foreign Affairs of Paraguay (a repository country of the agreements ratified by the bloc's members), and MERCOSUR's SIAM. My objective was to investigate the negotiation processes which occur in SGT nº6 and the RMMA, from the preparatory and technical stages all the way to the decision stage in the decision-making processes of the GMC and CMC, between 2009 to 2019, a period of relative geoeconomic stability starting with the recovery from the 2008 global financial crisis and ending before the beginning of the COVID-19 pandemic and before the Bolsonaro government ended up fundamentally changing the dynamics of regional politics by changing Brazil's position on numerous issues.

I identified, catalogued, and analysed topics on the agendas of the meetings of these bodies; the texts of the minutes; the participation of member states, external guests, and their respective positions; and the resulting documents. This research composes the fourth chapter of my doctoral thesis, "Challenges of South American Integration: The Environmental and Transport Policies in the MERCOSUR (2009–2019)", developed in the Postgraduate Programme in Human Geography of the University of São Paulo, Brazil. This is the first time the data is being compiled and published.

Between 2009 and 2019, 24 meetings (ordinary and extraordinary) of SGT nº6 were held. The main topics listed in the meeting agendas concerning MERCOSUR's environmental policy were the following (as compiled by the author):

- Discussions related to the implementation of the Additional Protocol to the Framework Agreement on the MERCOSUR's Environment on Cooperation and Assistance in the Face of Environmental Emergencies;
- Action plans for fire management, management of hazardous chemicals, environmental management of special waste, and post-consumption liability;
- Attempts to establish a regional regime for environmental impact assessments;
- Desertification and the fight against soil degradation and drought: MERCOSUR-FAO Cooperation and MERCOSUR-UNEP Cooperation;
- Biological diversity: action plan for the prevention, monitoring, and control of invasive alien species;
- Working programme of SGT nº6 and reports on the fulfilment of activities;

- Proposed agenda and support of the RMMA;
- MERCOSUR-AECID Cooperation: SIAM implementation;
- MERCOSUR-European Union Cooperation: ECONORMAS Project;
- Discussions related to the implementation of the MERCOSUR Policy for Promotion and Cooperation in Sustainable Production and Consumption;
- Exchange of positions in international environmental forums;
- Preparations for the Rio+20 Conference, held in Brazil;
- Agenda 2030.

From the documents on the aforementioned websites, it is clear that the minutes published are brief. Moreover, most complementary documents are not accessible to the public. This makes it impossible to identify the arguments of the technical representatives of the member states regarding the environmental topics negotiated. Lack of public access is one of the limitations of the environmental agenda negotiated in the bloc.

Following the identification of the phases in the decision-making processes, the documents referring to the 13 meetings held by the RMMA between 2009 and 2019 were analysed. The main topics negotiated in the RMMA in this timeframe were as follows:

- Climate change;
- Desertification and the fight against soil degradation and drought;
- Financing for MERCOSUR's environmental plans;
- The SIAM database project;
- MERCOSUR-European Union Cooperation: ECONORMAS Project;
- Exchange of views on international environmental forums and possible joint declarations;
- Preparations for the Rio+20 Conference, held in Brazil;
- MERCOSUR's environmental agenda for after Rio+20;
- Agenda 2030: specific topics within MERCOSUR's scope.

This research revealed that most RMMA minutes are detailed. They expose countries' positions on the topics proposed in the negotiation agendas, note the advances and limitations of policies and actions related to the environment, and highlight alignments and difficulties associated with MERCOSUR's environmental policy.

In this first stage of the analysis of MERCOSUR documents published between 2009 and 2019, correlations among the issues discussed during meetings of SGT nº6 and the RMMA were identified; these links demonstrated the intersection of the agendas of both technical and political bodies. Indeed, some points of convergence and divergence were found in the investigated minutes. This made it possible to infer that there have been limitations and advances in environmental policy at the regional level. For example, it was possible to confirm that the representatives of member states and associates presented their positions, improvements, and domestic difficulties on various environmental issues, especially climate change, during RMMA meetings. However, despite the proposition to build strategies and action plans, the environment ministers chose not to assume a joint stance at the 16th Conference of the Parties (COP16) of the United Nations Climate Change Conference, held in Cancun in 2010.

Variations in domestic, commercial interests, levels of performance in the institutional structures, and the specific national legislations available to deal with climate change have possibly influenced the delegations in their decisions on individual positioning in negotiations related to international climate governance. During the Rio+20 Conference, when Brazil was responsible for organizing and hosting it, the RMMA and environment ministers created a joint positioning document entitled *Declaration of Buenos Aires of the MERCOSUR's Environment Ministers and Chile as an Associated State*. The document was published in May 2012, with the bloc's guidelines based on the pillars of sustainable development, green economy, and governance. The aim was to eradicate poverty and promote social inclusion, based on principles of common but differentiated responsibility. Additionally, MERCOSUR environment ministers wanted to position themselves against protectionist measures applied to trade, with the justification of environmental preservation, to defend the need for international financing for sustainable development projects, and to highlight the responsibility of developed countries to allocate 0.7% of their gross domestic product (GDP) for such purposes (Garcia, 2019).

The second stage of analysis of MERCOSUR documents was aimed at finding out whether the environmental issues negotiated by SGT nº6 and the RMMA were forwarded to MERCOSUR's decision-making bodies. To this end, the minutes and documents resulting from the meetings of the CMC and the GMC, made available by the MERCOSUR Secretariat in the Regulations of the Decision-making MERCOSUR's Bodies database from 2009 to 2019, were investigated.

The CMC expresses itself using decisions, which are binding for member states, and recommendations when it establishes general guidelines, action plans, or incentive initiatives that corroborate integration, but which are not binding. The GMC issues resolutions that are binding for member states, some of which must be formalized in the respective countries as a decree or law after ratification; others, however, do not need to be incorporated into the legal system of the member states, because they regulate aspects related to MERCOSUR's operations. There are also declarations, which are public positions of member states on an issue in question, but which are not binding.

The GMC is MERCOSUR's executive body and is responsible for SGT n°6 and the ad-hoc groups dealing with environmental issues. Technically, resolutions for environmental issues are published and implemented by the GMC, and the CMC rarely makes decisions on environmental issues. For example, in 2022, the GMC created the Ad-hoc Group on Trade and Sustainable Development, based on an issue related to one of the chapters of the EU-MERCOSUR Free Trade Agreement. This issue, however, was not decided by the GMC. Proposals from the RMMA are directed to the CMC; however, the handling of environmental issues is done by the GMC.

Five hundred and twenty-six (526) resolutions passed by the GMC between 2009 and 2019 were investigated. Most of the resolutions approved in this period dealt with intra-bloc and extra-bloc trade, such as phytosanitary, animal health, and pharmaceutical measures, standardization to improve the movement of goods, and nomenclatures and correspondence regarding TECs, among others. Only nine resolutions were related to environmental issues, as shown in Table 9.1.

Table 9.1. GMC resolutions with environmental themes (direct or indirect) (2009–2019)

Year	Documents
2009	N°41/09: Financing Agreement for the Support Programme for the Deepening of MERCOSUR's Process of Economic Integration and Sustainable Development (ECONORMAS Project)
2010	N°44/10: Understanding Memorandum on Cooperation between MERCOSUR and the United Nations' Food and Agriculture Organization (FAO)
2012	N°38/12: Extension of the Understanding Memorandum between MERCOSUR and the Spanish Agency for International Development Cooperation (AECID)
2013	N°18/13: Understanding Memorandum between MERCOSUR and the Spanish Agency for International Development Cooperation (AECID)
2015	N°36/15: Cooperation between MERCOSUR and the Spanish Agency for International Development Cooperation (AECID) N°27/15: Guidelines for the Sanitary Management of Solid Waste, Wastewater and Drinkable Water at Ports, Airports, International Cargo and Passenger Terminals and Land Border Crossings in MERCOSUR
2017	N°18/17: Extension of the Understanding Memorandum between MERCOSUR and the Spanish Agency for International Cooperation for Development (AECID)
2018	N°59/18: Understanding Memorandum between MERCOSUR and the United Nations' Environment Programme (UNEP)
2019	N°38/19: Guidelines for the Preparation of a Plan for the Prevention, Monitoring, Control and Mitigation of Invasive Exotic Species

Source: Created by the author; based on Garcia (2019, pp. 193–194).

Among the issues previously addressed by SGT n°6 and the RMMA that were negotiated and approved in GMC resolutions, the following stand out:

- Technical and financial cooperation between MERCOSUR and AECID for the construction of a database for SIAM;
- The ECONORMAS Project is a partnership between MERCOSUR and the European Union that involves financial and technical assistance for the former to establish and implement sustainability standards;
- The Understanding Memorandum for Cooperation between MERCOSUR-FAO and MERCOSUR-UNEP. FAO and UNEP have participated in various meetings of SGT n°6 and the RMMA to collaborate on strategies to implement MERCOSUR's environmental agenda. Themes have included desertification and drought, climate change, and biodiversity, among others related to Rio+20 and Agenda 2030;
- The Guidelines for the Preparation of a Plan for the Prevention, Monitoring, Control and Mitigation of Invasive Exotic Species is probably a result of the discussions and proposals of SGT n°6 and the RMMA;
- The proposal for Resolution n°27/15, whose scope extends beyond the environmental agenda, was possibly presented by other technical bodies of the bloc, such as SGT n°5 Transport or SGT n°11 Health.

There were no GMC resolutions on environmental issues in 2011, 2014, and 2016. Regarding the meetings and documents produced by the CMC, 408 decisions made between 2009 and 2019 were investigated. Almost all of these documents dealt with issues related to intra- and extra-bloc trade, the creation and harmonization of standards, measures to consolidate integration, MERCOSUR's institutional structure, budgets of technical bodies, policies, and funds, among others. Decisions and approvals that indirectly dealt with environmental topics, such as basic sanitation, were probably previously negotiated by other technical and political bodies of the bloc, not by SGT n°6 and the RMMA. Table 9.2 lists the few documents that were approved by the CMC that directly or indirectly dealt with environmental issues in 2009, 2010, 2012, 2015, 2017, and 2018.

Table 9.2. CMC decisions on environmental themes (direct or indirect) (2009–2019)

Year	Documents
2009	Nº03/09: Creation of the Specialized Meeting on Natural Disaster Risk Reduction, Civil Defence, Civil Protection and Humanitarian Assistance (REHU)
2010	Nº05/10: MERCOSUR Structural Convergence Fund: "Expansion of the Sanitary Sewerage System of Ponta Porã MS" Project • *Observation 1*: This project was presented by the Federative Republic of Brazil Nº18/10: Approval of Internal Rules of the Environment Ministers' Meeting Nº51/10: MERCOSUR Structural Convergence Fund: "Sanitary Sewage System Engineering Works in the City of São Borja RS" Project Observation: This project was presented by the Federative Republic of Brazil Nº67/10: MERCOSUR's Strategic Social Action Plan • *Observation 2*: Guideline 22: To consolidate the environmental issue as a crosscutting theme of public policies • *Observation 3*: Guideline 23: To promote changes towards more sustainable patterns of production and consumption
2012	Nº30/12: MERCOSUR's Fund for Structural Convergence: "Integrated Urban Sanitation Aceguá/Brazil and Aceguá/Uruguay" Project
2015	Nº47/15: Meeting of Ministers and High Authorities on Integral Disaster Risk Management (RMAGIR)
2017	Nº13/17: Understanding Memorandum on International Cooperation between MERCOSUR and the FAO for the Promotion of Food and Nutritional Security, the Right for Development and the Fight against Poverty
2018	Nº02/18: Framework Agreement between MERCOSUR and the Financial Fund for the Development of the La Plata Basin (FONPLATA)

Source: Created by the author; based on Garcia (2019, pp. 195–197)

Only two documents appear to have been prepared and forwarded by SGT nº6 and the RMMA—Decision nº18/10 and Decision nº67/10. The latter has two guidelines related to public policies and sustainable production and consumption, which are probably associated with an unfolding of the ECONORMAS Project.

The recommendations produced by the CMC between 2009 and 2019, for the most part, referred to labour-related themes, gender issues and valuing/protecting women, promoting family agriculture, combating child labour, and public policies for rural youth. Those which were indirectly related to environmental issues covered basic sanitation, disaster risk management, and food security.

While investigating the CMC's declarations published by member states (which are not binding), I identified and analysed those that had some correlation with environmental issues (Table 9.5).

Table 9.3. CMC declarations on environmental themes (direct or indirect) (2009–2019)

Year	Declarations (Non-binding)
2010	Declaration of MERCOSUR's Presidents of the Member States on the Guaraní Aquifer Declaration of MERCOSUR's Presidents and Associated States on the Exploitation of Non-renewable Natural Resources in the Argentinean Continental Platform • *Observation 1*: Rejection of the exploitation of non-renewable natural resources in the Argentinean platform by the United Kingdom and Northern Ireland • *Observation 2*: Support of sovereignty over the question of the Falkland Islands in the Declaration of MERCOSUR's Presidents and Associated States on the Falklands
2012	Declaration of Mendonza on the Use, Conservation and Sovereign and Sustainable Exploitation of Natural Resources and Natural Wealth of MERCOSUR's Member States and Associated States Declaration on the Question of the Falkland Islands • *Observation 1:* Rejection of the exploitation of renewable and non-renewable natural resources on the Argentinean platform by the United Kingdom and Northern Ireland • *Observation 2:* Exchange of information among MERCOSUR's member states and associated states on research and naval artefacts related to the question of the Malvinas Islands
2015	Declaration on the Exploitation of Hydrocarbons on the Argentinean Continental Platform in Proximity to the Falkland Islands • *Observation:* Rejection of the exploitation of hydrocarbons on the Argentinean continental platform in the Falkland Islands.
2017	Declaration of MERCOSUR's Member States and Associated States on Illegal, Unreported and Unregulated Fishing Declaration of MERCOSUR's Member States and Associated States on the Commitment to the Paris Agreement MERCOSUR's Declaration on the 2030 Agenda for Sustainable Development Declaration on the Bioceanic Integration Rail Corridor Project • *Observation:* Correlated to the construction of the railway linking it to the Paraná-Paraguay Waterway

Source: Created by the author; based on data from Garcia (2019, pp. 197–198).

The declarations published between 2009 and 2019 reinforce commitments negotiated by SGT nº6 and the RMMA, whose issues transcend the political borders of the bloc and form part of the international environmental agenda. Two examples are the declarations referring to the Paris Agreement (Climate Change) and the Agenda 2030. The declarations relate to the Falkland Islands, where Argentina has made a claim to the United Kingdom's territory, which is a geopolitical issue that also touches on the exploitation of fossil resources (hydrocarbons) and thus is also related to environmental issues. The Declaration on the Bioceanic Integration Rail Corridor Project correlates this future investment with the Paraná-Paraguay Waterway, a subject with historical, environmental, economic, and geopolitical aspects. The declaration on the Guaraní Aquifer is the only document with a clear environmental focus, but it was not negotiated by SGT nº6 or the RMMA in the period investigated.

Leite (2018) argues that the Agreement on the Guaraní Aquifer was signed by MERCOSUR's member states in August 2010, based on the studies of the Ad-hoc High-level Group on the Guaraní Aquifer, a provisional and auxiliary body of the CMC. The aim of this agreement is the establishment of greater cooperation regarding the knowledge and responsible management of the transboundary groundwater resources of the region. However, this agreement has not yet been ratified by Paraguay; meanwhile, Brazil (2017), Argentina (2012), and Uruguay (2012) have ratified it.

Despite the strategic importance of the waters of the La Plata Basin and the Guaraní Aquifer for MERCOSUR's member states, which are direct beneficiaries of these resources and have historically had conflicting and cooperative relations, this issue is not on the negotiation agendas of MERCOSUR's technical, political, and decision-making bodies that deal with environmental issues. This is probably because the presidents of the countries in this region have chosen to leave the issues related to the La Plata Basin and the Guaraní Aquifer to be dealt with by other regional organizations, such as the CIC Plata and FONPLATA. It is evident that the shared management of water resources is not covered in MERCOSUR's environmental policy, highlighting one of its limitations.

9.5 Limitations of MERCOSUR's environmental policy

The first aspect that limits the progress of MERCOSUR's environmental policy stems from the large gaps and differences in public policies, legislation, technical capacities, and domestic institutions dedicated to environmental issues in each of the bloc's member states. Brazil is more advanced in managing environmental issues compared to Argentina, Uruguay, and Paraguay. Moreover, the internal regulatory and institutional frameworks of these countries are influenced by diverse political, economic, and social actors as well as by national, regional, and international conjunctures. At certain times, the importance of advancing sustainable development is recognized; at others, the priority is strictly economic, commercial, and financial issues, resulting in the marginalization of socio-environmental issues.

Article 225 of the Constitution of Brazil (1988) states that every person has the right to live in an ecologically balanced environment since it is essential to a healthy quality of life. Moreover, it says that the government should defend and preserve the environment for present and future generations. The principles set out in this article are in line with the aim of achieving more sustainable development. Brazil pioneered the construction of a broad legislative and institutional framework to address specific environmental issues, such as water, conservation units, and solid waste, among others.

Argentina, Paraguay, and Uruguay also have constitutional texts that deal with environmental protection. However, complementary legislation was practically non-existent before they joined MERCOSUR. Although the constitutional texts have a common origin and list concerns related to environmental issues, achieving environmental legislative harmonization has demanded joint efforts by nations (Oliveira and Espindola, 2015).

At the national level, states have advanced significantly, with the creation of legislations, institutions, and public policies aimed at dealing with the diversity of issues that make up the environmental dimension, such as biodiversity, forests, protected areas, and climate change, among others. The inspection of actions that violate environmental laws is the responsibility of national agencies. Based on these pre-conditions, the measures and actions taken by states first depend on the level of engagement with the issues at hand, with the knowledge of relevant people in key positions, and the quality of normative and institutional frameworks that each member state has at its disposal internally. Then there is the possibility to take it to the regional arena and be willing to advance, or not, in the establishment of common standards or projects.

Braga (2014) claims that the environmental regulations produced by the bloc have more bureaucratic than practical effects because each member state produces legal environmental measures and institutions according to its internal demands. Clearly, environmental issues are first discussed at the local and national levels, before regional commitments can be considered. This limitation is also a factor of the diversity of measures and projects, without standardization and common goals, which do not present tangible results or have significant repercussions and products. Besides, it also reinforces that Brazil and Argentina are more active than the others in dealing with environmental issues.

Another aspect that limits the evolution of the bloc's Environmental Policy is the intergovernmental decision-making process and the lack of multi-level governance; this forces non-state actors legitimately interested in environmental issues to lead MERCOSUR negotiations. Indeed, MERCOSUR member states opted for an intergovernmental decision-making process, with power concentrated in the central governments and three institutions: the CMC, GMC, and CCM. The meetings of these bodies are attended by the presidents and/or foreign and economy ministers of the member states. The choice to centralize decision-making to the executive branch of the member states was justified to avoid bureaucracy and delays in achieving the bloc's objectives. Depending on the issues at hand, MERCOSUR member states, representatives of the economic and social sectors of the member states, international organizations, and other groups from the countries are invited to attend meetings but without the right to vote.

MERCOSUR's negotiations have two stages. During the preparatory stage, technical experts from member countries participate in the technical subgroups, and direct representatives of the national governments hold specialized meetings to work on formulating proposals. In the decision-making stage, the proposals are forwarded to the higher authorities, composed exclusively of presidents or ministers of the member states. If proposals are approved by consensus, the standards are rendered mandatory. Following this, if necessary, the standards need to be incorporated into the national legal systems through procedures provided by the legislative framework in each country. Indeed, Rocha (2011) confirms that the bloc does not have regional laws or common jurisprudence precisely because it does not have supranational prerogatives.

Medeiros et al. (2015) report that MERCOSUR's institutional design is held up by intergovernmental pillars to ensure the integration process takes place in an effective and pragmatic way that is adapted to the needs of the member states. The result is an institutional framework that prioritizes intergovernmental cooperation, with a clear hierarchy — at the top is the Common Market Council (CMC), then is the Common Market Group (GMC), and finally the Mercosur Trade Commission (CCM). Although the European Union serves as a model for MERCOSUR, the latter has not yet evolved to include autonomous supranational bodies; for instance, the regional legislative body Parlasur is merely consultative. MERCOSUR has also yet to implement multi-level governance, and involve non-state actors in decision-making processes.

During the literature review and document analysis, I confirmed that SGT nº6 answers to the GMC, and that the RMMA is the interlocutor with the GMC and hierarchically linked to the CMC. In light of this institutional design, it was assumed that the proposals previously negotiated by technicians and ministers specialized in environmental issues would be taken to the decision-making bodies and negotiated until they were turned into resolutions, decisions, declarations, or even new norms to be implemented at the national or regional levels. However, these phases of the negotiation and decision-making process were not fully confirmed when comparing the meeting agendas, minutes, and documents from between 2009 and 2019. This revealed the limitations arising from the competition between issues and the priority given to those that directly impact intraregional trade and trade with external partners. Such conditions also hinder the evolution of the bloc's Environmental Policy.

Another aspect detected in the literature review and document analysis is the lack of participation of organized civil society and university experts in technical and political organizations with formal access to the MERCOSUR structure to collaborate in the construction of the Environmental Policy. The last record of participation by a non-governmental organization (NGO) was in a meeting of SGT nº6 in 2009. The non-participation of civil society representatives and universities shows the lack of multi-level governance in the technical scope negotiations for environmental issues in the bloc. In comparison to other MERCOSUR bodies, when it comes to technical negotiations related to transport, representatives from the interested economic and professional sectors participate indirectly, with the right to speak but not to vote.

Dias (2001) points out that in the early years of the bloc, NGOs provided technical information and sent proposals that would assist the public bodies of member countries when the governments had little competence and few specialized staff. In parallel, these NGOs organized the Conferences on MERCOSUR, the Environment and Transboundary Aspects, entitled ECOSUR.

According to Hochstetler (2003), MERCOSUR's own institutions made it difficult to deal with environmental issues in decision-making processes, with suggestions coming from NGOs. This is because the main representative channel, the Economic and Social Consultative Forum (FCES), favoured the participation of trade unions and companies. In 1995, NGOs and the private sector participated in SGT nº6's meeting, but under unequal conditions. Given this history of low participation of organized civil society and university representatives in the negotiations of MERCOSUR's specialized bodies for the environment, it can be inferred that there were constraints on the progress and effectiveness of the bloc's Environmental Policy. Indeed, there was a lack of actors that could generate greater legitimacy and commitment at multiple scales and across sectors.

Despite the importance of natural landscapes and environmental resources in South America, and the geopolitical history of the La Plata Basin region, the creation of environmental policies in the Latin American context is limited due to political instability, institutional fragility, and the intrinsic needs of social development associated with economic and productive growth. This impedes the establishment of a collective management mechanism for transboundary natural resources in MERCOSUR.

Water resources are an example, as despite their historical and strategic importance, several attempts were made to include them in the agendas of SGT nº6 and the RMMA, but no progress was made. The cross-cutting issue, its impact on other sectors, the difficulties associated with articulating the issue between MERCOSUR bodies, and the differences between national environmental bodies prevented the region from achieving more concrete results to jointly deal with the issue. Although environmental protection can serve to converge the interests of states, commercial and economic issues end up prevailing in meetings of MERCOSUR's decision-making bodies. Furthermore, SGT nº6 and the RMMA rarely dialogue with other technical bodies in the bloc.

The difficulties and limitations associated with building common sectoral policies and joint instruments for effective MERCOSUR action are a direct reflection of the existing asymmetries between member countries and their external vulnerabilities. The forums for debate on environmental issues have little political and operational weight, as does the political and institutional organization of the bloc. This leads to the marginalization of environmental issues within the integration process in favour of trade issues, as previously mentioned.

The lack of a shared vision by central governments as well as their lack of thinking about policies based on sustainability guidelines also hinders the progress and effectiveness of MERCOSUR's environmental policy. This has been true for decades, but has recently led to the stagnation of the bloc's environmental agenda.

In 2019, after more than two decades of negotiations, the CMC approved an institutional reform of the bloc through Decision no. 90/19, with the justification of the need for mergers and exclusion of bodies that had already fulfilled their mandate/objective or had been inactive for two years. In compliance with the instructions issued by this higher body, SGT n°6 eliminated the ad-hoc groups from its internal structure. This was made official in Minute n°02/20 of its 13th Extraordinary Meeting, held on 14 and 15 October 2020 (MERCOSUR, 2020).

My hypothesis is that the demobilization of these ad-hoc groups, which conduct studies on environmental issues, was in part to meet the institutional reform of the bloc and attempt to streamline integration. Additionally, it was because of the low concern about the environment among the MERCOSUR federal governments that were in power in that period.

Historically, Brazil has led MERCOSUR's environmental negotiations. However, several times between 2019 and 2022, Brazilian President Jair Bolsonaro and his Environment Minister Ricardo Salles publicly positioned themselves as sceptical that humans were the cause of environmental problems, such as climate change. They also argued that environmental conservation should not hinder trade, demonstrating their blinkered vision and lack of theoretical and practical knowledge on the nuances of sustainability. Before coming into power, shortly after he had been elected, Bolsonaro requested the withdrawal of Brazil's candidacy to host the United Nations Climate Change Conference (COP25), which was to be held in 2019, on the grounds of cost containment.

9.6 Conclusion

MERCOSUR's environmental policy was built over almost three decades of negotiations, which resulted in the introduction of specialized technical and political bodies, ad-hoc study groups, agendas with negotiating schedules, recommendations, resolutions, decisions, declarations, environmental agreements, and protocols. Additionally, the negotiations amounted to the harmonization of environmental legislation in the member states; the signing and implementation of international cooperation projects of a financial and technical nature with European countries and United Nations bodies; and the exchange of experiences at international environmental conferences and alignment of member states, which reverberate across multiple levels of power. MERCOSUR's aim was not to create a single environmental legislation for all member states, or supranational standards, but to establish a set of common criteria for environmental issues, while considering the specific conditions in each state and the productive sectors.

It should be acknowledged that negotiations in the bloc's technical, political, and decision-making bodies have served to reinforce dialogue and strengthen the commitments established at the national and international levels. These commitments were related to the environmental and sustainable development agendas. The processes have contributed to environmental governance by connecting the national, regional, and international arenas, despite the barriers imposed by prevailing conjunctures, periods of tension between the member states, political and economic crises, and decisions of the bloc's high-level bodies being focused on trade.

Although dealing with environmental issues was not the main objective of cooperation, MERCOSUR has made a great contribution to the environmental negotiations in South America. It has negotiated environmental issues, considering the institutional frameworks of its member states, and complementing the South American environmental governance system, together with the Amazon Cooperation Treaty Organization and other regional organizations that deal with water resources and conduct environmental studies.

Limitations and difficulties still persist in the advancement of environmental norms at the regional level, highlighting the concentration of decision-making power in the central governments. There is evidence of strong intergovernmentalism and a lack of supranational democracy to address environmental issues. These factors, in addition to the prevailing commercial interests, marginalize the impacts that some systems of production and occupation of the territory have on the environment. Moreover, they are aggravated by the endurance of technical, normative, and institutional asymmetries between member states, and non-existence of a shared management policy for natural resources, such as the waters of the La Plata Basin and the Guaraní Aquifer.

Between 2019 and 2023, MERCOSUR has faced a series of challenges, such as the COVID-19 pandemic, as well as political and ideological divergences among the presidents of member states. These domestic and cross-border factors influenced the dynamics of this regional arena, not only on issues related to the environment, but also on intraregional and extra-regional trade, the movement of people and goods, and other issues relevant to the various bodies in the organizational structure and the objectives of the bloc. During this period, the governments in power showed little will to find joint solutions to minimize these challenges. At times, there was estrangement and tension, which led to the weakening of the bloc. In this context, MERCOSUR's environmental policy has suffered apparent stagnation as the marginalization of environmental issues reverberates across nations; this phenomenon has been most clearly epitomized by the position of Brazil's central government.

As mentioned, there are also external variables—extra-bloc actors and events occurring on a global scale—that can influence the dynamics of regional environmental politics, by prioritizing or neglecting issues in MERCOSUR's agendas and decision-making processes. A recent example is the European Union-MERCOSUR Free Trade Agreement, signed in 2019, which mandates all members to implement previously signed international environmental agreements, such as the Paris Agreement (COP21).

Despite the limitations identified, it is not possible to entirely disregard the normative and institutional framework that constitutes the bloc's Environmental Policy and its contribution, even if indirect, to environmental governance at national, regional, and international levels. At this moment, with the newly elected governments in South America, it would be worth noting the weight that the current political actors assign to the environment and regional integration processes. This might include a consideration of the instruments used to strengthen relations with neighbouring countries; the efforts undertaken to overcome the challenges that have worsened in recent times as well as the extent to which there will be political rhetoric or actions related to the 17 sustainable development goals of the 2030 Agenda and, consequently, the evolution of MERCOSUR's environmental policy.

The transnationality of these issues requires continuous dialogue to enable alignments and collective action, while respecting the environmental, socio-cultural, political, and institutional realities of each state and its societies. There must be a focus on the valuation of natural resources and sustainable systems relevant to the production and circulation of goods (domestic, intraregional, and international), and associated with the convergence of multiple factors and interests. This would enable the formulation and implementation of regional strategies aimed at promoting sustainable development and reducing the bloc's dependence on extra-regional countries and products.

References

Braga, L. M. (2014) 'O histórico da incipiente política ambiental do MERCOSUL', *Mundorama*, (82), pp. 1–6.

Brazilian Chamber of Deputies (2003) *Decreto legislativo n°333, de 2003*. Available at: http://www2.camara.leg.br/legin/fed/decleg/2003/decretolegislativo-333-24-julho-2003-494160-acordo-quadro-1-pl.html (Accessed: October 2019).

Dias, R. (2001) *A política ambiental do MERCOSUL (1991–1999): um novo espaço de articulação*. Unpublished PhD thesis. Universidade Estadual de Campinas.

Garcia, T. S. L. (2019) *Desafios da integração Sul-Americana: as políticas de meio ambiente e de transportes no MERCOSUL (2009–2019)*. PhD thesis. Universidade de São Paulo. Available at: https://www.teses.usp.br/teses/disponiveis/8/8136/tde-16062020-122911/publico/2019_TatianaDeSouzaLeiteGarcia_VOrig.pdf (Accessed: 8 June 2023).

Garcia, T. S. L. and Jesus, B. O. (2019) 'Fronteiras na bacia do Prata: geopolítica, história e contemporaneidade', in: Costa, W. M. and Vasconcelos, D. B. (eds.), *Geografia e geopolítica da América do Sul: integrações e conflitos*. São Paulo: FFLCH/USP. pp. 318–336.

Hochstetler, K. (2003). 'Fading Green? Environmental Politics in the Mercosur Free Trade Agreement', *Latin American Politics and Society*, 45(4), pp. 1–32.

Irachande, A. M., Almeida, L. B. and Vieira, M. M. A. (2010) 'O MERCOSUL e a construção de uma política ambiental para os países do Cone Sul', *Sociologia & Política*, 9 (16), pp. 205–223. Available at: https://repositorio.unb.br/handle/10482/24563 (Accessed: May 2023).

Leite, M. L. T. A. (2018) *O Acordo Aquífero Guarani e Ótica da Integração Regional*. Master's thesis. UNESP/UNICAMP/PUC-SP. São Paulo. Available at: https://repositorio.unesp.br/handle/11449/154202 (Accessed: May 2023).

Mariano, K. P. (2007) 'Globalização, integração e o Estado', *Lua Nova*, 71, pp. 123–168.

Medeiros, M. A., Meunier, I. and Cockles, M. (2015) 'Processos de difusão política e legitimidade no MERCOSUL: mimetismo institucional e mecanismos de internacionalização de normas comunitárias', *Contexto Internacional*, 37 (2), pp. 537–570.

Mello, L. I. A. (1997) *A geopolítica do Brasil e a bacia do Prata*. Manaus: Universidade do Amazonas.

MERCOSUR (1991) *Tratado de asunción para la constitución de un mercado común*. Available at: http://www.mercosur.int/innovaportal/fle/719/1/CMC_1991_TRATADO_ES_Asuncion.pdf (Accessed: October 2019).

MERCOSUR (2001) *Acuerdo marco sobre medio ambiente del MERCOSUR*. Available at: http://servicios.infoleg.gob.ar/infolegInternet/anexos/90000-94999/91816/norma.htm (Accessed: October 2019).

MERCOSUR (2006) *Medio ambiente en el MERCOSUR*. Available at: http://www.mercosur.int/msweb/SM/es/Publicaciones/Medio%20Ambiente%20en%20el%20Mercosur.pdf (Accessed: October 2019).

MERCOSUR (2008) *A temática ambiental no MERCOSUL: Evolução e perspectivas. IX Reunião de Ministros do Meio Ambiente do MERCOSUL*. Available at: https://documentos.mercosur.int/public/reuniones/doc/3862 (Accessed: October 2019).

MERCOSUR (2020) *Declaração de ministros do meio ambiente do MERCOSUL. XXV Reunião Ordinária de Ministros do Meio Ambiente, os Ministros do Meio Ambiente dos Estados Partes do MERCOSUL.* Available at: https://documentos.mercosur.int/public/reuniones/8805 (Accessed: October 2019).

MERCOSUR (2020) *XIII reunión extraordinaria del subgrupo de trabajo nº6 medio ambiente.* Available at: https://documentos.mercosur.int/public/reuniones/8803 (Accessed: November 2022).

Oliveira, C. M. and Espindola, I. B. (2015) 'Harmonização das normas jurídicas ambientais nos países do MERCOSUL', *Ambiente & Sociedade*, 28 (4), pp. 1–18.

Presidency of Brazil (2013) *Decreto nº7.940, de 20 de fevereiro de 2013.* Available at: http://www.planalto.gov.br/ccivil_03/_Ato2011-2014/2013/Decreto/D7940.htm (Accessed: October 2019).

Reboratti, C. E. (2007) 'América de sul, Brasil e la cuestión ambiental', in: Costa, S., Sangmeister, H. and Steckbauer, S. (eds.), *O Brasil na América Latina: interações, percepções e interdependências.* São Paulo: Annablume, Adlaf and Fundação Heirinch Böll, pp. 163–176.

Ribeiro, W. C. (2017) 'Uso compartilhado da água transfronteiriça na bacia do prata: utopia ou realidade?' *Ambiente & Sociedade*, 20 (3), pp. 263–276.

Rocha, M. E. G. T. (2011) 'A incorporação das normativas Mercosulinas e as constituições dos estados-partes: o desafio das superações da normatividade estatal', *Universitas: Relações Internacionais*, 9 (1), pp. 1–37.

Simões, T. N. and Garcia, T. S. L. (2022) 'MERCOSUL aos trintas anos: geopolítica, avanços, impasses e desafios', in: Costa, W. M. and Garcia, T. S. L. (eds.), *América do Sul: geopolítica, arranjos regionais e relações internacionais.* São Paulo: FFLCH/USP, pp. 95–119.

Torres, A. (2012) 'Politicas ambientales: el convidado de piedra de la integración regional', in: Caetano, G. (ed.), *El MERCOSUR de las políticas regionales.* Montevideo: Centro de Formacion para la Integración Regional, pp. 219–228.

Chapter 10

Regional environmental efforts in Mesoamerica: Achievements and modes of cooperation

Alina Gamboa Combs
Universidad Anáhuac México, México

Dircea Arroyo Buganza
Universidad Anáhuac México, México

Abstract

This chapter employs a regional institutionalist approach to analyse the activities and efficacy of the environmental efforts of Proyecto Mesoamerica (PM), a regional cooperation and integration project that includes the southeastern states of Mexico, Central America, Colombia and the Dominican Republic. The PM is divided into two pillars, economic and social; the former has a larger budget while the latter has a smaller one but can receive external funding. Environmental sustainability forms part of the social pillar, and it incorporates the pre-existing Mesoamerican Biological Corridor (MBC), as well as other environmental initiatives in Mexico and Central America. This chapter argues that the source of financial support largely determines the outcome of an environmental project; when funding is provided through international bodies that demand accountability, it produces promising results. However, when funding is provided by member states, then outcomes are only accountable to them and little or no progress ensues.

Keywords: Proyecto Mesoamerica, environmental sustainability, Mesoamerican Biological Corridor, international funding, accountability, regional institutionalism

***

10.1 Introduction

Mesoamerica is a natural pathway that has historically enabled the migration of wildlife and the interchange of genetic information between North and South America (Lambert and Carr, 1998). This exchange has enhanced diversity in the Mesoamerican land bridge as well as throughout the Americas. Since the 1970s, there has been a growing awareness of this area's importance in maintaining biodiversity and combating climate change, but political unrest, civil wars, and natural disasters hindered conservation efforts for several decades. The relative peace that prevailed in Central America during the 1990s created opportunities for reforming previous regional integration projects and initiating new ones. With the help of external international institutions, these regional initiatives reiterated the importance of environmental conservation in the mid-1990s. Projects like the Mesoamerican Biological Corridor (MBC) showed promise in safeguarding the biodiversity found in the land bridge, albeit plagued by difficulties and setbacks. With the integration of the MBC into the larger regional development project, Proyecto Mesoamérica, there was potential to institutionalize successful implementation and expand regional environmental efforts. Recent patterns of deforestation, land erosion, and changes in precipitation in Central America have resulted in the formation of what is called the "Central American Dry Corridor", bringing new urgency to safeguarding the existing natural resources and reversing degradation. This chapter focuses on the environmental elements of Proyecto Mesoamérica, analysing the effectiveness of its institutional structure, its policies, and the role of involved external (or associated) international institutions.

In 2008, the governments of Belize, Costa Rica, El Salvador, Guatemala, Honduras, Mexico,[1] Nicaragua, and Panama announced the Mesoamerican Integration and Development Project, known as Proyecto Mesoamérica, to stimulate economic and social development through region-wide social, infrastructure, and interconnectivity projects. Its predecessor, the more ambitious and highly controversial Plan Puebla Panamá (PPP), lasted seven years (2001–2008). The PPP launched within the Tuxtla Mechanism for Dialogue and Cooperation (hereafter the Tuxtla Mechanism), a permanent forum between Mexico and Central America that began in 1991 after the cessation of civil wars in Central America. The Mexican government was instrumental in brokering the Central American peace agreements, and the Tuxtla Mechanism ensured continuous dialogue about cross-border issues in

---

[1] Proyecto Mesoamerica only includes the south-eastern Mexican states of Campeche, Guerrero, Oaxaca, Puebla, Quintana Roo, Tabasco, Veracruz, and Yucatán. Colombia and the Dominican Republic joined in 2009.

the region. The transition from the PPP to Proyecto Mesoamérica involved institutional restructuring and a reduction in the number of projects to better coordinate with the various regional organizations (Gamboa, 2019; Bosco, 2008).

The PPP increased cooperation between Mexico and Central America and achieved some of its objectives, mainly through large infrastructure projects and increased trade within Mesoamerica. It also stimulated collaboration between Mexico and Central America, but there were obvious difficulties in carrying out regional projects that required implementation at a local level (Organization for Economic Co-operation and Development, 2006). Regional nongovernmental organizations (NGOs) protested against the PPP and formed the Mesoamerican forums that met each year to discuss the shortcomings of the regional project and propose alternatives. The forums began after the PPP launched, with the participation of organized civil society groups (Bull, 2005). They complained that they received the project in the form of a completed document and, therefore, had no opportunity to give feedback or suggestions. They also had serious concerns about the priorities in the initial public documents, particularly in regard to how the project would affect indigenous populations and the environment. Several authors rejected the Mesoamerican initiatives established in the PPP directed at environmental management on the premise that they went against the attitude towards nature held by the region's peoples (Bartra, 2002). Forero and Pérez (2002) and Rioja Peregrina (2002) highlighted the fact that the environmental policies in the region were derived not only based on the interests of the Mexican government but also on the globalizing nature of the economy. They drew attention to the environmental richness of the area and alleged that the PPP and MBC projects stemmed from the government's desire to capitalize on the potential economic benefits. The then-Mexican president, Vicente Fox, hinted that the MBC would be part of the PPP; however, it was never officially incorporated.

In 2007, during the yearly summit of the Tuxtla Mechanism, the member heads of state agreed to strengthen and restructure the PPP to enable continued cooperation for development between the eight southeastern Mexican states and Central American countries. The national leaders presented Proyecto Mesoamerica the following year in Villahermosa, Mexico. The environmental ministers also introduced their new initiative (which we will explain in further detail), including the MBC as part of Proyecto Mesoamérica's environmental focus (Proyecto Integración y Desarrollo de Mesoamerica, 2012). When the Mexican and Central American presidents first announced the formation of the PPP—that is, Proyecto Mesoamérica's predecessor—some authors have criticized the term "Mesoamerica" as it diverged from previous geographic definitions. They also argued against giving the eight Mexican states the same status as the Central American Countries (Forero and Pérez, 2002). As Grandia (2007) points out, the definition of "Mesoamerica" varies depending on whether you are talking to archaeologists, historians, politicians, or economists—there is no consensus. In 2009, Proyecto Mesoamérica expanded to include Colombia and the Dominican Republic. It has been in place for 15 years and is steadfast in reinforcing its "Mesoamerican identity", which in practice means being part of Proyecto Mesoamérica (Agency for International Development Cooperation, PNUD and Proyecto Mesoamérica, 2019).

Proyecto Mesoamérica centres on activities that have a region-wide impact on economic growth, which are organized as two pillars (or axes): economic and social. Within the economic pillar lie the activities related to transport (highways and infrastructure), energy (electric grid connectivity and sustainable energy sources), trade (border crossings, trade agreements, and competitiveness), and telecommunications (networks). This first pillar accounts for approximately 94% of the 2019 budget (USD 5951.5 million of the 6345.4 million total).[2]

The social pillar includes environmental sustainability, public health, natural disaster risk management, housing, and food security (incorporated in 2015). The total expenditure in 2019 for this pillar was USD 393.8 million.[3] In contrast, the economic pillar has garnered the most attention, with substantially larger funding provisions (both from within the region and from external sources) and visible advances (Martínez and Sánchez, 2020).

This chapter focuses on the environmental sustainability aspect of the project, which is part of the social pillar. Although the official strategy is the Mesoamerican Environmental Sustainability Strategy (EMSA), we focus on the MBC, the longest-running component, given that it is the most varied and about which the most information is available. First, we explain our theoretical framework—which will allow us to analyse the effectiveness of using a regional integration project to foster cooperation on environmental issues—and our research methods. Then, we explain how Proyecto Mesoamérica fits in with other regional institutions and how it developed its environmental strategy, including how the MBC emerged and was incorporated into Proyecto Mesoamerica. Finally, we discuss the relevant lessons to reflect on and end with some concluding remarks.

---

[2] Budget allocations (in USD million): 3931.6 for transport, 1835.0 for energy, 167.6 on trade, and 17.3 on telecommunications. See: http://www.proyectomesoamerica.org

[3] Expenditure (in USD million): 323.3 on health, 59.6 on housing, 1.9 on risk management for natural disasters, 6.8 on food security, and 2.2 on the environment. See: http://www.proyectomesoamerica.org

Proyecto Mesoamerica is an intergovernmental organization for regional cooperation. Although it does have a central office based in San Salvador that is administrative and consultative, this secretariat does not have the authority to implement projects without the consent of its members. In addition to Proyecto Mesoamérica, the 10 member countries all participate in other regional organizations and agreements, notably the Central American Integration System (SICA), the Latin American Economic System (SELA), the Organization of American States (OAS), the Central American–US Free Trade Agreement (CAFTA), the Mexico–Central America Free Trade Agreement, the US–Mexico–Canada Agreement (USMCA), and various other free trade agreements (see Table 10.1). One of Proyecto Mesoamérica's goals is to ensure communication and coordination among the overlapping regional organizations, trade agreements, and other regional projects. The regulations that were adopted during the founding of the PPP and, subsequently, Proyecto Mesoamérica are unambiguous in maintaining the intergovernmental design, with no intent to create any supranational authority. Instead, there are mechanisms in place that grant veto power and protect national sovereignty (Estados Unidas Mexicanos, 2008; Presidencia de la República, 2001).

10.2 Regional integration theory and methodology of this study

Defining whether a project is considered a "regional integration" project is complicated. Two bodies of literature on integration theory roughly follow two main "waves" of integration (Gamble and Payne, 1996). The first body of literature stems from the functionalist integration model, as explained by Bela Balassa (1962). This model shows a linear progression from trade agreements to the free movement of people, goods, and capital as well as a coordinated macroeconomic policy and the presence of supranational regional bodies. For Belassa, this distinguishes "integration" from "cooperation". However, the more recent literature concurs that regionalism does not have to take form in a specific institutional manner (Söderbaum, 2015). Regional integration occurs when regions become more cohesive and participating national governments work together to tackle common issues (Mansfield and Milner, 1997).

Even so, a region forms through a conscious process; it doesn't just exist. "[R]egions do not have fixed borders, instead, they are constantly being reassessed by political actors who negotiate who is 'in' and who is 'out'" (Grugel and Hout, 1999, p. 9), and even though regions clearly have a geographical element, geography is not necessarily the most important defining factor. In the past, the emphasis was on "natural regions", which were based on geographical proximity, language, or shared identities. However, not all regions form this way. The modern region can shift and change through the actions of its members. Proyecto Mesoamerica expanded its original membership by adding Colombia and the Dominican Republic in 2009. Currently, it excludes Mexico's central and northern states, but it could grow to cover the rest of the nation if there were a reason to do so.

The first wave of regionalism focused on acts of regional integration initiated by state activity; conversely, the new regional literature is more concerned with explaining the differences among regional cooperation schemes and how these fit into the Post-Cold War structures. It explores different political, economic, and social aspects related to or affected by the integration process. Whereas during the Cold War, most regions were "either political or mercantile clusters of neighbouring countries that had a place in the larger international system" (Väyrynen, 2003, p. 26), post–cold war regionalism, or what is currently known as "new" regionalism, encompasses a broader range of political and economic cooperation between nations. Hettne (2000) tentatively defines "new regionalism" as a multidimensional form of integration, including political, social, and cultural aspects. He notes that in the newer generation of regionalist projects, the goal is not just creating region-based free trade regimes or security alliances; "rather the political ambition of establishing regional coherence and identity seems to be of primary importance" (Ibid., p. xvi). The second wave of regional integration is linked to the resurgence of regional integration across Europe during the 1980s, marked especially by the single-market policy, suggesting further social, political, and economic integration (Breslin et al., 2002). Although the European Union (EU) remains the most discussed and studied regional organization – partly because it is the most established and most integrated one —in some ways, the EU undermines the study of regional integration altogether as it takes the spotlight and other regional organizations appear to be less successful in comparison. Integration projects in Latin America, such as the Central American Common Market (CACM) or the Southern Cone Common Market (MERCOSUR), have tried to implement structures similar to those of the EU but have achieved limited results. Technical assistance and cooperation schemes from the EU have been welcomed (European Commission, 2007; European Union, 2002), as well as the funds accompanying them. Some success is seen when the EU builds accountability structures into the assistance and projects.

The proliferation of preferential trade agreements (PTAs) or free trade agreements (FTAs) between states that began in the 1990s provided impetus for the second wave and added a new dimension to regionalism. Although many agreements took place between neighbouring countries (the North American Free Trade Agreement (NAFTA) or MERCOSUR), others were signed between countries that were not geographically contiguous (i.e., Mexico–Chile Free Trade Agreement or Asia-Pacific Economic Cooperation (APEC)). Recognizing that the form and context of these PTAs and other forms of regional cooperation are different from those of previous accords, scholars have coined the term "new regionalism" to describe them. But just as this "new regionalism" is very diverse and covers a vast spectrum of cooperation, so is the literature analysing it. For example, writers like Hettne (2000) and Väyrynen (2003) diverge from the previous functionalist (based on institutionalization, the scope of activity, and the level of institutional authority) approach and adopt a more constructivist approach, focused on the approach of exploring international politics as an intersubjective social reality.

Nevertheless, designing a collective management system is vital to increasing integration and implementing regional projects. Regional institutions and the relevant national governments are the facilitators of much of the integration activity, and they need to safeguard the continuance of projects whose durations are typically longer than national government terms. We agree that there is no specific type of regional institutional structure that defines regional integration; however, it should be noted that the institutional structure and governance systems influence the effectiveness and outcomes of a project.

Proyecto Mesoamérica falls under Hettne's category of "developmental regionalism", where the project is not only used as a means for improving collective bargaining positions and increasing economic cooperation, but also for stabilizing the economy, reinforcing societal viability, facing common problems (i.e., natural disasters), and managing the environment and resources of the region (Hettne, 2000). Environmental issues, such as climate change and other environmental matters, are much more likely to be dealt with on a regional level rather than on a global scale (Hurrell, 1995).

Although the different approaches to regionalism are beneficial in providing insights into the way regions form and function, they still need do not reflect the reality of integration projects in Latin America as a whole. This chapter presents a new perspective on regionalism in Latin America, proposing a new approach in the form of institutional regionalism. Institutional regionalism highlights the need for institutions or organizations to facilitate state cooperation within regional projects. External international institutions, especially, play a crucial role in ensuring that projects are carried out. In most cases, states invite international institutions to get involved in a project to provide funding and, in some cases, technical assistance, but beyond this, international institutions will introduce an element of accountability into the project. This ensures that the project is monitored, expenses are justified, and outcomes are publicly available. When the institutions involved in the project ensure effective accountability, it has a positive effect on the project's duration.

Also, the institutions and their involvement influence the support of subnational and local governments. This is relevant because if there is external support (i.e., financing), governments will emphasize project compliance.

Without support, however, governments are likely to change the projects at their convenience without complying with the agreements they committed to. Using regional institutionalism as part of our analysis permits us to reinstate some functionalist elements into the construction of a region. A region does not need institutional frameworks to exist, but institutional frameworks help it to function and meet its goals. Furthermore, when regional institutions are weak or their underlying governance structures are fragmented (as in Mesoamerica), external regional or international institutions can help provide mechanisms such as continuity and accountability to support the project.

Proyecto Mesoamérica is a multipurpose regional organization that has several goals, and its activities range from economic issues to health and the environment (see Söderbaum, 2015). Yet its coverage of regional problems is not comprehensive. For example, the economic pillar excludes trade agreements[4] and the social pillar leaves out critical regional issues such as regional security and migration (Toussaint and Garzón, 2017). Nevertheless, the Tuxtla Mechanism provides a forum for these specific issues, which are dealt with in other intra-governmental mechanisms involving the United States.

Regional governance is essential for regional integration mechanisms, particularly when several organizations coexist and have a high degree of interdependence (Hveem, 2003). Governance is not limited to the government, and "a variety of actors and agencies, both public and private, are involved in efforts to create order" (Sasuga, 2002, p. 16). Thus, governance explores the development of networking linkages through the various strategic interactions among diverse levels of political and economic activity. When designing implementation mechanisms for a regional project, it is important to identify the existing governance structures, so that compatibility can be ensured.

Many actors participate in constructing the Mesoamerican region, not just the formal institutions. NGOs, businesses, multinational corporations (MNCs), other international organizations (particularly for funding), and national and sub-national government representatives play an essential role in shaping regional policy (Machuca, 2005). Since each state determines the extent of its participation according to its national interests, the individual head of state plays a crucial role in deciding to what degree the state is willing to engage in the regional project. Internal politics, government efficacy, and corruption levels also determine the level of commitment.

---

[4] However, early on an effort to consolidate pre-existing trade agreements among the members resulted in the 2011 Mexico–Central America Free Trade Agreement (Gamboa, 2019).

Our research highlights how it is the individual national governments that influence the progress of and commitment to the projects more, rather than the institutional structure of Proyecto Mesoamérica. Furthermore, we find that the economic and technical aid provided by external international institutions supports the implementation of the project, serving to bridge the fractured governance structures and bringing continuity and accountability.

Environmental issues tend to defy political divisions among countries, so tackling them at a regional level yields better results. Animals roam across borders for feeding and mating, forests and jungles don't stop at borders, and hurricanes and droughts transcend the lines drawn by humans. Natural spaces show that national boundaries are "blurry" or "porous". Projects like the MBC are essential to integration as, according to Machuca, they return "the environmental and geographic continuity to the Mexican and Central American territory to integrate on an ecological level that political borders have separated" (Machuca, 2005, p. 68).

We conducted most of our research with the help of documents and reports published by Proyecto Mesoamerica and other participatory regional and international institutions, such as the SICA, United Nations Development Programme (UNDP), Economic Commission for Latin America and the Caribbean (ECLAC, or CEPAL in Spanish), the World Bank (WB), the Global Environment Fund, and the Interamerican Development Bank (IDB). We also gathered information from the Secretariat of the Environment and Natural Resources (SEMARNAT) of the Mexican Environmental Ministry and the Mexican National Commission for the Knowledge and Use of Biodiversity (CONABIO). Some of the data is readily available online, and we requested the respective offices to share data when it was not available online. We also interviewed a member of Pronatura (an environmental NGO based in Mexico), who was involved in the MBC before it was part of Proyecto Mesoamerica, and the leader of the communal (*ejido*) *Sayachaltun* in Yucatán, whose ecotourism project received funds from the MBC. There was a significant backlog for many reports and assessments as a result of the COVID-19 lockdown. Although some webinars from the MBC from 2020 are on YouTube, very little was published during 2020 and even during 2021; more importantly, the Proyecto Mesoamerica website had few updates. In addition, the government that came to power after the Mexican presidential elections of 2018 set other priorities for the southeast of Mexico. Regional environmental groups have challenged one of the projects, the Tren Maya (a regional train that is to span the Yucatán peninsula), since the tracks cut through jungle areas and go over the underground rivers of the peninsula. The Tren Maya represents territorial reordering in the southeast of Mexico, along with two other projects, Sembrando Vida (agricultural) and an interoceanic corridor (Flores, Deniau and Prieto, 2019). The Mexican government also changed the funding mechanism for CONABIO (in charge of the MBC at the time), prohibiting the use of private contributions, thus leaving them with scarce resources.

10.3 Environmental protection and Proyecto Mesoamerica

Mesoamerica represents one of the world's most biodiverse areas: it constitutes just 0.5% of the global mass but includes almost 10% of the registered global biodiversity. It also has one of the highest deforestation rates as well as rates of loss of animal and plant species (CEPAL, 2015). Urbanization has caused fragmentation in the natural environment. This means that species become isolated, which can limit the gene pool, causing an increase in diseases and biodiversity loss. The foundational purpose of the MBC was to establish biological corridors and protected areas that would connect or maintain the existing connections among, the paths required for the movement of species. Its natural ecosystems range from coral reefs to pine savannas, semiarid woodlands, grasslands, lowland rainforests, high mountain forests, and mangrove forests. The Mesoamerican reef system is the second-largest coral reef in the world, running along the coasts from Mexico to Honduras.

Panama alone has approximately 929 known species of birds, and Belize has about 150 different mammals, 540 birds, and 152 amphibians and reptiles. Mexico is home to 717 different reptiles and 4,000 plants with potential medicinal uses. Guatemala and Honduras have unique endemic plants in the high mountains.

Unfortunately, Mesoamerica's environmental heritage has declined steadily over the past century. Cities continue to grow, and large ranches and farms have been established to provide food for the area. Over 235 million people live in the region, but there is significant income inequality (CEPAL, 2015). People in rural areas cut trees and burn the jungles and forests to make way for subsistence farming (called temporal farming). Earlier, they would farm for about two to four years on their *milpa*[5] to grow staples such as corn, beans, and courgettes and then move on to other plots to repeat the process, leaving the depleted land for 8 to 10 years to allow it to regenerate (Díaz-Gallegos, Mas and Velazquez Montes, 2008). Although this form of agriculture was sustainable for over a millennium, due to population growth and the corresponding increase in food needs, currently, the land is farmed again before it has the opportunity to recover.

---

[5] This is a small field cleared from the forest and cropped for a few seasons. It usually implies traditional farming where corn is intercropped with other products.

Finding ways of generating economic benefits from these unique ecosystems without causing damage is a high priority for the region. Engaging with a population that is diverse in terms of culture and languages and often lives in isolated areas is also challenging (Independent Evaluation Group, 2011).

Central American governments prioritize agricultural production since the export of produce (sugar, coffee, cacao, etc.) is a vital source of income. Deforestation has increased due to livestock production and the felling of trees to create roads or clear land for agriculture. For example, in Panama, the state created the National Institute of Renewable Natural Resources (IPRENARE) in 1986. However, this did not help because forest reserves were not maintained according to IPRENARE standards (Lao, 1993).

During the 1990s, specialists had warned that this area was vulnerable because local governments did not have the capacity or the capital to maintain the parks or ecological reserves that were in place then. One proposed solution is to create sustainable economic activities that would help the communities financially while preserving the integrity of the ecosystems (Hartshorn, 1989).

Around 60% of the close to 40 million people who live in the Central American isthmus are considered poor (Barboza Lizano, 2011), especially those who live in rural areas. This is not unique to Mesoamerica; in 1999, CEPAL estimated that rural poverty reached 51% across Latin America. However, it was above 50% in 6 of the 12 countries with data, and Mexico (53%), Colombia (54%), El Salvador (62%), and Guatemala (75%) are part of this region (Sadoulet and de Janvry, 2000). In addition, there is a deficit of 4.1 million houses, and in rural areas, many people do not have access to running water or electricity in their homes (Economic Commission for Latin America and the Caribbean, 2019). To further complicate the issue, Mesoamerica is located in a high seismic hazard area and within a hurricane corridor, making its population vulnerable to natural disasters. In addition, civil wars, corruption, violence, and lack of technological advancement have widened the gap between the rich and the poor, so it is a region with high levels of income inequality (Corredor Biológico Mesoamericano, 2005).

The question is, how can the needs of a growing population be met without decimating Mesoamerica's natural richness? According to Machuca, "sustainable development is the minimal rational requirement for using natural resources" (Machuca, 2005, p. 69), and we find that there is ample leeway in the definition of "sustainable".

One popular solution is ecotourism, where the community is committed to protecting the environment while creating regional jobs. This is the case of the Tropical Science Center (TSC) in Costa Rica, which was created in 1962. In 1986, it formulated a strategy to produce and sell sustainable forest products (Lázaro,

Pariona and Simeone, 1993). Similarly, in 1989, the National Institute for Biodiversity in Costa Rica (INBio) emerged, an NGO committed to the non-damaging use of natural resources for economic development. INBio followed a novel model—it created a programme to inventory the country's biodiversity and then apply this knowledge to economic activities, encouraging research by MNCs in Costa Rica's conservation areas (Ramírez, 2008). INBio was successful because it engaged the local population and universities and shared the information obtained freely, both for commercial and noncommercial use.

The seven years of existence of the PPP serve to illustrate the need for coordination among regional institutions and projects. The inability to coordinate effectively caused setbacks because necessary and timely action could not be taken to achieve the goals required for sustainable development. Infrastructure projects, however, were easier to design, fund, and build because there was access to public and private funds. They also required less political negotiation as they are highly visible and the economic impact is tangible. Environmental policies, on the other hand, relied on national and local governments to coordinate and cooperate. They also need to be handled carefully because while pointing out that a road or electrical connection is behind schedule or needs more funding is straightforward, signalling the lack of compliance on conservation matters could be interpreted as criticism or interfering in matters of "national sovereignty".

Central America had cooperation mechanisms in place even before the PPP (see Table 10.1), so once the PPP emerged, Mexico needed to coordinate with pre-existing entities such as the Central American Commission for the Environment and Development (CCAD), the leading regional organization for the environment in Central America. The CCAD is part of the SICA, and it continues to be the party that engages in regional cooperation to safeguard the environment. This includes implementing the objectives of the Environmental Plans of the Central American Region (PARCA) and the Central American Alliance for Sustainable Development (ALIDES). ALIDES's main initiative is the development of public policies oriented towards sustainability and fulfilling international cooperation commitments (Martínez and Sánchez, 2020).

The transition of the PPP to Proyecto Mesoamérica required organizational changes to coordinate the overlapping activities among the members and other regional organizations. To this end, Proyecto Mesoamérica had to involve the CCAD and all the environmental ministries of the member states and align with their activities, including PARCA and ALIDES. In addition, most regional trade agreements have some environmental regulations embedded into their framework, which is a necessary initiative considering that economic growth and trade have been prioritized over the environment. However, having many environmental clauses alone does not ensure protection of the environment or a regional strategy per se. On the contrary, there is the risk that they might get overlooked or diluted unless there is coordinated reading of the clauses. In the next section, we will discuss the origins of the MBC, its evolution, and its integration into Proyecto Mesoamérica.

Table 10.1 Overlapping environmental regionalisms in Mesoamerica

Regional projects	Participating countries	Environmental aspect
Proyecto Mesoamerica, 2008. Office of the Permanent Secretariat located in San Salvador	México (nine states), Guatemala, Nicaragua, Belize, Honduras, Costa Rica, El Salvador, Panamá, Colombia, Dominican Republic	Environmental axis within the Social Pillar. ESMA (and MBC)
Central American Integration System, 1962 (addendum 1991). Offices located in San Salvador, El Salvador (SICA)	Belize, Costa Rica, El Salvador, Guatemala, Honduras, Nicaragua, Panama, Dominican Republic as an associated state; Mexico, Chile, and Brazil as regional observers; Taiwan, Spain, and Germany as extra-regional observers	The Central American Commission for Environment and Development (CCAD): develop a regional framework for environmental cooperation and integration and implement the Environmental Plans of the Central American Region (PARCA)
		PARCA I: (2000–2004) Operate the Central American Alliance for Sustainable Development (ALIDES)
		PARCA II: (2005–2009) Develop environmental management instruments and establish regional cross-sector alliances
		PARCA III: (2010–2014) Environmental governance
Central America, Dominican Republic: USA Free Trade Agreement (DR-CAFTA), 2006	United States, Guatemala, El Salvador, Honduras, Nicaragua, Costa Rica, and Dominican Republic (Costa Rica hasn't ratified as of date)	CAFTA-DR Environmental Cooperation Program, CAFTA-DR: Strengthen environmental protection, improve the environmental performance of the private sector, and promote public participation in environmental decision-making
Association of Caribbean States (ACS), 1994. Office of the Secretariat in Port of Spain, Trinidad, and Tobago	Antigua and Barbuda, Bahamas, Barbados, Belize, Colombia, Costa Rica, Cuba, Dominica, Dominican Republic, El Salvador, Grenada, Guatemala, Guyana, Haiti, Honduras, Jamaica, Mexico, Nicaragua, Panama, St Kitts and Nevis, St Lucia, St Vincent and the Grenadines, Suriname, Trinidad and Tobago, Venezuela. Associate members: Aruba, British Virgin Islands, Curacao, France on behalf of (French Guiana and Saint Barthelemy), Guadeloupe, Martinique, Montserrat, Saint Martin, and the Netherlands Antilles on behalf of Saba and Sint Eustatius	ASC Disaster Risk Reduction Commission, Environment and Caribbean Sea Directorate. Strengthen regional cooperation and integration processes to create an enhanced economic space in the region; preserve the environmental integrity of the Caribbean Sea; and promote the sustainable development of the Greater Caribbean. ACS has many extra-regional observer countries as well as observer organizations (like ECLAC and SICA)
US–Mexico–Canada Free Trade Agreement (USMCA), 2020 (renegotiated the 1994 NAFTA in 2018)	Mexico, United States, Canada	Chapter 24: Environment
		Enforce environmental law and cooperate in areas of biodiversity, protection, marine conservation, etc.

Central American Economic Integration Bank (BCIE), 1960. Offices in Tegucigalpa, Honduras	Founding members: Guatemala, El Salvador, Honduras, Costa Rica, Nicaragua, Panama (non-regional members: Mexico, the Republic of China, Argentina, Colombia, and Spain; beneficiary member: Belize). Observers: the WB, IDB, AEO, OMC, CEPAL, USAID	Environmental sustainability is part of its 2020–2024 institutional strategy; programmes and projects have an environmental analysis before approval; green bonds; sustainable cities; regional movement with zero emissions
Association Agreement Central America–European Union, 2012	EU member countries; Costa Rica, El Salvador, Guatemala, Honduras, Nicaragua, Panama	Trade and sustainable development (title VII of the trade pillar): respect and effectively implement the conventions on labour and the environment that they have signed internationally; promote trade compatible with sustainable development—fair and ethical trade, eco-labelling and organic production, corporate social responsibility, and accountability

Source: Created by the authors based on data from CCAD, MBC & PM (2013), European Commission (2007) and Proyecto Mesoamérica (2023).

10.4 History of the Mesoamerican Biological Corridor

Before the biological corridor came into being, there was no regional effort to care for the environment. Most conservation took place locally, in fragments, with each community taking responsibility. In member states with a highly centralized government structure, policies changed every time government officials changed, making the participation of local communities essential to prevent loss of continuity (Heckadon, 1993).

In 1990, the Wildlife Conservation Society began a project known as the Path of the Panther (Paseo Pantera). Paseo Pantera was designed to protect and allow the passage of large animals throughout the region. This was the first attempt to create a corridor in the area (Goethals, 1991). Shortly after that, in 1992, a summit was held in Rio de Janeiro to analyse and propose solutions to environmental problems. The participants of the Earth Summit (as it is known) signed the Convention on Biological Biodiversity,[6] which focused on maintaining sustainable biological diversity and recovering ecosystems through international cooperation. The Summit emphasized regional activities and the equitable sharing of resources.

In October 1994, the Central American Ecological Summit for Sustainable Development was held, where Costa Rica, Nicaragua, Honduras, Guatemala, and Panama established the importance of respecting nature. A recurring theme throughout the summit was seeking equitable economic growth without

---

[6] See: https://www.cbd.int/

damaging and overexploiting natural resources. In order to do so, they agreed on a definition of sustainable economic activities (Ankersen, 1994).

In 1997, in light of the positive experience with the Paseo Pantera, Central American countries decided to continue some of their activities through the MBC. However, this new project was modelled after INBio in Costa Rica, not the Paseo Pantera. The goal was to develop and maintain a policy between states that supported a connection between the ecosystems of North America and South America through a system of biological corridors that would address species conservation from the Mexican Selva Maya to Darien in Panama.

A biological corridor is "a delimited geographical space that provides connectivity between landscapes, ecosystems, and habitats, natural or modified, and ensures the maintenance of biological diversity, evolutionary and ecological processes" (CCAD-PNUD/GEF, 2002, p. 17).

The MBC's objective was to develop regional policies that supported connections among Mesoamerican ecosystems. To achieve this goal, international organizations such as the UNDP, the Global Environment Facility, the WB, and the German and Danish Governments provided funding and technical assistance (Independent Evaluation Group, 2011). Each country underwent an MBC design process, resulting in a regional proposal pertaining to existing and proposed protected areas. Most of these areas were selected because of the endemic or endangered flora and fauna, unique natural ecosystems, or tourist-worthy landscapes or because they provided essential services, such as access to water (Heckadon, 1993).

Mexico joined in 2002,[7] shortly after the PPP was announced. Mexico's protected natural areas include national parks, biosphere reserves, national shrines, and areas voluntarily designated for conservation. Government policy proposes maintaining the genetic diversity of species and preserving different ecosystems.

The MBC's overarching objective was strengthening local communities' sustainability, with the aim of preserving or creating a culture that maintained the biodiversity of different zones. Its motto, *naturalmente unidos*, or naturally united, expresses the intention to link protected areas into larger corridors. The territory encompassed in the corridor is divided into core zones, buffer zones, multiple-use zones, and corridor zones. The core zones are the highly protected areas (many were already designated as national parks or forests) and are surrounded by buffer zones, which are in place to decrease the impact of potential threats. Corridor zones link the core zones, so that there is a wild cover

---

[7] The Mexican states that participated were Campeche, Chiapas, Quintana Roo, Tabasco, Oaxaca, and Yucatán.

that ensures the movement of animals and that also allows plants to spread. Finally, since there is extensive human economic activity in multiple-use zones, the MBC must ensure that enough landscapes remain available for the movement of wild species. All zones in the MBC should provide environmental and socioeconomic benefits to the communities (Gamboa, 2019; Independent Evaluation Group, 2011; Global Environment Facility, 1999).

A key element to the programme's success was the involvement of the local community, who were invited to organize, plan, and establish connections among the corridor zones. Although there was regional planning (mainly through the Global Environmental Fund), each country appointed national coordinators who trained people to make proposals, approach donors, and work together across borders. The MBC had two goals: (1) maintain biodiversity and (2) encourage sustainable economic use of resources. After assessing the current state of the ecosystems and their status as a protected area, the field workers went on to identify areas for investment, such as ecotourism, pharmaceutical prospecting, or environmentally friendly agriculture (Corredor Biológico Mesoamericano, 2005). The MBC facilitated a series of workshops in March 2005 that brought together the people already working on individual, sustainable projects with the aim of demonstrating how their efforts fit in with the overall plan. The documentary resulting from these meetings (*Sendero de vidas*, 2015) shows some of the workshop's activities as well as the positive reactions of the participants.

An example of an MBC-supported project is Laguna Sayachaltún in Yucatán. This project began in 2002 with a group of fishermen who were unable to support their families with their earnings. As part of an *ejido*,[8] they used their land to create new economic opportunities through ecotourism. They received technical assistance to learn how to care for the mangroves in the lagoon, plant new ones, and measure the water's salinity. In turn, they would go to other areas and help train others to care for mangroves. They received funding from the MBC for some of their infrastructure (like solar panels and public toilets). SEMARNAT, which was in charge of the technical training, ensured that the buildings and facilities did not damage the environment (Ortega, 2022). However, dissension among the 50 original fishermen caused the project to end in 2010, but in 2017, 23 fishermen bought out the rest and decided to relaunch. Several families still live off the project, employing local youths for tours; they

---

[8] An *ejido* is a communal property intended for agriculture where members have usufruct rights more than they have actual ownership rights. After the 1992 reform, there is more flexibility in the processes regarding the sale of *ejidos*, but it entails a complicated legal process and applies only to Mexican nationals. Close to 55% of cultivated land in Mexico belongs to *ejidos*.

also opened a successful restaurant in 2020. Although they did not receive money from the MBC in their second launch, the project's original purpose remains.

Several authors (Ramírez, 2008; Bartra, 2002; Rioja Peregrina, 2002), however, considered these projects "biopiracy" and exploitation of the area. Rioja Peregrina goes as far as to compare this new form of piracy of the environment with the plundering of the sixteenth and seventeenth centuries because, in both cases, the "pirates" had the support of their home government (Rioja Peregrina, 2002). The actors, on the one hand, are indigenous and campesino communities and, on the other hand, include universities, governments, and agro-industrial, pharmaceutical, and other multinational companies (Rioja Peregrina, 2002).

Governments and companies promote bioprospecting, the official term for identifying and investigating live organisms, and consider it harmless to indigenous communities. Bartra (2002) and Rioja Peregrina (2002) argue that although researchers rely on the knowledge of local communities, once their final product is patented, the patent is only used by the investigating party, and the indigenous community who provided invaluable information is excluded from commercializing their knowledge in the future. Companies buy cheap and sell high whatever they extract from biogenetics. They do not share or distribute the knowledge they gain, and neither do they share the uses or benefits of whatever they extract with the original owners (Rioja Peregrina, 2002; Saldívar, 2003). Those who oppose bioprospecting argue that because natural resources are appropriated by capitalist organizations, it becomes another form of exploitation of the communities and not a source of development—a "free market" environmentalism of a sort (Finley-Brook, 2007). Instead, they propose that local and indigenous communities should have the right to care for and make the best use of their natural resources, as they see fit (Saldívar, 2003).

The MBC finished its initial stage in 2005, and even though there are final project reports and audits on the use of funds, as Grandia mentions, "the fuzziness of the MBC framework is precisely what makes it such a slippery subject for analysis and evaluation" (Grandia, 2007, p. 480). This fuzziness is partly the reason for the mixed reviews and criticism that the MBC generates. Despite the mixed reactions from academics wanting hard data for comparative analysis, the WB and the Global Environmental Fund published positive reviews on the results, noting that areas within the corridor had better environmental management than those that were not (Cristina Carrillo Hernández et al., 2022; Díaz-Gallegos, Mas and Velazquez Montes, 2008; Corredor Biológico Mesoamericano, 2005).

10.5 Mesoamerican sustainable environment strategy

In 2007, as part of the PPP, the environmental ministers of Mesoamerica gathered to create a regional ecological strategy. After meeting with regional experts, they defined priorities and areas for cooperation that they grouped under three strategic heads: (1) biodiversity and forests, (2) climate change, and (3) sustainable competitiveness (Proyecto Integración y Desarrollo de Mesoamerica, 2012). These three areas are the foundation of the EMSA, which strives to be a structured but flexible environmental strategy promoting sustainable development in the Mesoamerican region (see Table 10.2). The ministers declared that "cooperation among Mesoamerican nations is a fundamental tool for affronting [sic] the environmental challenges faced by sustainable development" (Proyecto Integración y Desarrollo de Mesoamerica, 2012, p. 2). They aimed to secure economic development without compromising Mesoamerica's environmental, social, and cultural wealth.

The environmental ministers signed the "Declaración de Campeche" that launched Proyecto Mesoamérica and announced that the MBC would form part of the new integration project. The ministers appointed "EMSA Ministerial Liaisons" to oversee the implementation of the EMSA. They met for the first time in Cuernavaca (Mexico) in October 2009, creating the first EMSA plan of action, 2013–2016. This first plan of action gathered a comprehensive agenda of activities to enact during 2013–2016.

The document reiterates that similar to other decisions in the EMSA and Proyecto Mesoamerica, it is the product of consensus among the Mesoamerican countries. It also states that the nature of the plan of action is non-binding and that each country's participation in the recommended activities depends on each member's national interests, circumstances, and legal framework (Proyecto Integración y Desarrollo de Mesoamerica, 2012). All participation in these regional mechanisms depends entirely on the political goodwill of the actors involved.

The EMSA Ministerial Liaisons Committee has published three plans of action thus far. The first was the 2013–2016 plan (see Table 10.2). Subsequently, the EMSA published the 2017–2019 plan and the 2020–2025 plan, but they are not publicly available. Although there is no official mechanism for monitoring the progress associated with each activity, upon presenting the 2020–2025 EMSA plan of action, they included an unofficial report of the most significant developments from the previous plan (Proyecto Integración y Desarrollo de Mesoamerica, 2023).

The three objectives of the EMSA, stated in its plan of action, are as follows: (1) reverse the diminishing, fragmenting, and deterioration of ecosystems in Mesoamerica; (2) increase the region's capacity to adapt to climate change and reduce its vulnerability to the effects of climate change; and (3) strengthen regional capabilities for adopting environmental management instruments by promoting sustainable and eco-efficient production and consumption, and the voluntary mitigation of climate change by prioritizing the adoption of renewable energy sources, transportation options, and sustainable production practices.

Table 10.2 The EMSA 2013–2016 plan of action

Strategic area	Actions
Biodiversity and forests	• Strengthen the Mesoamerican Biological Corridor and facilitate cooperation and coordination among all the regional biological corridors • Install regional systems of protected areas and connectivity • Incorporate integral management of the watersheds expert network • Employ a Mesoamerican system for economic and social ecosystem assessment
Climate change	• Adjustment programme for communities, productive systems, and ecosystems in the context of climate change • Local plans of action facing the Climate Change Network (PLACC) based on the SICA commitments • Mesoamerican technical abilities network for forest conservation and maintaining their ecosystems • Mesoamerican programme for the conservation and sustainable use of marine and coastal resources
Sustainable competitiveness	• Integrated waste management network • National programmes for strengthening environmental management abilities, asymmetry reduction, and regulatory compliance monitoring • Good eco-competitive practices that promote a sustainable production and consumption framework • A programme for the development of instruments and mechanisms for control and minimization of regional environmental impacts

Source: Adapted by the authors based on data from EMSA (2012).

Although the MBC could fit within any of the three objectives, the EMSA catalogues it under biodiversity and forests. During the action plan from 2013 to 2016, the MBC was one of the main activities of the EMSA.

Besides the MBC, Central American countries have also obtained financing through other institutions to mitigate environmental change. An example of the above is the Republic of Honduras. This state has worked jointly with the Japan International Cooperation Agency (JICA) in the Biological Union Corridor Project (CBLU) for the sustainable use and conservation of biodiversity. This project sought to draw on the lessons learnt from the MBC and incorporate them into four new municipalities. It also gave significantly more importance to the sustainability of communities (Japan International Cooperation Agency, 2018).

Since 2008, the MBC is no longer an independent regional project but part of Proyecto Mesoamérica. Funding is still primarily obtained through international organizations such as the UNDP, the Global Environmental Fund, and the WB. However, as part of the ESMA, there should be more coordination with the other environmental elements of the plan. One of the criticisms of the MBC was that it was donor-driven and not community-driven (Finley-Brook, 2007). Even if the ideal situation of having community benefits as the foremost priority is not possible, comprehensive design mechanisms are needed to format proposals for regional environmental projects and accountability mechanisms need to be in place in order to ensure the completion (or continuance) of such projects. It is the regional funding institutions that have provided this function for the MBC.

The WB Independent Evaluation Group report on the MBC published in 2011 found that a "clear delineation and coordination of the roles of national and regional institutions" was necessary to achieve their regional aims (Independent Evaluation Group, 2011, p. xxi). The WB requested the "establishment of a coordinating body for regional environmental integration separate from states' interest ... (and) to give national staff the mandate and budget resources to internalize the priorities set at the regional level" (Independent Evaluation Group, 2011). However, throughout the report, the lack of regional strategies is mentioned repeatedly, and most strategies were implemented country-wise, not regionally. The result was that, in some instances, they sponsored activities that were not aligned with the regional vision but, instead, were national priorities. Although these activities were relevant to environmental conservation, they were not part of the corridor connectivity goals.

Additionally, the report mentions that the individual national projects made progress but failed to achieve alignment with regional strategies. The funds procured from different international organizations would be divided among projects and used for maintaining the regional offices; only sometimes would they be used for operating the corridors. Implementation suffered as a result of political strife. In Nicaragua, activities were suspended for two years due to the government's inability to meet the WB conditions, and Mexico put the MBC on hold for about half of its duration due to a change in the administration after the presidential elections (Independent Evaluation Group, 2011).

In the case of Mexico, on 16 March 1992, the CONABIO was created to formulate a strategy with a clear action plan to tackle the exploitation of natural resources and establish sustainable use. Its functions included creating and promoting programmes to classify, document, and maintain ecosystems. In addition, it was established as a consultative institution for citizens and government agencies (Diario Oficial, 1992). From 2002 (until 2018), CONABIO was responsible for maintaining the MBC in Mexico, but the Global Environmental Fund continued to provide funding (Álvarez-Icaza, 2013). The MBC assisted the Mexican government in developing social and economic sustainability programmes and improving public policies for managing natural resources by establishing biological corridors connecting Mexico all the way to Colombia (World Bank, 2000).

In 2013, the EMSA reported that the initiative achieved greater regional cooperation and increased sustainability. However, no hard data were available in the report to support these claims. The only reference found was related to forestry, as regional forest monitoring was implemented with financial support from the Norwegian Government through the UN-REDD Program (2014–2015; CONAFOR, 2017).

As of 2020, the Mexican Agency for International Development Cooperation (AMEXCID) has taken charge of environmental cooperation relations from CONABIO, with the support of the Ministry of the Environment (SEMARNAT). Even though during the last Tuxtla Mechanism summit, the leaders gave approval to the MBC for plan revision and update for 2030 (Proyecto Integración y Desarrollo de Mesoamerica, 2023), there is no evidence that it continues in Mexico. CONABIO, which was in charge of Mexico's part of the MBC, has confirmed that they are not involved, and there has been no announcement from the Mexican government that another government body is taking its place. SEMARNAT, also, has not declared ownership. The MBC office that used to be in Chetumal is officially closed. Although the Proyecto Mesoamérica website announces meetings where the EMSA and MBC present their results, no documents are available, nor do they provide factual evidence to substantiate their claims. However, funding bodies such as the Global Environment Fund, the WB, UNDP, and the ECLAC have published reports and reviews and analysed the impact of the projects they funded (United Nations Development Programme, 2020; Economic Commission for Latin America and the Caribbean, 2019; CEPAL, 2015; Independent Evaluation Group, 2011).

There is growing awareness regarding a new environmental challenge in Central America: an increasing "dry corridor". A dry corridor is a group of ecosystems of tropical forests that become dry and separated from one another. This dry corridor "... begins in Chiapas, Mexico; and, in a strip, it covers the lowlands of the Pacific slope and a large part of the premontane central region of Guatemala, El Salvador, Honduras, Nicaragua, and part of Costa Rica (up to Guanacaste); in Honduras, it also includes fragments that come close to the Caribbean coast" (Food and Agriculture Organization, 2012, p. 8). Diaz Bolaños (2019) concludes that this corridor is a consequence of the agricultural activities and livestock rearing that are inevitable when there are large human settlements (Diaz Bolaños, 2019). Although the Central American region has always been vulnerable to extreme climatic events and natural disasters and is characterized by intermittent periods of drought and heavy rain, the rapid growth of the dry corridor presents an imminent threat.

Inequity and poverty are problems throughout Latin America, which are exacerbated in Mesoamerica. To survive and produce food, the communities choose to convert forests and jungles into farmland or grazing land for cattle, resulting in further deforestation. A regional study by PROARCA established that the rate of felling was an alarming "... 48 hectares per hour, which is equivalent to between 375,000 and 400,000 hectares per year" (Rodriguez Quiroz, 2005, p. 29). The loss of forests generates a multitude of problems. Among the most serious are "... soil erosion; ... changes [in] the composition of the vegetation and, as an additional consequence, changes [in] climatic conditions" (CEPAL, 1993, p. 7).

Governments have attempted to solve the problem of deforestation by conducting workshops and educating the population. But the economic reality is that deforestation provides immediate gains to the community, albeit long-term destruction and loss. We suggest that they incorporate areas at risk of, or suffering deforestation into the biological corridor to maintain and preserve the ecosystems and reduce the effects of climate change, which are already apparent. This would provide training, funding, and economic benefit to the communities whilst focusing on conservation. Many corridors in the MBC have shown lower deforestation rates than the rest of Mesoamerica (ranging from 1.4% to 2.1% of loss yearly). Deforestation rates range from 0.6% in the Calakmul biosphere to 0.8% in the Montes Azules biosphere (Diaz-Gallegos, Mas and Velazquez Montes, 2008), but they can be improved further. Still, there is enough difference to argue in favour of using corridors for environmental management. The WB report shows that forest cover was higher and deleterious changes in forest characteristics were lower in the MBC areas, but since there is little baseline data and studies were done too early, the causal link to the MBC might be coincidental. However, the WB analysis shows that considerable deforestation continues in agricultural areas that border the corridors, and these threaten to disrupt connectivity (Independent Evaluation Group, 2011).

10.6 Conclusion

There are several lessons that could be learned from this study. Firstly, communities need to be involved in all aspects of regional environmental projects. Only when a project includes the local communities do they have ownership. The MBC included communities, listened to them, and incorporated their suggestions. In addition, local community leaders participated in MBC-led workshops and received training (Rosas Hernández and Álvarez Icaza Longoria, 2018). If stakeholders participate in the design of a project and help set its objectives, they are more likely to understand its functions and expected outcomes.

Communities and NGOs accepted the MBC (especially before it became part of Proyecto Mesoamerica) because it had a participatory element, bringing together the priorities set by experts and the needs of the community. Local people need to benefit from the projects, and whether it is in the form of ecotourism, carbon bonds, [9] or any other income-generating activity, these need to be more profitable than the alternative—namely, cutting down trees and burning the jungle for subsistence.

Nevertheless, there is strong support for community involvement since "where MBC projects have been community supported and/or officially enforced, evidence points to lower rates of habitat destruction and benefits to local communities" (Independent Evaluation Group, 2011, p. xvii).

Secondly, governance structures need to be considered when designing projects. Regional institutions need to involve local governments to support their efforts. Local governments provide the groundwork for these projects. They define borders and supply basic infrastructure, such as sewage or water extraction, which can help or hinder efforts. Grassroots support to communities helps legitimize the projects and build community awareness of the importance of the environment. However, this also needs to be supplemented with concrete actions by government authorities. The regional organization involved in the project needs a holistic vision to shape and connect community activities, as communities would not know what is happening beyond their local area. If the regional body is weak or fragmented, then international organizations can provide continuity and ensure that all arms of the project work together.

Thirdly, governments must support their commitments with legal action to prevent non-binding projects and activities from remaining just wishful thinking. Territorial organization is essential, and designating areas as "protected" and not just "important" will enforce compliance. Without legal impetus, these projects only work when funds are assigned. If an area is designated as "protected", it is safe even when no funding is available; no one can build highways or resorts in these areas because the site is legally protected. In the past, what has happened is that in areas of the MBC recognized by authorities only as "important" but not "protected" legally, the work progresses and conservation efforts continue while there is funding. However, when

---

[9] The Mexican administration (2012–2018) was very interested in receiving certified emission reductions (CERs) and helped communities create projects that would qualify for funding. International funding is available for conservation programmes such as mangrove regeneration, and communities benefit from the funds and a healthier environment. The subsequent administration, however, did not continue these programmes (Acosta, 2022).

funding isn't available, conservation work stops, and environmental destruction resumes:

> The problem is that if you protect everything, nothing is protected. You can't include everything; people will invade. Environmental Ministries have to prioritize. They don't have enough resources to patrol everything, and economic activity needs to continue. They have to find balance. (Acosta, 2022).

Finally, since no supranational institution oversees the implementation of the Proyecto Mesoamérica projects for the environmental sustainability pillar, there should be better coordination among the environmental ministries of the member states. While there is a regional plan in the EMSA, each country implements its section independently. When one of the member states acts against the priorities of the EMSA, the non-binding nature of the EMSA takes precedence. The López Obrador administration (2018–2024) has spearheaded a new tourist-oriented train known as the "Tren Maya", which cuts through areas of the MBC. Although many Mexican NGOs have protested and spoken up against the project, citing the deforestation that is taking place and the placing of train tracks over water sources,[10] SEMARNAT has given the go-ahead (Flores, Deniau and Prieto, 2019). Neither the EMSA nor the CCAD have expressed any opinions on the matter. The López Obrador administration abolished the MBC in Mexico because it would have been a hurdle for the construction of the Tren Maya.

Integrating an environmental element into Proyecto Mesoamérica is a necessary measure to ensure that the rich natural resources, landscapes, and biodiversity in Mesoamérica are preserved. Although there are many shortcomings to the EMSA and its implementation throughout the region, there is at least an intent to implement a regional environmental strategy. However, all 10 member countries must implement the EMSA through their national environmental ministries, not through a regional body. Proyecto Mesoamerica's official publications show a general list of accomplishments and milestones reached in the EMSA, but they don't publish a holistic assessment of the outcomes of the projects. Reports from individual countries don't identify projects as part of Proyecto Mesoamérica but as activities of the environmental ministry, and this makes it difficult to differentiate between the outcomes of regional cooperation efforts and those of an individual country's policies. In addition, administration changes also lead to disruptions as new government bodies come up with their own priorities and visions for the future.

---

[10] The Yucatán peninsula does not have surface rivers; most of the peninsula's water is found in underground rivers and cenotes.

The MBC is a good example of regional institutionalism—as compared to other elements of the EMSA—where having external bodies fund and review the projects provided better results (which are at least quantifiable) and continuity to the MBC. International organizations were able to fill in some of the cracks in the fragmented governance structures in Mesoamerica and pressure governments to work together and prioritize the regional environment over the national political agenda. Although there are clear exceptions (such as Mexico ending the MBC so that it could go ahead with the Tren Maya project), international institutions can enable regional projects and provide follow-up and continuity. In Latin America, these institutions can manage regional projects and report on their advances, successes, and shortcomings, in contrast to regional institutions, which are not equipped to do this because of the loose and non-binding nature of their regulations. This is especially important for regional conservation efforts, where advances made by one state can be undermined by the actions of one or more of its neighbours. It is, therefore, crucial for all states to work together towards a regional environmental vision.

References

Acosta, E. (2022) Personal interview. Conducted by Alina Gamboa Combs at Pronatura.

Agency for International Development Cooperation, PNUD and Proyecto Mesoamerica (2019) *Decálogo de la Cooperación Sur-Sur.* Available at: https://www.undp.org/es/mexico/publications/dec%C3%A1logo-de-cooperaci%C3%B3n-sur-sur-y-triangular-en-mesoam%C3%A9rica#:~:text=El%20Dec%C3%A1logo%20de%20Cooperaci%C3%B3n%20Sur,el%20Instituto%20de%20Investigaciones%20Dr (Accessed: 1 June 2023).

Álvarez-Icaza, P. (2013) 'Corredor Biológico Mesoamericano en México', *Biodiversitas*, 110, pp. 2-13.

Ankersen, C. (1994) 'A Clausewitzian framework for analysis', in: *The politics of civil-military cooperation.* London: Palgrave Macmillan, pp. 51–70.

Balassa, B. (1962) *The theory of economic integration.* London: Allen & Unwin.

Barboza Lizano, O. (2011) 'Corredor Biológico Mesoamericano: ¿Un ejemplo de Integración Regional para America Latina?' *Latinidade*, 1, pp. 184–199.

Bartra, A. (2002) 'Hacia una nueva colonización del sureste', in: Alvarez, A., Barreda, V. and Banra, A. (eds.), *Economía política del Plan Puebla Panamá.* Mexico City: Itaca, pp. 81–109.

Bosco, M. A. (2008) 'Proyecto Mesoamérica: Fortaleciendo la integración y el desarrollo regional', *Revista mexicana de política exterior*, 152, pp. 9-39.

Breslin, S., Higgot, R., Rosamond, R., Breslin, S., Hughes, C., Phillips, N. and Rosamond, B. (2002) 'The EU and world regionalism', in: Breslin, S., Hughes, C., Phillips, N. and Rosamond, B. (eds.), *New regionalisms in the global political economy.* London: Routledge, pp. 1–19.

Bull, B. (2005) 'Between Bush and Bolívar: change and continuity in the remaking of Mesoamerica', in: Shaw, T. M. and Marchand, M. (eds.), *The political economy of regions and regionalisms*. London: Palgrave Macmillan, pp. 13–32.

CCAD, MBC & PM (2013) *Plan Director CBM 2020 Gestión territorial sostenible en el Corredor Biológico Mesoamericano*. Available at: https://www.oas.org/en/sedi/dsd/Biodiversity/Mesoamerica2020/3.%20%C3%81lvarez-Icaza%20LongoriaCBM%202020_junio%202014.pdf (Accessed: 3 June 2023).

CCAD-PNUD/GEF (2002) *Proyecto para la consolidación del corredor biológico mesoamericano*. Available at: http://www.bio-nica.info/Biblioteca/CBM2002PlataformaDesarrolloSostenible.pdf (Accessed: 22 May 2023).

CEPAL (1993) *Centroamérica: La protección de los recursos forestales y el medio ambiente con la modernización de la actividad productiva*. Santiago: CEPAL. Available at: https://repositorio.cepal.org/bitstream/handle/11362/27010/LCmexL224_es.pdf?sequence=1&isAllowed=y (Accessed: 1 June 2023).

CEPAL (2015) *Una mirada a los países del Proyecto Mesoamérica*. Santiago: CEPAL. Available at: http://repositorio.cepal.org/bitstream/handle/11362/38426/S1500579_es.pdf?sequence=4&isAllowed=y (Accessed: 1 June 2023).

CONAFOR (2017) *Primer resumen de información sobre la forma en que se están abordando y respetando todas las salvaguardas mencionadas en la decisión 1/CP.16, apéndice I, en México*. Jalisco: CONAFOR. Available at: https://redd.unfccc.int/files/primer_resumen_de_informacion_de_salvaguardas.pdf (Accessed: 1 June 2023).

Corredor Biológico Mesoamericano (2005) *Corredor Biológico Mesoamericano: Instrumentos para su consolidación*. Managua: Editarte.

Cristina Carrillo Hernández, A., Ortega-Argueta, A., María Gama Campillo, L., Bello-Baltazar, E. and Rioja Nieto, R. (2022) 'Effectiveness of management of the Mesoamerican Biological Corridor in Mexico', *Landscape and Urban Planning*, 226, pp. 1–11.

Diario Oficial (1992) *Diario Oficial de la Federación de México, Secretaria de Desarrollo Urbano y Ecología, Acuerdo por el que se crea la Comisión Nacional para el Conocimiento y Uso de la Biodiversidad*. Available at: https://dof.gob.mx/nota_detalle.php?codigo=4655751&fecha=16/03/1992 (Accessed: 1 June 2023).

Diaz Bolaños, R. E. (2019) 'El Corredor Seco Centroamericano en perspectiva histórica', *Anuario De Estudios Centroamericanos*, 45, pp. 297–322.

Diaz-Gallegos, J. R., Mas, J. and Velazquez Montes, A. (2008) 'Monitoreo de los patrones de deforestación en el corredor biológico Mesoamericano, México', *Interciencia*, 33 (12), pp. 882–890. Available at: http://ve.scielo.org/scielo.php?script=sci_arttext&pid=S0378-18442008001200006#:~:text=La%20p%C3%A9rdida%20global%20de%20bosques,con%2093%25%20(315000ha) (Accessed: 1 June 2023).

Economic Commission for Latin America and the Caribbean (2019) *A glance at member countries of the Mesoamerica Integration and Development Project*. Mexico City: United Nations (LC/MEX/TS.2019/12).

EMSA (2012) *Plan de Acción de la Estrategia Mesoamericana de Sustentabilidad Ambiental 2013-2016 (P-EMSA)*. Available at: http://www.proyectomesoamerica.org/images/Anexos/Foro.Sectorial/medioambiente/Plan-de-Accin-EMSA-2013-2016-aprob.pdf (Accessed: 28 April 2023).

Estados Unidas Mexicanos (2008) *X Cumbre de Jefes de Estado y de Gobierno del Mecanismo de Diálogo y Concertación de Tuxtla: Declaración de Villahermosa*.

Available at: http://www.sice.oas.org/tpd/cacm_mex/negotiations/villahermosa_decl_280608_s.doc (Accessed: 1 June 2023).

European Commission (2007) *Regional strategy paper for Central America 2007-2013*. Available at: https://eur-lex.europa.eu/EN/legal-content/summary/regional-strategy-for-central-america-2007-2013.html (Accessed: 1 June 2023).

European Union (2002) *Regional strategy paper for Central America 2002-2006*. Available at: http://aei.pitt.edu/38380/ (Accessed: 1 June 2023).

Finley-Brook, M. (2007) 'Green neoliberal space: the Mesoamerican Biological Corridor', *Journal of Latin American Geography*, 6(1), pp. 101-124. Available at: http://www.jstor.org/stable/25765160 (Accessed: 1 June 2023).

Flores, A., Deniau, Y. and Prieto, S. (2019) *El Tren Maya: Un nuevo proyecto de articulación territorial en la Península de Yucatán*. México: GeoComunes/Consejo Civil Mexicano Para La Silvicultura Sostenible.

Food and Agriculture Organization (2012) *Estudio de caracterización del Corredor Seco Centroamericano*. Rome: Food and Agriculture Organization. Available at: http://humanright2water.org/wp-content/uploads/2020/03/12 12-Corredor-Seco-Centroamericano.pdf (Accessed: 1 June 2023).

Forero, E. A. S. and Pérez, R. S. (2002) *Lectura crítica del Plan Puebla Panamá*. Buenos Aires: LibrosEnRed.

Gamble, A. and Payne, A. (1996) *Regionalism and world order*. London: Macmillan.

Gamboa, A. (2019) *Regional integration, development, and governance in Mesoamerica*. London: Springer Nature.

Global Environment Facility (1999) *The Global Environment Facility and its programme of work*. Washington, DC: Global Environment Facility.

Goethals, H. (1991) 'A unifying environmental purr-pose (Paseo Pantera, a new conservation program by the Wildlife Conservation International and the Caribbean Conservation Corporation)', *Américas (English Edition)*, 43 (1), p. 3.

Grandia, L. (2007) 'Between Bolivar and bureaucracy: the Mesoamerican Biological Corridor. *Conservation and Society*, 5 (4), pp. 478-503. Available at: http://www.jstor.org/stable/26392900 (Accessed: 1 June 2023).

Grugel, J. and Hout, W. (1999) 'Regions, regionalism and the South', in: Grugel, J. and Hout, W. (eds.), *Regionalism across the North/South divide: state strategies and globalization*. London: Routledge, pp. 3-13.

Hartshorn, G. (1989) 'Forest loss and future options in Central America', in: Hagan III, J. and Johnston, D. (eds.), *Ecology and conservation of neotropical migrant landbirds*. Washinton, DC: Smithsonian Institution Press, pp. 13-19.

Heckadon, S. (1993) *Agenda ecológica y social para Bocas del Toro: actas de los seminarios talleres*. Available at: http://bdigital.binal.ac.pa/bdp/descarga.php?f=agenda%20ecological.pdf (Accessed: 1 June 2023).

Hettne, B. (2000) 'The new regionalism: a prologue', in: Hettne, B., Inotal, A. and Sunkel, O. (eds.), *National perspectives on the new regionalism in the South*. London: Macmillan, pp. xv-xxxi.

Hurrell, A. (1995) 'Regionalism in theoretical perspective', in: Fawcett, L. and Hurrell, A. (eds.), *Regionalism in world politics: regional organization and international order*. Oxford: Oxford University Press, pp. 37-73.

Hveem, H. (2003) 'The regional project in global governance', in: Söderbaum, F. and Shaw, T. M. (eds.), *Theories of new regionalism: a Palgrave reader*. London: Palgrave Macmillan, pp. 81–98.

Independent Evaluation Group (2011) 'The Mesoamerican Biological Corridor', *Regional Program Review*, 5 (2). Available at: https://openknowledge.worldbank.org/entities/publication/e471dc4d-4a1f-5a41-a286-126e45ead3ba (Accessed: 1 June 2023).

Japan International Cooperation Agency (2018) *Proyecto Corredor Biológico La Unión (CBLU), para el Uso Sostenible y Conservación de la Biodiversidad*. Available at: https://www.jica.go.jp/project/spanish/honduras/004/materials/c8h0vm0000bk9y9y-att/materials_12.pdf (Accessed: 1 June 2023).

Lambert, D. J. and Carr, M. H. (1998) 'The Paseo Pantera Project: a case study using GIS to improve continental-scale conservation plannin', in: Lacher, T. E. and Savitsky, B. G. (eds.), *GIS methodologies for developing conservation strategies: tropical forest recovery and wildlife management in Costa Rica*. New York: Columbia University Press, pp. 138–147.

Lao, E. (1993) 'Los Bosques de la zona Atlántica y el Darien de Panamá: Una vía del paseo Pantera', in: Heckadon, S. (ed.), Agenda ecológica y social para Bocas del Toro: actas de los seminarios talleres. Panama and Bocas del Toro: Paseo Pantera and Smithsonian Tropical Research Institute, pp. 73–106.

Lázaro, M., Pariona, M. and Simeone, R. (1993) 'A natural harvest: the Yanesha forestry cooperative in Peru combines western science and indigenous knowledge', *Cultural Survival Quarterly*, 17 (1), pp. 48–51.

Machuca, R. J. A. (2005) 'Reconfiguración de las fronteras y reestructuración territorial: el Corredor Biológico Mesoamericano', *Alteridades*, 15 (30), pp. 61–73.

Mansfield, E. D. and Milner, H. V. (1997) 'The political economy of regionalism: an overview', in: Mansfield, E. D. and Milner, H. V. (eds.), *The political economy of regionalism*. New York: Columbia University Press, pp. 1–19.

Martínez, H. and Sánchez, G. (2020) 'Integración y desarrollo de Mesoamérica', *InterNaciones*, 19, pp. 179–220.

Organization for Economic Co-operation and Development (2006) *OECD territorial reviews: the Mesoamerican region: southeastern Mexico and central America*. Paris: Organization for Economic Co-operation and Development.

Ortega, R. (2022) Personal interview. Conducted by Alina Gamboa Combs at Laguna Sayachaltun.

Presidencia de la República (2001) *Plan Puebla-Panamá: Capítulo México, Documento Base*. Available at: http://www.diputados.gob.mx/comisiones/asunindi/dgmxuno.pdf (Accessed: 23 May 2023).

Proyecto Integración y Desarrollo de Mesoamerica (2012) *Plan de Acción de la Estrategia Mesoamericana de Sustentabilidad Ambiental 2013–2016 (P-EMSA)*. Available at: http://www.proyectomesoamerica.org/images/Anexos/Foro.Sectorial/medioambiente/Plan-de-Accin-EMSA-2013-2016-aprob.pdf (Accessed: 1 June 2023).

Proyecto Integración y Desarrollo de Mesoamerica (2023) *Proyecto Mesoamerica*. Available at: http://www.proyectomesoamerica.org (Accessed: 1 June 2023).

Proyecto Mesoamérica (2023) Official Website. Available at: www.proyectomesoamerica.org (Accessed: 28 April)

Ramírez, I. R. (2008) 'Mercantilización de la biodiversidad: la actividad de bioprospección del INBio en Costa Rica', *Economía Y Sociedad*, 13 (33-34), pp. 21–38.

Rioja Peregrina, L. H. (2002) 'Biopirateria y la lucha política en el contexto del PPP', in: Forero, E. A. S. and Pérez, R. S. (eds.), *Lectura Crítica Del Plan Puebla Panamá*, Colección Insumisos, pp. 99–116.

Rodriguez Quiroz, J. E. (2005) *Centroamerica en el Límite Forestal: desafíos para la implementación de las políticas forestales en el Istmo*. Available at: https://cidoc.marn.gob.sv/documentos/centroamerica-en-el-limite-forestal-desafios-para-la-implementacion-de-las-politicas-forestales-en-el-istmo/ (Accessed: 1 June 2023).

Rosas Hernández, M. I. and Álvarez Icaza Longoria, P. (2018) *El Corredor Biológico Mesoamericano: Cooperación Regional para el desarrollo social incluyente*. CONABIO. Available at: http://proyectomesoamerica.org/images/Documentos-de-soporte-CT-CAF-DEPM/cuaderno3/cuaderno3a.pdf (Accessed: 1 June 2023).

Sadoulet, E. and de Janvry, A. (2000) 'Rural poverty in Latin America: determinants and exit paths'. *Food Policy*, 25, pp. 389–409. Available at: https://are.berkeley.edu/esadoulet/wp-content/uploads/2018/10/rural-poverty-determinants-and-exit-paths.pdf (Accessed: 1 June 2023).

Saldívar, E. (2003) 'Indigenismo legal: la política indigenista de los noventa', *Revista Mexicana de Ciencias Políticas y Sociales*, 46 (188-9), pp. 311–337.

Sasuga, K. (2002) *The dynamics of cross-border micro-regionalisation among Guangdong, Taiwan and Japan: sub-national governments, multinational corporations and the emergence of multi-level governance*. PhD Thesis at the University of Warwick.

Sendero de vidas: Corredor Biológico Mesoamericano (2015) Directed by E. Herrera [Video/DVD]. Available at: https://www.youtube.com/watch?v=nRYj6pHE9vY (Accessed: 1 June 2023).

Söderbaum, F. (2015) *Rethinking regionalism*. London: Macmillan International Higher Education.

Toussaint, M. and Garzón, M. (2017) 'El Proyecto Mesoamérica: ¿éxito o fracaso? Límites de la cooperación de México hacia Centroamérica', *EntreDiversidades: Revista de Ciencias Sociales y Humanidades*, 1, pp. 15–52.

United Nations Development Programme (2020) *Enhancing jaguar corridors and strongholds through improved management and threat reduction*. Available at: https://info.undp.org/docs/pdc/Documents/BLZ/PIMS_6397_Enhancing%20jaguar%20corridors%20and%20strongholds%20through%20improved%20management%20and%20threat%20reduction%20PRODOC_signed.pdf (Accessed: 1 June 2023).

Väyrynen, R. (2003) 'Regionalism: old and new', *International Studies Review*, 5 (1), pp. 25–51.

World Bank (2000) *Project appraisal document on a proposed grant for the Global Environment Facility Trust Fund, for a Mesoamerican Biological Corridor*. Washington, DC: Global Environment Facility.

Chapter 11

Lessons from the Escazú Agreement for environmental and human rights protection in Africa

Fernand Guevara Mekongo Mballa
Centre for Regional Integration, Cameroon

Abstract

This chapter explores lessons that can be drawn from the Escazú Agreement and applied to Africa. In Latin America, public participation in debates on environmental issues has shed light on human rights violations and highlighted the need for an adapted legal instrument to ensure the effective protection of human rights. This inspired the Regional Agreement on Access to Information, Public Participation and Justice in Environmental Matters in Latin America and the Caribbean, better known as the Escazú Agreement. Its main innovations are the specific dispositions it contains for Environmental Human Rights Defenders (EHRDs). Similar to Latin America, Africa is also a developing region which faces comparable issues in the areas of environmental protection and human rights. This chapter argues that these can be addressed through adopting measures inspired by the Escazú Agreement, in terms of both substantive as well as procedural innovations that protect the environment, EHRDs, and local communities.

Keywords: Latin America, Africa, Escazú Agreement, human rights, environmental protection, international treaty

***

11.1 Introduction

The bitter experiences of WWI and, more specifically, WWII necessitated the universal protection of human rights in order to guarantee global peace and security, and led to the creation of the United Nations (UN) and the subsequent adoption of its charter. Despite such measures, human rights violations persist, risking global security in the process. Given the impact they have on human rights, environmental threats to peace and security are progressively taking centre stage in world diplomacy. In the *Kawas-Fernández v. Honduras* (2009) case, the Inter-American Court of Human Rights (IAmCHR) acknowledged the "undeniable linkage" between environmental protection and the effectiveness of other human rights. This trend is also illustrated by the global focus on climate change. Beyond this specific issue, environmental threats to peace and security are manifold, as they also concern pollution, loss of biodiversity, increased episodes of drought, and growing desertification, among other matters. Indeed, climate change is the amalgamation of all those environmental threats. Environmental issues have a large-scale influence, but they may give rise to specific preoccupations in some regions of the world. In Europe, such was the case with public participation, which prompted the adoption of the Aarhus Convention to enable the public to play a stronger role in tackling Europe's environmental challenges (Pánovics, 2020). In Latin America, public participation in environmental issues has shed light on human rights violations and highlighted the need for an adapted legal instrument to ensure the effective protection of human rights.

Thus, the Regional Agreement on Access to Information, Public Participation and Justice in Environmental Matters in Latin America and the Caribbean, better known as the Escazú Agreement, was adopted on 4 March 2018 by 24 countries in Latin America and the Caribbean. It became available for signature and ratification by the 33 countries of the region on 27 September 2018 but only entered into force on 22 April 2021. This agreement was adopted by Latin American countries in the aftermath of the Rio+20 Conference held in 2012. It contains a preamble, 26 articles, and one annex. Though regional in scope, the UN Secretary-General believes that the agreement has the potential to unlock structural change and address key challenges of our times (Ituarte-Lima, 2021) more broadly. In other words, the principles of the Escazú Agreement could be effective beyond Latin America and, therefore, contribute to the preservation of global peace and security.

In this chapter, I aim to investigate what lessons can be drawn from the Escazú Agreement for implementation in Africa. The chapter is divided into two parts. In the first part, I present the main features of the agreement and their contribution to human rights and the preservation of the environment in Latin America. In the second part, I assess what inspiration can be taken from the agreement for better protection of human rights and the environment in Africa.

11.2 The Escazú Agreement: a regional instrument to ensure the protection of human rights and the environment in Latin America

Similar to the Aarhus Convention, the Escazú Agreement (United Nations, 2018) is rooted in Principle 10 of the Rio Declaration, which stipulates that:

> Environmental issues are best handled with the participation of all concerned citizens, at the relevant level. At the national level, each individual shall have the appropriate access to information concerning the environment that is held by public authorities, including information on hazardous materials and activities in their communities, and the opportunity to participate in decision-making processes. States shall facilitate and encourage public awareness and participation by making information widely available. Effective access to judicial and administrative proceedings, including redress and remedy, shall be provided (United Nations, 1992).

In other words, the more the potentially impacted populations engage with a project established in their community, the lesser chance it has of impacting them as well as their environment negatively. However, if they are affected, they should have unrestricted access to judicial and administrative procedures to obtain reparations.

There are various cases of human rights violations and environmental damages caused by economic projects that are intended to help developing countries prosper by enforcing the right to development. For instance, the construction of the Barro Blanco hydroelectric dam on the Tabasara River in the Chiriquí province, Panama, flooded the habitats of the Ngabe community and encumbered the rights they were enjoying (Grossman, 2018). Likewise, a Global Witness (2022) report records numerous human rights and environmental violations in relation to economic activities. The *quilombola* territory on Ilha da Maré island in Brazil suffers from water pollution and air contamination, which have resulted in the poisoning of the local community. A study conducted in 2005 found high levels of heavy metals in the hair and blood samples of children living in the region (Paraguassú, 2022). Similarly, in Magdalena Medio, Colombia, children suffer from respiratory problems and skin conditions resulting from the mercury-poisoned landfill that contaminates the water supply of the Patio Bonito village in Barrancabermeja because of the various extractive activities in the region. They have been nicknamed "the children of garbage" (Global Witness, 2023).

Furthermore, the killings of environmental human rights defenders (EHRDs)— who advocate the right to a healthy environment in their communities along with other socioeconomic rights that are threatened mostly by extractive projects in various parts of the region are vivid. The aforementioned report by

Global Witness (2023) also indicates that in Magdalena Medio, defending human rights and nature can be fatal: at least 3 EHRDs were killed in 2022. It also reports that 54 EHRDs were killed in Mexico in 2021. In 2016, Berta Caceres was killed in Honduras because of her opposition to the construction of the Agua Zarca dam on the Gualcarque River, which threatened the ancestral territory of the Lenca people. According to the Business & Human Rights Resource Centre (2017), at least 11 EHRDs of communities affected by dam construction projects in Guatemala were murdered in 2017 and 36 were imprisoned. The killings of EHRDs in Latin America were estimated to be 29 in Brazil, 25 in Colombia, 12 in Honduras, nine in Peru, five in Guatemala, three in Paraguay, three in Mexico, one in Ecuador, and one in Costa Rica (Frost, 2016). A coalition of various organizations wrote a letter to John Knox (the UN independent expert on human rights and environment at the time) in 2013, which states that at least one member of the M10—the indigenous movement defending the Tabasara river—was murdered in relation to his activities (Bodero et al., 2013). These examples underline the human rights violations and environmental damages that are incurred when the potentially impacted populations are not consulted in decision-making processes.

The Escazú Agreement (United Nations, 2018) has also been adopted in great part to avoid the repetition of such events. Thus, it aims to ensure a right to a healthy environment and sustainable development. This objective is in tandem with Article 2 of the Rio Declaration, which stipulates that all concerned citizens should have "appropriate access of information", "opportunity to participate in decision-making processes", and "effective access to judicial and administrative processes" (Anderson, 2020). The by-laws of the Escazú Agreement can be classified into two categories: the positive obligations of the parties towards the public and the specific obligations of the parties towards EHRDs.

The Escazú Agreement (United Nations, 2018) provides inclusive guarantees for the populations that may be impacted by a project. Before the agreement was adopted, the economic aspect of any project had pre-eminence over all other factors. Large-scale developments or investment projects that were motivated by international demands for goods and raw materials were considered at the macroeconomic levels—in terms of the revenues they would generate for the investors and the country as well as the employment they would generate directly and indirectly—at the expense of all other considerations. Such an approach notably excluded the environmental impacts and/or the preservation of the rights of local populations. This policy often led to social and environmental conflicts that emerged mostly at the feasibility and implementation or construction stages because of "deficient planning reduced access to resources, lack of community benefits and lack of adequate consultation" (Watkins et al., 2017, p. 4), as illustrated by the case of the Saramaka

People v. Suriname (2008). In this case, the government of Suriname had awarded logging and mining concessions on territories possessed by the Saramaka tribe without consultation. The project resulted in damages to the environment (pollution, land degradation, and deforestation) and hostility from local communities.

With the implementation of the Escazú Agreement (United Nations, 2018), legal steps have been taken to bar the exclusion of local communities from any project that would impact them and their environment. The dispositions for inclusivity are centred on three fundamental, interrelated, and interdependent access rights, as mentioned in the third paragraph of the preamble:

a. Access to environmental information;

b. Public participation in the environmental decision-making process;

c. Access to justice in environmental matters.

Articles 5 and 6 of the agreement focus on access to environmental information. Article 5 describes the norms guiding the attitude of the authorities regarding information requests from an applicant. States should provide unconditional access to information to the public at their request. This obligation specifically applies to groups in vulnerable situations. Any eventual denial of information should be explained by authorities on legal provisions, specifically when the requested information falls within the exception made by domestic legislation. In any case, the exceptions should be motivated by the desire to protect the environment and maintain peace and security. Also, taking into consideration the public interest, the authorities' refusal to provide information should be applied restrictively. The requested information should be provided on time. Article 5 establishes a maximum duration of 30 days— and, on exception, 40 or less, if specified by the national legislation—for the same. The authorities must refer the applicant to the appropriate source if they do not have the requested information. If the requested information is unavailable, the authorities must inform the applicant within 30 days (exceptionally, 40 days). In any case, the information must be provided at no cost but for reproduction, which may be charged to the applicant. Finally, each Party must establish an independent body to ensure transparency in access to environmental information and compliance with the rules. This body may also be endowed with sanctioning powers.

Article 6 describes the norms for information generation and dissemination from the authorities. In accordance with their resources, each of the parties must ensure that the concerned authorities actively collect the environmental information related to their function and make it accessible at local levels. They must also have an up-to-date information system that provides all environmental information about the Party (legal, institutional, and implementation reports on various environmental multilateral agreements; environmental studies; environmental impact assessments; pollution, waste, and administrative sanctions on environmental matters, etc.).

They must also implement certain steps to render environmental information available more conveniently:

a. Establish a pollutant release and transfer register;
b. Publish a national report on the environment at least every five years;
c. Create and regularly update their archive system;
d. Develop an early warning system in case of threat to public health and the environment.

Parties should also encourage public and private companies to provide environmental information and independent environmental performance reviews. They should produce environmental information in languages and formats accessible to vulnerable persons and groups and also disclose environmental information on products and services that consumers purchase and that may affect their health.

Public participation in the environmental decision-making process is described in Article 7 of the Escazú Agreement. The parties are required "to implement open and inclusive participation in environmental decision-making processes based on domestic and international normative frameworks". The Parties should establish mechanisms to ensure public participation in the various decision-making processes in projects and activities that may have an impact on the environment and their health. The same applies to environmental matters of public interest, for example, land use planning, policies, strategies, plans, programmes, rules, and regulations. Public participation should take effect from the early stages and due consideration must be given to its observations. To enforce these directives, the public must be provided with adequate information in a timely and comprehensive manner. Electronic, oral, or custom channels can be used to inform the public. The information must include the environmental decision under consideration, the authorities in charge of the decision, the procedure for public participation, and the authorities to be referred to for eventual additional information and the procedure for reaching out to them. The public must also be informed of the decision made and its rationale. The decisions resulting from public participation should be made available in the appropriate format.

The parties are also encouraged to promote public participation and negotiations on environmental matters on international forums. They may also participate at the national level in matters of international environmental forums. The parties should encourage inclusive participation of the public through the use of appropriate spaces for consultation, local knowledge, the identification and adequate support to vulnerable persons, the identification of the public potentially impacted by a project and ensuring its participation. Stipulations also include due observance of the national and international legislation related to the participation of local populations. Article 7 outlines the type of information to be provided to the public for its participation:

1. The description of the area to be impacted and its physical and technical characteristics;
2. The potential environmental impacts of the project;
3. The mitigation measures related to those impacts;
4. A summary of the aforementioned actions in non-technical language;
5. The opinion of the involved entities addressed to the public authority related public authorities addressed to the expected project or activity;
6. A description of the technologies to be used and the eventual backup location of the project;
7. The actions taken to implement the results of the environmental impact assessment measures.

Article 8 elaborates on access to justice in environmental matters. It stipulates that each of the parties ensure effective access to justice in environmental matters in accordance with the guarantees of due process. More specifically, the internal legislation of each of the parties should provide the public with access to judicial and administrative mechanisms to challenge and appeal any decision, action or omission related to environmental information, public participation in the decision-making process on environmental matters, or any of the aforementioned situations that violate environmental laws and regulations. Furthermore, to ensure effective access to justice in environmental matters, each Party, considering its specific situation, shall have:

a. Competent bodies with access to environmental expertise;
b. Affordable, open, equitable, effective, timely, and unbiased procedures;
c. Internal legislation that allows for effective defence of the environment;
d. The capacity to undertake proactive actions to protect the environment like precautionary and provisory measures, to prevent further damages or to restore the environment;
e. Facilitative dispositions regarding environmental damage like the reversal of the burden of proof and its dynamic;

f. The capacities to enforce judicial and administrative decisions on time, to implement environmental restoration, and compensation, to assist affected persons and provide guarantees of non-repetition.

Parties should also endeavour to facilitate access to justice on environmental matters for the public by eliminating the impediments to public access to this service by disseminating judicial and administrative decisions, translating them into the local language when necessary, raising awareness of the right of access to justice and the subsequent procedures, taking into account the needs of persons or groups in vulnerable situations, and providing them with technical and free of charge assistance whenever necessary, as well as with the rationale behind every administrative and judicial decision, and promoting alternative resolution dispute mechanisms.

Although the UN General Assembly adopted the Declaration on the Right and Responsibility of Individuals, Groups and Organs of Society to Promote and Protect Universally Recognized Human Rights and Fundamental Freedoms, also known as the Declaration on Human Rights Defenders, in March 1999, the number of EHRDs killed in Latin America continued to rise. According to the Mesoamerican Women Human Rights Defenders Initiative (MWHRDI), most of the attacks on women were against those who defended land territory and natural resources: 37.66% in 2014, 15.82% in 2013, and 37.92% in 2012 (López and Vidal, 2015). The Global Witness (2015) report *How Many More?* reveals that 477 deaths were reported in Brazil between 2002 and 2014. In 2014, 87 of the 116 EHRDs killed worldwide were from Latin American countries. As already mentioned, the assassination of the Honduran EHRD Berta Caceres also generated global indignation and condemnation. This occurred two years after the assassination of another popular EHRD in Peru, Edwin Chota, who was a defender of the indigenous and forest rights of the Tamaya-Saweto community. The Escazú Agreement was adopted merely two years after the Berta Caceres episode, signalling that too much had been tolerated and that the member states ought to do something to ensure the protection of EHRDs.

The Escazú Agreement contains specific dispositions concerning the protection of EHRDs in environmental matters. According to the United Nations, EHRDs can be defined as:

> Individuals and groups who, in their personal or professional capacity and in a peaceful manner, strive to protect and promote human rights relating to the environment, including water, air, land, flora and fauna (United Nations, 2016, paragraph 7).

According to Article 9, parties are required to provide a safe and adequate environment for persons, groups, and organizations that promote and defend human rights in environmental matters to enable them to act in safety. The expected actions from the parties are to provide them with safety, ensure their right to life, physical integrity, freedom of opinion and expression, right to peaceful assembly and association, freedom of movement, and their ability to exercise their access rights in regard with each Party's international obligations about human rights, constitution, and legal system.

Overall, the Escazú Agreement appears to be a much-needed legal instrument for the Latin American and Caribbean region, given the extent of human rights violations in relation to environmental protection, the rights of indigenous populations, and EHRDs. Its appraised innovation is about the specific dispositions it provides for EHRDs. It establishes common ground for public participation and the protection of EHRDs in Latin America, but also has a progressive seed, as it stipulates the principle of non-regression and a progressive realization— the latter a novelty in international environmental law (Barchiche, Hedge, Napoli, 2019)—and also encourages Parties to take further measures to ensure public participation and protect the rights of EHRDs. All these provisions contribute to better protection of human rights in the Organization of American States (OAS) system.

It can be argued that the Escazú Agreement received an international consecration with the adoption of Resolution 40/11 in March 2019 by the United Nations Human Rights Council on "recognizing the contribution of human rights defenders to the enjoyment of human rights, environmental protection and sustainable development". Having received such an indirect consecration, the Escazú Agreement may inspire the protection of the environment and human rights in Africa.

11.3 The Escazú Agreement as a template for the protection of human rights and the environment in Africa

The issues of public participation, environmental damages, and the effective protection of EHRDs are not restricted to Latin America. As discussed in section 1.2, the Aarhus Convention was the first regional instrument that addressed these issues in Europe. The articles of the Escazú Agreement are the obligations of the Parties towards EHDR because of the dangers they face in the region. In the same vein, public participation in the decision-making process could have a positive impact on these issues in Africa as well.

Consider the *Endorois Welfare Council v. Kenya* (2010) case from the African region. The government expelled the Endorois from their ancestral land around Lake Bogoria in the 1970s without consultation and appropriate compensation. The case was submitted to the African Commission on Human People's Rights (AfCHPR) on 25 November, 2009. During its forty-sixth session, from 11 November to 25 November that year, the AfCHPR ruled that the Kenyan government had violated Articles 1 on the duty of every Party to implement the dispositions of the Charter, 8 on the freedom of conscience, 14 on the right to property, 17 on the right to freely take part in the cultural life of his community, 21 (on free disposal of wealth and natural resources), and 22 on the right to development. Those violations were against the dispositions of the African Charter of Human and People's Rights (ACHPR).

Social and Economic Rights Action Center & the Center for Economic and Social Rights v. Nigeria (2002), better known as the SERAC case, also comes to mind when discussing human rights violations and environmental damages in Africa. In their complaint to the ACHPR, the plaintiffs argued that the then-military government of Nigeria had direct responsibility for the contamination of the environment of the Ogoni people, and for the consequent environmental degradation and health problems that had resulted from oil production in the region. On its thirtieth ordinary session from 13 October to 27 October, the ACHPR ruled that the Nigerian government had violated Articles 2 on the enjoyment of the rights and freedoms recognized and guaranteed by the African Charter, 4 on the inviolability of human beings, 14 on the right to property, 16 on the best attainable state of physical and mental health, 18.1 on family protection, 21 on free disposal of wealth and natural resources, and 24 on satisfactory environment favourable for development.

EHRDs are not only threatened in Latin America but in Africa too. According to Global Witness (2022), 200 EHRDs were killed globally in 2021, of whom 10 were in Africa: 8 in the Democratic Republic of Congo, 1 in Gabon, and 1 in Kenya. The United Nations report on the situation of human rights defenders mentions the case of Sikhosiphi Rhadebe, who was assassinated because of his opposition to mining operations in Xolobeni in 2016.

Latin America has always been a source of inspiration for Africa on the matter of human rights preservation. For example, in the aforementioned case in Kenya, the complainants mention that IAmCHR had determined that expulsion from the lands central to the practice of religion constitutes a violation of religious freedoms in *Dianna Ortiz v. Guatemala* (2016). They also refer to the *Moiwana Community v. Suriname* (2005) and *Saramaka People v. Suriname* (2008) cases in their complaint. This stems from the fact that contentions regarding public participation as well as the violations of human rights are almost always the same: land grabbing for mineral and oil exploitation and subsequent environmental damages, coupled with the deprivation of the rights of ingenuous people.

A study by Green Advocates International (2021) reveals that although only 10% of the killings are reported in Africa, it has been observed that those killings mostly occur in the Congo Basin which ranks second only to the Amazon Basin.

Meanwhile, a surge in the killings of EHRDs has also been observed in Amazonia, especially in Brazil. The same study also suggests that:

> Despite the policies and conventions aimed to address the issue and the global recognition of the problem, serious barriers to implementation remain due to the type and nature of attacks on HRDs in West Africa especially attacks on Frontline Grassroots HRDs [...] Research has found that environmental HRD are three times more likely to suffer attacks than other HRDS and that 77% of HRDs that were killed in 2018 worked on land, indigenous peoples, or environmental rights. Thus, human rights preservation in the West and Central Africa region is the need of the hour for EHRDs as well as the indigenous communities (Green Advocates International, 2021, p. 2).

Based on these similarities, the Escazú Agreement is an opportunity for a new paradigm in the protection and promotion of human rights from a South-South perspective (Anderson, 2020). I propose to elaborate on the lessons from the Escazú Agreement in two steps: public participation and the other obligations outlined in the document.

It is interesting to examine the procedure that led to the adoption of the Escazú Agreement because it bears the seed of public participation in the adoption of a legal instrument at the regional level. The most common approach in the adoption of legal instruments pertaining to environmental issues and/or human rights is to bring forth a panel of experts or diplomats representing the potential Parties. Thereafter, they hold various meetings under specialized committees to find common ground before reaching an agreement and opening the legal instrument to signature. This generally requires years and, in most cases, the general public is unaware of the negotiation procedures and their content.

The Escazú Agreement took a different approach: the general public was associated throughout the negotiation process. Following the Rio+20 Conference, the Declaration on the Application of Principle 10 of the Rio Declaration on Environment and Development in Latin America and the Caribbean was adopted. This declaration was followed by four preparatory meetings, which lasted two years (2012–2014), and the negotiation phase, which lasted four years (2014–2018). As expressed in the Modalities for Participation of the Public in The Negotiating Committee of The Escazú Agreement (United Nations, 2018), which were adopted during the third meeting of the negotiating committee, "the promotion of broad and diverse participation by the public is grounded in the ultimate object of this regional process". The agreement also stipulates that the negotiation process of the regional agreement on access to information, participation, and justice in environmental matters in Latin America and the Caribbean will provide for the participation of the interested public to contribute to the fulfilment of the mandate of the negotiating committee. With the objective of straightening the inclusiveness and legitimacy of the process, these modalities intend to:

a. Ensure the provision of information on the negotiation of the regional agreement;

b. Establish both specific and broad opportunities for participation.

Furthermore, the modalities of participation were also defined. They included attendance, reporting, and making statements. Such dispositions provided for large public participation through the submission of written proposals during the negotiation phase. The public participation mechanism also provided for more rigorous consideration of popular proposals if they were supported by at least one country from the negotiation committee. Additionally, the public of other regions could participate in those preparatory meetings with the authorization of the signatory countries. These conditions ensured massive participation of the public (individuals, NGOs, EHRDs, etc.), which decisively influenced the content of the Escazú Agreement. The specific obligations the agreement provides for EHRDs are the most praised, but other substantial obligations may also be attributed to public participation, such as the obligation to establish a register of polluted areas by the type of pollutant and its location, the principles of non-regression and prevention, and the mechanisms to ensure access to justice on environmental issues (Barchiche, Hege and Napoli, 2019).

All in all, it can be said that public participation in the preparatory phase of the Escazú Agreement yielded positive results. As the host secretariat of the Escazú Agreement, the Economic Commission for Latin America (CEPAL) also launched a public consultation on the Escazú Agreement implementation guide from 11 April to 25 May 2022. Interested stakeholders were asked to provide suggestions. As the Escazú Agreement is just entering its implementation phase, it remains to be seen to what extent it will be able to protect EHRDs. In this respect, it will also be interesting to see what actions the Parties take to reinforce state capacities to protect EHRDs and local communities in matters of corporate impunity and the subsequent violation of human rights of the local communities. Nevertheless, public participation in the implementation guide of the Escazú Agreement is a good omen.

In Africa, public participation in the formulation of environmental legal instruments is yet to be seen. However, environmental considerations at the regional level are not uncommon. For example, the African Convention on the Conservation of Nature and Natural Resources was adopted in Algiers in 1968, well before the Stockholm Conference which heralded growing environmental concerns at the global level. Further back in time, the Convention for the Preservation of Wild Animals, Birds and Fish in Africa was adopted in Africa in 1900 and its purpose was to protect animals on the continent. At the national level, the right to a clean and healthy environment and the right to information and participation are enshrined in the constitutions of many African countries but their effectiveness remains problematic (Donoumassou, 2013). Moreover, poor implementation of the existing laws pertaining to the protection of natural resources, scarcity of sanctions, inaccessibility to environmental information, and the almost nonexistent public participation in Africa (Ibid.) are compelling reasons to pay closer attention to the Escazú Agreement.

In Africa, the preparation and adoption of such legal instruments happen via the traditional channels of diplomats and experts, as already mentioned. At this level, the endogenous content of environmental treaties is generally considered in broad generalist terms. International agreements abound with convened expressions such as "in the implementation of this agreement, due consideration shall be given to the case/situation of indigenous people", but little space is provided for public participation in the elaboration of the agreement.

In an article about the role of subregional organizations in the integration of international environmental law in the Central African region, Parfait Oumba (2013) points out that its subregional integration organizations endeavour to appropriate and valorise international environmental law. However, these efforts are vertical, as they are generally implemented in a top-down approach. For example, in 1999, the Yaoundé Declaration was adopted at the Summit of Central African Heads of State on the Conservation and Sustainable Management of Tropical Forests (Central African Heads of State, 1999). This summit was a proclamation of biodiversity preservation as well as social and economic development. It was followed by the establishment of the Conference of Ministers in Charge of Forests in Central Africa (COMIFAC). The process eventually led to the creation of the Central African Forests Commission (CAFC), which is in charge of the orientation, harmonization, and follow-up of environmental policies in the Central Africa region (Assembe Mvondo, 2006). There was no room for direct public participation in this whole process. The recent regional instruments in Africa are no exception to this trend: both the Abidjan and Nairobi Conventions on regional seas, the Bamako Convention on dangerous waste, or the African Charter on Human and Peoples' Rights.

This situation seems paradoxical because, based on anthropological evidence, there are various practices which advocate for public participation in the elaboration of environmental norms in Africa. Professor Maurice Kamto argues that ecological considerations were not uncommon in the African traditional law. In some cases, traditional law and customary practices were more efficient in environmental protection than modern-day law. As an example, he cites that contrary to modern law, water was never perceived as a private resource but rather a public resource at the disposal of individuals (Kamto, 2014). Other examples mentioned in his work are the role of sacred forests in preserving biodiversity and the various traditional knowledge accumulated in selecting the best and most resistant seeds (Ibid.). Moreover, the 1996 legal framework on the environment in Cameroon stipulates that whenever a traditional practice or a rule inspired by customary law better protects the environment than a modern law rule, the pre-existing one shall prevail (Ibid.).

According to Kamto, the parliamentarians are presumably closer to the population and, consequently, best able to promote laws that are embedded in the cultural context of the population. This certainly works at the national level. Public participation in the elaboration (indigenization) of environmental law may be achieved indirectly by the parliamentarians who can propose laws based on the milieu or following direct consultations with populations. The Escazú Agreement had massive public participation because of the democratization of technology. A larger proportion of the Latin American population has internet access. The internet penetration rate in Africa is not the same as in Latin America. For example, according to the statistics of the United Nations (2021), in 2019, the percentage of individuals using the internet in Latin America and the Caribbean was 67.4%, while in sub-Saharan Africa it was 17.8%. Hence, adopting the same approach in Africa may not bring about as much participation, even in the urban areas of the continent where the internet is more accessible. Consequently, a legal fracture would follow the digital fracture because of the even lower internet penetration rate in rural areas, despite the progress in urban areas.

Nevertheless, the technological difference should not be an impediment to the adoption of an Escazú Agreement–inspired text in Africa, although a different approach may be required. From a comparative perspective, Africa is not a homogenous continent like Latin America. In Africa, various subregions that broadly share the same physical features coexist. These subregions have created subregional organizations such as the ECOWAS, which regroups the western region, the ECCAS, which regroups the centre, and the SADC, which aligns the austral subregions.

The physical features of the ECCAS may seem the most indicative of the adoption of an instrument similar to the Escazú Agreement. It is a region endowed with oil reserves. Furthermore, the Congo Basin forest is generally considered the second lung of the world after the Amazonian forest. Both forests are transnational. In both regions, minorities' rights are under threat from the extractive activities of corporations. In Cameroon, a member of the

Bagyeli pygmies' community revealed that during the construction of a pipeline linking Chad to the Cameroonian town of Kribi, the community only learned about this and other projects under the aegis of the CAFC by chance. The pygmies were told about the development of such projects by non-pygmies people riding motorcycles, who were passing by and barely made a stop in their villages.

The same member of the Bagyeli pygmies' community also went on to say that most of the projects aimed at his community during the construction of the pipeline were implemented without their consent (Biankola-Biankola, 2016). The lack of communication with local communities and the absence of an attempt to obtain consent from them is a severe issue which can be found across a variety of projects and activities of the CAFC. The Chad–Cameroon pipeline case demonstrates the importance of the forests in central Africa and highlights the need for transnational instruments to protect local populations, such as pygmies, as well as EHRDs. It also should be noted that of the 10 killings of EHRDs reported in Africa (Global Witness, 2022), 8 were in the Democratic Republic of Congo, which occupies the largest area of the forests in the region, and the other one was in Gabon, a country mostly covered in forests, with an internationally acclaimed policy of forest conservation.

In this respect, almost all countries are members of the support program for the preservation of biodiversity and ecosystems in Central Africa, best known by its French acronym ECOFAC6, and have pygmy populations. Hence, the broad features they share in common are indicative of an Escazú-like agreement among them. In Article 4 of the objectives, ECCAS (2020) states that:

> It shall be the aim of the Community to promote and strengthen harmonious cooperation and balanced and self-sustained development in all fields of economic and social activity, particularly in the fields of …energy, agriculture, natural resources…

Article 56 (a) (Ibid.), which is about the promotion of cooperation in energy and natural resources, reads that the Member States shall, among other things, "harmonize their policies for prospecting, producing and processing mineral resources…". Such dispositions offer incentives for the implementation of an Escazú-like agreement.

ECCAS's consultative commission should be in charge of such an operation. It could engage in public consultations with not only the executives of the member states but with its citizens as well. An inclusive approach would necessitate direct consultations with the deputies in each of the countries. As the ECCAS does not have a parliament, the deputies of each country would submit their received proposals to their national assemblies. The presidents, in turn, may synthesize the proposals and submit them to the commissary in charge of the environment, natural resources, agriculture, and rural development. The latter could then work on a document to be submitted to heads of each member state for discussion and adoption in a future conference.

ECOWAS (1993) includes some dispositions to ensure public participation and protection of EHRDs. Article 3§2 (b) of the revised treaty of the ECOWAS (Ibid.) is on the "harmonization and coordination of the policies for the protection of the environment". The same article reads:

> the encouragement, strengthening of the relations and the promotion of the flow of information particularly among rural populations, women and youth organizations and socio-professional organizations such as the associations of the media, business men and women, workers, trade unions (ECOWAS, 1993, Articles 3§2b).

Article 3§ 2 (m) states that "the adoption of a community population policy which takes into account the need for a balance between demographic factors and socio-economic development" (Ibid.).

> Article 4 on fundamental principles mentions, among others,
> g) recognition, promotion and protection of human and people's rights in accordance with the provisions of the African Charter of Human People's Rights; h) accountability, economic and social justice and popular participation in development (Ibid.).

According to Article 63§2, (a) and (b) on women and development,

> Member States shall take measures to a) identify and assess all constraints that inhibit women from maximising their contribution to regional development efforts and b) provide a framework within which the constraints will be addressed for the incorporation of women's concerns and needs into the normal operations of the society (Ibid.).

Finally, Article 64§2 (a) and (c) on population and development stipulate that the Member States agree to,

> a) Include population issues as central components in formulating and implementing national policies and programmes for accelerated and balanced socioeconomic development; c) undertake public sensitization on population matters, particularly operations of the society (Ibid.).

Consequently, the Council of Ministers of the ECOWAS, in collaboration with the technical commission on environment and natural resources, may launch public participation debates in each of the member countries in view of making propositions to the heads of state for the adoption of an agreement on the protection of local communities and environment.

Concerning public access to information, the Escazú Agreement requires Parties to map polluted areas. Given the extreme vulnerability of African populations to pollution and the possibility that unofficial polluted areas may exist, as demonstrated by the Probo Koala incident (United Nations, 2009), populations should be allowed to inform the relevant authorities of any polluted area. Concerning access to justice in environmental matters, as mentioned earlier, more importance should be given to local practices and customs. Access to modern justice may be arduous for local populations for financial, technical, geographical, or legal reasons.

In the ECOWAS, populations can directly file complaints against the violations of human rights at the regional court without exhausting the procedure at the regional level. However, given the aforementioned difficulties, this facility may not be accessible or known to grassroots defenders. The reinforcement of the powers of traditional tribunals—when they exist—on environmental matters could be an efficient approach concerning access to justice. The Escazú Agreement requires Parties to provide the public with information to facilitate the acquisition of knowledge on access rights. This disposition should be applied in African states while prioritising the local language of the populations potentially impacted.

The Escazú Agreement attributes the power to deliver environmental information, or not, to competent authorities. This power should be shared with traditional Chiefs or rulers who are close to the population. The authorities should endeavour to provide these community leaders with all the authorized information on environmental issues impacting their communities. This would shorten the time required to collect information and allow applicants to make informed decisions in a timely manner. At local levels, independent oversight mechanisms—similar to those mentioned in Article 18 of the Escazú Agreement—to oversee compliance with rules and monitor, report on, and guarantee the right of access to information should be vested in local assemblies. They should also be enabled to take legal action. The early warning systems, such as those established by the Escazú Agreement, should not just be vertical. Similar to the Lake Nyos catastrophe in Cameroon (1986), populations may feel impending catastrophes before the authorities can react. Thus, it is important to implement both top-down and bottom-up warning systems so that populations may alert the authorities for action and protection when needed. During the tsunami of 2004 in Banda Aceh, Indonesia, integration of the local knowledge of the Simelue tribe into the disaster response would have averted the high death toll. Given the limited resources of developing countries, the progressive principle should be adopted in the implementation of a regional agreement on public participation and justice in environmental matters.

At the regional level, the African Continental Free Trade Area (ACFTA), in line with the Lagos Plan of Action established by the African Unity Organization in 1980, is supposed to be the legal instrument that assembles all the subregional ones to achieve free movement of goods and persons in the continent. Theoretically, it is through the ACFTA that rights like those protected under the Escazú Agreement would be implemented more efficiently because of its continental scope. The ACFTA aims to create a single marketplace comprising of the 1.3 billion people in the continent, and the World Bank estimates it could lift 30 million people out of extreme poverty. However, such an achievement cannot be accomplished without addressing some inevitable challenges. Among them is the due concern for environmental issues.

In its preamble, although focused on free trade, the member states of the African Union recognize the "importance of international security, democracy, human rights, gender equality and the rule of law, for the development of international trade and economic cooperation" (African Union, 2018, p. 1). It also reaffirms "the right of State Parties to regulate within their territories and the State Parties flexibility to achieve legitimate policy objectives in areas including public health, safety, environment, public morals and the promotion and protection of cultural diversity" (African Union, 2018, p. 2).

As hinted by the same preamble, environmental dispositions are scattered all over the agreement and do not constitute a specific focus (Moussavou, 2020). Article 3 (e) stipulates that the ACFTA's objectives are to "promote and attain sustainable and inclusive socio-economic development, gender equality and structural transformation in the State Parties" (African Union, 2018, p. 4). According to Article 26, on protocol on goods, states are free to adopt or enforce measures that are "b) necessary to protect human, animal or plant life on earth" and "g) relating to the conservation of exhaustible natural resources if such measures are made effective in conjunction with restrictions on domestic production or consumption" (African Union, 2018, p. 27). Regarding the protocol on trade and services, its preamble recognizes,

> The right of State Parties to regulate in pursuit of national policy objectives, and to introduce new regulations, on the supply of services, within their territories, in order to meet legitimate national policy objectives…the particular need for State Parties to exercise this right, without compromising consumer protection, environmental protection and overall sustainable development.

Article 3 stipulates that its specific objectives "promote sustainable development with the Sustainable Development Goals (SDGs)". Article 7 on special differential treatment stipulates that parties shall "provide special consideration to the progressive liberalization of service sector commitments and modes of supply which will promote critical sectors of growth, social and sustainable economic development". Article 15 on general exceptions states that nothing in the protocol shall be interpreted to prevent the adoption by any state party of measures which should protect people, animals or the environment. Hence, the specific dispositions regarding the implementation of environmental dispositions are left to the appreciation of the parties.

The ACTFA is scheduled to be implemented through successive rounds of negotiations and is at the incipient stage. The Phase Two negotiations concern intellectual property rights, investment, and competition policy. Investment and competition policies retain our attention because they can hardly be separated. Investors will be attracted to places that offer the best invitation to invest. In most cases, investors prefer places that offer less stringent investment conditions, especially regarding the protection of the environment or the ECSR of the local/indigenous populations. Consequently, parties with more effective environmental considerations may be at a disadvantage. As many African countries seek to attract foreign investment, such a disposition could lead to a race on the environmental bottom (Moussavou, 2020). This approach seems at odds with the already felt and expected consequences of climate change in the continent. Increased drought and flooding are on the rise, thus putting the agriculture on which the majority of the continent depends under threat.

In this respect, EHRDs mostly come to the frontline about investments in areas affecting the Economic, Social and Cultural Rights (ESCR) of their communities. States allowing minimal environmental considerations at the expense of economic advantages could be winners in the short term but will be losers in the end. Hence, according due consideration to the protection of the rights of EHRDs and the communities they defend would benefit African countries, given the circumstances created by climate change.

11.4 Conclusion

The Escazú Agreement was adopted to meet the regional needs of Latin America concerning environmental issues—environmental damages and the violations of the rights of local communities sacrificed on the altar of the exploitation of natural resources had become unbearable. Thus, this is why State Parties decided to focus on public participation and the protection of EHRDs. The Escazú Agreement is rich in substantive as well as procedural innovations that protect the environment, EHRDs, and local communities. Though it seems to have gotten off to a good start, it remains to be seen how effective it will be.

The conditions in Africa are not very different from the ones which motivated the adoption of this instrument in Latin America. Although social practices as well as the consequences of climate change, argue in favour of a similar instrument in Africa, no such instrument has been devised to this day. Even if the technological divide indicates the need for a different approach to public participation in Africa, it must be implemented given the challenges to be faced. Viewed this way, existing subregional organizations may provide the necessary legal basis for such an instrument.

At the regional level, the ACFTA favours the economy at the expense of the protection of the environment. Instead of reversing the pendulum, an equilibrium must be sought. This could be achieved by devoting an entire section of the ACFTA to the relationship between economic activities and the necessary protection of the environment or establishing gateways with the African Charter on the protection of nature and natural resources (Moussavou, 2020). The aim should be the regeneration of the resources exploited and the preservation of the rights of impacted communities.

From a larger perspective, environmental issues have become a global concern. It seems that after two centuries of reckless predation of mankind towards nature, her patience has reached its limits. It is time for mankind to face the crank return. Nature does not distinguish us among humans because she has served and protected us indistinctively from the earliest beginnings. She was there long before us and will certainly survive us after we are long gone, should the trends climate change portend increase. If every nation in the world has a right to development, it does not have the right to do so at the cost of others. Thus, there is a need to implement sustainable development effectively. We have inherited the present environment from past generations as well as the mistakes they have made. The environment is not an abstraction but, as the ICJ points out in its advisory opinion on the legality of the threat or use of nuclear weapons, it "represents the living space, the quality of life and the very health of human beings, including generations unborn" (International Court of Justice, 1996, p. 226). We must bequeath it to future generations in equal quality, if not better. Nevertheless, better is achievable now because we possess the knowledge our past generations did not. It is worth retaining cognizance of Principle 3 of the Rio Declaration, "[t]he right to development must be fulfilled so as to equitably meet developmental and environmental needs of present and future generations" as well as of Principle 4, "in order to achieve sustainable development, environmental protection shall constitute an integral part of the development process and cannot be considered in isolation from it".

Therefore, the issues of public participation, environmental protection, justice, and the protection of EHRDs are important and not limited to one region of the world. The challenge now is whether and how nations in Africa, and worldwide, will learn from the Escazú Agreement. If such an instrument is successfully implemented, it will certainly contribute to making the "utopia" of sustainable development (Boukongou, 2016) a reality in Africa.

References

African Union (2018) *Agreement establishing the African Continental Free Trade Area*. 21 March. Available at: https://au.int/sites/default/files/treaties/36437-treaty-consolidated_text_on_cfta_-_en.pdf (Accessed: 15 March 2023).

Anderson, W. (2020) *Why the Escazú Agreement matters: Environmental rights, justice and public participation in the Caribbean*. University of West Indies St Augustine Public Lecture, 23 January.

Assembe Mvondo, S. (2006) 'Dynamiques de gestion transfrontalière des forêts du bassin du Congo: Une analyse du traité relatif à la conservation et la gestion des écosystèmes forestiers d'Afrique Centrale', *Journal du droit de l'environnement et du développement*, 2/1, pp. 106–115. Available at: http://www.lead-journal.org/content/06106.pdf (Accessed: 22 April 2023).

Barchiche, D., Hege, E. and Napoli, A. (2019) *The Escazú Agreement: An ambitious example of a multilateral treaty in support of environmental law?* Issue Brief No. 03/19. Paris: Institute for Sustainable Development and International Relations.

Biankola-Biankola, M. B. (2016) 'La prévention et la répression des violations des droits des populations autochtones en république du Congo', *Cahier Africain des droits de l'Homme*, 13, pp. 177–194.

Bodero, T. A., Arredondo, L. A., Carrasquilla, O., Jordán, O., and Sogandares, O. (2013) Letter to Mr. John Knox, 24 June. Available at: https://carbonmarketwatch.org/wp-content/uploads/2013/06/Letter-to-John-Knox-Barro-Blanco-24-June-2013.pdf (Accessed: 3 April 2023).

Boukongou, J. D. (2016) 'Le développement durable: Une utopie raisonnable', *Cahier Africain des droits de l'Homme*, 13, December, pp. 9–12.

Business & Human Rights Resource Centre (2017) *Denuncian ante la CIDH violaciones de derechos humanos y ataques a defensores/as por proyectos hidroelectricos en Guatemala*. Available at: https://www.business-humanrights.org/es/ultimas-npticias/denuncian-ante-lacidh-violaciones-de-derechos-humanos-y-ataques-a-defensoresas-por-proyectos-hidroelectricos-en-guatemala (Accessed: 24 April 2023).

Central African Heads of State (1999) *Déclaration de Yaoundé*. Sommet des chefs d'Etats d'Afrique centrale sur la conservation et la gestion durable des forêts tropicales, 17 March. Available at: https://pfbc-cbfp.org/files/docs/key_docs/COMIFAC/declarationyaounde.pdf (Accessed: 28 March 2023).

Dianna Ortiz v. Guatemala (2016) Case 10.526, Report No. 31/96, Inter-American Commission on Human Rights, OEA/Ser.L/V/II.95 Doc. 7 rev. at 332 (1997). Available at: https://www.refworld.org/cases,IACHR,3ae6b61c4.html (Accessed: 22 April 2023).

Donoumassou, S. (2013) 'La démocratie environnementale pour une protection durable de l'environnement en Afrique', *African journal of Environmental Law*, 00, pp. 95–102.

ECCAS (2020) *Revised treaty establishing the economic community of Central African States.* Available at: https://www.gazettes.africa/archive/rw2020/rw-government-gazette-dated-2020-07-07-no-Special.pdf (Accessed: 24 April 2023).

ECOWAS (1993) *Revised treaty of the economic community of West African States.* Available at: https://www.refworld.org/docid/492182d92.html (Accessed: 24 April 2023).

Endorois Welfare Council v. Kenya (2010) Case 276/2003, African Commission on Human and Peoples' Rights. Available at: https://www.refworld.org/cases,ACHPR,4b8275a12.html (Accessed: 22 April 2023).

Frost, M. (2016) *A deadly shade of green: Threats to environmental and human rights defenders in Latin America,* CIEL, Vermont Law School and Sida. Available at: https://www.article19.org/data/files/Deadly_shade_of_green_A5_72pp_report_hires_PAGES_PDF.pdf (Accessed: 24 April 2023).

Global Witness (2015) *How many more?* Available at: https://www.globalwitness.org/en/campaigns/environmental-activists/how-many-more/#:~:text=As%20well%20documenting%20fatalities,so-called%development (Accessed: 24 April 2023).

Global Witness (2022) *Decade of Defiance: Ten years of reporting land and environmental activism worldwide.* Available at: https://www.globalwitness.org/en/campaigns/environmental-activists/decade-defiance (Accessed: 24 April 2023).

Global Witness (2023) 'Scarred for life: How a "toxic" landfill bought by French giant Veolia has devastated lives and biodiversity in Colombia', May 2023. Available at: https://www.globalwitness.org/en/campaigns/environmental-activists/scarred-life/ (Accessed: 27 May 2023).

Green Advocates International (2021) *Securing the firewall and connecting the unconnected: Frontline defenders across West Africa baseline report.* Available at: https://law.yale.edu/system/files/area/center/schell/final_hdr_executivesummary1.pdf (Accessed: 5 April 2023).

Grossman, D. (2018) 'Dam lies: Despite promises, an indigenous community's land is flooded', Pulitzer Center, 6 March. Available at: https://pulitzercenter.org/stories/dam-lies-despite-promises-indigenous-communitys-land-flooded (Accessed: 27 April 2023).

International Court of Justice (1996) *Legality of the threat or use of nuclear weapons, Advisory Opinions,* ICJ Reports, p. 226. Available at: https://www.icj-cij.org/public/files/case-related/95/095-19960708-ADV-01-00-EN.pdf (Accessed: 24 April 2023).

Ituarte-Lima, C. (2021) 'The Escazú Agreement and the right to a healthy environment', *Environmental Governance Programme,* 2 June. Available at: https://www.environmentalgovernanceprogramme.org/the-Escazú-agreement-the-right-to-a-healthy-environment (Accessed: 1 April 2023).

Kamto, M. (2014) 'L'impératif de l'inculturation (« endogénéisation ») du droit de l'environnement en Afrique', *African Journal of Environmental Law,* 1, pp. 153–154.

Kawas-Fernández v. Honduras (2009) IAmCHR. Available at: https://www.refworld.org/cases,IACRTHR,5e67c8ab4.html (Accessed: 22 April 2023).

López, M. and Vidal, V. (2015) *Violence against women and human rights defenders in Mesoamerica 2012–2014 report.* Available at: https://www.awid.org/sites/

default/files/atoms/files/286224690-violence-against-whrds-in-mesoamerica-2012-2014-report.pdf (Accessed: 24 April 2023).

Moiwana Community v. Suriname (2005) IAmCHR Series C No. 124. Available at: https://www.refworld.org/cases,IACRTHR,4721bb292.html (Accessed: 22 April 2023).

Moussavou, F. L. (2020) 'La protection de l'environnement dans l'accord portant création de la zone de libre- échange continentale Africaine', *African Journal of Environmental Law*, 5, pp. 223–230.

Oumba, P. (2013) 'Le rôle des organisations sous régionales dans l'intégration et le développement du droit international de l'environnement en Afrique centrale', *African Journal of Environmental Law*, 00, pp. 42–54.

Pánovics, A. (2020) 'The Escazú Agreement and the protection of environmental human rights defenders', *Pécs Journal of International and European Law*, 1, pp. 23–34.

Paraguassú, E. (2022) 'Brazil: We live a silent war against an invisible monster', *Global Witness*, 29 September. Available at: https://www.globalwitness.org/en/campaigns/environmental-activists/decade-defiance/ (Accessed: 22 April 2023).

Saramaka People v. Suriname (2008) IAmCHR Series C No. 185, IHRL 3058. Available at: https://opil.ouplaw.com/display/10.1093/law:ihrl/3058iachr08.case.1/law-ihrl-3058iachr08 (Accessed: 22 April 2023).

Social and Economic Rights Action Center & the Center for Economic and Social Rights v. Nigeria (2002) Communication No. 155/96. Available at: https://www.escr-net.org/caselaw/2006/social-and-economic-rights-action-center-center-economic-and-social-rights-v-nigeria (Accessed: 22 April 2023].

United Nations (1992) 'Annex I: Rio Declaration on environment and development', in *Report of the United Nations Conference on Environment and Development, A/CONF.151/26, Vol. 1*. New York: United Nations.

United Nations (1998) *Convention on access to information, public participation in decision-making and access to justice in environmental matters.* Treaty Series, 2161, p. 447. Available at: https://treaties.un.org/Pages/ViewDetails.aspx?src=IND&mtdsg_no=XXVII-13&chapter=27 (Accessed: 24 April 2023).

United Nations (2009) *Toxic waste: UN Expert releases report on 'Probo Koala' incident*, 16 September. Available at: https://www.ohchr.org/en/press-releases/2009/10/toxic-waste-un-expert-releases-report-probo-koala-incident (Accessed: 7 February 2023).

United Nations (2016) *Report of the Special Rapporteur on the situation of human rights defenders, A/71/281*. Available at: https://www.refworld.org/pdfid/57d2a3364.pdf (Accessed: 24 April 2023).

United Nations (2018) *Regional agreement on access to information, public participation and justice in environmental matters in Latin America and the Caribbean.* Treaty series, 3397C.N.195.2018. Available at: https://treaties.un.org/Pages/ViewDetails.aspx?src=IND&mtdsg_no=XXVII18&chapter=27&clang=_en (Accessed: 24 April 2023).

United Nations (2021) *Statistical Yearbook*, pp. 451–455. Available at: https://unstats.un.org/unsd/publications/statistical-yearbook/files/syb64/T31_Internet.pdf (Accessed: 21 April 2023).

Watkins, G. G., Mueller, S. G., Meller, H., Ramirez, M. C., Serebrisky, T., and Georgoulias, A. (2017) *Lessons from 4 decades of infrastructure project related conflicts in Latin America and the Caribbean.* Washington, DC: Inter-American Development Bank.

Index

A

A(H1N1), 156
Aarhus Convention, 294-295, 301
Abdo Benitez, Mario, 48, 49, 205, 209
Abinader, Luis, 183
abstention, 195, 198
ACFTA, 310, 312
ACN or CAN or Andean Community, 5, 9, 42-43, 68, 84, 179, 180, 205-6
ACTO, xxiv, 217, 224-228
ad-hoc group, 242-250, 258
AECID, 244, 248-251
African Charter of Human Rights and People, 302, 308
African Union, 203, 310
AIR, 226, 228,
ALADI, 203, 204, 207, 237
ALALC, 204
ALBA, 3, 5, 6, 8, 13-14, 17-19, 22, 23, 25, 27-30, 40-41, 43-35, 203-205, 207, 211
ALCA, 39-40
ALIDES, 274-275
Almagro, Luis, 18, 23-24, 50, 204
alternative resolution dispute mechanism, 300
Amazon Basin, 225-226, 302
Amazon River Basin, xxii, xxiv, 217
Amazon+10, 227
AMEXCID, 283
América Crece Program, 98
Andean Pact, 204
Áñez, Jeanine, 20-22, 45, 180, 205, 209
anti-Americanism, 8
anti-corruption, 74, 92, 110, 199

Antonio Noriega, Manuel, 183
APEC, 140, 143, 145, 268
APNT, xxiv, 91-114,
Arauz, Andres, 187, 214
Arce, Luis, 206, 213
Aristide, Jean-Bertrand, 7-8
armed conflict, xxii, 61, 66, 71, 77-78, 80, 84
armed forces, 10, 29, 45, 54, 75, 78, 181, 220
Aráujo, Ernesto, 49
Asfura, Nasry, 199
Asia Pacific, 40
asylum seekers, 70
authoritarian or authoritarianism, 4, 24, 38, 51, 79, 85, 92, 199
autocratic tendencies or autocratic rule, 92, 96
autonomy, 9, 52, 108, 112, 114, 185, 205- 213

B

Bachelet, Michelle, 9, 182
Bagyeli pygmies, 307
balance of power, 25, 62-65, 71, 73, 83, 236
Bamako Convention, 305
Ban Ki-Moon, 109
Barbacoas, 79
Barro Blanco hydroelectric dam, 295
benevolent hegemony, 44
Berta Caceres, 296, 300
Biden, Joe, 52-53, 94, 98, 110
bilateral agreements, 193
bilateral treaties, 207
biological terrorism, 127-128, 148, 153-155

biopiracy, 279
Blue Tide or conservative wave, 3, 6, 18-19, 22, 27, 29, 45
Bolivar, Simon, xix, 8, 213
Bolivarianist, 50-52, 55-56
Bolsonaro, Jair, 41, 44-45, 49, 53, 156, 180, 184, 200, 209, 211, 214, 247, 258,
Boluarte, Dina, 181, 198
border crime, 75, 219
border management, 78
Boric, Gabriel, 26, 45, 49, 197, 201
BRICS, 54, 130, 139, 143, 145, 150, 151, 152, 155-157
Buenos Aires Consensus, 40
Bukele, Nayib, 44, 192, 195
Bush, George W., 44
BWC, 133

C

CACM, 268
CAFC, 305, 307
CAFTA, 207, 267, 275
CAIS, 42
CALC, 207-8
Calderón, Felipe, 98, 181
Canela Declaration, 240
capitalism, 39, 40, 239
Carchi, 76
CARICOM, 3, 8, 26, 28, 166, 167, 174
CARSI, 92, 98, 110, 118
Castillo, Pedro, 197-198, 201, 206-207, 213-214
Castro, Fidel, 180
Castro, Raúl, 208
Castro, Xiomara, 99, 199, 201
Catatumbo, 74
Cauca, 79
CBLU, 281
CCAD, 274-277, 286

CELAC, 3, 5, 17-19, 22, 25-30, 40, 41, 44, 48, 52, 71, 128, 191-192, 203, 207-209, 211-214
CELAG, 202
Central African Heads of State, 305
Central American Dry Corridor, 264
Central American Integration Bank, 15
Central American Security Strategy, 42
CEPAL, 105, 167-174, 194, 220, 271-276, 283-284, 304
Chavez, Hugo, 7, 9, 16, 18, 22-23, 40, 43, 68, 69, 184, 204, 210
Chiapas, 277, 283
chikungunya virus, 155, 225
Chilean Spring, 48
Chomsky, Noam, 13
Chota, Edwin, 300
CIC Plata, 236, 254
CICIES, 99
CICIG, 93, 98, 101, 111
citizen security, 92, 100
civil security, 47
civil society, 92, 94, 96-97, 102, 104, 109-110, 113-114, 170, 226, 245-246, 256-257, 265
climate change, 97, 114, 180, 209, 212, 246, 248-249, 251, 253, 255, 258, 264, 269, 280, 281, 284, 294, 311-312,
closed regionalism, 39
CMC, 246-253, 258
CMG or GMC, 241-251, 256
Cold War, xx, 46, 180, 239, 268
collective identity, 156
COMIFAC, 305
commodity prices, 38
common market, 207, 238, 241, 243, 256, 268
CONABIO, 271-272, 282-283,

Index

CONAFOR, 283
Concordia Americas Summit, 53-54, 56
conditionality, 96, 108
CONFAP, 227
confidence-building measures, 43, 67
conflict of interests, 134
Congo Basin, 302, 306
congressional elections, 198
Constitution of Brazil, 254
constitutional crisis, 24
constructivism or constructivist, 61-62, 156, 169
contagion, 192, 195-196, 202
Convention on Biological Biodiversity, 276
COP16, 249
Correa, Rafael, 9-11, 77-78, 178, 196-197, 205, 208
corruption scandal, 74
cosmopolitanism, 41
COVAX, 193, 212
CPLP, 138-140, 143-145
Cristopher Figuera, Manuel Ricardo, 28
Curfews, 169, 195
customs union, 238, 242
cyber defence, 47
Cúcuta, 65, 70-74

D

Damas de Blanco, 70
Darien, 277
death toll, 200, 309
debt, 166, 173-174, 178, 180, 237
decentralization, 103, 197, 224
deforestation, 264, 272-273, 284, 286, 297

deglobalization or (de)globalization, xxiii, 37-39, 41
democracy, 4, 5, 12, 16, 18-19, 23-25, 28-29, 39, 42, 45, 47-52, 55, 198, 205, 208-209, 213, 237-238, 259, 310
dengue fever, 225
desertification, 242-243, 247-248, 251, 294
Dianna Ortiz v. Guatemala, 302
digital, 49, 226, 244, 306
disaster risk management, 47, 252, 266
displacement or forced migration, 71, 74-76, 78, 93, 97, 109
distrust, 40, 49, 201
division of labour, 39
donor or donors or donorship, xxiv, 43, 91, 95-96, 99-100, 102-103, 221, 278, 282
drought, 242, 247-248, 251, 271, 283, 294, 311
drug patents, 152
drug traffickers or drug trafficking, 16, 68-69, 72-73, 75, 77, 82-87, 92, 97-99, 114, 179, 199, 219-220
Duque, Iván, 45, 48, 81, 209, 211
Díaz-Canel, Miguel, 180

E

early warning system, 298, 309
Earth Summit, 276
Ebola, 124-126, 147, 150, 157
ECCAS, 306-307
ECLAC, 98, 172, 184, 194, 194, 196, 199, 271, 275, 283
ECOFAC6, 307
economic benefits, 265, 273, 278
economic blockage, 15

economic development or socio-economic development, xxi, 5, 45, 67, 68, 102, 107, 109, 111, 172, 181, 207, 211, 213, 220, 227, 240, 243, 274, 280, 305, 308, 310-311
ECONORMAS, 248-252
ECOSUR, 257
ecotourism, 271, 273, 278, 285
ECOWAS, 306
education, 93, 100-106, 110, 138, 171, 173, 175, 197, 221, 224, 236, 240, 244-245
EHRD or EHRDs, 293, 295-296, 300-304, 307-308, 311-312
ejido, 217, 278
Elcano Institute, 46
electoral observation mission, 20
electoral participation, 201-202
electoral processes, xxiv, 192, 195-196, 199, 201
electricity, 273
elite interviews, 127
embargo or embargoes, 25, 180
emergency meeting, 11
emigration, 22, 45
EMSA, 266, 280-283, 286-287
Endorois Welfare Council v. Kenya, 301
energy, xxii, 67, 86, 100, 102, 104, 107, 171, 236-238, 241, 243, 266, 281, 207
enforcement, 21, 53, 92, 130
environmental conservation, 240, 258, 264, 282
environmental crimes, 219, 243
environmental security, 46, 151
environmental sustainability, 77, 265-266, 276, 286
environmental threats, 294

epidemic or epidemics, xxiv, 48, 123-128, 147, 150, 151, 155-157, 171, 223
epidemiological surveillance, 224
Esmeraldas, 76
Esquipulas II, 177
EsSalud, 223-224
EU, xx, 9, 26, 250, 268, 276
exploitation, 66, 72, 73, 75, 78, 85, 113, 253, 279, 282, 302, 311
export, 15, 56, 60, 79, 83, 110, 132, 150, 168, 173, 184, 219, 236, 242, 273
extortion, 69, 72-73, 82
extractive activities, 295, 306
extreme poverty, 105, 173-174, 194, 210, 310

F

FANB, 70
FARC, 72, 74, 76-80, 82-83, 85
FCES, 257
feminist, 197
Fernandez, Alberto, 26, 49, 183, 206, 213
Fernández de Kirchner, Cristina, 53, 183
field interviews, xxiv
fieldwork observations, 91, 95
FILAC, 225
Fiocruz, 221-223, 227
FONPLATA, 236, 252, 254
food security, 100, 218, 252, 266
forced displacement, 93, 97
foreign investment, 107, 111, 113, 183, 311
Fox, Vicente, 181, 265
FPGHI, 137-145, 155
Franco, Federico, 15
França, Carlos, 49
fraud, 20-21, 23, 199

free market, 199, 279
free trade agreement or free trade agreements, 41, 112, 204, 207, 250, 260, 267-268, 270, 275
free trade zone, 238
FSLN, 198
FTAA, xxi, 207
Funasa, 222
functionalist integration, 267

G

G20, 46, 150, 152, 154
GATT, 128
Gaviria, César, 179
GDP, 105-106, 164, 166-167, 171-174, 178, 196-197, 210, 218, 222, 249
gender equality, 197, 212, 310
gender-based violence, 75
General Assembly, 18, 24, 300
geopolitics, 49, 91, 236
GHSI, 124, 130, 135-136, 138-139, 141, 143, 145, 147, 148, 150, 153-157
Gini Index, 174
global community, 39
Global Health Security Index, 223
Global South, 40
Globalism, 41
good living or living well or buen vivir, xxii, 77
government responses, 165, 185
Great Lockdown, 164, 166-168, 171-172, 174-175
GTZ, 246
Guaidó, Juán, 22-24, 26, 28, 45, 50, 51, 195, 206
Guaraní Aquifer, 235, 253-254, 259
Guerrillas, 67-68, 79-80

H

hard power, 56, 166
Harris, Kamala, 98
health crisis, xxiii, 197-198, 200, 214
health diplomacy, 221-227
healthcare, xi-xxiv, 44, 49, 171, 191-192, 217-218, 220-228
hegemonic vision, 94
hegemony, 5, 38-39, 44, 181, 213
Henrique Cardoso, Fernando, 184, 219
Hernández, Juan Orlando, 92-94, 104, 106, 199, 201, 202, 279, 284
historical sociology, 191-192, 212
HIV-AIDS, 127, 171
homicide rate, 62
Hubei, 193
Humala, Ollanta, 201
human security, 45, 47, 50
human trafficking, 72-73, 82
humanitarian aid, 24, 44, 54, 97
humanitarian crisis, 84-85
hurricane damage, 199
hybrid governance, 65-66, 86
hybrid security, xxiii, 61, 83, 86
hydro-politics, 236
hydrocarbons, 168, 253
hyperinflation, 22

I

IADC, 12, 16, 23
IBSA, 151-152
IDB, 93, 94, 99-114, 271, 276
ideology, 5, 16, 155-156, 211
IHR, 124-125, 127-128, 135, 147, 154
illegal activities, 71, 72, 78
illicit actors, 66
illicit markets, 72

Imbabura, 82
IMCI, 165
Immigration, 72, 91-99, 106-114, 180
Impeachment, 4, 15-16, 18-19, 184, 198
INBio, 274, 277
inclusive regionalism, xxi
income inequality, 272-273
Indepaz, 79-80
Independent Evaluation Group, 273, 277-278, 282-285
indigenous communities, 225, 279, 303
indigenous people or indigenous populations, 48, 219, 224-226, 228, 303, 305, 311
inequality, xxii, 39, 92, 105, 184, 194, 200, 204, 210, 272, 273
influenza, 124-125, 129, 148, 153, 155, 171,
informal employment, 73
infrastructure projects, 113, 225, 228, 265, 274
insecurity, 44, 64, 75, 77, 81, 84, 93, 97-98, 106
institutional capacity, 14, 96, 146
institutional design, 28, 29, 41, 124-125, 128, 144, 154, 156, 256
institutional reform, 258
institutional regionalism, 269
instrumental effectiveness, 96
integration mechanisms, 210-211, 270
Inter-American Democratic Charter, 50
inter-state war, xxii, 61
intergovernmental cooperation, 38, 129, 155, 256
international aid, 95
international cooperation, 38, 44, 45, 92, 95, 97, 99, 103, 106, 125, 130, 221, 237, 250, 252, 252, 259, 274, 276, 281
international financial crisis, 207
international institutions, 50, 95, 127-128, 131, 152, 264, 269, 271, 287
international law, 25, 27-28, 38, 54
international organizations, xii, 9, 66, 123, 124, 127, 129, 150, 173, 198, 236, 255, 270, 277, 282, 285, 287
international peacekeeping, 43, 48
international preferences and coalitions, 95
international relations, 39, 54, 56, 135, 239-240
internet penetration rate, 306
IPRENARE, 273
ISO 14000, 241-242
Itaipú Treaty, 17

J

JICA, 281

K

Kast, Jose Antonio, 197
Kawas-Fernández v. Honduras, 294
Kirchner, Néstor, 11, 53, 183
Knox, John, 296
Kribi, 307

L

La Plata Basin, 235-238, 252, 254, 257, 259
Lacalle Pou, Luis Alberto, 178, 205, 209, 211
Lagos Plan of Action, 310
Laguna Sayachaltun, 271, 278

Lake Bogoria, 301
Lake Nyos catastrophe, 309
land grabbing, 302
Lasso, Guillermo, 178, 209, 211
law enforcement agencies, 53, 92
legislative elections, 195, 199
legislature, 95, 96, 134
legitimacy, xix, xxii, 3-4, 12, 14, 18-19, 20, 22-23, 24-27, 29, 46, 65, 113, 114, 138, 141, 157, 198, 209, 257, 304
liberal democracy, 39
liberal order or liberal world order, 39, 46, 55
liberalization, xx, 96, 310
liberals, 55, 173
LIBRE, 199, 201
Lima Group, 4, 21-29, 45, 51, 206, 213
limited statehood, 65
Lisbon Concept, 52
Lobo Sosa, Porfirio, 12, 199, 201,
Los Rastrojos, 72, 74, 80
Lugo, Fernando, 15-17, 205
Lula da Silva, Luiz Inácio, 8, 18, 30, 54-55, 184, 200, 206-207
López Obrador, Andrés Manuel, 22, 44, 183, 192, 203, 207, 208, 286,

M

M10, 296
MACCIH, 93, 99, 111
Macri, Mauricio, 40, 49, 183, 205, 209
Madrid Summit, 53
Maduro Moros, Nicolás, 21-27, 30, 48-52, 54, 69, 70, 195, 206, 210
Maduro, Ricardo, 103
Magdalena Medio, 295-296
Magüi-Payan, 79

Malvinas Islands, 53, 253
mano dura policies, 93
Manta military base, 77-78
Manuel Santos, Juan, 53, 69, 86, 179
Mariscal Estigarribia, 16
maritime negotiations, 68
MAS, 195, 206
MBC, xxv, 263-266, 271-272, 275-286
MCI, 165-166, 171
MCM, 67
measles, 223
medical services, 223
medicinal uses, 272
membership, 12, 14-15, 28, 129-130, 132, 154, 155, 207, 267
Mercocidades, 243
MERCOSUR, xxiv, 3, 16-17, 28, 49-45, 52, 203-205, 213, 223, 235-260, 268
Merino, Manuel, 198
Micheletti, Roberto, 12, 14
migration crisis, 50, 73, 98
Miguel Insulza, José, 11-12
military aid, 100, 111
military base, 13, 16, 69, 77-78
military spending, 76, 170
military–industrial complex, 47, 53
milpa, 272
MNCs, 270, 274
Moiwana Community v. Suriname, 302
money laundering, 68, 85
Monroe Doctrine, 204, 213
Montevideo Mechanism, 3, 23, 26, 28
Morales, Evo, 9-10, 20-22
Moreno, Lenin, 178, 180, 196-197, 201, 205, 209
Moreno, Maikel, 28

mortality rate, 198
MSF, 146-147, 157
multi-level governance, 255-257
multidimensional security, 42-45, 47, 49, 54
multilateralism, 41, 49, 212
multiple-use zones, 277-278
multipolar world or multipolarity, 40, 44
Mérida Initiative, 92, 98

N

NACOBPI, 129, 130, 138, 139-140, 143, 145, 150
NAFTA, 41, 112, 207, 268, 275
Nairobi Convention, 305
NAPAPI, 129
narco-politics, 92
narcotics, 17, 66, 80, 102, 104,
Nariño, 76, 78-84
nation state or nation-state, 38, 203, 210, 213
national interests, 17, 95, 204, 270, 280
national parks, 227, 277
National Party of Honduras, 199
NATO, 43, 52-56
natural disasters, 97, 100, 209, 246, 264, 266, 269, 273, 283
natural ecosystems, 272, 277
neoclassical economics, 107
neoliberal interventionism, 94
neoliberalism or neoliberal globalization or neoliberal economy, 39-41, 205, 209
network cooperation, 132
new Cold War, 46
new regionalism, 268-269
Ngabe community, 295
NGOs, 109, 113, 146, 157, 257, 265, 270, 285-286, 304

non-state actors, xix, 62, 64, 235, 255-256
non-state armed actors, 62, 64, 67, 72
non-trade integration, 40-41
Norte de Santander, 67, 74, 84
NSAGs, 66, 72-75, 79, 80, 84-85
núcleo de poder, 45

O

OAS, 5-24, 37, 42, 49-52, 204, 206, 212
Obama, Barack, 44, 93, 98, 107, 111
obligation, 45, 129, 152, 154, 219, 238, 242, 296-297, 301-304
ODA or official development assistance, 99, 174-175
OECD, 53, 85, 172, 174
Ogoni people, 302
oil exploitation, 302
oil prices, 22, 178
online surveys, 127
open regionalism, xx, 30, 39, 237
Operation for the People's Liberation, 70
organized crime, xxii, 4, 38, 46, 47, 69, 72-73, 81-82, 92-93, 98, 220, 227
Orinoco watershed, 219
Orito-Vides, 83
Ortega, Daniel, 92
Oslo Agreement, 177

P

Pacific Alliance, 40-42, 207
PAHO, 217, 220-221, 223, 225, 226-227
PAN, 181

Pan-Americanism, xix, 40, 46, 204, 213
pan-regional sovereignty, 40
Panama Congress, 213
Paraguay-Paraná Waterway System, 237, 241
paramilitary groups, 20, 69, 81, 87
Parlasur, 243, 256
Path of the Panther or Paseo Pantera, 276-277
Patio Bonito village, 295
PDVSA, 184
peace agreement, 77-78, 81, 264
peace process, 68-69, 80, 177
peer-to-peer monitoring, 132, 149
Permanent Council of the OAS, 12, 16, 18, 23-24, 50
Peronism or Peronists, 40, 207
Petro, Gustavo, 45, 56
Petrocaribe, 27
Peña Nieto, Enrique, 181
Peña, Ximena, 196-197
pharmaceutical industry or pharmaceutical companies, 203, 212 222
PHEICs, 125, 135, 139
physical isolation, 223
Pink Tide or marea rosa, 3, 5-7, 9-12, 18-20, 22, 27-29
Pinochet, Augusto, 181, 197,
Piñera, Sebastián, 26, 45, 89, 182, 197, 201, 208
Plan Colombia, 68, 76, 78, 109
policy change or policy reform, 94, 97, 111
policy-making, xxiv, 108
political crisis, 22, 76, 181, 198, 201, 205
political elite, 77, 95, 114
political goodwill, 280
pollution, 294-298, 309
Porvenir massacre, 9

post-emergency reconstruction, 101
post-hegemonic regionalism or postliberal regionalism, xxiii, 3, 6, 22, 28-30, 42, 43, 46, 52, 56
PPP, 98, 264-267, 274, 277, 280
presidential and legislative elections, 195, 199
presidential election, 26, 191-201, 271, 281
Probo Koala incident, 309
progressive governments, 204-206, 211-212
PROSUR, xxiii, 3, 26, 28-29, 37, 41, 47-49, 51, 55, 206, 213
Proyecto Mesoamérica, xxv, 263-287
PTAs, 268
public administration, 111, 237
public expenditure, 174
public health, xxii, 124-125, 134, 141, 192, 221, 223, 226, 228, 266, 298, 310
public participation, 275, 293-294, 298-313
public policy or public policies, 82, 93, 126, 165, 195, 204, 210, 214, 240, 245, 252, 254, 255, 274, 283
public services, xxi, 105
public spending, 96, 114, 169, 173-174
Puerto Santander, 74
Putumayo, 76-83, 227
Pérez Molina, Otto, 92, 106

Q

quilombola territory, 295

R

R4W, 50
rational choice or rationalism, 127, 131, 152, 154, 156
realist paradigm, 166
referendum, 7, 96, 197
refugee crisis, 78
regional cooperation, xi, xxv, xxvii, 106, 236, 263, 267-268, 274-275, 283, 286
regional development, 71, 243, 264, 308
regional governance, xi, xxv, 5, 27, 34, 62, 86, 270
regional institutions, 266, 269, 270, 274, 282, 285, 287
regional integration, xix-xxi, 19, 25, 86, 191-192, 203, 205-206, 213-214, 217, 228, 240-242, 260, 264, 267-270, 305
regional organizations, xi, xix-xxiv, 3-7, 12, 15-30, 66, 71, 110, 123, 222, 254, 259, 265, 267-268, 274, 305-306, 312
regional policy, 270
regional power or regional powers, 176, 179, 184, 238
regional projects, xix, 67, 265, 267, 269, 275, 287
regional security governance, 62-64, 84,
regional strategies, 260, 282
regional threats, 148, 153
REMA, 241
Resolution 40/11, 301
RESP-AL, 221
revisionist powers, 44
Reyes, Raúl, 69, 76
Rhadebe, Sikhosiphi, 302
right to a healthy environment, 295-296
Rio Declaration, 295-296, 303, 312
Rio Group, 128, 207-208
Rio+20, 248-249, 251, 294, 303
Rio-92, 240
RMMA, 241-244, 247-253, 256-257
Rodríguez, Delcy, 24
Rosenthal, Yani, 199
Rousseff, Dilma, 18-19, 40, 184, 205
rubella, 223
rural population, 106, 308
rural poverty, 273
Río de la Plata Basin, 235-236

S

Saca, Elías Antonio, 101
SADC, 43, 53, 306
Sagasti, Francisco, 198
Samper, Ernesto, 19, 179
San António del Táchira, 70
San Salvador Protocol, 40
sanctions, 14-16, 23-24, 27, 41, 46, 50, 183-184, 202, 298, 305
Santiago Declaration, 48
Santos, Juan Manuel, 53, 69, 86, 179
Saramaka People v. Suriname, 302
SARS outbreak, 136
Sayachaltun, 271, 278
securitization, 43-45, 55, 108-109, 114
security agenda, xxiii, 37-39, 42, 46-47, 52, 54-56
security community or security communities, 42-45, 49, 54-55, 62-65, 71, 83
security governance, 39, 61-67, 76, 83-87
security studies, 61-62, 83
security threat, xxii, 124, 131, 138, 148, 155

Index 327

Segunda Marquetalia, 79-80
SELA, 267
self-determination, 23, 25, 40
Selva Maya, 277
SEMARNAT, 271, 278, 283, 286
Sembrando Vida, 271
separation of powers, 92
SERAC case, 302
SGT nº6, 241-253, 256-258
Shannon, Thomas, 13
SHC, 221
SIAM, 244-251
SICA, 3, 15, 28, 110, 203, 213, 271, 274-275-281
Sinaloa Cartel, 73-74
Slim Foundation, 212
SMCI, 165, 171
smuggling, 67, 68, 70, 72, 82, 220
social control, 75
social development, 16, 204-210, 214, 235, 237, 240, 242, 245, 257, 264
social distancing, 200, 202, 223
social goods, 75
social programs, 198
socialism, 20, 25, 41, 195, 206-207
soft power, 171, 174
solidarity, 9, 11, 13, 14, 19, 23, 25, 27, 40-41, 46, 84
South American pan-nationalism or sudamericanización, 47
South–South cooperation, 221
sovereignty, xx, 23, 25-27, 29, 40, 44, 55, 78, 131, 134, 154, 253, 267, 274
species conservation, 277
state authority, 64-65
state modernization, 91, 92, 100, 104
stock markets, 168
successful coup, 3, 6, 11, 12, 18, 28, 30

Sucumbíos, 76, 83
supra-national organizations, xx
Supreme Court, 7, 12, 24, 28, 199
sustainability, 77, 220, 235, 241, 246, 251, 258, 263, 266, 274, 276-277, 281-283, 286
sustainable development, xxii, 208, 220, 225, 228, 242-243, 245, 249-250, 253, 254, 259-260, 273-276, 280, 296, 301, 310, 312-313
sustainable economic development, xxi
Sánchez Cerén, Salvador, 101, 106

T

Tabasara River, 295-296
Tamaya-Saweto community, 300
technical assistance, 98, 221, 227, 242, 244, 251, 268, 269, 277-278
technical cooperation, 220
technological advancement, 273
telecommunications, 174-175, 266
Telembí, 79
telemedicine, 226
Temer, Michel, 18-19, 40, 49, 184
terrorism, 44, 49, 52-53, 78, 127-128, 148, 153, 155, 181, 212, 219
TGNs, xxiv, 123-157
30-S, 10, 11
TIAR, 204
Torrijos, Omar, 183
traditional tribunals, 309
Trans-Pacific Partnership, 41
transatlantic cooperation, 52
transborder cooperation, 75
transnational crime or transnational organized crime, 4, 47, 93
transnational social violence, 62-63
transnationalism, 40

Tren Maya, 271, 286-287
Triple-Border Area or tri-border area, 42, 46
Trochas, 67, 73
tropical forests, 283, 305
Trump, Donald, 22, 41, 50, 53, 55, 94, 98, 111-113, 168-180
TSC, 273
tuberculosis, 150-152
Tumaco, 79, 83
Tuxtla Mechanism, 264, 265, 270, 283
Táchira, 67

U

UN, 5, 9, 11, 25-26, 46, 50, 99, 151, 212, 218, 294, 296, 300
UNASUR, 3, 5, 8, 9-11, 13-14, 16, 17-19, 21-22, 25-26, 28-29, 30, 40-41, 43-45, 47-49, 53, 55, 71, 83, 86, 135, 138, 140-146, 155-157, 203-207, 211, 213, 221
UNDP, 271, 277, 282-283
unemployment, 67, 72, 199, 200
ungoverned spaces, 64
UNHCR, 70
unipolarity, 39
United Nations Human Rights Council, 301
universal health coverage, 155, 218
urbanization, 272
Uribe, Álvaro, 69
US ambassador, 9, 21
US foreign policy, 20, 97
US hegemony, 5, 38
US interests, xxiii, 3, 6, 18, 21, 24-27, 94, 132, 149
USAID, 112, 276
Ushuaia Protocol, 238
USMCA, 267, 275
US–China, 38, 39, 46

V

vaccination or vaccine, 44, 48, 138, 193-194, 200, 203, 210, 212, 222-225
Vazquez, Tabare, 178, 205
Venezuelan crisis, 3, 21-22, 24, 27, 45, 49-50, 54, 55, 184
veto power, 267
violent peace, xxii, 62
Vizcarra, Martín, 181, 198
VNSAs, 64-66, 76-81
voluntary isolation, 219, 224-225, 228
vulnerable persons and groups, 298

W

Washington Consensus, 204, 206
white paper, 45, 53, 219
Wildlife Conservation Society, 276
WOLA, 94
wood trafficking, 82
Workers' Party, 53
World Bank Independent Evaluation Group, 282
World Bank, 99, 100, 104, 157, 166, 204, 271, 310
world order, 38, 54-55
WPI, xxiv, 163, 165-166, 171, 174, 176-177, 179-185
WTO, 41, 128, 153, 168
Wuhan, 193

X

xenophobic narratives, 95
Xolobeni, 302

Y

Yacyretá hydroelectric power
    plant, 237
Yalta-Potsdam system, 39
Yaoundé Declaration, 305
yellow fever, 155, 223
Yucatán, 264, 271, 277

Z

Zelaya, Manuel, 12-15, 199
ZIF, 68, 84
Zika virus, 155, 225
zones of peace, 42, 62

www.ingramcontent.com/pod-product-compliance
Lightning Source LLC
Chambersburg PA
CBHW071233290426
44108CB00013B/1400